May Your Name be Inscribed in the BOOK of LIFE

INTRODUCTION

The first followers of Yeshua* were all Jewish. As Gentiles began to follow the Jewish Messiah, they brought their culture into their expressions of worship. Since there were many more Gentiles than Jews, the Jewish culture was gradually eliminated and replaced with Gentile (Hellenistic) expressions.

According to the Jewish historian Neander, by the end of the first century C.E., when belief in Messiah was still Jewish in culture and expression, more than one million followers of Messiah were Jewish.

Although some have suggested that this Book is non-Jewish—or possibly even anti-Jewish—the allegation does not fit the facts. As the twentieth century's premier archaeologist and expert on the ancient Middle East, William F. Albright, emphatically stated:

> . . . [it] was written entirely by Jews, with a spiritual and literary background in the Bible and the proto-rabbinic culture, so it remains a Jewish work. . . . In the light of these [Dead Sea Scrolls] finds . . . [it] becomes more Jewish than we had thought—as truly Jewish as the Old Testament is Israelite.

If this is true, why was it "banned" for us as Jews? Because of misunderstanding and misuse, no doubt, but mainly because it spoke of *that man*. For years, we have not spoken his name out of fear, spite, and hatred. Yet, he stands as the pinnacle of human history. As Napoleon observed:

> Superficial minds see a resemblance between him and the founders of empires and the gods of other religions. That resemblance does not exist. . . . Between him and whoever else in the world, there is no possible term of comparison. He is truly a being by himself. I search in vain in history to find the similar to him.

This estimation is not only the opinion of Gentiles, but is shared by some of the best Jewish thinkers. Albert Einstein admitted:

> I am a Jew, but I am enthralled by the luminous figure of the Nazarene. . . . Jesus is too colossal for the pen of the phrasemongers, however artful.

Martin Buber acknowledged:

> I am more than ever certain that a great place belongs to him in Israel's history of faith and that this place cannot be described by any usual categories.

Israeli scholar, Dr. Pinchas Lapide, pointed out:

> In this respect you must believe me, for I do know my Talmud more or less. . . . This Jesus was as faithful to the law as I

* Yeshua: The name of Jesus in Hebrew. It means "Salvation".

iii

would hope to be. But I suspect that Jesus was more faithful to the law than I am—and I am an orthodox Jew.

Einstein expressed it well:

No man can read the Gospels without feeling the actual presence of Jesus. His personality pulsates in every word. No myth is filled with such life. How different, for instance, is the impression which we receive from an account of the legendary heroes of antiquity like Theseus! Theseus and other heroes of his type lack the authentic vitality of Jesus.

David Flusser, professor of religious history at Hebrew University in Jerusalem, said of him:

I do not think that many Jews would object if the Messiah—when he came—was the Jew Jesus.

The intention of this New Covenant is to help us to rediscover the original Jewishness of this Jewish Book, written by Jewish men, fulfilling prophecy about the Jewish Messiah.

Read this Book, and decide for yourself about *that man*.

QUESTIONS ABOUT MESSIANIC JUDAISM

What are the major beliefs of Messianic Judaism?
Messianic Jews believe:
- In the one God of Abraham, Isaac, and Jacob.
- The Jewish Scriptures (Old and New Covenant) are the inspired words of God.
- Yeshua is the Messiah of Israel.
- By Yeshua's voluntary, self-sacrificing death and resurrection, we have atonement before God for all our sins.
- In preserving our identity as Jews.
- In supporting Israel by prayers, financial assistance, and Aliyah (immigration to Israel).

How Jewish were Paul and others after they became Followers of Messiah?
Paul always identified himself as Jewish (Acts 21:39; 22:3; 23:6). He spoke Hebrew (Acts 21:40) and observed Jewish holidays and rituals (Acts 18:21; 20:16; 28:17). There were thousands of Jews who believed (like Paul) and they were all zealous for the Torah! (Acts 21:20).

"But Paul said, I am a Jew . . ." (Acts 21:39)

". . . Brought up in this city at the feet of Gamaliel, and taught according to the perfect manner of the law of the fathers . . ." (Acts 22:3)

"Men and brethren, I am a Pharisee, the son of a Pharisee . . ." (Acts 23:6)

" . . . He spoke to them in the Hebrew language . . ." (Acts 21:40)

"I must by all means keep this coming feast in Jerusalem . . ." (Acts 18:21)

". . . For he [Paul] was hurrying to be at Jerusalem, if possible, on the Day of Shavuoth." (Acts 20:16)

"I have done nothing against our people or the customs of our fathers . . ." (Acts 28:17)

". . . You see, brother, how many thousands of Jews there are who believe, and they are all zealous for the Torah" (Acts 21:20)

How can you be so sure Yeshua is the Messiah?
Because the Jewish Prophets predicted hundreds of *specific* facts describing Him as Messiah. Yeshua fulfilled them all. These are a few to consider. The rest can be looked up in the Old Covenant by referring to footnotes in this New Covenant.

He would be born in Bethlehem:
> But thou, *Bethlehem* Ephrathah, though thou be little among the thousands of Judah, yet out of thee shall one come forth unto me that is to be ruler in Israel; whose goings forth are from of old, from everlasting.
> —Micah 5:1 (5:2 in some versions)

He would be from the ancestry of David:
> Behold, the days come, saith the Lord, that I will raise
> unto *David* a righteous Branch . . . and shall execute judg-
> ment and justice in the earth.
>
> —Jeremiah 23:5

> The book of the genealogy of Yeshua ha Mashiach, the
> Son of David. . . .
>
> —Matthew 1:1

He would not be recognized by His own Jewish people:
> Who would have believed our report? . . . We hid as it
> were our faces from him; he was despised, and we es-
> teemed him not.
>
> —Isaiah 53:1, 3

He would die before the destruction of the Second Temple:
> . . . Messiah shall be cut off, but not for himself: and the
> people of the prince that shall come shall destroy the city
> and the sanctuary . . .
>
> —Daniel 9:26

Why don't ALL Jewish people believe in Yeshua?

Throughout Jewish history, it has always been a minority who
obeyed God. Moses and the Prophets of God were rejected by the people of Israel while false Messiahs were accepted. The Jewish Scriptures
said the Jewish people as a nation would reject the Messiah at His first
appearance:

> He is despised and rejected of men; a man of sorrows, and
> acquainted with grief: and we hid as it were our faces from
> him; he was despised, and we esteemed him not.
>
> —Isaiah 53:3

He was scheduled to make two appearances: the first time He came
to die as atonement for sin.

> But he was wounded for our transgressions, he was bruised for
> our iniquities: the chastisement of our peace was upon him;
> and with his stripes we are healed.
>
> —Isaiah 53:5

> . . . He was cut off out of the land of the living: for the trans-
> gression of my people was he stricken.
>
> —Isaiah 53:8b

His second appearance will bring peace on earth (Isaiah 11:1-10).

> They shall not hurt nor destroy in all my holy mountain: for
> the earth shall be full of the knowledge of the Lord, as the
> waters cover the sea.
>
> —Isaiah 11:9

Many Jewish people only see the prophecies of His second coming
and disregard the prophecies fulfilled at His first appearance.

Do Jewish people believe in Original Sin?

In Psalm 51:5, David wrote, "Behold, I was shapen in iniquity; and in sin did my mother conceive me." From Ecclesiastes 7:20, we learn "there is not a just man upon earth," who continually does good and who never sins. Scriptures point out that the person who sins is separated from God.

> . . . The soul that sinneth, it shall die.
>
> —Ezekiel 18:4

Can prayers, mitzvoth (good deeds) or synagogue attendance cleanse us from sin?

No. Leviticus 1:5 and 17:11 require the death of a sacrificial animal *in the Temple* for forgiveness of sin.

> For the life of the flesh is in the blood: and I have given it to
> you upon the altar to make an atonement for your souls: for it
> is the blood that maketh an atonement for the soul.
>
> —Leviticus 17:11

God provided our final sacrificial Lamb, the Messiah, before He allowed the Temple to be destroyed in 70 C.E. Although prayers, mitzvoth, and synagogue attendance are important, they do not provide atonement (covering) for sin.

The Rabbis reaffirmed this principle:

"They asked the Torah, 'What is the punishment of the sinner?' Torah answered, 'Let him bring a guilt offering and it shall be forgiven unto him, as it is said, "And it shall be accepted for him to make atonement for him (Leviticus 1:4)." ' " [Makkot 31d, Jerusalem Talmud]

"Does not atonement come through the blood, as it is said: For it is the blood that maketh atonement by reason of the life." [Yoma 5a, Talmud]

Why do you pray through Yeshua rather than praying directly to God?

Jewish people have always required a mediator to approach God. This mediator is necessary because, as the Bible says, "For there is not a just man upon earth, that doeth good, and sinneth not" (Ecclesiastes 7:20). The result of sin is separation from God. "But your sins have separated between you and your God" (Isaiah 59:2). Just as the High Priest was necessary to be our mediator in the Temple, Yeshua is our mediator today.

MAY YOUR NAME BE INSCRIBED IN THE BOOK OF LIFE!

. . . And at that time thy people shall be delivered, every one that shall be found written in the Book [of Life].

And many of them that sleep in the dust of the earth shall awake, some of everlasting life, and some to shame and everlasting contempt.

—Daniel 12:1, 2

A PRAYER TO KNOW YOUR NAME IS INSCRIBED IN THE BOOK OF LIFE

Messiah Yeshua, I admit that I have sinned.
I believe that you have provided the forgiveness for me.
I receive you as my Messiah.

For more information about Messianic Judaism, write to:
THE MESSIANIC VISION
P.O. Box 34462
Washington, DC 20034
U.S.A.

The Good News According To
MATTHEW

The Genealogy of Yeshua ha Mashiach[1]

THE book of the genealogy of Yeshua ha Mashiach,[1] the Son of David,[2] the Son of Abraham:[3]

2 Abraham begot Isaac, Isaac begot Jacob, and Jacob begot Judah and his brothers.

3 Judah begot Perez and Zerah by Tamar, Perez begot Hezron, and Hezron begot Ram.

4 Ram begot Amminadab, Amminadab begot Nahshon, and Nahshon begot Salmon.

5 Salmon begot Boaz by Rahab, Boaz begot Obed by Ruth, Obed begot Jesse,

6 and Jesse begot David the king.

David the king begot Solomon by her who had been the wife of Uriah.

7 Solomon begot Rehoboam, Rehoboam begot Abijah, and Abijah begot Asa.

8 Asa begot Jehoshaphat, Jehoshaphat begot Joram, and Joram begot Uzziah.

9 Uzziah begot Jotham, Jotham begot Ahaz, and Ahaz begot Hezekiah.

10 Hezekiah begot Manasseh, Manasseh begot Amon, and Amon begot Josiah.

11 Josiah begot Jeconiah and his brothers about the time they were carried away to Babylon.

12 And after they were brought to Babylon, Jeconiah begot Shealtiel, and Shealtiel begot Zerubbabel.

13 Zerubbabel begot Abiud, Abiud begot Eliakim, and Eliakim begot Azor.

14 Azor begot Zadok, Zadok begot Achim, and Achim begot Eliud.

15 Eliud begot Eleazar, Eleazar begot Matthan, and Matthan begot Jacob.

16 And Jacob begot Joseph [4] the husband of Miriam, of whom was born Yeshua who is called the Messiah.

17 So all the generations from Abraham to David are fourteen generations, from David until the captivity in Babylon are fourteen generations, and from the captivity in Babylon until the Messiah are fourteen generations.

The Messiah Born of Miriam

18 Now the birth of Yeshua ha Mashiach was thus: After His

---

1 The Hebrew form of the name of Jesus the Messiah.   *2* Jeremiah 23:5, 6
3 Genesis 22:15–18; 26:3, 4; 35:11

4 This is Joseph's genealogy. The genealogy of Miriam, Yeshua's mother, is found in Luke, chapter 3.

mother Miriam was betrothed to Joseph, before they came together, she was found with child of the Holy Spirit.

19 Then Joseph her husband, being a just man, and not wanting to make her a public example, was minded to put her away secretly.

20 But while he thought about these things, behold, an angel of the Lord appeared to him in a dream, saying, "Joseph, son of David, do not be afraid to take to you Miriam your wife, for that which is conceived in her is of the Holy Spirit.

21 "And she will bring forth a Son, and you shall call His name YESHUA,[5] for He will save His people from their sins."

22 Now all this was done that it might be fulfilled which was spoken by the Lord through the prophet, saying:

23 *"Behold, the virgin will be with child, and will bring forth a Son, and they will call His name Immanuel,"* [6] which is translated, "God with us."

24 Then Joseph, being aroused from sleep, did as the angel of the Lord commanded him and took to him his wife,

25 and did not know her till she had brought forth her firstborn Son. And he called His name YESHUA.

Wise Men from the East

2 Now after Yeshua was born in Bethlehem of Judea in the days of Herod the king, behold, wise men from the East came to Jerusalem,

2 saying, "Where is He who has been born King of the Jews? For we have seen His star in the East and have come to worship Him."

3 When Herod the king had heard these things, he was troubled, and all Jerusalem with him.

4 And when he had gathered all the chief priests and scribes of the people together, he inquired of them where the Messiah was to be born.

5 And they said to him, "In Bethlehem of Judea, for thus it is written by the prophet:

6 *'And you, Bethlehem, in the land of Judah,*
    Are not the least among the rulers of Judah;
    For out of you will come a Ruler
    Who will shepherd My people Israel.'" [7]

7 Then Herod, when he had secretly called the wise men, determined from them what time the star appeared.

8 And he sent them to Bethlehem and said, "Go and search diligently for the young Child, and when you have found Him, bring back word to me, that I may come and worship Him also."

9 When they had heard the king, they departed; and behold, the star which they had seen in the East went before them, till it came and stood over where the young Child was.

10 When they saw the star, they rejoiced with exceedingly great joy.

11 And when they had come into the house, they saw the young

---

5 The Hebrew word "Yeshua" means "Salvation."   6 Isaiah 7:14

7 Micah 5:2 (5:1 in some versions)

Child with Miriam His mother, and fell down and worshiped Him. And when they had opened their treasures, they presented gifts to Him: gold, frankincense, and myrrh.

12 And being warned by God in a dream that they should not return to Herod, they departed for their own country another way.

The Flight into Egypt

13 And when they had departed, behold, an angel of the Lord appeared to Joseph in a dream, saying, "Arise, take the young Child and His mother, flee to Egypt, and stay there until I bring you word; for Herod will seek the young Child to destroy Him."

14 When he arose, he took the young Child and His mother by night and departed into Egypt,

15 and was there until the death of Herod, that it might be fulfilled which was spoken by the Lord through the prophet, saying, *"Out of Egypt I have called My Son."* [8]

Massacre of the Innocents

16 Then Herod, when he saw that he was deceived by the wise men, was exceedingly angry; and he sent forth and put to death all the male children who were in Bethlehem and in all that region, from two years old and under, according to the time which he had determined from the wise men.

17 Then was fulfilled what was spoken by Jeremiah the prophet, saying:

18 *"A voice was heard in Ra-*
mah,

Lamentation, weeping, and
great mourning,
Rachel weeping for her chil-
dren;
And she would not be com-
forted, because they are no
more." [9]

The Home in Nazareth

19 But when Herod was dead, behold, an angel of the Lord appeared in a dream to Joseph in Egypt,

20 saying, "Arise, take the young Child and His mother, and go into the land of Israel, for those who sought the young Child's life are dead."

21 And he arose, took the young Child and His mother, and came into the land of Israel.

22 But when he heard that Archelaus was reigning in Judea instead of his father Herod, he was afraid to go there. And being warned by God in a dream, he turned aside into the region of Galilee.

23 And he came and dwelt in a city called Nazareth, that it might be fulfilled which was spoken by the prophets, "He will be called a Nazarene."

John Prepares the Way [10]

3 In those days John the Baptizer came preaching in the wilderness of Judea

2 and saying, "Repent, for the kingdom of heaven is at hand!"

3 For this is he who was spoken of by the prophet Isaiah, saying:

8 Hosea 11:1

9 Jeremiah 31:15 (31:14 in some versions)
10 The call to repent, undergo mikveh (immersion), and be ready for the coming Messiah.

"The voice of one crying in
the wilderness:
'Prepare the way of the
LORD,
Make His paths
straight.' " [11]

4 And John himself was clothed
in camel's hair, with a leather belt
around his waist; and his food was
locusts and wild honey.

5 Then Jerusalem, all Judea,
and all the region around the Jordan went out to him

6 and were immersed by him in
the Jordan, confessing their sins.

7 But when he saw many of the
Pharisees and Sadducees coming
to his immersion, he said to them,
"O brood of vipers! Who has
warned you to flee from the wrath
to come?

8 "Therefore bear fruits worthy
of repentance,

9 "and do not think to say to
yourselves, 'We have Abraham as
our father.' For I say to you that
God is able to raise up children to
Abraham from these stones.

10 "And even now the ax is laid
to the root of the trees. Therefore
every tree which does not bear
good fruit is cut down and thrown
into the fire.

11 "I indeed immerse you in water to repentance, but He who is
coming after me is mightier than
I, whose sandals I am not worthy
to carry. He will immerse you in
the Holy Spirit and fire.

12 "His winnowing fan is in His
hand, and He will thoroughly
purge His threshing floor, and
gather His wheat into the barn;
but He will burn up the chaff with
unquenchable fire."

John Immerses Yeshua

13 Then Yeshua came from
Galilee to John at the Jordan to be
immersed by him.

14 But John tried to prevent
Him, saying, "I have need to be
immersed by You, and are You
coming to me?"

15 And Yeshua answered and
said to him, "Permit it to be so
now, for thus it is fitting for us to
fulfill all righteousness." Then he
allowed Him.

16 And Yeshua, when He had
been immersed, came up immediately from the water; and behold,
the heavens were opened to Him,
and He saw the Spirit of God descending like a dove and alighting
upon Him.

17 And suddenly a voice came
from heaven, saying, "This is My
beloved Son, in whom I am well
pleased."

Satan Tempts Yeshua

4 Then Yeshua was led up by
the Spirit into the wilderness
to be tempted by the devil.

2 And when He had fasted
forty days and forty nights, afterward He was hungry.

3 And when the tempter came
to Him, he said, "If You are the
Son of God, command that these
stones become bread."

4 But He answered and said,
"It is written, *'Man shall not live
by bread alone, but by every word
that proceeds out of the mouth of
God.'* " [12]

5 Then the devil took Him up
into the holy city, set Him on the
pinnacle of the temple,

6 and said to Him, "If You are

---

[11] Isaiah 40:3

[12] Deuteronomy 8:3

the Son of God, throw Yourself down. For it is written:

'He will give His angels
    charge concerning you,'

and,

'In their hands they will bear
    you up,
Lest you dash your foot
    against a stone.'" [13]

7 Yeshua said to him, "It is written again, *You shall not tempt the LORD your God.*'" [14]

8 Again, the devil took Him up on an exceedingly high mountain, and showed Him all the kingdoms of the world and their glory.

9 And he said to Him, "All these things I will give You if You will fall down and worship me."

10 Then Yeshua said to him, "Away with you, Satan! For it is written, *You shall worship the LORD your God, and Him only you shall serve.*'" [15]

11 Then the devil left Him, and behold, angels came and ministered to Him.

Yeshua in Galilee

12 Now when Yeshua had heard that John had been put in prison, He departed to Galilee.

13 And leaving Nazareth, He came and dwelt in Capernaum, which is by the sea, in the regions of Zebulun and Naphtali,

14 that it might be fulfilled which was spoken by Isaiah the prophet, saying:

15 *"The land of Zebulun and
    the land of Naphtali,
The way of the sea, beyond
    the Jordan,
Galilee of the Gentiles:*

16 *The people who sat in dark-
    ness saw a great light,
And to those who sat in the
    region and shadow of death
    Light has dawned."* [16]

17 From that time Yeshua began to preach and to say, "Repent, for the kingdom of heaven is at hand."

Four Fishermen

18 And Yeshua, walking by the Sea of Galilee, saw two brothers, Simon called Peter, and Andrew his brother, casting a net into the sea; for they were fishermen.

19 And He said to them, "Follow Me, and I will make you fishers of men."

20 And they immediately left their nets and followed Him.

21 And going on from there, He saw two other brothers, James the son of Zebedee, and John his brother, in the boat with Zebedee their father, mending their nets. And He called them,

22 and immediately they left the boat and their father, and followed Him.

Yeshua Heals a Great Multitude

23 And Yeshua went about all Galilee, teaching in their synagogues, preaching the good news of the kingdom, and healing all kinds of sickness and all kinds of disease among the people.

24 And His fame went throughout all Syria; and they brought to Him all sick people who were afflicted with various diseases and torments, and those who were demon-possessed, epileptics, and paralytics; and He healed them.

---

13 Psalm 91:11, 12   *14* Deuteronomy 6:16   *15* Deuteronomy 6:13, 14

16 Isaiah 9:1, 2 (8:23—9:1 in some versions)

25 And great multitudes followed Him—from Galilee, and from Decapolis, Jerusalem, Judea, and beyond the Jordan.

The Blessings

5 And seeing the multitudes, He went up on a mountain, and when He was seated His disciples came to Him.

2 And He opened His mouth and taught them, saying:

3 "Blessed are the poor in spirit,
     For theirs is the kingdom of heaven.

4 Blessed are those who mourn,
     For they shall be comforted.

5 Blessed are the gentle,
     For they shall inherit the earth.[17]

6 Blessed are those who hunger and thirst for righteousness,
     For they shall be filled.

7 Blessed are the merciful,
     For they shall obtain mercy.

8 Blessed are the pure in heart,
     For they shall see God.

9 Blessed are the peacemakers,
     For they shall be called sons of God.

10 Blessed are those who are persecuted for righteousness' sake,
     For theirs is the kingdom of heaven.

11 "Blessed are you when they revile and persecute you, and say all manner of evil against you falsely for My sake.

12 "Rejoice and be exceedingly glad, for great is your reward in heaven, for so they persecuted the prophets who were before you.

Believers Are Salt and Light

13 "You are the salt of the earth; but if the salt loses its flavor, how shall it be seasoned? It is then good for nothing but to be thrown out and trampled under foot by men.

14 "You are the light of the world. A city that is set on a hill cannot be hidden.

15 "Nor do they light a lamp and put it under a basket, but on a lampstand, and it gives light to all who are in the house.

16 "Let your light so shine before men, that they may see your good works and glorify your Father who is in heaven.

Messiah Fulfills the Torah

17 "Do not think that I have come to destroy the Torah or the Prophets. I have not come to destroy but to fulfill.

18 "For assuredly, I say to you, till heaven and earth pass away, one yod[18] or one mark[19] will by no means pass from the Torah till all is fulfilled.

19 "Whoever therefore breaks one of the least of these commandments, and teaches men so, he will be called least in the kingdom of heaven; but whoever does and teaches them will be called great in the kingdom of heaven.

20 "For I say to you, that unless

---

17 Psalm 37:11

18 Smallest letter in the Hebrew alphabet.

19 Hebrew: *tag,* an elaboration, functional or ornamental, of a line or stroke in a Hebrew letter.

your righteousness exceeds the righteousness of the scribes and Pharisees, you will by no means enter the kingdom of heaven.

Murder Begins in the Heart

21 "You have heard that it was said to those of old, 'You shall not murder,' [20] and whoever murders will be in danger of the judgment.

22 "But I say to you that whoever is angry with his brother without a cause will be in danger of the judgment. And whoever says to his brother, 'Raca!' [21] will be in danger of the council. But whoever says, 'You fool!' will be in danger of hell fire.

23 "Therefore if you bring your gift to the altar, and there remember that your brother has something against you,

24 "leave your gift there before the altar, and go your way. First be reconciled to your brother, and then come and offer your gift.

25 "Agree with your adversary quickly, while you are on the way with him, lest your adversary deliver you to the judge, the judge hand you over to the officer, and you are thrown into prison.

26 "Assuredly, I say to you, you will by no means get out of there till you have paid the last penny.

Adultery in the Heart

27 "You have heard that it was said to those of old, 'You shall not commit adultery.' [22]

28 "But I say to you that whoever looks at a woman to lust for her has already committed adultery with her in his heart.

29 "And if your right eye causes you to sin, pluck it out and cast it from you; for it is profitable for you that one of your members perish, and not that your whole body be cast into hell.

30 "And if your right hand causes you to sin, cut it off and cast it from you; for it is profitable for you that one of your members perish, and not that your whole body be cast into hell.

Marriage Is Sacred and Binding

31 "Furthermore it has been said, 'Whoever puts away his wife, let him give her a certificate of divorce.' [23]

32 "But I say to you that whoever divorces his wife, except for sexual immorality,[24] causes her to commit adultery; and whoever marries a woman who is divorced commits adultery.

Yeshua Forbids Oaths

33 "Again you have heard that it has been said to those of old, 'You shall not swear falsely, but shall perform your oaths to the Lord.'

34 "But I say to you, do not swear at all: neither by heaven, for it is God's throne;

35 "nor by the earth, for it is His footstool; nor by Jerusalem, for it is the city of the great King.

---

20 Exodus 20:13; Deuteronomy 5:17
21 Aramaic: "empty-head" or "good-for-nothing."
22 Exodus 20:14; Deuteronomy 5:18 (5:17 in some versions)

23 Deuteronomy 24:1
24 Lit. "prostitution, unchastity, fornication." This is a general term referring to any kind of illicit sexual intercourse.

36 "Nor shall you swear by your head, because you cannot make one hair white or black.

37 "But let your 'Yes' be 'Yes,' and your 'No,' 'No.' For whatever is more than these is from the evil one.

Go the Second Mile

38 "You have heard that it has been said, '*An eye for an eye and a tooth for a tooth.*' [25]

39 "But I tell you not to resist an evil person. But whoever slaps you on your right cheek, turn the other to him also.

40 "And if anyone wants to sue you and take away your tunic, let him have your cloak also.

41 "And whoever shall compel you to go one mile, go with him two.

42 "Give to him who asks you, and from him who wants to borrow from you do not turn away.

Love Your Enemies

43 "You have heard that it has been said, '*You shall love your neighbor*[26] *and hate your enemy.*'

44 "But I say to you, love your enemies, bless those who curse you, do good to those who hate you, and pray for those who spitefully use you and persecute you,

45 "that you may be sons of your Father who is in heaven; for He makes His sun rise on the evil and on the good, and sends rain on the just and on the unjust.

46 "For if you love those who love you, what reward have you? Do not even the tax collectors do the same?

47 "And if you greet your brethren only, what do you do more than others? Do not even the tax collectors do so?

48 "Therefore you shall be perfect, just as your Father in heaven is perfect.

Do Good to Please God

6 "Take heed that you do not do your charitable deeds before men to be seen by them. Otherwise you have no reward from your Father who is in heaven.

2 "Therefore, when you do a charitable deed, do not sound a trumpet before you as the hypocrites do in the synagogues and in the streets, that they may have glory from men. Assuredly, I say to you, they have their reward.

3 "But when you do a charitable deed, do not let your left hand know what your right hand is doing,

4 "that your charitable deed may be in secret; and your Father who sees in secret will Himself reward you openly.

The Model Prayer

5 "And when you pray, you shall not be like the hypocrites. For they love to pray standing in the synagogues and on the corners of the streets, that they may be seen by men. Assuredly, I say to you, they have their reward.

6 "But you, when you pray, go into your room, and when you have shut your door, pray to your Father who is in secret; and your Father who sees in secret will reward you openly.

25 Exodus 21:24; Leviticus 24:20; Deuteronomy 19:21   26 Leviticus 19:18

7 "But when you pray, do not use vain repetitions as the heathen do. For they think that they will be heard for their many words.

8 "Therefore do not be like them. For your Father knows the things you have need of before you ask Him.

9 "In this manner, therefore, pray:

Our Father in heaven,
Hallowed be Your name.
10 Your kingdom come.
Your will be done
On earth as it is in heaven.
11 Give us this day our daily
bread.
12 And forgive us our debts,
As we forgive our debtors.
13 And do not lead us into
temptation,
But deliver us from the evil
one.
For Yours is the kingdom
and the power and the
glory forever. Amen.

14 "For if you forgive men their trespasses, your heavenly Father will also forgive you.

15 "But if you do not forgive men their trespasses, neither will your Father forgive your trespasses.

Fasting to Be Seen Only by God

16 "Moreover, when you fast, do not be like the hypocrites, with a sad countenance. For they disfigure their faces that they may appear to men to be fasting. Assuredly, I say to you, they have their reward.

17 "But you, when you fast, anoint your head and wash your face,

18 "so that you do not appear to men to be fasting, but to your Father who is in secret; and your Father who sees in secret will reward you openly.

Lay Up Treasures in Heaven

19 "Do not lay up for yourselves treasures on earth, where moth and rust destroy and where thieves break in and steal;

20 "but lay up for yourselves treasures in heaven, where neither moth nor rust destroys and where thieves do not break in and steal.

21 "For where your treasure is, there your heart will be also.

The Lamp of the Body

22 "The lamp of the body is the eye. If therefore your eye is good, your whole body will be full of light.

23 "But if your eye is bad, your whole body will be full of darkness. If therefore the light that is in you is darkness, how great is that darkness!

You Cannot Serve God and Riches

24 "No one can serve two masters; for either he will hate the one and love the other, or else he will hold to the one and despise the other. You cannot serve God and mammon.

Do Not Worry

25 "Therefore I say to you, do not worry about your life, what you will eat or what you will drink; nor about your body, what you will put on. Is not life more than food and the body more than clothing?

26 "Look at the birds of the air, for they neither sow nor reap nor

gather into barns; yet your heavenly Father feeds them. Are you not of more value than they?

27 "Which of you by worrying can add one cubit to his stature?

28 "And why do you worry about clothing? Consider the lilies of the field, how they grow: they neither toil nor spin;

29 "and yet I say to you that even Solomon in all his glory was not arrayed like one of these.

30 "Now if God so clothes the grass of the field, which today is, and tomorrow is thrown into the oven, will He not much more clothe you, O you of little faith?

31 "Therefore do not worry, saying, 'What shall we eat?' or, 'What shall we drink?' or, 'What shall we wear?'

32 "For after all these things the Gentiles seek. For your heavenly Father knows that you need all these things.

33 "But seek first the kingdom of God and His righteousness, and all these things will be added to you.

34 "Therefore do not worry about tomorrow, for tomorrow will worry about its own things. Sufficient for the day is its own trouble.

Do Not Judge

7 "Judge not, that you be not judged.

2 "For with what judgment you judge, you will be judged; and with the same measure you use, it will be measured back to you.

3 "And why do you look at the speck that is in your brother's eye, but do not consider the plank that is in your own eye?

4 "Or how can you say to your brother, 'Let me take the speck out of your eye'; and look, a plank is in your own eye?

5 "You hypocrite! First remove the plank from your own eye, and then you will see clearly to take the speck out of your brother's eye.

6 "Do not give what is holy to the dogs; nor cast your pearls before swine, lest they trample them under their feet, and turn and tear you in pieces.

Keep Asking, Seeking, Knocking

7 "Ask, and it will be given to you; seek, and you will find; knock, and it will be opened to you.

8 "For everyone who asks receives, and he who seeks finds, and to him who knocks it will be opened.

9 "Or what man is there among you who, if his son asks for bread, will give him a stone?

10 "Or if he asks for a fish, will he give him a serpent?

11 "If you then, being evil, know how to give good gifts to your children, how much more will your Father who is in heaven give good things to those who ask Him!

12 "Therefore, whatever you want men to do to you, you also do to them, for this is the Torah and the Prophets.

The Narrow Way

13 "Enter in at the narrow gate; for wide is the gate and broad is the way that leads to destruction, and there are many who go in through it.

14 "Because narrow is the gate and difficult is the way which

leads to life, and there are few who find it.

You Will Know Them by Their Fruits

15 "Beware of false prophets, who come to you in sheep's clothing, but inwardly they are ravenous wolves.

16 "You will know them by their fruits. Do men gather grapes from thornbushes or figs from thistles?

17 "Even so, every good tree bears good fruit, but a bad tree bears bad fruit.

18 "A good tree cannot bear bad fruit, nor can a bad tree bear good fruit.

19 "Every tree that does not bear good fruit is cut down and thrown into the fire.

20 "Therefore by their fruits you will know them.

I Never Knew You

21 "Not everyone who says to Me, 'Lord, Lord,' will enter the kingdom of heaven, but he who does the will of My Father who is in heaven.

22 "Many will say to Me in that day, 'Lord, Lord, have we not prophesied in Your name, cast out demons in Your name, and done many wonderful works in Your name?'

23 "And then I will declare to them, 'I never knew you; depart from Me, you who practice lawlessness!'

Build on the Rock

24 "Therefore whoever hears these sayings of Mine, and does them, I will liken him to a wise man who built his house on the rock:

25 "and the rain descended, the floods came, and the winds blew and beat on that house; and it did not fall, for it was founded on the rock.

26 "And everyone who hears these sayings of Mine, and does not do them, will be like a foolish man who built his house on the sand:

27 "and the rain descended, the floods came, and the winds blew and beat on that house; and it fell. And great was its fall."

28 And it came to pass, when Yeshua had ended these sayings, that the people were astonished at His teaching,

29 for He taught them as one having authority, and not as the scribes.

Yeshua Cleanses a Leper

8 When He had come down from the mountain, great multitudes followed Him.

2 And behold, a leper came and worshiped Him, saying, "Lord, if You are willing, You can make me clean."

3 And Yeshua put out His hand and touched him, saying, "I am willing; be cleansed." And immediately his leprosy was cleansed.

4 And Yeshua said to him, "See that you tell no one; but go your way, show yourself to the priest, and offer the gift that Moses commanded, as a testimony to them." [27]

27 Leviticus 14:1-32

Yeshua Heals a Centurion's Servant

5 And when Yeshua had entered Capernaum, a centurion came to Him, pleading with Him,

6 saying, "Lord, my servant is lying at home paralyzed, terribly tormented."

7 And Yeshua said to him, "I will come and heal him."

8 The centurion answered and said, "Lord, I am not worthy that You should come under my roof. But only speak a word, and my servant will be healed.

9 "For I also am a man under authority, having soldiers under me. And I say to this one, 'Go,' and he goes; and to another, 'Come,' and he comes; and to my servant, 'Do this,' and he does it."

10 When Yeshua heard it, He marveled, and said to those who followed, "Assuredly, I say to you, I have not found such great faith, not even in Israel!

11 "And I say to you that many will come from the east and west, and sit down with Abraham, Isaac, and Jacob in the kingdom of heaven.

12 "But the sons of the kingdom will be cast out into outer darkness. There will be weeping and gnashing of teeth."

13 And Yeshua said to the centurion, "Go your way; and as you have believed, so let it be done for you." And his servant was healed that same hour.

Peter's Mother-in-Law Healed

14 And when Yeshua had come into Peter's house, He saw his wife's mother lying sick with a fever.

15 And He touched her hand, and the fever left her. And she arose and served them.

Many Healed After Sabbath Sunset

16 When evening had come, they brought to Him many who were demon-possessed. And He cast out the spirits with a word, and healed all who were sick,

17 that it might be fulfilled which was spoken by Isaiah the prophet, saying:

"He Himself took our infirmities
And bore our sicknesses." [28]

The Cost

18 Now when Yeshua saw great multitudes about Him, He gave a command to depart to the other side.

19 And a certain scribe came and said to Him, "Rabbi, I will follow You wherever You go."

20 And Yeshua said to him, "Foxes have holes and birds of the air have nests, but the Son of Man has nowhere to lay His head."

21 And another of His disciples said to Him, "Lord, let me first go and bury my father."

22 But Yeshua said to him, "Follow Me, and let the dead bury their own dead."

Wind and Wave Obey Yeshua

23 And when He got into a boat, His disciples followed Him.

24 And suddenly a great tempest arose on the sea, so that the boat was covered with the waves. But He was asleep.

25 And His disciples came to Him and awoke Him, saying,

[28] Isaiah 53:4

"Lord, save us! We are perishing!"

26 And He said to them, "Why are you fearful, O you of little faith?" Then He arose and rebuked the winds and the sea. And there was a great calm.[29]

27 And the men marveled, saying, "What kind of Man is this, that even the winds and the sea obey Him!"

Two Demon-Possessed Men Healed

28 And when He had come to the other side, to the country of the Gergesenes, there met Him two demon-possessed men, coming out of the tombs, exceedingly fierce, so that no one could pass that way.

29 And suddenly they cried out, saying, "What have we to do with You, Yeshua, You Son of God? Have You come here to torment us before the time?"

30 And a good way off from them there was a herd of many swine feeding.

31 So the demons begged Him, saying, "If You cast us out, permit us to go away into the herd of swine."

32 And He said to them, "Go." And when they had come out, they went into the herd of swine. And suddenly the whole herd of swine ran violently down the steep place into the sea, and perished in the water.

33 And those who kept them fled; and they went away into the city and told everything, including what had happened to the demon-possessed men.

34 And behold, then the whole city came out to meet Yeshua. And when they saw Him, they begged Him to depart from their region.

Yeshua Forgives and Heals a Paralytic

9 And He got into a boat, crossed over, and came to His own city.

2 And behold, they brought to Him a paralytic lying on a bed. And Yeshua, seeing their faith, said to the paralytic, "Son, be of good cheer; your sins are forgiven you."

3 And at once some of the scribes said within themselves, "This Man blasphemes!"

4 And Yeshua, knowing their thoughts, said, "Why do you think evil in your hearts?

5 "For which is easier, to say, 'Your sins are forgiven you,' or to say, 'Arise and walk'?

6 "But that you may know that the Son of Man has power on earth to forgive sins"—then He said to the paralytic, "Arise, take up your bed, and go to your house."

7 And he arose and departed to his house.

8 But when the multitudes saw it, they marveled and glorified God who had given such power to men.

Matthew the Tax Collector

9 And as Yeshua passed on from there, He saw a man named Matthew sitting at the tax office. And He said to him, "Follow Me." And he arose and followed Him.

---

29 This suggests what was declared of God, who controls the seas, in Psalm 107:28, 29.

10 And so it was, as Yeshua sat at the table in the house, behold, many tax collectors and sinners came and sat down with Him and His disciples.

11 And when the Pharisees saw it, they said to His disciples, "Why does your Rabbi eat with tax collectors and sinners?"

12 But when Yeshua heard that, He said to them, "Those who are well have no need of a physician, but those who are sick.

13 "But go and learn what this means: 'I desire mercy and not sacrifice.' [30] For I did not come to call the righteous, but sinners, to repentance."

Yeshua Is Questioned About Fasting

14 Then the disciples of John came to Him, saying, "Why do we and the Pharisees fast often, but Your disciples do not fast?"

15 And Yeshua said to them, "Can the friends of the bridegroom mourn as long as the bridegroom is with them? But the days will come when the bridegroom will be taken away from them, and then they will fast.

16 "No one puts a piece of unshrunk cloth on an old garment; for the patch pulls away from the garment, and the tear is made worse.

17 "Nor do people put new wine into old wineskins, or else the wineskins break, the wine is spilled, and the wineskins will be ruined. But they put new wine into new wineskins, and both are preserved."

A Girl Restored to Life and a Woman Healed

18 While He spoke these things to them, behold, a ruler came and worshiped Him, saying, "My daughter has just died, but come and lay Your hand on her and she will live."

19 And Yeshua arose and followed him, and so did His disciples.

20 And suddenly a woman who had a flow of blood for twelve years came behind Him and touched the hem of His garment;[31]

21 for she said to herself, "If only I may touch His garment, I shall be made well."

22 But Yeshua turned around, and when He saw her He said, "Be of good cheer, daughter; your faith has made you well." And the woman was made well from that hour.

23 And when Yeshua came into the ruler's house, and saw the flute players and the noisy crowd wailing,

24 He said to them, "Make room, for the girl is not dead but sleeping." And they laughed Him to scorn.

25 But when the crowd was put outside, He went in and took her by the hand, and the girl arose.

26 And the report of this went out into all that land.

Two Blind Men Healed

27 And when Yeshua departed from there, two blind men followed Him, crying out and saying, "Son of David, have mercy on us!"

---

30 Hosea 6:6

31 Fringes (tzitzit), Numbers 15:38–41.

28 And when He had come into the house, the blind men came to Him. And Yeshua said to them, "Do you believe that I am able to do this?" They said to Him, "Yes, Lord."

29 Then He touched their eyes, saying, "According to your faith let it be to you."

30 And their eyes were opened. And Yeshua sternly warned them, saying, "See that no one knows it."

31 But when they had departed, they spread the news about Him in all that country.

The Mute Speaks

32 As they went out, behold, they brought to Him a man, mute and demon-possessed.

33 And when the demon was cast out, the mute spoke. And the multitudes marveled, saying, "It was never seen like this in Israel!"

34 But the Pharisees said, "He casts out demons by the ruler of the demons."

The Compassion of Yeshua

35 And Yeshua went about all the cities and villages, teaching in their synagogues, preaching the good news of the kingdom, and healing every sickness and every disease among the people.

36 But when He saw the multitudes, He was moved with compassion for them, because they were weary and scattered, like sheep having no shepherd.

37 Then He said to His disciples, "The harvest truly is plentiful, but the laborers are few.

38 "Therefore pray the Lord of the harvest that He will send out laborers into His harvest."

The Twelve

10 And when He had called His twelve disciples to Him, He gave them power over unclean spirits, to cast them out, and to heal all kinds of sickness and all kinds of disease.

2 Now the names of the twelve apostles are these: first, Simon, who is called Peter, and Andrew his brother; James the son of Zebedee, and John his brother;

3 Philip and Bartholomew; Thomas and Matthew the tax collector; James the son of Alphaeus, and Lebbaeus, whose surname was Thaddaeus;

4 Simon the Canaanite, and Judas Iscariot, who also betrayed Him.

Sending Out the Twelve

5 These twelve Yeshua sent out and commanded them, saying: "Do not go into the way of the Gentiles, and do not enter a city of the Samaritans.

6 "But go rather to the lost sheep of the house of Israel.

7 "And as you go, preach, saying, 'The kingdom of heaven is at hand.'

8 "Heal the sick, cleanse the lepers, raise the dead, cast out demons. Freely you have received, freely give.

9 "Provide neither gold nor silver nor copper in your money-belts,

10 "nor bag for your journey, nor two tunics, nor sandals, nor staffs; for a worker is worthy of his food.

11 "And whatever city or town you enter, inquire who in it is worthy, and stay there till you go out.

12 "And when you go into a household, greet it.

13 "And if the household is worthy, let your peace come upon it. But if it is not worthy, let your peace return to you.

14 "And whoever will not receive you nor hear your words, when you depart from that house or city, shake off the dust from your feet.

15 "Assuredly, I say to you, it will be more tolerable for the land of Sodom and Gomorrah in the day of judgment than for that city!

Persecutions Are Coming

16 "Behold, I send you out as sheep in the midst of wolves. Therefore be wise as serpents and harmless as doves.

17 "But beware of men, for they will deliver you up to councils and scourge you in their synagogues.

18 "And you will be brought before governors and kings for My sake, as a testimony to them and to the Gentiles.

19 "But when they deliver you up, do not worry about how or what you will speak. But it will be given to you in that hour what you will speak;

20 "for it is not you who speak, but the Spirit of your Father who speaks in you.

21 "And brother will deliver up brother to death, and a father his child; and children will rise up against parents and cause them to be put to death.

22 "And you will be hated by all for My name's sake. But he who endures to the end will be saved.

23 "But when they persecute you in this city, flee to another. For assuredly, I say to you, you shall not have gone through the cities of Israel before the Son of Man comes.

24 "A disciple is not above his teacher, nor a servant above his master.

25 "It is enough for a disciple that he be like his teacher, and a servant like his master. If they have called the master of the house Beelzebub, how much more will they call those of his household!

26 "Therefore do not fear them. For there is nothing covered that will not be revealed, and hidden that will not be known.

Yeshua Teaches the Fear of God

27 "What I tell you in the darkness, speak in the light; and what you hear in the ear, preach on the housetops.

28 "And do not fear those who kill the body but cannot kill the soul. But rather fear Him who is able to destroy both soul and body in hell.

29 "Are not two sparrows sold for a copper coin? And not one of them falls to the ground apart from your Father's will.

30 "But the very hairs of your head are all numbered.

31 "Do not fear therefore; you are of more value than many sparrows.

Confess the Messiah Before Men

32 "Therefore whoever confesses Me before men, him I will also confess before My Father who is in heaven.

33 "But whoever denies Me before men, him I will also deny before My Father who is in heaven.

The Messiah Brings Division

34 "Do not think that I have come to bring peace on earth. I did not come to bring peace but a sword.

35 "For I have come to *'set a man against his father, a daughter against her mother, and a daughter-in-law against her mother-in-law.'*

36 "And *'a man's foes will be those of his own household.'* [32]

37 "He who loves father or mother more than Me is not worthy of Me. And he who loves son or daughter more than Me is not worthy of Me.

38 "And he who does not take his cross and follow after Me is not worthy of Me.

39 "He who finds his life will lose it, and he who loses his life for My sake will find it.

A Cup of Cold Water

40 "He who receives you receives Me, and he who receives Me receives Him who sent Me.

41 "He who receives a prophet in the name of a prophet will receive a prophet's reward. And he who receives a righteous man in the name of a righteous man will receive a righteous man's reward.

42 "And whoever gives one of these little ones only a cup of cold water in the name of a disciple, assuredly, I say to you, he will by no means lose his reward."

John Sends Messengers to Yeshua

11 And it came to pass, when Yeshua finished commanding His twelve disciples, that He departed from there to teach and to preach in their cities.

2 Now when John had heard in prison about the works of the Messiah, he sent two of his disciples

3 and said to Him, "Are You the Coming One, or do we look for another?"

4 Yeshua answered and said to them, "Go and tell John the things you hear and see:

5 "The blind receive their sight and the lame walk, the lepers are cleansed and the deaf hear, the dead are raised up and the poor have the good news preached to them.

6 "And blessed is he who is not offended because of Me."

7 And as they departed, Yeshua began to say to the multitudes concerning John: "What did you go out into the wilderness to see? A reed shaken by the wind?

8 "But what did you go out to see? A man clothed in soft garments? Indeed, those who wear soft clothing are in kings' houses.

9 "But what did you go out to see? A prophet? Yes, I say to you, and more than a prophet.

10 "For this is he of whom it is written:

'Behold, I send My messenger before Your face,
Who will prepare Your way before You.' [33]

11 "Assuredly, I say to you, among those born of women there has not risen one greater than John the Baptizer; but he who is least in the kingdom of heaven is greater than he.

12 "And from the days of John

32 Micah 7:6

33 Malachi 3:1

the Baptizer until now the kingdom of heaven suffers violence, and the violent take it by force.

13 "For all the prophets and the Torah prophesied until John.

14 "And if you are willing to receive it, he is Elijah who is to come.[34]

15 "He who has ears to hear, let him hear!

16 "But to what shall I liken this generation? It is like children sitting in the marketplaces and calling to their companions,

17 "and saying:

'We played the flute for you,
And you did not dance;
We mourned to you,
And you did not lament.'

18 "For John came neither eating nor drinking, and they say, 'He has a demon.'

19 "The Son of Man came eating and drinking, and they say, 'Look, a gluttonous man and a winebibber, a friend of tax collectors and sinners!' But wisdom is justified by her children."

Woe to the Impenitent Cities

20 Then He began to upbraid the cities in which most of His mighty works had been done, because they did not repent:

21 "Woe to you, Chorazin! Woe to you, Bethsaida! For if the mighty works which were done in you had been done in Tyre and Sidon, they would have repented long ago in sackcloth and ashes.

22 "But I say to you, it will be more tolerable for Tyre and Sidon in the day of judgment than for you.

23 "And you, Capernaum, who are exalted to heaven, will be brought down to Hades; for if the mighty works which were done in you had been done in Sodom, it would have remained until this day.

24 "But I say to you that it will be more tolerable for the land of Sodom in the day of judgment than for you."

Yeshua Gives True Rest

25 At that time Yeshua answered and said, "I thank You, O Father, Lord of heaven and earth, because You have hidden these things from the wise and prudent and have revealed them to babes.

26 "Even so, Father, for so it seemed good in Your sight.

27 "All things have been delivered to Me by My Father, and no one knows the Son but the Father. Nor does anyone know the Father but the Son, and he to whom the Son wills to reveal Him.

28 "Come to Me, all you who labor and are heavy laden, and I will give you rest.

29 "Take My yoke upon you and learn from Me, for I am gentle and lowly in heart, and you will find rest for your souls.

30 "For My yoke is easy and My burden is light."

Yeshua Teaches Concerning the Sabbath

12 At that time Yeshua went through the grainfields on the Sabbath. And His disciples were hungry, and began to pluck heads of grain and to eat.

2 But when the Pharisees saw it, they said to Him, "Look, Your

---

34 Malachi 4:5 (3:23 in some versions)

disciples are doing what is not lawful to do on the Sabbath!"

3 But He said to them, "Have you not read what David did when he was hungry, he and those who were with him:

4 "how he entered the house of God and ate the showbread which was not lawful for him to eat, nor for those who were with him, but only for the priests?[35]

5 "Or have you not read in the Torah that on the Sabbath the priests in the temple profane the Sabbath, and are blameless?[36]

6 "But I say to you that in this place there is One greater than the temple.

7 "But if you had known what this means, '*I desire mercy and not sacrifice,*'[37] you would not have condemned the guiltless.

8 "For the Son of Man[38] is Lord even of the Sabbath."

A Man with a Withered Hand Healed on the Sabbath

9 And when He had departed from there, He went into their synagogue.

10 And behold, there was a man who had a withered hand. And they asked Him, saying, "Is it lawful to heal on the Sabbath?"—that they might accuse Him.

11 And He said to them, "What man is there among you who has one sheep, and if it falls into a pit on the Sabbath, will not lay hold of it and lift it out?

12 "Of how much more value then is a man than a sheep?

Therefore it is lawful to do good on the Sabbath."

13 Then He said to the man, "Stretch out your hand." And he stretched it out, and it was restored as whole as the other.

14 Then the Pharisees went out and took counsel against Him, how they might destroy Him.

Behold My Servant

15 But when Yeshua knew it, He withdrew from there; and great multitudes followed Him, and He healed them all.

16 And He warned them not to make Him known,

17 that it might be fulfilled which was spoken by Isaiah the prophet, saying:

18 "*Behold, My Servant whom I have chosen,*
    My Beloved in whom My soul is well pleased;
    I will put My Spirit upon Him,
    And He will declare justice to the Gentiles.

19 *He will not quarrel nor cry out,*
    Nor will anyone hear His voice in the streets.

20 *A bruised reed He will not break,*
    And smoking flax He will not quench,
    Till He sends forth justice to victory.

21 *And in His name Gentiles will trust.*"[39]

A House Divided Cannot Stand

22 Then one was brought to Him who was demon-possessed,

---

35 1 Samuel 21:1-6

36 Numbers 28:9, 10　　37 Hosea 6:6

38 A title of Messiah, Daniel 7:13, 14.

39 Isaiah 42:1-4

blind and mute; and He healed him, so that the blind and mute man both spoke and saw.

23 And all the multitudes were amazed and said, "Could this be the Son of David?"

24 But when the Pharisees heard it they said, "This fellow does not cast out demons except by Beelzebub, the ruler of the demons."

25 And Yeshua knew their thoughts and said to them: "Every kingdom divided against itself is brought to desolation, and every city or house divided against itself will not stand.

26 "And if Satan casts out Satan, he is divided against himself. How then will his kingdom stand?

27 "And if I cast out demons by Beelzebub, by whom do your sons cast them out? Therefore they will be your judges.

28 "But if I cast out demons by the Spirit of God, then the kingdom of God has come to you.

29 "Or else how can one enter a strong man's house and plunder his goods, unless he first binds the strong man? And then he will plunder his house.

30 "He who is not with Me is against Me, and he who does not gather with Me scatters abroad.

The Unpardonable Sin

31 "Therefore I say to you, every sin and blasphemy will be forgiven men, but the blasphemy against the Holy Spirit will not be forgiven men.

32 "And whoever speaks a word against the Son of Man, it will be forgiven him; but whoever speaks against the Holy Spirit, it will not be forgiven him, either in this age or in the age to come.

A Tree Known by Its Fruits

33 "Either make the tree good and its fruit good, or else make the tree bad and its fruit bad; for a tree is known by its fruit.

34 "O brood of vipers! How can you, being evil, speak good things? For out of the abundance of the heart the mouth speaks.

35 "A good man out of the good treasure of his heart brings forth good things; and an evil man out of the evil treasure brings forth evil things.

36 "But I say to you that for every idle word men may speak, they will give account of it in the day of judgment.

37 "For by your words you will be justified, and by your words you will be condemned."

The Scribes and Pharisees Ask for a Sign

38 Then some of the scribes and Pharisees answered, saying, "Rabbi, we want to see a sign from You."

39 But He answered and said to them, "An evil and adulterous generation seeks after a sign, and no sign will be given to it except the sign of the prophet Jonah.

40 "For as Jonah was three days and three nights in the belly of the great fish, so will the Son of Man be three days and three nights in the heart of the earth.[40]

41 "The men of Nineveh will rise in the judgment with this generation and condemn it, because they repented at the preaching of Jonah;[41] and indeed a greater than Jonah is here.

40 Jonah 1:17
41 Jonah 3:5

42 "The queen of the South will rise up in the judgment with this generation and condemn it, for she came from the ends of the earth to hear the wisdom of Solomon;[42] and indeed a greater than Solomon is here.

An Unclean Spirit Returns

43 "When an unclean spirit goes out of a man, he goes through dry places, seeking rest, and finds none.

44 "Then he says, 'I will return to my house from which I came.' And when he comes, he finds it empty, swept, and put in order.

45 "Then he goes and takes with him seven other spirits more wicked than himself, and they enter and dwell there; and the last state of that man is worse than the first. So it also will be with this wicked generation."

Yeshua's Mother and Brothers Send for Him

46 While He was still talking to the multitudes, behold, His mother and His brothers stood outside, seeking to speak with Him.

47 Then one said to Him, "Look, Your mother and Your brothers are standing outside, seeking to speak with You."

48 But He answered and said to the one who told Him, "Who is My mother and who are My brothers?"

49 And He stretched out His hand toward His disciples and said, "Here are My mother and My brothers!

50 "For whoever does the will of My Father who is in heaven is My brother and sister and mother."

The Parable of the Sower

13 The same day Yeshua went out of the house and sat by the seaside.

2 And great multitudes were gathered together to Him, so that He got into a boat and sat; and the whole multitude stood on the shore.

3 And He spoke many things to them in parables, saying: "Behold, a sower went out to sow.

4 "And as he sowed, some seed fell by the wayside; and the birds came and devoured them.

5 "Some fell on stony places, where they did not have much earth; and they immediately sprang up because they had no depth of earth.

6 "But when the sun was up they were scorched, and because they had no root they withered away.

7 "And some fell among thorns, and the thorns sprang up and choked them.

8 "But others fell on good ground and yielded a crop: some a hundredfold, some sixty, some thirty.

9 "He who has ears to hear, let him hear!"

The Purpose of Parables

10 And the disciples came and said to Him, "Why do You speak to them in parables?"

11 He answered and said to them, "Because it has been given to you to know the mysteries of the kingdom of heaven, but to them it has not been given.

42 2 Chronicles 9:1-12

12 "For whoever has, to him will be given, and he will have more abundance; but whoever does not have, even what he has will be taken away from him.

13 "Therefore I speak to them in parables, because seeing they do not see, and hearing they do not hear, nor do they understand.

14 "And in them the prophecy of Isaiah is fulfilled, which says:

'By hearing you will hear
    and shall not understand,
And seeing you will see and
    not perceive;

15 For the heart of this people
    has grown dull.
Their ears are hard of hear-
    ing,
And their eyes they have
    closed,
Lest they should see with
    their eyes,
Hear with their ears,
Should understand with
    their heart,
And should turn,
And I should heal them.'[43]

16 "But blessed are your eyes for they see, and your ears for they hear;

17 "for assuredly, I say to you that many prophets and righteous men have desired to see those things which you see, and have not seen them, and to hear those things which you hear, and have not heard them.

The Parable of the Sower Explained

18 "Therefore hear the parable of the sower:

19 "When anyone hears the word of the kingdom, and does not understand it, then the wicked one comes and snatches away what was sown in his heart. This is he who received seed by the wayside.

20 "But he who received the seed on stony places, this is he who hears the word and immediately receives it with joy;

21 "yet he has no root in himself, but endures only for a while. For when tribulation or persecution arises because of the word, imme-diately he stumbles.

22 "Now he who received seed among the thorns is he who hears the word, and the cares of this world and the deceitfulness of riches choke the word, and he be-comes unfruitful.

23 "But he who received seed on the good ground is he who hears the word and understands it, who indeed bears fruit and produces: some a hundredfold, some sixty, some thirty."

The Parable of the Wheat and the Tares

24 Another parable He put forth to them, saying: "The kingdom of heaven is like a man who sowed good seed in his field;

25 "but while men slept, his ene-my came and sowed tares[44] among the wheat and went his way.

26 "But when the grain had sprouted and produced a crop, then the tares also appeared.

27 "So the servants of the owner came and said to him, 'Sir, did you not sow good seed in your field? How then does it have tares?'

---

43 Isaiah 6:9, 10

44 Or, darnel, a weed resembling wheat.

28 "He said to them, 'An enemy has done this.' The servants said to him, 'Do you want us then to go and gather them up?'

29 "But he said, 'No, lest while you gather up the tares you also uproot the wheat with them.

30 'Let both grow together until the harvest, and at the time of harvest I will say to the reapers: First gather together the tares and bind them in bundles to burn them, but gather the wheat into my barn.'"

The Parable of the Mustard Seed

31 Another parable He put forth to them, saying: "The kingdom of heaven is like a mustard seed, which a man took and sowed in his field,

32 "which indeed is the least of all the seeds; but when it is grown it is greater than the herbs and becomes a tree, so that the birds of the air come and nest in its branches."

The Parable of the Leaven

33 Another parable He spoke to them: "The kingdom of heaven is like leaven, which a woman took and hid in three measures of meal till it was all leavened."

Prophecy and the Parables

34 All these things Yeshua spoke to the multitude in parables; and without a parable He did not speak to them,

35 that it might be fulfilled which was spoken by the prophet, saying:

"*I will open My mouth in parables;*

I will utter things which have been kept secret from the foundation of the world."[45]

The Parable of the Tares Explained

36 Then Yeshua sent the multitude away and went into the house. And His disciples came to Him, saying, "Explain to us the parable of the tares of the field."

37 He answered and said to them: "He who sows the good seed is the Son of Man.

38 "The field is the world, the good seeds are the sons of the kingdom, but the tares are the sons of the wicked one.

39 "The enemy who sowed them is the devil, the harvest is the end of the age, and the reapers are the angels.

40 "Therefore as the tares are gathered and burned in the fire, so it will be at the end of this age.

41 "The Son of Man will send out His angels, and they will gather out of His kingdom all things that offend, and those who practice lawlessness,

42 "and will cast them into the furnace of fire. There will be wailing and gnashing of teeth.

43 "Then the righteous will shine forth as the sun in the kingdom of their Father. He who has ears to hear, let him hear!

The Parable of the Hidden Treasure

44 "Again, the kingdom of heaven is like treasure hidden in a field, which, when a man found, he hid; and for joy over it he goes

45 Psalm 78:2

and sells all that he has and buys that field.

The Parable of the Pearl of Great Price

45 "Again, the kingdom of heaven is like a merchant seeking beautiful pearls,

46 "who, when he had found one pearl of great price, went and sold all that he had and bought it.

The Parable of the Dragnet

47 "Again, the kingdom of heaven is like a dragnet that was cast into the sea and gathered some of every kind,

48 "which, when it was full, they drew to shore; and they sat down and gathered the good into vessels, but threw the bad away.

49 "So it will be at the end of the age. The angels will come forth, separate the wicked from among the just,

50 "and cast them into the furnace of fire. There will be wailing and gnashing of teeth."

51 Yeshua said to them, "Have you understood all these things?" They said to Him, "Yes, Lord."

52 Then He said to them, "Therefore every scribe instructed concerning the kingdom of heaven is like a householder who brings out of his treasure things new and old."

Yeshua Rejected at Nazareth

53 And it came to pass, when Yeshua had finished these parables, that He departed from there.

54 And when He had come to His own country, He taught them in their synagogue, so that they were astonished and said, "Where did this Man get this wisdom and these mighty works?

55 "Is this not the carpenter's son? Is not His mother called Miriam? And His brothers James, Joses, Simon, and Judas?

56 "And His sisters, are they not all with us? Where then did this Man get all these things?"

57 And they were offended at Him. But Yeshua said to them, "A prophet is not without honor except in his own country and in his own house."

58 And He did not do many mighty works there because of their unbelief.

John Is Beheaded

14 At that time Herod the tetrarch heard the report about Yeshua

2 and said to his servants, "This is John the Baptizer; he is risen from the dead, and therefore these powers are at work in him."

3 For Herod had laid hold of John and bound him, and put him in prison for the sake of Herodias, his brother Philip's wife.

4 For John had said to him, "It is not lawful for you to have her."

5 And although he wanted to put him to death, he feared the multitude because they counted him as a prophet.

6 But when Herod's birthday came, the daughter of Herodias danced before them and pleased Herod.

7 Therefore he promised with an oath to give her whatever she would ask.

8 And she, having been prompted by her mother, said,

"Give me the head of John the Baptizer here on a platter."

9 And the king was sorry; nevertheless, because of the oaths and because of those who sat with him at the table, he commanded it to be given to her.

10 And he sent and beheaded John in prison.

11 And his head was brought on a platter and given to the girl, and she brought it to her mother.

12 And his disciples came and took away the body, buried it, and went and told Yeshua.

Feeding the Five Thousand

13 When Yeshua heard it, He departed from there by boat to a deserted place by Himself. And when the multitudes heard it, they followed Him on foot from the cities.

14 And when Yeshua went out He saw a great multitude; and He was moved with compassion for them, and healed their sick.

15 And when it was evening, His disciples came to Him, saying, "This is a deserted place, and the hour is already late. Send the multitudes away, that they may go into the villages and buy themselves food."

16 But Yeshua said to them, "They do not need to go away. You give them something to eat."

17 And they said to Him, "We have here only five loaves and two fish."

18 He said, "Bring them here to Me."

19 And He commanded the multitudes to sit down on the grass. And He took the five loaves and the two fish, and looking up to heaven, He blessed and broke and gave the loaves to His disciples; and the disciples gave to the multitudes.

20 And they all ate and were filled, and they took up twelve baskets full of the fragments that remained.

21 And those who had eaten were about five thousand men, besides women and children.

Yeshua Walks on the Sea

22 And immediately Yeshua made His disciples get into the boat and go before Him to the other side, while He sent the multitudes away.

23 And when He had sent the multitudes away, He went up on a mountain by Himself to pray. And when evening had come, He was alone there.

24 But the boat was now in the middle of the sea, tossed by the waves, for the wind was contrary.

25 And in the fourth watch of the night [46] Yeshua went to them, walking on the sea.

26 And when the disciples saw Him walking on the sea, they were troubled, saying, "It is a ghost!" And they cried out for fear.

27 But immediately Yeshua spoke to them, saying, "Be of good cheer! It is I; do not be afraid."

28 And Peter answered Him and said, "Lord, if it is You, command me to come to You on the water."

29 And He said, "Come." And when Peter had come down out of the boat, he walked on the water to go to Yeshua.

30 But when he saw that the

46 Between 3 and 6 a.m.

wind was boisterous, he was afraid; and beginning to sink he cried out, saying, "Lord, save me!"

31 And immediately Yeshua stretched out His hand and caught him, and said to him, "O you of little faith, why did you doubt?"

32 And when they got into the boat, the wind ceased.

33 Then those who were in the boat came and worshiped Him, saying, "Truly You are the Son of God."

Many Touch Him and Are Made Well

34 And when they had crossed over, they came to the land of Gennesaret.

35 And when the men of that place recognized Him, they sent out into all that surrounding region, brought to Him all who were sick,

36 and begged Him that they might only touch the hem of His garment. And as many as touched it were made perfectly well.

Defilement Is from Within

15 Then the scribes and Pharisees who were from Jerusalem came to Yeshua, saying,

2 "Why do Your disciples transgress the tradition of the elders? For they do not wash their hands when they eat bread."

3 But He answered and said to them, "Why do you also transgress the commandment of God because of your tradition?

4 "For God commanded, saying, 'Honor your father and your mother';[47] and, 'He who curses father or mother, let him be put to death.'[48]

5 "But you say, 'Whoever says to his father or his mother, "Whatever you might be profited by me is a gift"—

6 'and does not honor his father or his mother, he will be free.' Thus you have made the commandment of God of no effect by your tradition.

7 "Hypocrites! Well did Isaiah prophesy about you, saying:

8 'This people draws near to
   Me with their mouth,
   And honors Me with their
   lips,
   But their heart is far from
   Me.
9 And in vain they worship
   Me,
   Teaching as doctrines the
   commandments of
   men.' "[49]

10 And He called the multitude and said to them, "Hear and understand:

11 "Not what goes into the mouth defiles a man; but what comes out of the mouth, this defiles a man."

12 Then His disciples came and said to Him, "Do You know that the Pharisees were offended when they heard this saying?"

13 But He answered and said, "Every plant which My heavenly Father has not planted will be uprooted.

14 "Let them alone. They are blind leaders of the blind. And if the blind leads the blind, both will fall into a ditch."

47 Exodus 20:12; Deuteronomy 5:16
48 Exodus 21:17   49 Isaiah 29:13

15 Then Peter answered and said to Him, "Explain this parable to us."

16 And Yeshua said, "Are you also still without understanding?

17 "Do you not yet understand that whatever enters the mouth goes into the stomach and is eliminated?

18 "But those things which proceed out of the mouth come from the heart, and they defile a man.

19 "For out of the heart proceed evil thoughts, murders, adulteries, fornications, thefts, false witness, blasphemies.

20 "These are the things which defile a man, but to eat with unwashed hands does not defile a man."

A Gentile Shows Her Faith

21 Then Yeshua went out from there and departed to the region of Tyre and Sidon.

22 And behold, a woman of Canaan came from that region and cried out to Him, saying, "Have mercy on me, O Lord, Son of David! My daughter is severely demon-possessed."

23 But He answered her not a word. And His disciples came and urged Him, saying, "Send her away, for she cries out after us."

24 But He answered and said, "I was not sent except to the lost sheep of the house of Israel."

25 Then she came and worshiped Him, saying, "Lord, help me!"

26 But He answered and said, "It is not good to take the children's bread and throw it to the little dogs."

27 And she said, "True, Lord, yet even the little dogs eat the crumbs which fall from their masters' table."

28 Then Yeshua answered and said to her, "O woman, great is your faith! Let it be to you as you desire." And her daughter was healed from that very hour.

Yeshua Heals Great Multitudes

29 And Yeshua departed from there, came near to the Sea of Galilee, and went up on the mountain and sat down there.

30 And great multitudes came to Him, having with them those who were lame, blind, mute, maimed, and many others; and they laid them down at the feet of Yeshua, and He healed them.

31 So the multitude marveled when they saw the mute speaking, the maimed made whole, the lame walking, and the blind seeing; and they glorified the God of Israel.

Feeding the Four Thousand

32 Then Yeshua called His disciples to Him and said, "I have compassion on the multitude, because they have now continued with Me three days and have nothing to eat. And I do not want to send them away hungry, lest they faint on the way."

33 And His disciples said to Him, "Where could we get enough bread in the wilderness to fill such a great multitude?"

34 And Yeshua said to them, "How many loaves do you have?" And they said, "Seven, and a few little fish."

35 And He commanded the multitude to sit down on the ground.

36 And He took the seven loaves and the fish, gave thanks, broke them, and gave them to His disciples; and the disciples gave to the multitude.

37 And they all ate and were filled; and they took up seven large baskets full of the broken pieces that were left.

38 And those who ate were four thousand men, besides women and children.

39 And He sent away the multitude, got into the boat, and came into the region of Magdala.

The Pharisees and Sadducees Seek a Sign

16 And the Pharisees and Sadducees came, and testing Him asked that He would show them a sign from heaven.

2 He answered and said to them, "When it is evening you say, 'It will be fair weather, for the sky is red';

3 "and in the morning, 'It will be foul weather today, for the sky is red and threatening.' Hypocrites! You know how to discern the face of the sky, but you cannot discern the signs of the times.

4 "A wicked and adulterous generation seeks after a sign, and no sign will be given to it except the sign of the prophet Jonah." And He left them and departed.

Beware of the Leaven of the Pharisees and Sadducees

5 And when His disciples had come to the other side, they had forgotten to take bread.

6 Then Yeshua said to them, "Take heed and beware of the leaven of the Pharisees and of the Sadducees."

7 And they reasoned among themselves, saying, "It is because we have taken no bread."

8 But when Yeshua perceived it, He said to them, "O you of little faith, why do you reason among yourselves because you have brought no bread?

9 "Do you not yet understand, or remember the five loaves of the five thousand and how many baskets you took up?

10 "Nor the seven loaves of the four thousand and how many large baskets you took up?

11 "How is it you do not understand that I did not speak to you concerning bread, but that you should beware of the leaven of the Pharisees and Sadducees?"

12 Then they understood that He did not tell them to beware of the leaven of bread, but of the doctrine of the Pharisees and Sadducees.

Simon Proclaims Yeshua as the Messiah

13 When Yeshua came into the region of Caesarea Philippi, He asked His disciples, saying, "Who do men say that I, the Son of Man, am?"

14 And they said, "Some say John the Baptizer, some Elijah,[50] and others Jeremiah or one of the prophets."

15 He said to them, "But who do you say that I am?"

16 And Simon Peter answered and said, "You are the Messiah, the Son of the living God."

17 And Yeshua answered and said to him, "Blessed are you, Simon Bar-Jonah, for flesh and

50 Malachi 4:5 (3:23 in some versions)

blood has not revealed this to you, but My Father who is in heaven.

18 "And I also say to you that you are Peter, and on this rock I will build My congregation, and the gates of Hades shall not prevail against it.

19 "And I will give you the keys of the kingdom of heaven, and whatever you bind on earth will be bound in heaven, and whatever you loose on earth will be loosed in heaven."

20 Then He commanded His disciples that they should tell no one that He was Yeshua the Messiah.

Yeshua Predicts His Death and Resurrection

21 From that time on Yeshua began to show to His disciples that He must go to Jerusalem, and suffer many things from the elders and chief priests and scribes, and be killed, and be raised again the third day.

22 Then Peter took Him aside and began to rebuke Him, saying, "Far be it from You, Lord; this shall not happen to You!"

23 But He turned and said to Peter, "Get behind Me, Satan! You are an offense to Me, for you are not mindful of the things of God, but the things of men."

Deny Yourself and Follow Him

24 Then Yeshua said to His disciples, "If anyone desires to come after Me, let him deny himself, take up his cross, and follow Me.

25 "For whoever desires to save his life will lose it, and whoever loses his life for My sake will find it.

26 "For what is a man profited if he gains the whole world, and loses his own soul? Or what will a man give in exchange for his soul?

27 "For the Son of Man will come in the glory of His Father with His angels, and then He will reward each according to his works.

28 "Assuredly, I say to you, there are some standing here who shall not taste death till they see the Son of Man coming in His kingdom."

Yeshua Transfigured on the Mount

17 And after six days Yeshua took Peter, James, and John his brother, brought them up on a high mountain by themselves,

2 and was transfigured before them. His face shone like the sun, and His clothes became as white as the light.

3 And behold, Moses and Elijah appeared to them, talking with Him.

4 Then Peter answered and said to Yeshua, "Lord, it is good for us to be here; if You wish, let us make here three tabernacles:[51] one for You, one for Moses, and one for Elijah."

5 While he was still speaking, behold, a bright cloud overshadowed them; and suddenly a voice came out of the cloud, saying, "This is My beloved Son, in whom I am well pleased. Hear Him!"

6 And when the disciples heard it, they fell on their faces and were greatly afraid.

7 And Yeshua came and

51 Hebrew: Sukkot, Leviticus 23:33f.; (cf. Zechariah 14:1-9, 16-19).

touched them and said, "Arise, and do not be afraid."

8 And when they had lifted up their eyes, they saw no one but Yeshua only.

9 And as they came down from the mountain, Yeshua commanded them, saying, "Tell the vision to no one until the Son of Man is risen from the dead."

10 And His disciples asked Him, saying, "Why then do the scribes say that Elijah must come first?"

11 And Yeshua answered and said to them, "Elijah truly is coming first and will restore all things.

12 "But I say to you that Elijah has come already, and they did not know him but did to him whatever they wished. Likewise the Son of Man is also about to suffer at their hands."

13 Then the disciples understood that He spoke to them of John the Baptizer.

A Boy Is Healed

14 And when they had come to the multitude, a man came to Him, kneeling down to Him and saying,

15 "Lord, have mercy on my son, for he is an epileptic and suffers severely; for he often falls into the fire and often into the water.

16 "And I brought him to Your disciples, and they could not cure him."

17 Then Yeshua answered and said, "O faithless and perverse generation, how long shall I be with you? How long shall I bear with you? Bring him here to Me."

18 And Yeshua rebuked him, and the demon came out of him; and the child was cured from that very hour.

19 Then the disciples came to Yeshua privately and said, "Why could we not cast him out?"

20 And Yeshua said to them, "Because of your unbelief; for assuredly, I say to you, if you have faith as a mustard seed, you will say to this mountain, 'Move from here to there,' and it will move; and nothing will be impossible for you.

21 "However, this kind does not go out except by prayer and fasting."

Yeshua Again Predicts His Death and Resurrection

22 And while they were staying in Galilee, Yeshua said to them, "The Son of Man is about to be betrayed into the hands of men,

23 "and they will kill Him, and the third day He will be raised up." And they were exceedingly sorrowful.

Peter and His Rabbi Pay Their Taxes

24 And when they had come to Capernaum, those who received the temple tax came to Peter and said, "Does your Rabbi not pay the temple tax?"

25 He said, "Yes." And when he had come into the house, Yeshua anticipated him, saying, "What do you think, Simon? From whom do the kings of the earth take customs or taxes, from their own sons or from strangers?"

26 Peter said to Him, "From strangers." Yeshua said to him, "Then the sons are free.

27 "Nevertheless, lest we offend

them, go to the sea, cast in a hook, and take the fish that comes up first. And when you have opened its mouth, you will find a piece of money; take that and give it to them for Me and you."

Who Is the Greatest?

18 At that time the disciples came to Yeshua, saying, "Who then is greatest in the kingdom of heaven?"

2 And Yeshua called a little child to Him, set him in the midst of them,

3 and said, "Assuredly, I say to you, unless you turn to God and become as little children, you will by no means enter the kingdom of heaven.

4 "Therefore whoever humbles himself as this little child is the greatest in the kingdom of heaven.

5 "And whoever receives one little child like this in My name receives Me.

Yeshua Warns of Offenses

6 "But whoever causes one of these little ones who believe in Me to sin, it would be better for him if a millstone were hung around his neck, and he were drowned in the depth of the sea.

7 "Woe to the world because of offenses! For offenses must come, but woe to that man by whom the offense comes!

8 "And if your hand or foot causes you to sin, cut it off and cast it from you. It is better for you to enter into life lame or maimed, rather than having two hands or two feet to be cast into the everlasting fire.

9 "And if your eye causes you to sin, pluck it out and cast it from you. It is better for you to enter into life with one eye, rather than having two eyes to be cast into hell fire.

The Parable of the Lost Sheep

10 "Take heed that you do not despise one of these little ones, for I say to you that in heaven their angels always see the face of My Father who is in heaven.

11 "For the Son of Man has come to save that which was lost.

12 "What do you think? If a man has a hundred sheep, and one of them goes astray, does he not leave the ninety-nine and go to the mountains to seek the one that is straying?

13 "And if he should find it, assuredly, I say to you, he rejoices more over that sheep than over the ninety-nine that did not go astray.

14 "Even so it is not the will of your Father who is in heaven that one of these little ones should perish.

Dealing with a Sinning Brother

15 "Moreover if your brother sins against you, go and tell him his fault between you and him alone. If he hears you, you have gained your brother.

16 "But if he will not hear you, then take with you one or two more, that *'by the mouth of two or three witnesses every word may be established.'* [52]

17 "And if he refuses to hear them, tell it to the congregation. But if he refuses even to hear the

52 Deuteronomy 19:15

congregation, let him be to you like a heathen and a tax collector.

18 "Assuredly, I say to you, whatever you bind on earth will be bound in heaven, and whatever you loose on earth will be loosed in heaven.

19 "Again I say to you that if two of you agree on earth concerning anything that they ask, it will be done for them by My Father who is in heaven.

20 "For where two or three are gathered together in My name, there I am in the midst of them."

The Parable of the Unforgiving Servant

21 Then Peter came to Him and said, "Lord, how often shall my brother sin against me, and I forgive him? Up to seven times?"

22 Yeshua said to him, "I do not say to you, up to seven times, but up to seventy times seven.

23 "Therefore the kingdom of heaven is like a certain king who wanted to settle accounts with his servants.

24 "And when he had begun to settle accounts, one was brought to him who owed him ten thousand talents.[53]

25 "But inasmuch as he was not able to pay, his master commanded that he, his wife and children, and all that he had be sold, and payment be made.

26 "The servant therefore fell down before him, saying, 'Master, have patience with me, and I will pay you all.'

27 "Then the master of that servant was moved with compassion, released him, and forgave him the debt.

28 "But the same servant went out and found one of his fellow servants who owed him a hundred denarii;[54] and he laid hands on him and took him by the throat, saying, 'Pay me what you owe!'

29 "So his fellow servant fell down at his feet and begged him, saying, 'Have patience with me, and I will pay you all.'

30 "And he would not, but went and threw him into prison till he should pay the debt.

31 "So when his fellow servants saw what had been done, they were very grieved, and came and told their master all that had been done.

32 "Then his master, after he had called him, said to him, 'O you wicked servant! I forgave you all that debt because you begged me.

33 'Should you not also have had compassion on your fellow servant, just as I had pity on you?'

34 "And his master was angry and delivered him to the torturers until he should pay all that was due him.

35 "So My heavenly Father also will do to you if each of you, from his heart, does not forgive his brother his trespasses."

Marriage and Divorce

19 And it came to pass, when Yeshua had finished these sayings, He departed from Galilee and came to the region of Judea beyond the Jordan.

---

53 About $225 million (One talent = about $22,500).

54 About $750.00 (One denarius = about $7.50).

2 And great multitudes followed Him, and He healed them there.

3 The Pharisees also came to Him, testing Him, and saying to Him, "Is it lawful for a man to divorce his wife for just any reason?"

4 And He answered and said to them, "Have you not read that He who made them at the beginning *'made them male and female,'*[55]

5 "and said, *'For this reason a man shall leave his father and mother and be joined to his wife, and the two shall become one flesh'?*[56]

6 "So then they are no longer two but one flesh. Therefore what God has joined together, let not man divide."

7 They said to Him, "Why then did Moses command to give a certificate of divorce, and to put her away?"

8 He said to them, "Moses, because of the hardness of your hearts, permitted you to divorce your wives, but from the beginning it was not so.

9 "And I say to you, whoever divorces his wife, except for sexual immorality,[57] and marries another, commits adultery; and whoever marries her who is divorced commits adultery."

10 His disciples said to Him, "If such is the case of the man with his wife, it is better not to marry."

11 But He said to them, "All men cannot accept this saying, but only those to whom it has been given:

12 "for there are some eunuchs who were born thus from their mother's womb, and there are some eunuchs who were made eunuchs by men, and there are eunuchs who have made themselves eunuchs for the kingdom of heaven's sake. He who is able to accept it, let him accept it."

Yeshua Blesses Little Children

13 Then little children were brought to Him that He might put His hands on them and pray, but the disciples rebuked them.

14 But Yeshua said, "Let the little children come to Me, and do not forbid them; for of such is the kingdom of heaven."

15 And He laid His hands on them and departed from there.

Yeshua Counsels the Rich Young Ruler

16 And behold, one came and said to Him, "Good Rabbi, what good thing shall I do that I may have eternal life?"

17 And He said to him, "Why do you call Me good? No one is good but One, that is, God. But if you want to enter into life, keep the commandments."

18 He said to Him, "Which ones?" Yeshua said, " *'You shall not murder,' 'You shall not commit adultery,' 'You shall not steal,' 'You shall not bear false witness,'*

19 *'Honor your father and your mother,'*[58] and, *'You shall love your neighbor as yourself.'* "[59]

---

55 Genesis 1:27; 5:2   56 Genesis 2:24
57 Lit. "prostitution, unchastity, fornication." This is a general term referring to any kind of illicit sexual intercourse.

58 Exodus 20:12–16; Deuteronomy 5:16–20 (5:16, 17 in some versions)
59 Leviticus 19:18 (19:17 in some versions)

20 The young man said to Him, "All these things I have kept from my youth. What do I still lack?"

21 Yeshua said to him, "If you want to be perfect, go, sell what you have and give to the poor, and you will have treasure in heaven; and come, follow Me."

22 But when the young man heard that saying, he went away sorrowful, for he had great possessions.

With God All Things Are Possible

23 Then Yeshua said to His disciples, "Assuredly, I say to you that it is hard for a rich man to enter the kingdom of heaven.

24 "And again I say to you, it is easier for a camel to go through the eye of a needle than for a rich man to enter the kingdom of God."

25 When His disciples heard it, they were exceedingly amazed, saying, "Who then can be saved?"

26 But Yeshua looked at them and said to them, "With men this is impossible, but with God all things are possible."

27 Then Peter answered and said to Him, "See, we have left all and followed You. Therefore what shall we have?"

28 And Yeshua said to them, "Assuredly, I say to you, that in the regeneration, when the Son of Man sits on the throne of His glory, you who have followed Me will also sit on twelve thrones, judging the twelve tribes of Israel.

29 "And everyone who has left houses or brothers or sisters or father or mother or wife or children or lands, for My name's sake, shall receive a hundredfold and inherit everlasting life.

30 "But many who are first will be last, and the last first.

The Parable of the Workers in the Vineyard

20 "For the kingdom of heaven is like a man who is a landowner who went out early in the morning to hire laborers for his vineyard.

2 "And when he had agreed with the laborers for a denarius a day, he sent them into his vineyard.

3 "And he went out about the third hour[60] and saw others standing idle in the marketplace,

4 "and said to them, 'You also go into the vineyard, and whatever is right I will give you.' And they went.

5 "Again he went out about the sixth and the ninth hour,[61] and did likewise.

6 "And about the eleventh hour[62] he went out and found others standing idle, and said to them, 'Why have you been standing here idle all day?'

7 "They said to him, 'Because no one hired us.' He said to them, 'You also go into the vineyard, and whatever is right you will receive.'

8 "So when evening had come, the owner of the vineyard said to his steward, 'Call the laborers and give them their wages, beginning with the last to the first.'

9 "And when those came who

60 9 a.m.

61 Noon and 3 p.m.   62 5 p.m.

were hired about the eleventh hour, they each received a denarius.

10 "But when the first came, they supposed that they would receive more; and they likewise each received a denarius.

11 "And when they had received it, they murmured against the landowner,

12 "saying, 'These last men have worked but one hour, and you made them equal to us who have borne the burden and the heat of the day.'

13 "But he answered one of them and said, 'Friend, I am doing you no wrong. Did you not agree with me for a denarius?

14 'Take what is yours and go your way. I want to give to this last man the same as to you.

15 'Is it not lawful for me to do what I want with my own things? Or is your eye evil because I am good?'

16 "So the last will be first, and the first last. For many are called, but few chosen."

Yeshua a Third Time Predicts His Death and Resurrection

17 And Yeshua, going up to Jerusalem, took the twelve disciples aside on the road and said to them,

18 "Behold, we are going up to Jerusalem, and the Son of Man will be betrayed to the chief priests and to the scribes; and they will condemn Him to death,

19 "and deliver Him to the Gentiles to mock and to scourge and to crucify. And the third day He will rise again."

Salome Asks a Favor

20 Then the mother of Zebedee's sons came to Him with her sons, kneeling down and asking something from Him.

21 And He said to her, "What do you wish?" She said to Him, "Grant that these two sons of mine may sit, one on Your right hand and the other on the left, in Your kingdom."

22 But Yeshua answered and said, "You do not know what you ask. Are you able to drink the cup that I am about to drink, and be baptized with the baptism[63] that I am baptized with?" They said to Him, "We are able."

23 And He said to them, "You shall indeed drink My cup, and be baptized with the baptism that I am baptized with; but to sit on My right hand and on My left is not Mine to give, but it is for those for whom it is prepared by My Father."

24 And when the ten heard it, they were moved with indignation against the two brothers.

25 But Yeshua called them to Himself and said, "You know that the rulers of the Gentiles lord it over them, and those who are great exercise authority over them.

26 "Yet it shall not be so among you; but whoever desires to become great among you, let him be your servant.

27 "And whoever desires to be first among you, let him be your slave—

63 Yeshua is asking if they are prepared to be obedient to God, even to the point of death, as He is.

28 "just as the Son of Man did not come to be served, but to serve, and to give His life a ransom for many."

Two Blind Men Receive Their Sight

29 And as they departed from Jericho, a great multitude followed Him.

30 And behold, two blind men sitting by the road, when they heard that Yeshua was passing by, cried out, saying, "Have mercy on us, O Lord, Son of David!"

31 And the multitude rebuked them, that they should be quiet. But they cried out all the more, saying, "Have mercy on us, O Lord, Son of David!"

32 And Yeshua stood still and called them, and said, "What do you want Me to do for you?"

33 They said to Him, "Lord, we want our eyes opened."

34 So Yeshua had compassion on them and touched their eyes. And immediately their eyes received sight, and they followed Him.

The Triumphal Entry

21 And when they drew near to Jerusalem, and came to Bethphage, at the Mount of Olives, then Yeshua sent two disciples,

2 saying to them, "Go into the village opposite you, and immediately you will find a donkey tied, and a colt with her. Loose them and bring them to Me.

3 "And if anyone says anything to you, you shall say, 'The Lord has need of them,' and immediately he will send them."

4 All this was done that it might be fulfilled which was spoken by the prophet, saying:

5 *"Tell the daughter of Zion,*
   'Behold, your King is coming to you,
   Humble, and sitting on a donkey,
   And a colt, the foal of a donkey.'" [64]

6 And the disciples went and did as Yeshua commanded them.

7 And they brought the donkey and the colt, laid their clothes on them, and set Him thereon.

8 And a very great multitude spread their garments on the road; others cut down branches from the trees and spread them on the road.

9 And the multitudes who went before and those who followed cried out, saying:

   "Hosanna to the Son of David!
   'Blessed is He who comes in the name of the LORD!' [65]
   Hosanna in the highest!"

10 And when He had come into Jerusalem, all the city was moved, saying, "Who is this?"

11 And the multitudes said, "This is Yeshua, the prophet from Nazareth of Galilee."

Yeshua Cleanses the Temple

12 And Yeshua went into the temple of God and drove out all those who bought and sold in the temple, and overturned the tables of the moneychangers and the seats of those who sold doves.

13 And He said to them, "It is written, *'My house shall be called*

64 Zechariah 9:9   65 Psalm 118:26

a house of prayer,[66] but you have made it a *'den of thieves.'* " [67]

14 And the blind and the lame came to Him in the temple, and He healed them.

15 But when the chief priests and scribes saw the wonderful things that He did, and the children crying out in the temple and saying, "Hosanna to the Son of David!" they were indignant

16 and said to Him, "Do You hear what these are saying?" And Yeshua said to them, "Yes. Have you never read, *'Out of the mouth of babes and nursing infants You have perfected praise'*?" [68]

17 And He left them and went out of the city to Bethany, and He lodged there.

The Fig Tree Withered

18 Now in the morning, as He returned to the city, He was hungry.

19 And when He saw a fig tree by the road, He came to it and found nothing on it but leaves, and said to it, "Let no fruit grow on you anymore forever." And immediately the fig tree withered away.

The Lesson of the Withered Fig Tree

20 And when the disciples saw it, they marveled, saying, "How did the fig tree wither away so soon?"

21 Yeshua answered and said to them, "Assuredly, I say to you, if you have faith and do not doubt, you will not only do this which was done to the fig tree, but also if

66 Isaiah 56:7   67 Jeremiah 7:11
68 Psalm 8:2 (8:3 in some versions)

you say to this mountain, 'Be removed and be cast into the sea,' it will be done.

22 "And all things, whatever you ask in prayer, believing, you will receive."

Authority of Yeshua Questioned

23 And when He had come into the temple, the chief priests and the elders of the people came to Him as He was teaching, and said, "By what authority are You doing these things? And who gave You this authority?"

24 And Yeshua answered and said to them, "I also will ask you one thing, which if you tell Me, I likewise will tell you by what authority I do these things:

25 "The immersion of John, where was it from? From heaven or from men?" And they reasoned among themselves, saying, "If we say, 'From heaven,' He will say to us, 'Why then did you not believe him?'

26 "But if we say, 'From men,' we fear the multitude, for all count John as a prophet."

27 And they answered Yeshua and said, "We do not know." And He said to them, "Neither will I tell you by what authority I do these things.

The Parable of the Two Sons

28 "But what do you think? A man had two sons, and he came to the first and said, 'Son, go work today in my vineyard.'

29 "He answered and said, 'I will not,' but afterward he regretted it and went.

30 "And he came to the second

and said likewise. And he answered and said, 'I go, sir,' and he did not go.

31 "Which of the two did the will of his father?" They said to Him, "The first." Yeshua said to them, "Assuredly, I say to you that tax collectors and harlots enter the kingdom of God before you.

32 "For John came to you in the way of righteousness, and you did not believe him; but tax collectors and harlots believed him; and when you saw it, you did not afterward regret it that you might believe him.

The Parable of the Wicked Vinedressers

33 "Hear another parable: There was a certain landowner who planted a vineyard, set a hedge around it, dug a winepress in it, and built a tower. And he leased it to vinedressers and went into a far country.

34 "And when the time for fruit drew near, he sent his servants to the vinedressers, that they might receive the fruit of it.

35 "And the vinedressers took his servants, beat one, killed one, and stoned another.

36 "Again he sent other servants, more than the first, and they did likewise to them.

37 "But last of all he sent his son to them, saying, 'They will respect my son.'

38 "But when the vinedressers saw the son, they said among themselves, 'This is the heir. Come, let us kill him and seize his inheritance.'

39 "And they caught him, cast him out of the vineyard, and killed him.

40 "Therefore, when the owner of the vineyard comes, what will he do to those vinedressers?"

41 They said to Him, "He will miserably destroy those wicked men, and lease his vineyard to other vinedressers who will render to him the fruits in their seasons."

42 Yeshua said to them, "Did you never read in the Scriptures:

'The stone which the builders rejected
Has become the chief cornerstone.
This is the LORD's doing,
And it is marvelous in our eyes'? [69]

43 "Therefore I say to you, the kingdom of God will be taken from you and given to a nation bearing the fruits of it. [70]

44 "And whoever falls on this stone will be broken; [71] but on whomever it falls, it will grind him to powder." [72]

45 And when the chief priests and Pharisees had heard His parables, they perceived that He was speaking of them.

46 But when they sought to lay hands on Him, they feared the multitudes, because they took Him for a prophet.

The Parable of the Wedding Feast

22 And Yeshua answered and spoke to them again by parables and said:

2 "The kingdom of heaven is

[69] Psalm 118:22, 23
[70] Authority to be taken from chief priests and Pharisees (see 21:45).
[71] Isaiah 8:14, 15   [72] Daniel 2:34, 35

like a certain king who arranged a marriage for his son,

3 "and sent out his servants to call those who were invited to the wedding; and they were not willing to come.

4 "Again, he sent out other servants, saying, 'Tell those who are invited: See, I have prepared my dinner; my oxen and fattened cattle are killed, and all things are ready. Come to the wedding.'

5 "But they made light of it and went their ways, one to his own farm, another to his business.

6 "And the rest seized his servants, treated them spitefully, and killed them.

7 "But when the king heard about it, he was furious. And he sent out his armies, destroyed those murderers, and burned up their city.

8 "Then he said to his servants, 'The wedding is ready, but those who were invited were not worthy.

9 'Therefore go into the highways, and as many as you find, invite to the wedding.'

10 "So those servants went out into the highways and gathered together all whom they found, both bad and good. And the wedding hall was filled with guests.

11 "But when the king came in to see the guests, he saw a man there who did not have on a wedding garment.

12 "And he said to him, 'Friend, how did you come in here without a wedding garment?' And he was speechless.

13 "Then the king said to the servants, 'Bind him hand and foot, take him away, and cast him into

outer darkness; there will be weeping and gnashing of teeth.'

14 "For many are called, but few are chosen."

The Pharisees: Is It Lawful to Pay Taxes to Caesar?

15 Then the Pharisees went and took counsel how they might entangle Him in His talk.

16 And they sent out to Him their disciples with the Herodians, saying, "Rabbi, we know that You are true and teach the way of God in truth; nor do You care about anyone, for You do not regard the person of men.

17 "Tell us therefore, what do You think? Is it lawful to pay taxes to Caesar, or not?"

18 But Yeshua perceived their wickedness, and said, "Why do you test Me, you hypocrites?

19 "Show Me the tax money." And they brought Him a denarius.

20 And He said to them, "Whose image and inscription is this?"

21 They said to Him, "Caesar's." Then He said to them, "Render therefore to Caesar the things that are Caesar's, and to God the things that are God's."

22 When they had heard these words, they marveled, and left Him and went their way.

The Sadducees: What About the Resurrection?

23 The same day the Sadducees, who say there is no resurrection, came to Him and asked Him,

24 saying: "Rabbi, Moses said that if a man dies, having no children, his brother shall marry his

wife and raise up offspring for his brother.[73]

25 "Now there were with us seven brothers. And the first died after he had married, and having no offspring, left his wife to his brother.

26 "Likewise the second also, and the third, even to the seventh.

27 "And last of all the woman died also.

28 "Therefore, in the resurrection, whose wife of the seven will she be? For they all had her."

29 Yeshua answered and said to them, "You are mistaken, not knowing the Scriptures nor the power of God.

30 "For in the resurrection they neither marry nor are given in marriage, but are like the angels of God in heaven.

31 "But concerning the resurrection of the dead, have you not read what was spoken to you by God, saying,

32 *'I am the God of Abraham, the God of Isaac, and the God of Jacob'*?[74] God is not the God of the dead, but of the living."

33 And when the multitudes heard this, they were astonished at His teaching.

The Scribes: Which Is the First Commandment of All?

34 But when the Pharisees heard that He had put the Sadducees to silence, they gathered together.

35 Then one of them, who was a lawyer,[75] asked Him a question, testing Him, and saying,

36 "Rabbi, which is the great commandment in the law?"

37 Yeshua said to him, "'*You shall love the* LORD *your God with all your heart, with all your soul, and with all your mind.*'[76]

38 "This is the first and great commandment.

39 "And the second is like it: *'You shall love your neighbor as yourself.'*[77]

40 "On these two commandments hang all the Law and the Prophets."

Yeshua: How Can David Call His Descendant Lord?

41 While the Pharisees were gathered together, Yeshua asked them,

42 saying, "What do you think about the Messiah? Whose Son is He?" They said to Him, "The Son of David."

43 He said to them, "How then does David in the Spirit call Him 'Lord,' saying:

44 *'The* LORD *said to my Lord,*
  "Sit at My right hand,
   Till I make Your enemies
    Your footstool"'?[78]

45 "If David then calls Him 'Lord,' how is He his Son?"

46 And no one was able to answer Him a word, nor from that day on did anyone dare ask Him any more questions.

Woe to the Hypocrites!

23 Then Yeshua spoke to the multitudes and to His disciples,

---

73 Deuteronomy 25:5   74 Exodus 3:6, 15
75 Lit. a master of Torah.

76 Deuteronomy 6:5
77 Leviticus 19:18   78 Psalm 110:1

2 saying, "The scribes and the Pharisees sit in Moses' seat.

3 "Therefore whatever they tell you to observe, that observe and do, but do not do according to their works; for they say, and do not do.

4 "For they bind heavy burdens, hard to bear, and lay them on men's shoulders; but they themselves will not move them with one of their fingers.

5 "But all their works they do to be seen by men. They make their phylacteries broad and enlarge the borders of their garments.[79]

6 "They love the best places at feasts, the best seats in the synagogues,

7 "greetings in the marketplaces, and to be called by men, 'Rabbi, Rabbi.'

8 "But you, do not be called 'Rabbi'; for One is your Teacher, the Messiah, and you are all brethren.

9 "And do not call anyone on earth your father; for One is your Father, He who is in heaven.

10 "And do not be called teachers; for One is your Teacher, the Messiah.

11 "But he who is greatest among you shall be your servant.

12 "And whoever exalts himself will be abased, and he who humbles himself will be exalted.

13 "But woe to you, scribes and Pharisees, hypocrites! For you shut up the kingdom of heaven against men; for you neither go in yourselves, nor do you allow those who are entering to go in.

79 Tallit or tzitzit.

14 "Woe to you, scribes and Pharisees, hypocrites! For you devour widows' houses, and for a pretense make long prayers. Therefore you will receive greater condemnation.

15 "Woe to you, scribes and Pharisees, hypocrites! For you go about on land and sea to make one proselyte, and when he is made, you make him twice as much a son of hell as yourselves.

16 "Woe to you, blind guides, who say, 'Whoever swears by the temple, it is nothing; but whoever swears by the gold of the temple, he is obligated.'

17 "Fools and blind! For which is greater, the gold or the temple that sanctifies the gold?

18 "And, 'Whoever swears by the altar, it is nothing; but whoever swears by the gift that is on it, he is obligated.'

19 "Fools and blind! For which is greater, the gift or the altar that sanctifies the gift?

20 "Therefore he who swears by the altar, swears by it and by all things on it.

21 "And he who swears by the temple, swears by it and by Him who dwells in it.

22 "And he who swears by heaven, swears by the throne of God and by Him who sits on it.

23 "Woe to you, scribes and Pharisees, hypocrites! For you pay tithe of mint and anise and cummin, and have neglected the weightier matters of the Torah: justice and mercy and faith. These you ought to have done, without leaving the others undone.

24 "Blind guides, who strain out a gnat and swallow a camel!

25 "Woe to you, scribes and Pharisees, hypocrites! For you cleanse the outside of the cup and the dish, but inside they are full of extortion and self-indulgence.

26 "Blind Pharisee, first cleanse the inside of the cup and dish, that the outside of them may be clean also.

27 "Woe to you, scribes and Pharisees, hypocrites! For you are like whitewashed tombs which indeed appear beautiful outwardly, but inside are full of dead men's bones and all uncleanness.

28 "Even so you also outwardly appear righteous to men, but inside you are full of hypocrisy and lawlessness.

29 "Woe to you, scribes and Pharisees, hypocrites! Because you build the tombs of the prophets and adorn the monuments of the righteous,

30 "and say, 'If we had lived in the days of our fathers, we would not have been partakers with them in the blood of the prophets.'

31 "Therefore you are witnesses against yourselves that you are sons of those who murdered the prophets.

32 "Fill up, then, the measure of your fathers' guilt.

33 "Serpents, brood of vipers! How can you escape the condemnation of hell?

34 "Therefore, indeed, I send you prophets, wise men, and scribes: some of them you will kill and crucify; and some of them you will scourge in your synagogues and persecute from city to city,

35 "that on you may come all the righteous blood shed on the earth, from the blood of righteous Abel to the blood of Zechariah, son of Berechiah, whom you killed between the temple and the altar.

36 "Assuredly, I say to you, all these things will come on this generation.

Yeshua Laments over Jerusalem

37 "O Jerusalem, Jerusalem, the one who kills the prophets and stones those who are sent to her! How often I wanted to gather your children together, as a hen gathers her chicks under her wings, and you were not willing!

38 "See! Your house is left to you desolate;

39 "for I say to you, you shall see Me no more till you say, *'Blessed is He who comes in the name of the LORD!'* [80]

Yeshua Predicts the Destruction of the Temple

24 And Yeshua went out and departed from the temple, and His disciples came to Him to show Him the buildings of the temple.

2 And Yeshua said to them, "Do you not see all these things? Assuredly, I say to you, not one stone shall be left here upon another that shall not be thrown down."

The Signs of the Times and the End of the Age

3 And as He sat on the Mount of Olives, the disciples came to Him privately, saying, "Tell us, when will these things be? And what will be the sign of Your coming, and of the end of the age?"

4 And Yeshua answered and

80 Psalm 118:26

said to them: "Take heed that no one deceives you.

5 "For many will come in My name, saying, 'I am the Messiah,' and will deceive many.

6 "And you will hear of wars and rumors of wars. See that you are not troubled; for all these things must come to pass, but the end is not yet.

7 "For nation will rise against nation, and kingdom against kingdom. And there will be famines, pestilences, and earthquakes in various places.

8 "All these are the beginning of sorrows.

9 "Then they will deliver you up to tribulation and kill you, and you will be hated by all nations for My name's sake.

10 "And then many will be offended, betray one another, and hate one another.

11 "And many false prophets will rise and deceive many.

12 "And because lawlessness will abound, the love of many will grow cold.

13 "But he who endures to the end will be saved.

14 "And this good news of the kingdom will be preached in all the world as a witness to all the nations, and then the end will come.

The Great Tribulation

15 "Therefore when you see the 'abomination of desolation,'[81] spoken of by Daniel the prophet, standing in the holy place" (whoever reads, let him understand),

16 "then let those who are in Judea flee to the mountains.

17 "Let him who is on the housetop not come down to take anything out of his house.

18 "And let him who is in the field not go back to get his clothes.

19 "And woe to those who are pregnant and to those with nursing babies in those days!

20 "But pray that your flight not be in winter or on the Sabbath.

21 "For then there will be great tribulation, such as has not been since the beginning of the world to this time, no, nor ever shall be.

22 "And unless those days were shortened, no flesh would be saved; but for the elect's sake those days will be shortened.[82]

23 "Then if anyone says to you, 'Look, here is the Messiah!' or 'There!' do not believe it.

24 "For false messiahs and false prophets will arise and show great signs and wonders so as to deceive, if possible, even the elect.

25 "See, I have told you beforehand.

26 "Therefore if they say to you, 'Look, He is in the desert!' do not go out; or 'Look, He is in the inner rooms!' do not believe it.

27 "For as the lightning comes from the east and flashes to the west, so also will the coming of the Son of Man be.

28 "For wherever the carcass is, there the eagles will be gathered together.

The Coming of the Son of Man

29 "Immediately after the tribulation of those days the sun will be darkened, and the moon will not

---

81 Daniel 11:31; 12:11

82 Daniel 12:1

give its light; the stars will fall from heaven, and the powers of the heavens will be shaken.[83]

30 "And then the sign of the Son of Man will appear in heaven, and then all the tribes of the earth will mourn, and they will see the Son of Man coming on the clouds of heaven with power and great glory.[84]

31 "And He will send His angels with a great sound of a shofar, and they will gather together His elect from the four winds, from one end of heaven to the other.

The Parable of the Fig Tree

32 "Now learn this parable from the fig tree: When its branch has already become tender and puts forth leaves, you know that summer is near.

33 "So you also, when you see all these things, know that He is near, even at the doors.

34 "Assuredly, I say to you, this generation will by no means pass away till all these things are fulfilled.

35 "Heaven and earth will pass away, but My words will by no means pass away.

No One Knows the Day or Hour

36 "But of that day and hour no one knows, no, not even the angels of heaven, but My Father only.

37 "But as the days of Noah were, so also will the coming of the Son of Man be.[85]

38 "For as in the days before the flood, they were eating and drinking, marrying and giving in marriage, until the day that Noah entered the ark,

39 "and did not know until the flood came and took them all away, so also will the coming of the Son of Man be.

40 "Then two men will be in the field: one will be taken and the other left.

41 "Two women will be grinding at the mill: one will be taken and the other left.

42 "Watch therefore, for you do not know what hour your Lord is coming.

43 "But know this, that if the master of the house had known what hour the thief would come, he would have watched and not allowed his house to be broken into.

44 "Therefore you also be ready, for the Son of Man is coming at an hour when you do not expect Him.

The Faithful Servant and the Bad Servant

45 "Who then is a faithful and wise servant whom his master made ruler over his household, to give them food in due season?

46 "Blessed is that servant whom his master, when he comes, will find so doing.

47 "Assuredly, I say to you that he will make him ruler over all his goods.

48 "But if that evil servant says in his heart, 'My master is delaying his coming,'

49 "and begins to beat his fellow servants, and to eat and drink with the drunkards,

83 Isaiah 13:10; 34:4
84 Daniel 7:13, 14   85 Genesis 6—8

50 "the master of that servant will come on a day when he is not looking for him and at an hour that he is not aware of,

51 "and will cut him in two, and will appoint him his portion with the hypocrites; there will be weeping and gnashing of teeth.

The Parable of the Wise and Foolish Virgins

25 "Then the kingdom of heaven shall be likened to ten virgins who took their lamps and went out to meet the bridegroom.

2 "And five of them were wise, and five were foolish.

3 "Those who were foolish took their lamps and took no oil with them,

4 "but the wise took oil in their vessels with their lamps.

5 "But while the bridegroom tarried, they all slumbered and slept.

6 "And at midnight there was a cry made: 'Behold, the bridegroom is coming; go out to meet him!'

7 "Then all those virgins arose and trimmed their lamps.

8 "And the foolish said to the wise, 'Give us some of your oil, for our lamps are going out.'

9 "But the wise answered, saying, 'No, lest there not be enough for us and you; but go rather to those who sell, and buy for yourselves.'

10 "And while they went to buy, the bridegroom came, and those who were ready went in with him to the wedding; and the door was shut.

11 "Afterward the other virgins came also, saying, 'Lord, Lord, open to us!'

12 "But he answered and said, 'Assuredly, I say to you, I do not know you.'

13 "Watch therefore, for you know neither the day nor the hour in which the Son of Man is coming.

The Parable of the Talents

14 "For the kingdom of heaven is like a man traveling into a far country, who called his own servants and delivered his goods to them.

15 "And to one he gave five talents, to another two, and to another one, to each according to his own ability; and right away he went on a journey.

16 "Then he who had received the five talents went and traded with them, and made another five talents.

17 "And likewise he who had received two gained two more also.

18 "But he who had received one went and dug in the ground, and hid his master's money.

19 "After a long time the master of those servants came and settled accounts with them.

20 "And so he who had received five talents came and brought five other talents, saying, 'Master, you delivered to me five talents; look, I have gained five more talents besides them.'

21 "His master said to him, 'Well done, good and faithful servant; you have been faithful over a few things, I will make you ruler over many things. Enter into the joy of your master.'

22 "He also who had received two talents came and said, 'Master, you delivered to me two talents; look, I have gained two more talents besides them.'

23 "His master said to him, 'Well done, good and faithful servant; you have been faithful over a few things, I will make you ruler over many things. Enter into the joy of your master.'

24 "Then he who had received the one talent came and said, 'Master, I knew you to be a hard man, reaping where you have not sown, and gathering where you have not scattered seed.

25 'And I was afraid, and went and hid your talent in the ground. Look, there you have what is yours.'

26 "But his master answered and said to him, 'You wicked and slothful servant, you knew that I reap where I did not sow, and gather where I have not scattered seed.

27 'Therefore you ought to have put my money with the bankers, and then at my coming I would have received back my own with interest.

28 'Therefore take the talent from him, and give it to him who has ten talents.

29 'For to everyone who has, more will be given, and he will have abundance; but from him who does not have will be taken away even what he has.

30 'And cast the unprofitable servant into the outer darkness. There will be weeping and gnashing of teeth.'

The Messiah of Israel Will Judge the Nations

31 "When the Son of Man comes in His glory, and all the holy angels with Him, then He will sit on the throne of His glory.[86]

32 "And all the nations will be gathered before Him, and He will separate them one from another, as a shepherd divides his sheep from the goats.

33 "And He will set the sheep on His right hand, but the goats on the left.

34 "Then the King will say to those on His right hand, 'Come, you blessed of My Father, inherit the kingdom prepared for you from the foundation of the world:

35 'for I was hungry and you gave Me food; I was thirsty and you gave Me drink; I was a stranger and you took Me in;

36 'I was naked and you clothed Me; I was sick and you visited Me; I was in prison and you came to Me.'

37 "Then the righteous will answer Him, saying, 'Lord, when did we see You hungry and feed You, or thirsty and give You drink?

38 'When did we see You a stranger and take You in, or naked and clothe You?

39 'Or when did we see You sick, or in prison, and come to see You?'

40 "And the King will answer and say to them, 'Assuredly, I say to you, inasmuch as you have done it to one of the least of these My brethren, you have done it to Me.'

86 Daniel 7:13, 14

41 "Then He will also say to those on the left hand, 'Depart from Me, you cursed, into the everlasting fire prepared for the devil and his angels:

42 'for I was hungry and you gave Me no food; I was thirsty and you gave Me no drink;

43 'I was a stranger and you did not take Me in, naked and you did not clothe Me, sick and in prison and you did not visit Me.'

44 "Then they will also answer Him, saying, 'Lord, when did we see You hungry or thirsty or a stranger or naked or sick or in prison, and did not minister to You?'

45 "Then He will answer them, saying, 'Assuredly, I say to you, inasmuch as you did not do it to one of the least of these, you did not do it to Me.'

46 "And these will go away into everlasting punishment, but the righteous into eternal life."

The Plot to Kill Yeshua

26 And it came to pass, when Yeshua had finished all these sayings, that He said to His disciples,

2 "You know that after two days is the Passover, and the Son of Man will be betrayed to be crucified."

3 Then the chief priests, the scribes, and the elders of the people assembled together at the palace of the high priest, who was called Caiaphas,

4 and plotted that they might take Yeshua by trickery and kill Him.

5 But they said, "Not during the feast, lest there be an uproar among the people."

The Anointing at Bethany

6 Now when Yeshua was in Bethany at the house of Simon the leper,

7 a woman came to Him having an alabaster flask of very costly fragrant oil, and she poured it on His head as He sat at the table.

8 But when His disciples saw it, they were indignant, saying, "To what purpose is this waste?

9 "For this fragrant oil might have been sold for much and given to the poor."

10 But when Yeshua was aware of it, He said to them, "Why do you trouble the woman? For she has done a good work for Me.

11 "For you have the poor with you always, but Me you do not have always.

12 "For in pouring this fragrant oil on My body, she did it for My burial.

13 "Assuredly, I say to you, wherever this good news is preached in the whole world, what this woman has done will also be told as a memorial to her."

Judas Agrees to Betray Yeshua

14 Then one of the twelve, called Judas Iscariot, went to the chief priests

15 and said, "What are you willing to give me if I deliver Him to you?" And they counted out to him thirty pieces of silver.[87]

16 And from that time he sought opportunity to betray Him.

Yeshua Celebrates Passover with His Disciples

17 Now on the first day of the Feast of the Unleavened Bread

---

87 Zechariah 11:12

the disciples came to Yeshua, saying to Him, "Where do You want us to prepare for You to eat the Passover?"[88]

18 And He said, "Go into the city to a certain man, and say to him, 'The Rabbi says: My time is at hand; I will keep the Passover at your house with My disciples.' "

19 And the disciples did as Yeshua had directed them; and they prepared the Passover.

20 Now when evening had come, He sat down with the twelve.

21 And as they were eating, He said, "Assuredly, I say to you, one of you will betray Me."

22 And they were exceedingly sorrowful, and each of them began to say to Him, "Lord, is it I?"

23 And He answered and said, "He who dipped his hand with Me in the dish will betray Me.[89]

24 "The Son of Man goes as it is written of Him, but woe to that man by whom the Son of Man is betrayed! It would have been good for that man if he had not been born."

25 Then Judas, who was betraying Him, answered and said, "Rabbi, is it I?" He said to him, "You have said it."

26 And as they were eating, Yeshua took matzah, blessed it and broke it, and gave it to the disciples and said, "Take, eat; this is My body."

27 And He took the cup, and gave thanks, and gave it to them, saying, "All of you drink from it.

28 "For this is My blood of the new covenant, which is shed for many for the remission of sins.

29 "But I say to you, I will not drink of this fruit of the vine from now on until that day when I drink it new with you in My Father's kingdom."

30 And when they had sung a hymn, they went out to the Mount of Olives.[90]

Yeshua Predicts Peter's Denial

31 Then Yeshua said to them, "All of you will be made to stumble because of Me this night, for it is written:

> 'I will strike the Shepherd,
> And the sheep of the flock
> will be scattered.'[91]

32 "But after I have been raised, I will go before you to Galilee."

33 Peter answered and said to Him, "Even if all shall be made to stumble because of You, yet I will never be made to stumble."

34 Yeshua said to him, "Assuredly, I say to you that this night, before the rooster crows, you will deny Me three times."

35 Peter said to Him, "Even if I have to die with You, yet I will not deny You!" And so said all the disciples.

The Prayer in the Garden

36 Then Yeshua came with them to a place called Gethsemane, and said to the disciples, "Sit here while I go and pray over there."

88 Exodus 12:24-26

89 Psalm 41:9 (41:10 in some versions)

90 Psalm 118 is one of the hymns sung at Passover. See Psalm 118:22, which makes a prediction about the Messiah, calling Him "the Stone". 91 Zechariah 13:7

37 And He took with Him Peter and the two sons of Zebedee, and He began to be sorrowful and deeply distressed.

38 Then He said to them, "My soul is exceedingly sorrowful, even to death. Stay here and watch with Me."

39 And He went a little farther, fell on His face, and prayed, saying, "O My Father, if it is possible, let this cup pass from Me; nevertheless, not as I will, but as You will."

40 And He came to the disciples, found them asleep, and said to Peter, "What, could you not watch with Me one hour?

41 "Watch and pray, lest you enter into temptation. The spirit indeed is willing, but the flesh is weak."

42 He went away again a second time and prayed, saying, "O My Father, if this cup may not pass away from Me unless I drink it, Your will be done."

43 And He came and found them asleep again, for their eyes were heavy.

44 And He left them, went away again, and prayed the third time, saying the same words.

45 Then He came to His disciples and said to them, "Sleep on now and take your rest. Behold, the hour is at hand, and the Son of Man is being betrayed into the hands of sinners.

46 "Rise, let us be going. See, he who betrays Me is at hand."

Betrayal and Arrest in Gethsemane

47 And while He was still speaking, behold, Judas, one of the twelve, with a great multitude with swords and clubs, came from the chief priests and elders of the people.

48 Now he who was betraying Him had given them a sign, saying, "Whomever I kiss, He is the One; seize Him."

49 And immediately he went up to Yeshua and said, "Greetings, Rabbi!" and kissed Him.

50 And Yeshua said to him, "Friend, why have you come?" Then they came and laid hands on Yeshua and took Him.

51 And, suddenly, one of those who were with Yeshua stretched out his hand and drew his sword, struck the servant of the high priest, and cut off his ear.

52 Then Yeshua said to him, "Put your sword in its place, for all who take the sword will perish by the sword.

53 "Or do you think that I cannot now pray to My Father, and He will provide Me with more than twelve legions of angels? [92]

54 "How then will the Scriptures be fulfilled, that it must be thus?"

55 In that hour Yeshua said to the multitudes, "Have you come out, as against a robber, with swords and clubs to take Me? I sat daily with you, teaching in the temple, and you did not seize Me.

56 "But all this was done that the Scriptures of the prophets might be fulfilled." Then all the disciples forsook Him and fled.

Yeshua Faces the Sanhedrin

57 And those who had laid hold of Yeshua led Him away to Caiaphas the high priest, where the

92 A legion contained about 6,000 soldiers.

scribes and the elders were assembled.

58 But Peter followed Him at a distance to the high priest's courtyard. And he went in and sat with the servants to see the end.

59 Now the chief priests, the elders, and all the council sought false testimony against Yeshua to put Him to death,[93]

60 but found none. Even though many false witnesses came forward, still they found none. But at last two false witnesses came forward

61 and said, "This fellow said, 'I am able to destroy the temple of God and to build it in three days.'"

62 And the high priest arose and said to Him, "Do You answer nothing? What is it these men testify against You?"

63 But Yeshua kept silent. And the high priest answered and said to Him, "I adjure You by the living God that You tell us if You are the Messiah, the Son of God."

64 Yeshua said to him, "It is as you said. Nevertheless, I say to you, hereafter you will see the Son of Man sitting at the right hand of the Power,[94] and coming on the clouds of heaven." [95]

65 Then the high priest tore his clothes, saying, "He has spoken blasphemy! What further need do we have of witnesses? Look, now you have heard His blasphemy!

66 "What do you think?" They answered and said, "He is guilty of death."

67 Then they spat in His face and beat Him; and others struck Him with the palms of their hands,[96]

68 saying, "Prophesy to us, You Messiah! Who is the one who struck You?"

Peter Denies Yeshua—and Weeps Bitterly

69 Now Peter sat outside in the courtyard. And a servant girl came to him, saying, "You also were with Yeshua of Galilee."

70 But he denied it before them all, saying, "I do not know what you are saying."

71 And when he had gone out to the entrance, another girl saw him and said to those who were there, "This fellow was also with Yeshua of Nazareth."

72 And again he denied with an oath, "I do not know the Man!"

73 And after a while, those who stood by came to him and said to Peter, "Surely you also are one of them, because your speech betrays you."

74 Then he began to curse and swear, saying, "I do not know the Man!" And immediately a rooster crowed.

75 And Peter remembered the word of Yeshua who had said to him, "Before the rooster crows, you will deny Me three times." And he went out and wept bitterly.

Yeshua Handed Over to Pontius Pilate

27 When morning came, all the chief priests and elders of the people took counsel against Yeshua to put Him to death.

---

93 Psalm 35:11
94 Psalm 110:1   95 Daniel 7:13, 14

96 Isaiah 50:6

2 And when they had bound Him, they led Him away and delivered Him to Pontius Pilate the governor.

Judas Hangs Himself

3 Then Judas, who had betrayed Him, when he saw that He had been condemned, felt remorse and brought back the thirty pieces of silver to the chief priests and elders,

4 saying, "I have sinned in that I have betrayed innocent blood." And they said, "What is that to us? You see to that!"

5 And he threw down the pieces of silver in the temple, departed, and went and hanged himself.

6 And the chief priests took the silver pieces and said, "It is not lawful to put them into the treasury, because they are the price of blood."

7 And they took counsel and bought with them the potter's field, to bury strangers in.

8 Therefore that field has been called the Field of Blood to this day.

9 Then was fulfilled what was spoken by Jeremiah the prophet, saying, *"And they took the thirty pieces of silver, the value of Him who was priced, whom they of the children of Israel priced,*

10 *"and gave them for the potter's field, as the* LORD *directed me."*[97]

Yeshua Faces Pilate

11 And Yeshua stood before the governor. And the governor asked Him, saying, "Are You the King of the Jews?" And Yeshua said to him, "It is as you say."

12 And while He was being accused by the chief priests and elders, He answered nothing.[98]

13 Then Pilate said to Him, "Do You not hear how many things they testify against You?"

14 And He answered him not one word, so that the governor marveled greatly.

Condemned in Our Place

15 Now at the feast the governor was accustomed to releasing to the multitude one prisoner whom they wished.

16 And they had then a notorious prisoner called Barabbas.

17 Therefore, when they had gathered together, Pilate said to them, "Whom do you want me to release to you? Barabbas, or Yeshua who is called the Messiah?"

18 For he knew that because of envy they had delivered Him.

19 While he was sitting on the judgment seat, his wife sent to him, saying, "Have nothing to do with that just Man, for I have suffered many things today in a dream because of Him."

20 But the chief priests and elders persuaded the multitudes that they should ask for Barabbas and destroy Yeshua.

21 The governor answered and said to them, "Which of the two do you want me to release to you?" They said, "Barabbas!"

22 Pilate said to them, "What then shall I do with Yeshua who is called the Messiah?" They all

97 Jeremiah 32:6-9; cf. Zechariah 11:12, 13

98 Isaiah 53:7

said to him, "Let Him be crucified!"

23 And the governor said, "Why, what evil has He done?" But they cried out all the more, saying, "Let Him be crucified!"

24 When Pilate saw that he could not prevail at all, but rather that a tumult was rising, he took water and washed his hands before the multitude, saying, "I am innocent of the blood of this just Person. You see to it."

25 And all the people answered and said, "His blood be on us and on our children."

26 Then he released Barabbas to them; but when he had scourged Yeshua, he delivered Him to be crucified.

Bruised for Our Iniquities

27 Then the soldiers of the governor took Yeshua into the Praetorium and gathered the whole band of soldiers around Him.

28 And they stripped Him and put a scarlet robe on Him.

29 And when they had twisted a crown out of thorns, they put it on His head, and a reed in His right hand. And they bowed the knee before Him and mocked Him, saying, "Hail, King of the Jews!"

30 And they spat on Him, and took the reed and struck Him on the head.

31 And when they had mocked Him, they took the robe off Him, put His own clothes on Him, and led Him away to crucify Him.

Wounded for Our Transgressions

32 And as they came out, they found a man of Cyrene, Simon by name. Him they compelled to bear His cross.

33 And when they had come to a place called Golgotha, that is to say, the Place of a Skull;

34 they gave Him sour wine mingled with gall to drink. And when He had tasted it, He would not drink.[99]

35 And they crucified Him, and divided His garments, casting lots, that it might be fulfilled which was spoken by the prophet:

"They divided My garments
    among them,
    And for My clothing they
      cast lots."[100]

36 And sitting down, they kept watch over Him there.

37 And they put up over His head the accusation written against Him:

THIS IS YESHUA
THE KING OF THE JEWS.

38 Then two robbers were crucified with Him, one on the right and another on the left.[101]

39 And those who passed by blasphemed Him, wagging their heads[102]

40 and saying, "You who destroy the temple and build it in three days, save Yourself! If You are the Son of God, come down from the cross."

41 Likewise the chief priests also, mocking with the scribes and elders, said,

42 "He saved others; Himself He cannot save. If He is the King of Israel, let Him now come down

---

99 Psalm 69:21 (69:22 in some versions)
100 Psalm 22:18 (22:19 in some versions)
101 Isaiah 53:9-12
102 Psalm 22:7, 8 (22:8, 9 in some versions)

from the cross, and we will believe Him.

43 "He trusted in God; let Him deliver Him now if He will have Him; for He said, 'I am the Son of God.' " [103]

44 Even the robbers who were crucified with Him reviled Him with the same thing.

An Offering for Sin

45 Now from the sixth [104] hour until the ninth [105] hour there was darkness over all the land.

46 And about the ninth hour Yeshua cried out with a loud voice, saying, *"Eli, Eli, lama sabachthani?"* that is, *"My God, My God, why have You forsaken Me?"* [106]

47 Some of those who stood there, when they heard that, said, "This Man is calling for Elijah!"

48 And immediately one of them ran, took a sponge and filled it with sour wine, put it on a reed, and gave it to Him to drink. [107]

49 The rest said, "Let Him alone; let us see if Elijah will come to save Him."

50 Yeshua, when He had cried out again with a loud voice, yielded up His spirit.

51 And behold, the curtain of the temple was torn in two from the top to the bottom; and the earth quaked, and the rocks were split,

52 and the graves were opened; and many bodies of the holy ones who had fallen asleep were raised;

53 and coming out of the graves after His resurrection, they went into the holy city and appeared to many.

54 Now when the centurion and those with him, who were guarding Yeshua, saw the earthquake and the things that had happened, they feared greatly, saying, "Truly this was the Son of God!"

55 And many women who followed Yeshua from Galilee, ministering to Him, were there looking on from afar,

56 among whom were Miriam of Magdala, Miriam the mother of James and Joses, and the mother of Zebedee's sons.

Yeshua Buried in Joseph's Tomb

57 Now when evening had come, there came a rich man [108] from Arimathea, named Joseph, who himself was also a disciple of Yeshua.

58 He went to Pilate and asked for the body of Yeshua. Then Pilate commanded the body to be given to him.

59 And when Joseph had taken the body, he wrapped it in a clean linen cloth,

60 and laid it in his own new tomb which he had hewn out of the rock; and he rolled a large stone against the door of the tomb and departed.

61 And Miriam of Magdala was there, and the other Miriam, sitting opposite the tomb.

Pilate Sets a Guard

62 Now the next day, which followed the Day of Preparation, the

---

103 Psalm 22:7, 8 (22:8, 9 in some versions) *104* Noon. *105* 3 p.m.
106 Psalm 22:1 (22:2 in some versions)
107 Psalm 69:21 (69:22 in some versions)

108 Isaiah 53:9

chief priests and Pharisees gathered together to Pilate,

63 saying, "Sir, we remember, while He was still alive, how that deceiver said, 'After three days I will rise.'

64 "Therefore command that the tomb be made secure until the third day, lest His disciples come by night, steal Him away, and say to the people, 'He has risen from the dead.' So the last deception will be worse than the first."

65 Pilate said to them, "You have a guard; go your way, make it as secure as you know how."

66 So they went and made the tomb secure, sealing the stone, and setting the guard.

He Is Risen

28 Now after the Sabbath, as the first day of the week began to dawn, Miriam of Magdala and the other Miriam came to see the tomb.

2 And behold, there was a great earthquake; for an angel of the Lord descended from heaven, and came and rolled back the stone from the door, and sat on it.

3 His countenance was like lightning, and his clothing as white as snow.

4 And the guards shook for fear of him and became like dead men.

5 And the angel answered and said to the women, "Do not be afraid, for I know that you seek Yeshua who was crucified.

6 "He is not here! For He is risen as He said. Come, see the place where the Lord lay.[109]

7 "And go quickly and tell His disciples that He is risen from the dead, and indeed He is going before you into Galilee; there you will see Him. Behold, I have told you."

8 And they departed quickly from the tomb with fear and great joy, and ran to bring His disciples word.

The Women Worship the Risen Lord

9 And as they went to tell His disciples, behold, Yeshua met them, saying, "Joy to you!" And they came and held Him by the feet and worshiped Him.

10 Then Yeshua said to them, "Do not be afraid. Go, tell My brethren to go to Galilee, and there they will see Me."

The Soldiers Bribed to Lie

11 Now while they were going, behold, some of the guard came into the city and reported to the chief priests all the things that had happened.

12 And when they had assembled with the elders and taken counsel, they gave a large sum of money to the soldiers,

13 saying, "Tell them, 'His disciples came at night and stole Him away while we slept.'

14 "And if this comes to the governor's ears, we will appease him and make you secure."

15 So they took the money and did as they were instructed, and this saying is commonly reported among the Jews until this day.

The Great Commission

16 Then the eleven disciples went away into Galilee, to the mountain which Yeshua had appointed for them.

17 And when they saw Him,

---

109 Psalm 16:10; cf. Isaiah 53:9, 10

they worshiped Him; but some doubted.

18 And Yeshua came and spoke to them, saying, "All authority has been given to Me in heaven and on earth.

19 "Go therefore and make disciples of all the nations, immersing them in the name of the Father and of the Son and of the Holy Spirit,

20 "teaching them to observe all things whatever I have commanded you; and behold, I am with you always, even to the end of the age." Amen.

The Good News According To
MARK

John Prepares the Way

THE beginning of the good news of Yeshua ha Mashiach, the Son of God.

2 As it is written in the Prophets:

"Behold, I send My messenger before Your face,
Who will prepare Your way before You." [1]

3 "The voice of one crying in the wilderness:
'Prepare the way of the LORD,
Make His paths straight.' " [2]

4 John came immersing in the wilderness and preaching the immersion of repentance for the remission of sins.

5 And all the land of Judea, and those from Jerusalem, went out to him and were all immersed by him in the Jordan River, confessing their sins.

6 And John was clothed with camel's hair and with a leather belt around his waist, and he ate locusts and wild honey.

7 And he preached, saying, "There comes One after me who is mightier than I, whose sandal strap I am not worthy to stoop down and loose.

8 "I indeed have immersed you in water, but He will immerse you in the Holy Spirit."

John Immerses Yeshua

9 And it came to pass in those days that Yeshua came from Nazareth of Galilee, and was immersed by John in the Jordan.

10 And immediately, coming up from the water, He saw the heavens opened and the Spirit descending upon Him like a dove.

11 And a voice came from heaven, "You are My beloved Son, in whom I am well pleased."

Satan Tempts Yeshua

12 And immediately the Spirit drove Him into the wilderness.

13 And He was there in the wilderness forty days, tempted by Satan, and was with the wild beasts; and the angels ministered to Him.

Yeshua Teaches in Galilee

14 Now after John was put in prison, Yeshua came to Galilee, preaching the good news of the kingdom of God,

15 and saying, "The time is fulfilled, and the kingdom of God is at hand. Repent and believe in the good news."

Four Fishermen Called as Disciples

16 Now as He walked by the Sea of Galilee, He saw Simon and An-

1 Malachi 3:1   2 Isaiah 40:3

drew his brother casting a net into the sea; for they were fishermen.

17 And Yeshua said to them, "Come after Me, and I will make you become fishers of men."

18 And immediately they left their nets and followed Him.

19 And when He had gone a little farther from there, He saw James the son of Zebedee, and John his brother, who also were in the boat mending their nets.

20 And immediately He called them, and they left their father Zebedee in the boat with the hired servants, and went after Him.

Yeshua Casts Out an Unclean Spirit

21 And they went into Capernaum, and immediately on the Sabbath He entered the synagogue and taught.

22 And they were astonished at His teaching, for He taught them as one having authority, and not as the scribes.

23 And there was a man in their synagogue with an unclean spirit. And he cried out,

24 saying, "Let us alone! What have we to do with You, Yeshua of Nazareth? Have You come to destroy us? I know who You are— the Holy One of God!"

25 And Yeshua rebuked him, saying, "Be quiet, and come out of him!"

26 And when the unclean spirit had convulsed him and cried out with a loud voice, he came out of him.

27 And they were all amazed, so that they questioned among themselves, saying, "What is this? What new doctrine is this? For

with authority He commands even the unclean spirits, and they obey Him."

28 And immediately His fame spread throughout all the region around Galilee.

Peter's Mother-in-Law Healed

29 And as soon as they had come out of the synagogue, they entered the house of Simon and Andrew, with James and John.

30 But Simon's wife's mother lay sick with a fever, and right away they told Him about her.

31 And He came and took her by the hand and lifted her up, and immediately the fever left her. And she served them.

Many Healed After Sabbath Sunset

32 And at evening, when the sun had set, they brought to Him all who were sick and those who were demon-possessed.

33 And the whole city was gathered together at the door.

34 And He healed many who were sick with various diseases, and cast out many demons; and He did not allow the demons to speak, because they knew Him.

In the Synagogues of Galilee

35 And in the morning, having risen a long while before daylight, He went out and departed to a solitary place; and there He prayed.

36 And Simon and those who were with Him searched for Him.

37 And when they had found Him, they said to Him, "Everyone is looking for You."

38 And He said to them, "Let us

go into the next towns, that I may preach there also, because for this purpose I have come forth."

39 And He was preaching in their synagogues throughout all Galilee, and casting out demons.

Yeshua Cleanses a Leper

40 And a leper came to Him, imploring Him, kneeling down to Him and saying to Him, "If You are willing, You can make me clean."

41 Then Yeshua, moved with compassion, put out His hand and touched him, and said to him, "I am willing; be cleansed."

42 And as soon as He had spoken, immediately the leprosy left him, and he was cleansed.

43 And He strictly warned him and sent him away at once.

44 And He said to him, "See that you say nothing to anyone; but go your way, show yourself to the priest, and offer for your cleansing those things which Moses commanded, as a testimony to them." [3]

45 But he went out and began to proclaim it freely, and to spread the matter, so that Yeshua could no longer openly enter the city, but was outside in deserted places; and they came to Him from every quarter.

Yeshua Forgives and Heals a Paralytic

2 And again He entered Capernaum after some days, and it was heard that He was in the house.

2 And immediately many gathered together, so that there was no longer room to receive them, not even near the door. And He preached the word to them.

3 And they came to Him, bringing a paralytic who was carried by four men.

4 And when they could not come near Him because of the crowd, they uncovered the roof where He was. And when they had broken through, they let down the bed on which the paralytic was lying.

5 When Yeshua saw their faith, He said to the paralytic, "Son, your sins are forgiven you."

6 But some of the scribes were sitting there and reasoning in their hearts,

7 "Why does this Man speak blasphemies like this? Who can forgive sins but God alone?"

8 And immediately, when Yeshua perceived in His spirit that they reasoned thus within themselves, He said to them, "Why do you reason about these things in your hearts?

9 "Which is easier, to say to the paralytic, 'Your sins are forgiven you,' or to say, 'Arise, take up your bed and walk'?

10 "But that you may know that the Son of Man has power on earth to forgive sins"—He said to the paralytic,

11 "I say to you, arise, take up your bed, and go your way to your house."

12 And immediately he arose, took up the bed, and went out in the presence of them all, so that all were amazed and glorified God, saying, "We never saw anything like this!"

[3] Leviticus 14:1-32

Matthew the Tax Collector

13 And He went out again by the sea; and all the multitude came to Him, and He taught them.

14 And as He passed by, He saw Levi the son of Alphaeus sitting at the tax office, and said to him, "Follow Me." And he arose and followed Him.

15 And it came to pass, as He was dining in Levi's house, that many tax collectors and sinners also sat together with Yeshua and His disciples; for there were many, and they followed Him.

16 And when the scribes and Pharisees saw Him eating with the tax collectors and sinners, they said to His disciples, "How is it that He eats and drinks with tax collectors and sinners?"

17 When Yeshua heard it, He said to them, "Those who are well have no need of a physician, but those who are sick. I did not come to call the righteous, but sinners, to repentance."

Yeshua Is Questioned About Fasting

18 And the disciples of John and of the Pharisees were fasting. And they came and said to Him, "Why do the disciples of John and of the Pharisees fast, but Your disciples do not fast?"

19 And Yeshua said to them, "Can the friends of the bridegroom fast while the bridegroom is with them? As long as they have the bridegroom with them they cannot fast.

20 "But the days will come when the bridegroom will be taken away from them, and then they will fast in those days.

21 "And no one sews a piece of unshrunk cloth on an old garment; or else the new piece pulls away from the old, and the tear is made worse.

22 "And no one puts new wine into old wineskins; or else the new wine bursts the wineskins, the wine is spilled, and the wineskins will be ruined. But new wine must be put into new wineskins."

Yeshua Teaches Concerning the Sabbath

23 And it came to pass that He went through the grainfields on the Sabbath. And as they went His disciples began to pluck the heads of grain.

24 And the Pharisees said to Him, "Look, why do they do what is not lawful on the Sabbath?"

25 And He said to them, "Have you never read what David did when he was in need and hungry, he and those who were with him:

26 "how he went into the house of God in the days of Abiathar the high priest, and ate the show-bread, which is not lawful to eat, except for the priests, and also gave some to those who were with him?" [4]

27 And He said to them, "The Sabbath was made for man, and not man for the Sabbath.

28 "Therefore the Son of Man is also Lord of the Sabbath."

A Man with a Withered Hand Healed on the Sabbath

3 And He entered the synagogue again, and a man was there who had a withered hand.

2 And they watched Him

4 1 Samuel 21:1-6

closely whether He would heal him on the Sabbath, so that they might accuse Him.

3 And He said to the man who had the withered hand, "Step forward."

4 And He said to them, "Is it lawful to do good on the Sabbath or to do evil, to save life or to kill?" But they kept silent.

5 And when He had looked around at them with anger, being grieved by the hardness of their hearts, He said to the man, "Stretch out your hand." And he stretched it out, and his hand was restored as whole as the other.

6 And the Pharisees went out and immediately took counsel with the Herodians against Him, how they might destroy Him.

A Great Multitude Follows Yeshua

7 But Yeshua withdrew with His disciples to the sea. And a great multitude from Galilee followed Him, and from Judea

8 and Jerusalem and Idumea and beyond the Jordan; and those from Tyre and Sidon, a great multitude, when they heard what great things He did, came to Him.

9 And He told His disciples that a small boat should be kept ready for Him because of the multitude, lest they should crush Him.

10 For He had healed many, so that as many as had afflictions pressed about Him to touch Him.

11 And the unclean spirits, whenever they saw Him, fell down before Him and cried out, saying, "You are the Son of God."

12 And He sternly warned them that they should not make Him known.

The Twelve Appointed

13 And He went up on the mountain and called to Him those He Himself wanted. And they came to Him.

14 And He appointed twelve, that they might be with Him, and that He might send them out to preach,

15 and to have power to heal sicknesses and to cast out demons:

16 Simon, to whom He gave the name Peter;

17 James the son of Zebedee and John the brother of James, to whom He gave the name Boanerges, that is, "Sons of Thunder";

18 Andrew, Philip, Bartholomew, Matthew, Thomas, James the son of Alphaeus, Thaddaeus, Simon the Canaanite;

19 and Judas Iscariot, who also betrayed Him. And they went into a house.

A House Divided Cannot Stand

20 And the multitude came together again, so that they could not so much as eat bread.

21 And when His own people heard about this, they went out to lay hold of Him, for they said, "He is out of His mind."

22 And the scribes who came down from Jerusalem said, "He has Beelzebub, and by the ruler of the demons He casts out demons."

23 And He called them to Him and said to them in parables: "How can Satan cast out Satan?

24 "And if a kingdom is divided against itself, that kingdom cannot stand.

25 "And if a house is divided against itself, that house cannot stand.

26 "And if Satan has risen up against himself, and is divided, he cannot stand, but has an end.

27 "No one can enter a strong man's house and plunder his goods, unless he first binds the strong man, and then he will plunder his house.

The Unpardonable Sin

28 "Assuredly, I say to you, all sins will be forgiven the sons of men, and whatever blasphemies they may utter;

29 "but he who blasphemes against the Holy Spirit never has forgiveness, but is subject to eternal condemnation"—

30 because they said, "He has an unclean spirit."

Yeshua's Mother and Brothers Send for Him

31 Then His brothers and His mother came, and standing outside they sent to Him, calling Him.

32 And a multitude was sitting around Him; and they said to Him, "Look, Your mother and Your brothers are outside seeking You."

33 And He answered them, saying, "Who is My mother, or My brothers?"

34 And He looked around in a circle at those who sat about Him, and said, "Here are My mother and My brothers!

35 "For whoever does the will of God is My brother and My sister and mother."

The Parable of the Sower

4 And again He began to teach by the seaside. And a great multitude was gathered to Him, so that He got into a boat and sat in it on the sea, and the whole multitude was on the land facing the sea.

2 And He taught them many things by parables, and said to them in His teaching:

3 "Listen! Behold, a sower went out to sow.

4 "And it happened, as he sowed, that some seed fell by the wayside; and the birds of the air came and devoured it.

5 "And some fell on stony ground, where it did not have much earth; and immediately it sprang up because it had no depth of earth.

6 "But when the sun was up it was scorched, and because it had no root it withered away.

7 "And some seed fell among thorns; and the thorns grew up and choked it, and it yielded no crop.

8 "And other seed fell on good ground and yielded a crop that sprang up, increased, and produced: some thirtyfold, some sixty, and some a hundred."

9 And He said to them, "He who has ears to hear, let him hear!"

The Purpose of Parables

10 And when He was alone, those who were around Him with the twelve asked Him about the parable.

11 And He said to them, "To you it has been given to know the mystery of the kingdom of God; but to those who are outsiders, all things come in parables,

12 "that

'Seeing they may see and not
perceive,
And hearing they may hear
and not understand;
Lest they should turn again,
And their sins be forgiven
them.' " 5

The Parable of the Sower Explained

13 And He said to them, "Do
you not understand this parable?
How then will you understand all
the parables?

14 "The sower sows the word.

15 "And these are the ones by
the wayside where the word is
sown. And when they hear, Satan comes immediately and takes
away the word that was sown in
their hearts.

16 "And these likewise are the
ones sown on stony ground who,
when they hear the word, immediately receive it with gladness;

17 "and they have no root in
themselves, and so endure only for
a time. Afterward, when tribulation or persecution arises for the
word's sake, immediately they
stumble.

18 "And these are the ones sown
among thorns; they are the ones
who hear the word,

19 "and the cares of this world,
the deceitfulness of riches, and the
desires for other things entering in
choke the word, and it becomes
unfruitful.

20 "And these are the ones sown
on good ground, those who hear
the word, accept it, and bear fruit:
some thirtyfold, some sixty, and
some a hundred."

5 Isaiah 6:9, 10

Light Under a Basket

21 And He said to them, "Is a
lamp brought to be put under a
basket or under a bed? Is it not to
be set on a lampstand?

22 "For there is nothing hidden
which will not be revealed, nor has
anything been kept secret but that
it should come to light.

23 "If anyone has ears to hear,
let him hear."

24 And He said to them, "Take
heed what you hear. With the
same measure you use, it will be
measured to you; and to you who
hear, more will be given.

25 "For he who has, to him will
be given; and he who does not
have, from him will be taken even
what he has."

The Parable of the Growing Seed

26 And He said, "The kingdom
of God is as if a man should scatter
seed on the ground,

27 "and should sleep by night
and rise by day, and the seed
should sprout and grow, he himself does not know how.

28 "For the earth yields crops by
itself: first the blade, then the
head, after that the full grain in
the head.

29 "But when the grain ripens,
immediately he puts in the sickle,
because the harvest has come."

The Parable of the Mustard Seed

30 And He said, "To what shall
we liken the kingdom of God? Or
with what parable shall we picture
it?

31 "It is like a mustard seed
which, when it is sown on the

ground, is smaller than all the seeds on earth;

32 "but when it is sown, it grows up, becomes greater than all herbs, and shoots out large branches, so that the birds of the air may nest under its shade."

Yeshua's Use of Parables

33 And with many such parables He spoke the word to them as they were able to hear it.

34 But without a parable He did not speak to them. And when they were alone, He explained all things to His disciples.

Wind and Wave Obey Yeshua

35 And the same day, when evening had come, He said to them, "Let us cross over to the other side."

36 And when they had sent away the multitude, they took Him along in the boat as He was. And other little boats were also with Him.

37 And a great windstorm arose, and the waves beat into the boat, so that it was already filling.

38 And He was in the stern, asleep on a pillow. And they awoke Him and said to Him, "Rabbi, do You not care that we are perishing?"

39 And He arose and rebuked the wind, and said to the sea, "Peace, be still!" And the wind ceased and there was a great calm.

40 And He said to them, "Why are you so fearful? How is it that you have no faith?"

41 And they feared exceedingly, and said to one another, "What kind of Man is this, that even the wind and the sea obey Him!"

A Demon-Possessed Man Healed

5 And they came to the other side of the sea, to the country of the Gadarenes.

2 And when He had come out of the boat, immediately there met Him out of the tombs a man with an unclean spirit,

3 who had his dwelling among the tombs; and no one could bind him, not even with chains,

4 because he had often been bound with shackles and chains. And the chains had been pulled apart by him, and the shackles broken to pieces; neither could anyone tame him.

5 And always, night and day, he was in the mountains and in the tombs, crying out and cutting himself with stones.

6 But when he saw Yeshua from afar, he ran and worshiped Him.

7 And he cried out with a loud voice and said, "What have I to do with You, Yeshua, Son of the Most High God? I implore You by God that You do not torment me."

8 For He said to him, "Come out of the man, unclean spirit!"

9 And He asked him, "What is your name?" And he answered, saying, "My name is Legion; for we are many."

10 And he begged Him earnestly that He would not send them out of the country.

11 Now a large herd of swine was feeding there near the mountains.

12 And all the demons begged Him, saying, "Send us to the swine, that we may enter them!"

13 And at once Yeshua gave

them permission. And the unclean spirits went out and entered the swine (there were about two thousand); and the herd ran violently down the steep place into the sea, and drowned in the sea.

14 And those who fed the swine fled, and they told it in the city and in the country. And they went out to see what it was that had happened.

15 And they came to Yeshua, and saw the one who had been demon-possessed and had the legion, sitting and clothed and in his right mind. And they were afraid.

16 And those who saw it told them how it happened to him who had been demon-possessed, and about the swine.

17 And they began to plead with Him to depart from their region.

18 And when He got into the boat, he who had been demon-possessed begged Him that he might be with Him.

19 However, Yeshua did not permit him, but said to him, "Go home to your friends, and tell them what great things the Lord has done for you, and how He has had compassion on you."

20 And he departed and began to proclaim in Decapolis what great things Yeshua had done for him; and all marveled.

A Girl Restored to Life and a Woman Healed

21 And when Yeshua had crossed over again by boat to the other side, a great multitude gathered to Him; and He was by the sea.

22 And behold, one of the rulers of the synagogue came, Jairus by name. And when he saw Him, he fell at His feet

23 and begged Him earnestly, saying, "My little daughter lies at the point of death. Come and lay Your hands on her, that she may be healed, and she will live."

24 And Yeshua went with him, and a great multitude followed Him and thronged Him.

25 And a certain woman had a flow of blood for twelve years,

26 and had suffered many things from many physicians. She had spent all that she had and was no better, but rather grew worse.

27 When she had heard about Yeshua, she came behind Him in the crowd and touched His garment;

28 for she said, "If only I may touch His clothes, I shall be made well."

29 And immediately the fountain of her blood was dried up, and she felt in her body that she was healed of the affliction.

30 And Yeshua, immediately knowing in Himself that power had gone out of Him, turned around in the crowd and said, "Who touched My clothes?"

31 And His disciples said to Him, "You see the multitude thronging You, and You say, 'Who touched Me?' "

32 And He looked around to see her who had done this thing.

33 But the woman, fearing and trembling, knowing what had happened to her, came and fell down before Him and told Him the whole truth.

34 And He said to her, "Daughter, your faith has made you well. Go in peace, and be healed of your affliction."

35 While He was still speaking, some came from the ruler of the synagogue's house who said, "Your daughter is dead. Why trouble the Rabbi any further?"

36 As soon as Yeshua heard the word that was spoken, He said to the ruler of the synagogue, "Do not be afraid; only believe."

37 And He permitted no one to follow Him except Peter, James, and John the brother of James.

38 And He came to the house of the ruler of the synagogue, and saw the tumult and those who wept and wailed loudly.

39 And when He had come in, He said to them, "Why make this commotion and weep? The child is not dead but sleeping."

40 And they laughed Him to scorn. But when He had put them all out, He took the father and the mother of the child, and those who were with Him, and entered where the child was lying.

41 And He took the child by the hand and said to her, *"Talitha, cumi,"* which is translated, "Little girl, I say to you, arise."

42 And immediately the girl arose and walked, for she was twelve years of age. And they were overcome with great amazement.

43 And He commanded them strictly that no one should know it, and said that something should be given her to eat.

Yeshua Rejected at Nazareth

6 And He went out from there and came to His own country, and His disciples followed Him.

2 And when the Sabbath had come, He began to teach in the synagogue. And many hearing Him were astonished, saying, "Where did this Man get these things? And what wisdom is this which is given to Him, that such mighty works are performed by His hands!

3 "Is this not the carpenter, the Son of Miriam, and brother of James, Joses, Judas, and Simon? And are not His sisters here with us?" And they were offended at Him.

4 But Yeshua said to them, "A prophet is not without honor except in his own country, among his own relatives, and in his own house."

5 And He could do no mighty work there, except that He laid His hands on a few sick people and healed them.

6 And He marveled because of their unbelief. And He went about the villages in a circuit, teaching.

Sending Out the Twelve

7 And He called the twelve to Him, and began to send them out two by two, and gave them power over unclean spirits.

8 And He commanded them that they should take nothing for their journey except a staff—no bag, no bread, no copper in their money belts—

9 but to wear sandals, and not to put on two tunics.

10 And He said to them, "In whatever place you enter a house, stay there till you depart from that place.

11 "And whoever will not receive you nor hear you, when you depart from there, shake off the dust under your feet as a testimony against them. Assuredly, I

say to you, it will be more tolerable for Sodom and Gomorrah in the day of judgment than for that city!"

12 And they went out and preached that people should repent.

13 And they cast out many demons, and anointed with oil many who were sick, and healed them.

John Beheaded

14 And King Herod heard of Him, for His name had become well-known. And he said, "John the Baptizer is risen from the dead, and therefore these powers are at work in him."

15 Others said, "It is Elijah." 6 And others said, "It is the Prophet, or like one of the prophets."

16 But when Herod heard, he said, "This is John, whom I beheaded; he has been raised from the dead!"

17 For Herod himself had sent and laid hold of John, and bound him in prison for the sake of Herodias, his brother Philip's wife; for he had married her.

18 For John had said to Herod, "It is not lawful for you to have your brother's wife."

19 Therefore Herodias held it against him and wanted to kill him, but she could not;

20 for Herod feared John, knowing that he was a just and holy man, and he protected him. And when he heard him, he did many things, and heard him gladly.

21 And an opportune day came when Herod on his birthday gave

a feast for his nobles, the high officers, and the chief men of Galilee.

22 And when Herodias' daughter herself came in and danced, and pleased Herod and those who sat with him, the king said to the girl, "Ask me whatever you want, and I will give it to you."

23 And he swore to her, "Whatever you ask me, I will give you, up to half of my kingdom."

24 And she went out and said to her mother, "What shall I ask?" And she said, "The head of John the Baptizer!"

25 And immediately she came in with haste to the king and asked, saying, "I want you to give me at once the head of John the Baptizer on a platter."

26 And the king was exceedingly sorry; yet, because of the oaths and because of those who sat with him, he did not want to refuse her.

27 And immediately the king sent an executioner and commanded his head to be brought. And he went and beheaded him in prison,

28 brought his head on a platter, and gave it to the girl; and the girl gave it to her mother.

29 And when his disciples heard of it, they came and took away his corpse and laid it in a tomb.

Feeding the Five Thousand

30 And the apostles gathered together to Yeshua and told Him all things, both what they had done and what they had taught.

31 And He said to them, "Come aside by yourselves to a deserted place and rest a while." For there were many coming and going, and they did not even have time to eat.

6 Malachi 4:5 (3:23 in some versions)

32 And they departed to a deserted place in the boat by themselves.

33 And the multitudes saw them departing, and many knew Him and ran there on foot from all the cities. They arrived before them and came together to Him.

34 And Yeshua, when He came out, saw a great multitude and was moved with compassion for them, because they were like sheep not having a shepherd. And He began to teach them many things.

35 And when the day was now far spent, His disciples came to Him and said, "This is a deserted place, and already the hour is late.

36 "Send them away, that they may go into the surrounding country and villages and buy themselves bread; for they have nothing to eat."

37 He answered and said to them, "You give them something to eat." And they said to Him, "Shall we go and buy two hundred denarii[7] worth of bread and give them something to eat?"

38 But He said to them, "How many loaves do you have? Go and see." And when they found out they said, "Five, and two fish."

39 And He commanded them to make them all sit down in groups on the green grass.

40 And they sat down in ranks, by hundreds and by fifties.

41 And when He had taken the five loaves and the two fish, He looked up to heaven, blessed and broke the loaves, and gave them to His disciples to set before them;

---

7 A denarius equals about $7.50.

and the two fish He divided among them all.

42 And they all ate and were filled.

43 And they took up twelve baskets full of the fragments and of the fish.

44 And those who had eaten the loaves were about five thousand men.

Yeshua Walks on the Sea

45 And immediately He made His disciples get into the boat and go before Him to the other side, to Bethsaida, while He sent the multitude away.

46 And when He had sent them away, He departed to the mountain to pray.

47 And when evening had come, the boat was in the middle of the sea; and He was alone on the land.

48 And He saw them straining at rowing, for the wind was against them. And about the fourth watch of the night He came to them, walking on the sea, and would have passed them by.

49 But when they saw Him walking on the sea, they supposed it was a ghost, and cried out;

50 for they all saw Him and were troubled. And immediately He talked with them and said to them, "Be of good cheer! It is I; do not be afraid."

51 And He went up into the boat to them, and the wind ceased. And they were greatly amazed in themselves beyond measure, and marveled.

52 For they had not understood about the loaves, because their heart was hardened.

Many Touch Him and Are Made Well

53 And when they had crossed over, they came to the land of Gennesaret and anchored near the shore.

54 And when they had come out of the boat, immediately the people recognized Him,

55 ran through that whole surrounding region, and began to carry about on beds those who were sick to wherever they heard He was.

56 And wherever He entered, into villages, cities, or the country, they laid the sick in the marketplaces, and begged Him that they might just touch the border[8] of His garment. And as many as touched Him were made well.

Defilement Is from Within

7 Then the Pharisees and some of the scribes came together to Him, having come from Jerusalem.

2 And when they saw some of His disciples eat bread with defiled, that is, with unwashed hands, they found fault.

3 For the Pharisees and all the Jews do not eat unless they wash their hands in a special way, holding the tradition of the elders.

4 And when they come from the marketplace, they do not eat unless they wash. And there are many other things which they have received and hold, like the washing of cups, pitchers, copper vessels, and couches.

5 Then the Pharisees and scribes asked Him, "Why do Your disciples not walk according to the tradition of the elders, but eat bread with unwashed hands?"

6 He answered and said to them, "Well did Isaiah prophesy of you hypocrites, as it is written:
'This people honors Me with
  their lips,
But their heart is far from
  Me.
7 And in vain they worship
  Me,
Teaching as doctrines the
  commandments of men.'[9]

8 "For laying aside the commandment of God, you hold the tradition of men—the washing of pitchers and cups, and many other such things you do."

9 And He said to them, "All too well you reject the commandment of God, that you may keep your tradition.

10 "For Moses said, 'Honor your father and your mother';[10] and, 'He who curses father or mother, let him be put to death.'[11]

11 "But you say, 'If a man says to his father or mother: Whatever you might be profited by me is Corban (that is, a gift), he shall be free';

12 "and you no longer let him do anything for his father or his mother,

13 "making the word of God of no effect through your tradition which you have handed down. And many such things you do."

14 And when He had called all the multitude to Him, He said to them, "Hear Me, everyone, and understand:

---

8 Tzitzit or fringes (Numbers 15:38-41).

9 Isaiah 29:13

10 Exodus 20:12; Deuteronomy 5:16

11 Exodus 21:17

15 "There is nothing that enters a man from outside which can defile him; but the things which come out of him, those are the things that defile a man.

16 "If anyone has ears to hear, let him hear!"

17 And when He had entered a house away from the people, His disciples asked Him concerning the parable.

18 And He said to them, "Are you thus without understanding also? Do you not perceive that whatever enters a man from outside cannot defile him,

19 "because it does not enter his heart but his stomach, and is eliminated, thereby purifying all foods?"

20 And He said, "What comes out of a man, that defiles a man.

21 "For from within, out of the heart of men, proceed evil thoughts, adulteries, fornications, murders,

22 "thefts, covetousness, wickedness, deceit, licentiousness, an evil eye, blasphemy, pride, foolishness.

23 "All these evil things come from within and defile a man."

A Gentile Shows Her Faith

24 And from there He arose and went to the region of Tyre and Sidon. And He entered a house and wanted no one to know it, but He could not be hidden.

25 For a woman whose young daughter had an unclean spirit heard about Him, and she came and fell at His feet.

26 The woman was a Greek, a Syro-Phoenician by birth, and she kept asking Him to cast the demon out of her daughter.

27 But Yeshua said to her, "Let the children be filled first, for it is not good to take the children's bread and throw it to the little dogs."

28 And she answered and said to Him, "Yes, Lord, yet even the little dogs under the table eat from the children's crumbs."

29 And He said to her, "For this saying go your way; the demon has gone out of your daughter."

30 And when she had come to her house, she found the demon gone out, and her daughter lying on the bed.

Yeshua Heals a Deaf Mute

31 And again, departing from the region of Tyre and Sidon, He came through the midst of the region of Decapolis to the Sea of Galilee.

32 And they brought to Him one who was deaf and had an impediment in his speech, and they begged Him to put His hand on him.

33 And He took him aside from the multitude, and put His fingers in his ears, and He spat and touched his tongue.

34 And looking up to heaven, He sighed, and said to him, *"Ephphatha,"* that is, "Be opened."

35 And immediately his ears were opened, and the impediment of his tongue was loosed, and he spoke plainly.

36 And He commanded them that they should tell no one; but the more He commanded them, the more widely they proclaimed it.

37 And they were astonished beyond measure, saying, "He has

done all things well. He makes both the deaf to hear and the mute to speak."

Feeding the Four Thousand

8 In those days, the multitude being very great and having nothing to eat, Yeshua called His disciples to Him and said to them,

2 "I have compassion on the multitude, because they have now been with Me three days and have nothing to eat.

3 "And if I send them away hungry to their own houses, they will faint on the way; for some of them have come from afar."

4 And His disciples answered Him, "How can one satisfy these people with bread here in the wilderness?"

5 And He asked them, "How many loaves do you have?" And they said, "Seven."

6 And He commanded the multitude to sit down on the ground. And He took the seven loaves, gave thanks, broke them, and gave them to His disciples to set before them; and they set them before the multitude.

7 And they had a few small fish; and having blessed them, He said to set them also before them.

8 So they ate and were filled, and they took up seven large baskets of the broken pieces that were left.

9 And those who had eaten were about four thousand. And He sent them away.

10 And immediately He got into the boat with His disciples and came to the region of Dalmanutha.

The Pharisees Seek a Sign

11 And the Pharisees came out and began to dispute with Him, seeking from Him a sign from heaven, testing Him.

12 And He sighed deeply in His spirit, and said, "Why does this generation seek after a sign? Assuredly, I say to you, no sign shall be given to this generation."

Beware of the Leaven of the Pharisees and Herod

13 And He left them, and getting into the boat again, departed to the other side.

14 Now the disciples had forgotten to take bread, and they did not have more than one loaf with them in the boat.

15 And He charged them, saying, "Take heed, beware of the leaven of the Pharisees and the leaven of Herod."

16 And they reasoned among themselves, saying, "It is because we have no bread."

17 And Yeshua, being aware of it, said to them, "Why do you reason because you have no bread? Do you not yet perceive nor understand? Is your heart still hardened?

18 "Having eyes, do you not see? And having ears, do you not hear? And do you not remember?

19 "When I broke the five loaves for the five thousand, how many baskets full of fragments did you take up?" They said to Him, "Twelve."

20 "And when I broke the seven for the four thousand, how many large baskets full of fragments did you take up?" And they said, "Seven."

21 And He said to them, "How is it you do not understand?"

A Blind Paralytic Healed at Bethsaida

22 And He came to Bethsaida; and they brought a blind man to Him, and begged Him to touch him.

23 And He took the blind man by the hand and led him out of the town. And when He had spit on his eyes and put His hands on him, He asked him if he saw anything.

24 And he looked up and said, "I see men like trees, walking."

25 After that He put His hands on his eyes again and made him look up. And he was restored and saw everyone clearly.

26 And He sent him away to his house, saying, "Neither go into the town, nor tell it to anyone in the town."

Simon Proclaims Yeshua as the Messiah

27 And Yeshua and His disciples went out to the towns of Caesarea Philippi; and on the road He asked His disciples, saying to them, "Who do men say that I am?"

28 And they answered, "John the Baptizer; but some say, Elijah; and others, one of the prophets."

29 And He said to them, "But who do you say that I am?" And Peter answered and said to Him, "You are the Messiah."

30 And He charged them that they should tell no one about Him.

Yeshua Predicts His Death and Resurrection

31 And He began to teach them that the Son of Man must suffer many things, and be rejected by the elders and chief priests and scribes, and be killed, and after three days rise again.

32 And He spoke this word openly. And Peter took Him aside and began to rebuke Him.

33 But when He had turned around and looked at His disciples, He rebuked Peter, saying, "Get behind Me, Satan! For you are not mindful of the things of God, but the things of men."

Deny Yourself and Follow Him

34 And when He had called the people to Him, with His disciples also, He said to them, "Whoever desires to come after Me, let him deny himself, take up his cross, and follow Me.

35 "For whoever desires to save his life will lose it, but whoever loses his life for My sake and the sake of the good news will save it.

36 "For what will it profit a man if he gains the whole world, and loses his own soul?

37 "Or what will a man give in exchange for his soul?

38 "For whoever is ashamed of Me and My words in this adulterous and sinful generation, of him the Son of Man [12] will also be ashamed when He comes in the glory of His Father with the holy angels."

9 And He said to them, "Assuredly, I say to you that there are some standing here who shall not taste death till they see the kingdom of God come with power."

---

12 A title of Messiah; see Daniel 7:13, 14.

Yeshua Transfigured on the Mount

2 And after six days Yeshua took Peter, James, and John, and led them up on a high mountain apart by themselves; and He was transfigured before them.

3 And His clothes became shining, exceedingly white, like snow, such as no launderer on earth can whiten them.

4 And Elijah appeared to them with Moses, and they were talking with Yeshua.

5 And Peter answered and said to Yeshua, "Rabbi, it is good for us to be here; and let us make three tabernacles:[13] one for You, one for Moses, and one for Elijah"—

6 because he did not know what to say, for they were greatly afraid.

7 And a cloud came and overshadowed them; and a voice came out of the cloud, saying, "This is My beloved Son. Hear Him!"

8 And suddenly, when they had looked around, they saw no one anymore, but only Yeshua with themselves.

9 And as they came down from the mountain, He commanded them that they should tell no one the things they had seen, till the Son of Man had risen from the dead.

10 And they kept this word to themselves, disputing with one another what the rising from the dead meant.

11 And they asked Him, saying, "Why do the scribes say that Elijah must come first?"[14]

12 And He answered and told them, "Elijah does come first, and restores all things. And how is it written concerning the Son of Man, that He must suffer many things and be treated with contempt?[15]

13 "But I say to you that Elijah also has come, and they have done to him whatever they wished, as it is written of him."

A Boy Is Healed

14 And when He came to the disciples, He saw a great multitude around them, and the scribes disputing with them.

15 And immediately, when they saw Him, all the people were greatly amazed, and running to Him, greeted Him.

16 And He asked the scribes, "What are you discussing with them?"

17 And one from the multitude answered and said, "Rabbi, I brought You my son, who has a mute spirit.

18 "And wherever he seizes him, he throws him down; he foams at the mouth, gnashes his teeth, and becomes rigid. And I spoke to Your disciples, that they should cast him out, and they could not."

19 He answered him and said, "O faithless generation, how long shall I be with you? How long shall I bear with you? Bring him to Me."

20 And they brought him to Him. And when he saw Him, immediately the spirit convulsed him, and he fell on the ground and wallowed, foaming at the mouth.

13 Hebrew: Sukkot; see Leviticus 23:33f.; (cf. Zechariah 14:1-9, 16-19).

14 Malachi 4:5, 6 (3:23 in some versions)

15 Isaiah 53:3

21 And He asked his father, "How long has this been happening to him?" And he said, "From childhood.

22 "And often he has thrown him both into the fire and into the water to destroy him. But if You can do anything, have compassion on us and help us."

23 Yeshua said to him, "If you can believe, all things are possible to him who believes."

24 And immediately the father of the child cried out and said with tears, "Lord, I believe; help my unbelief!"

25 When Yeshua saw that the people came running together, He rebuked the unclean spirit, saying to him, "You deaf and dumb spirit, I command you, come out of him, and enter him no more!"

26 And the spirit cried out, convulsed him greatly, and came out of him. And he became as one dead, so that many said, "He is dead."

27 But Yeshua took him by the hand and lifted him up, and he arose.

28 And when He had come into the house, His disciples asked Him privately, "Why could we not cast him out?"

29 And He said to them, "This kind can come out by nothing except by prayer and fasting."

Yeshua Again Predicts His Death and Resurrection

30 And they departed from there and passed through Galilee, and He did not want anyone to know it.

31 For He taught His disciples and said to them, "The Son of Man is being delivered into the hands of men, and they will kill Him. And after He is killed, He will rise the third day."

32 But they did not understand this saying, and were afraid to ask Him.

Who Is the Greatest?

33 And He came to Capernaum. And when He was in the house He asked them, "What was it you disputed among yourselves on the road?"

34 But they kept silent, for on the road they had disputed among themselves who would be the greatest.

35 And He sat down, called the twelve, and said to them, "If anyone desires to be first, he shall be last of all and servant of all."

36 And He took a little child and set him in the midst of them. And when He had taken him in His arms, He said to them,

37 "Whoever receives one of these little children in My name receives Me; and whoever receives Me, receives not Me but Him who sent Me."

Yeshua Emphasizes Unity

38 And John answered Him, saying, "Rabbi, we saw someone who does not follow us casting out demons in Your name, and we forbade him because he does not follow us."

39 But Yeshua said, "Do not forbid him, for no one who works a miracle in My name can soon afterward speak evil of Me.

40 "For he who is not against us is on our side.

A Cup of Water

41 "For whoever gives you a cup of water to drink in My name, because you belong to Messiah, assuredly, I say to you, he will by no means lose his reward.

Yeshua Warns of Offenses

42 "And whoever causes one of these little ones who believe in Me to stumble, it would be better for him if a millstone were hung around his neck, and he were thrown into the sea.

43 "And if your hand makes you sin, cut it off. It is better for you to enter into life maimed, than having two hands, to go to hell, into the fire that never shall be quenched—

44 "where *their worm does not die and the fire is not quenched.'*[16]

45 "And if your foot makes you sin, cut it off. It is better for you to enter life lame, than having two feet, to be cast into hell, into the fire that never shall be quenched—

46 "where *their worm does not die and the fire is not quenched.'*[16]

47 "And if your eye makes you sin, pluck it out. It is better for you to enter the kingdom of God with one eye, than having two eyes, to be cast into hell fire—

48 "where *their worm does not die and the fire is not quenched.'*[16]

Believers Must Have Salt

49 "For everyone will be seasoned with fire, and every sacrifice will be seasoned with salt.

50 "Salt is good, but if the salt loses its saltiness, how will you season it? Have salt in yourselves, and have peace with one another."

Marriage and Divorce

10 And He arose from there and came to the region of Judea by the other side of the Jordan. And the people gathered to Him again, and as He was accustomed, He taught them again.

2 And the Pharisees came and asked Him, "Is it lawful for a man to divorce his wife?" testing Him.

3 And He answered and said to them, "What did Moses command you?"

4 And they said, "Moses permitted writing a certificate of divorce, and to put her away." [17]

5 And Yeshua answered and said to them, "Because of the hardness of your heart he wrote you this precept.

6 "But from the beginning of the creation, God *'made them male and female.'*[18]

7 *'For this reason a man shall leave his father and mother and be joined to his wife,*

8 *and the two shall become one flesh';*[19] so then they are no longer two, but one flesh.

9 "Therefore what God has joined together, let not man divide."

10 And in the house His disciples asked Him again about the same matter.

11 And He said to them, "Whoever divorces his wife and marries another commits adultery against her.

16 Isaiah 66:24

17 Deuteronomy 24:1
18 Genesis 1:27; 5:2   19 Genesis 2:24

12 "And if a woman divorces her husband and marries another, she commits adultery."

Yeshua Blesses Little Children

13 And they brought young children to Him, that He might touch them; but the disciples rebuked those who brought them.

14 But when Yeshua saw it, He was greatly displeased and said to them, "Let the little children come to Me, and do not forbid them; for of such is the kingdom of God.

15 "Assuredly, I say to you, whoever does not receive the kingdom of God as a little child will by no means enter it."

16 And He took them up in His arms, put His hands on them, and blessed them.

Yeshua Counsels the Rich Young Ruler

17 And as He was going out on the road, one came running, knelt before Him, and asked Him, "Good Rabbi, what shall I do that I may inherit eternal life?"

18 And Yeshua said to him, "Why do you call Me good? No one is good but One, that is, God.

19 "You know the commandments: *'Do not commit adultery,' 'Do not murder,' 'Do not steal,' 'Do not bear false witness,'* 'Do not defraud,' *'Honor your father and your mother.'* " [20]

20 And he answered and said to Him, "Rabbi, all these I have observed from my youth."

21 Then Yeshua, looking at him, loved him, and said to him, "One thing you lack: Go your way, sell whatever you have and give to the poor, and you will have treasure in heaven; and come, take up the cross, and follow Me."

22 And he was sad at this word, and went away grieved, for he had great possessions.

With God All Things Are Possible

23 And Yeshua looked around and said to His disciples, "How hard it is for those who have riches to enter the kingdom of God!"

24 And the disciples were astonished at His words. But Yeshua answered again and said to them, "Children, how hard it is for those who trust in riches to enter the kingdom of God!

25 "It is easier for a camel to go through the eye of a needle than for a rich man to enter the kingdom of God."

26 And they were astonished beyond measure, saying among themselves, "Who then can be saved?"

27 And Yeshua looking at them said, "With men it is impossible, but not with God; for with God all things are possible."

28 And Peter began to say to Him, "See, we have left all and followed You."

29 And Yeshua answered and said, "Assuredly, I say to you, there is no one who has left house or brothers or sisters or father or mother or wife or children or lands, for My sake and the good news',

30 "who shall not receive a hundredfold now in this time—houses and brothers and sisters and mothers and children and lands, with persecutions—and in the age to come, eternal life.

20 Exodus 20:12–16; Deuteronomy 5:16–20

31 "But many who are first will be last, and the last first."

Yeshua a Third Time Predicts His Death and Resurrection

32 And they were on the road, going up to Jerusalem, and Yeshua was going before them; and they were amazed. And as they followed they were afraid. And He took the twelve aside again and began to tell them the things that would happen to Him:

33 "Behold, we are going up to Jerusalem; and the Son of Man will be delivered to the chief priests and to the scribes, and they will condemn Him to death and deliver Him to the Gentiles;

34 "and they will mock Him and scourge Him and spit on Him and kill Him. And the third day He will rise again."

Greatness Is Serving

35 And James and John, the sons of Zebedee, came to Him, saying, "Rabbi, we want You to do for us whatever we ask."

36 And He said to them, "What do you want Me to do for you?"

37 They said to Him, "Grant us that we may sit, one on Your right hand and the other on Your left, in Your glory."

38 But Yeshua said to them, "You do not know what you ask. Can you drink the cup that I drink, and be baptized with the baptism[21] that I am baptized with?"

39 And they said to Him, "We can." And Yeshua said to them,

"You shall indeed drink the cup that I drink, and with the baptism I am baptized with you will be baptized;

40 "but to sit on My right hand and on My left is not Mine to give, but it is for those for whom it is prepared."

41 And when the ten heard it, they began to be greatly displeased with James and John.

42 But Yeshua called them to Himself and said to them, "You know that those who are considered rulers over the Gentiles lord it over them, and their great ones exercise authority over them.

43 "Yet it shall not be so among you; but whoever desires to become great among you shall be your servant.

44 "And whoever of you desires to be first shall be slave of all.

45 "For even the Son of Man did not come to be served, but to serve, and to give His life a ransom for many."

Yeshua Heals Blind Bartimaeus

46 And they came to Jericho. And as He went out of Jericho with His disciples and a great multitude, blind Bartimaeus, the son of Timaeus, sat by the road begging.

47 And when he heard that it was Yeshua of Nazareth, he began to cry out and say, "Yeshua, Son of David,[22] have mercy on me!"

48 And many warned him that he should be quiet; but he cried out all the more, "Son of David, have mercy on me!"

---

21 Yeshua is asking if they are prepared to be obedient to God, even to the point of death, as He is.

22 A title of Messiah (cf. Jeremiah 23:5, 6).

49 And Yeshua stood still and commanded him to be called. And they called the blind man, saying to him, "Be of good cheer. Rise, He is calling you."

50 And throwing aside his garment, he rose and came to Yeshua.

51 And Yeshua answered and said to him, "What do you want Me to do for you?" The blind man said to Him, "*Rabboni*, that I may receive my sight."

52 And Yeshua said to him, "Go your way; your faith has made you well." And immediately he received his sight and followed Yeshua on the road.[23]

The Triumphal Entry

11 And when they came near to Jerusalem, to Bethphage and Bethany, at the Mount of Olives, He sent out two of His disciples;

2 and He said to them, "Go your way into the village opposite you; and as soon as you have entered it, you will find a colt tied, on which no one has ever sat. Loose it and bring it.

3 "And if anyone says to you, 'Why are you doing this?' say, 'The Lord has need of it,' and immediately he will send it here."

4 And they went their way and found the colt tied by the door outside on the street, and they loosed it.

5 And some of those who stood there said to them, "What are you doing, loosing the colt?"

6 And they spoke to them just as Yeshua had commanded. And they let them go.

7 And they brought the colt to Yeshua and threw their garments on it, and He sat on it.

8 And many spread their garments on the road, and others cut down leafy branches off the trees and spread them on the road.

9 And those who went before and those who followed cried out, saying:

"Hosanna!
*Blessed is He who comes in
the name of the LORD!'* [24]

10 Blessed is the kingdom of our
father David
That comes in the name of
the Lord!
Hosanna in the highest!"

11 And Yeshua entered into Jerusalem and into the temple. And when He had looked around at all things, as the hour was already late, He went out to Bethany with the twelve.

The Fig Tree Withered

12 And the next day, when they had come out from Bethany, He was hungry.

13 And seeing from afar a fig tree having leaves, He went to see if perhaps He might find something on it. And when He came to it, He found nothing but leaves, for it was not the season for figs.

14 And Yeshua answered and said to it, "Let no one eat fruit from you anymore forever." And His disciples heard it.

Yeshua Cleanses the Temple

15 And they came to Jerusalem. And Yeshua went into the temple and began to drive out those who bought and sold in the temple,

---

23 Isaiah 42:1-7

24 Psalm 118:26

and overturned the tables of the moneychangers and the seats of those who sold doves.

16 And He would not allow anyone to carry a vessel through the temple.

17 And He taught, saying to them, "Is it not written, '*My house shall be called a house of prayer for all nations*'?²⁵ But you have made it a '*den of thieves.*'"²⁶

18 And the scribes and chief priests heard it and sought how they might destroy Him; for they feared Him, because all the people were astonished at His teaching.

19 And when evening had come, He went out of the city.

The Lesson of the Withered Fig Tree

20 And in the morning, as they passed by, they saw the fig tree dried up from the roots.

21 And Peter, remembering, said to Him, "Rabbi, look! The fig tree which You cursed has withered away."

22 And Yeshua answered and said to them, "Have faith in God.

23 "For assuredly, I say to you, whoever says to this mountain, 'Be removed and be cast into the sea,' and does not doubt in his heart, but believes that those things he says will come to pass, he will have whatever he says.

24 "Therefore I say to you, whatever things you ask when you pray, believe that you receive them, and you will have them.

Forgiveness and Prayer

25 "And whenever you stand praying, if you have anything against anyone, forgive him, that your Father who is in heaven may also forgive you your trespasses.

26 "But if you do not forgive, neither will your Father who is in heaven forgive your trespasses."

Authority of Yeshua Questioned

27 And they came again to Jerusalem. And as He was walking in the temple, the chief priests, the scribes, and the elders came to Him.

28 And they said to Him, "By what authority are You doing these things? And who gave You this authority to do these things?"

29 And Yeshua answered and said to them, "I will also ask you one question; then answer Me, and I will tell you by what authority I do these things:

30 "The immersion of John— was it from heaven or from men? Answer Me."

31 And they reasoned among themselves, saying, "If we say, 'From heaven,' He will say, 'Why then did you not believe him?'

32 "But if we say, 'From men'"—they feared the people, for all counted John to have been a prophet indeed.

33 And they answered and said to Yeshua, "We do not know." And Yeshua, answering, said to them, "Neither will I tell you by what authority I do these things."

The Parable of the Wicked Vinedressers

12 And He began to speak to them in parables: "A man planted a vineyard, set a hedge around it, dug a place for the wine vat, and built a tower. And he

25 Isaiah 56:7   26 Jeremiah 7:11

leased it to vinedressers and went into a far country.

2 "And at harvesttime he sent a servant to the vinedressers, that he might receive from the vinedressers some of the fruit of the vineyard.

3 "And they took him, beat him, and sent him away empty-handed.

4 "And again he sent to them another servant, and at him they threw stones, wounded him in the head, and sent him away shamefully treated.

5 "And again he sent another, and him they killed; and many others, beating some and killing some.

6 "Therefore still having one son, his beloved, he also sent him to them last, saying, 'They will respect my son.'

7 "But those vinedressers said among themselves, 'This is the heir. Come, let us kill him, and the inheritance will be ours.'

8 "And they took him, killed him, and cast him out of the vineyard.

9 "Therefore what will the owner of the vineyard do? He will come and destroy the vinedressers, and give the vineyard to others.

10 "And have you not read this Scripture:

'The stone which the builders rejected
Has become the chief cornerstone.

11 This was the LORD's doing,
And it is marvelous in our eyes'?" [27]

12 And they sought to lay hold of Him, but feared the multitude, for they knew He had spoken the parable against them. And they left Him and went away.

The Pharisees: Is It Lawful to Pay Taxes to Caesar?

13 And they sent to Him some of the Pharisees and the Herodians, to catch Him in His words.

14 And when they had come, they said to Him, "Rabbi, we know that You are true and care about no one; for You do not regard the person of men, but teach the way of God in truth. Is it lawful to pay taxes to Caesar, or not?

15 "Shall we pay, or shall we not pay?" But He, knowing their hypocrisy, said to them, "Why do you test Me? Bring Me a denarius that I may see it."

16 And they brought it. And He said to them, "Whose image and inscription is this?" And they said to Him, "Caesar's."

17 And Yeshua answered and said to them, "Render to Caesar the things that are Caesar's, and to God the things that are God's." And they marveled at Him.

The Sadducees: What About the Resurrection?

18 Then the Sadducees, who say there is no resurrection, came to Him; and they asked Him, saying:

19 "Rabbi, Moses wrote to us that if a man's brother dies, leaves his wife behind, and leaves no children, his brother should take his wife and raise up offspring for his brother. [28]

---

27 Psalm 118:22, 23

28 Deuteronomy 25:5

20 "Now there were seven brothers. And the first took a wife, and dying, left no offspring.

21 "And the second took her, and he died; nor did he leave any offspring. And the third likewise.

22 "And the seven had her and left no offspring. Last of all the woman died also.

23 "Therefore, in the resurrection, when they rise, whose wife will she be? For all seven had her as wife."

24 And Yeshua answered and said to them, "Are you not therefore mistaken, because you do not know the Scriptures nor the power of God?

25 "For when they rise from the dead, they neither marry nor are given in marriage, but are like angels who are in heaven.

26 "But concerning the dead, that they rise, have you not read in the book of Moses, in the burning bush passage, how God spoke to him, saying, *'I am the God of Abraham, the God of Isaac, and the God of Jacob'*? [29]

27 "He is not the God of the dead, but the God of the living. You are therefore greatly mistaken."

The Scribes: Which Is the First Commandment of All?

28 And one of the scribes came, and having heard them reasoning together, perceiving that He had answered them well, asked Him, "Which is the first commandment of all?"

29 And Yeshua answered him, "The first of all the commandments is: *'Hear, O Israel, the* LORD *our God is one* LORD.

30 *'And you shall love the* LORD *your God with all your heart, with all your soul, with all your mind, and with all your strength.'* [30] This is the first commandment.

31 "And the second, like it, is this: *'You shall love your neighbor as yourself.'* [31] There is no other commandment greater than these."

32 And the scribe said to Him, "Well said, Rabbi. You have spoken the truth, for there is one God, and there is no other but He.

33 "And to love Him with all the heart, with all the understanding, with all the soul, and with all the strength, and to love one's neighbor as oneself, is more than all the whole burnt offerings and sacrifices."

34 And when Yeshua saw that he answered wisely, He said to him, "You are not far from the kingdom of God." And after that no one dared ask Him any question.

Yeshua: How Can David Call His Descendant Lord?

35 And Yeshua answered and said, while He taught in the temple, "How is it that the scribes say that the Messiah is the Son of David?

36 "For David himself said by the Holy Spirit:

'The LORD *said to my Lord,*
"Sit at My right hand,
Till I make Your enemies
Your footstool."' [32]

---

30 Deuteronomy 6:4, 5

31 Leviticus 19:18   32 Psalm 110:1

29 Exodus 3:6, 15

37 "Therefore David himself calls Him 'Lord'; how is He then his Son?" And the common people heard Him gladly.

Beware of the Scribes

38 And He said to them in His teaching, "Beware of the scribes, who desire to go around in long robes, love greetings in the marketplaces,

39 "the best seats in the synagogues, and the best places at feasts,

40 "who devour widows' houses, and for a pretense make long prayers. These will receive greater condemnation."

The Widow's Two Mites

41 And Yeshua sat opposite the treasury and saw how the people put money into the treasury. And many who were rich put in much.

42 And a certain poor widow came and threw in two mites, which make a quadrans.[33]

43 And He called His disciples to Him and said to them, "Assuredly, I say to you that this poor widow has put in more than all those who have given into the treasury;

44 "for they all put in out of their abundance, but she out of her poverty put in all that she had, her whole livelihood."

Yeshua Predicts the Destruction of the Temple

13 And as He went out of the temple, one of His disciples said to Him, "Rabbi, see what

manner of stones and what buildings are here!"

2 And Yeshua answered and said to him, "Do you see these great buildings? Not one stone shall be left upon another that shall not be thrown down."

The Signs of the Times and the End of the Age

3 And as He sat on the Mount of Olives opposite the temple, Peter, James, John, and Andrew asked Him privately,

4 "Tell us, when will these things be? And what will be the sign when all these things will be fulfilled?"

5 And Yeshua, answering them, began to say: "Take heed that no one deceives you.

6 "For many will come in My name, saying, 'I am He,' and will deceive many.

7 "And when you hear of wars and rumors of wars, do not be troubled; for such things must happen, but the end is not yet.

8 "For nation will rise against nation, and kingdom against kingdom. And there will be earthquakes in various places, and there will be famines and troubles. These are the beginnings of sorrows.

9 "But watch out for yourselves, for they will deliver you up to councils, and you will be beaten in the synagogues. And you will be brought before rulers and kings for My sake, for a testimony to them.

10 "And the good news must first be preached to all the nations.

11 "But when they arrest you and deliver you up, do not worry

---

33 A quadrans equals 1/64 of a denarius, or about 12¢.

beforehand, or premeditate what you will speak. But whatever is given you in that hour, speak that; for it is not you who speak, but the Holy Spirit.

12 "Now brother will betray brother to death, and a father his child; and children will rise up against parents and cause them to be put to death.

13 "And you will be hated by all men for My name's sake. But he who endures to the end will be saved.

The Great Tribulation

14 "But when you see the 'abomination of desolation,'[34] spoken of by Daniel the prophet, standing where it ought not" (let the reader understand), "then let those who are in Judea flee to the mountains.

15 "And let him who is on the housetop not go down into the house, nor enter to take anything out of his house.

16 "And let him who is in the field not go back to get his garment.

17 "But woe to those who are pregnant and to those with nursing babies in those days!

18 "And pray that your flight not be in winter.

19 "For in those days there will be tribulation, such as has not been from the beginning of creation which God created to this time, nor ever shall be.

20 "And unless the Lord had shortened those days, no flesh would be saved; but for the elect's sake, whom He chose, He shortened the days.[35]

21 "And then if anyone says to you, 'Look, here is the Messiah!' or, 'Look, He is there!' do not believe it.

22 "For false messiahs and false prophets will rise and show signs and wonders to deceive, if possible, even the elect.

23 "But take heed; see, I have foretold you all things.

The Second Coming of the Messiah

24 "But in those days, after that tribulation, the sun will be darkened, and the moon will not give its light;[36]

25 "the stars of heaven will fall, and the powers in heaven will be shaken.[37]

26 "And then they will see the Son of Man coming in the clouds with great power and glory.[38]

27 "And then He will send His angels, and gather together His elect from the four winds, from the farthest part of earth to the farthest part of heaven.

The Parable of the Fig Tree

28 "Now learn this parable from the fig tree: When its branch has already become tender, and puts forth leaves, you know that summer is near.

29 "So you also, when you see these things happening, know that it is near, even at the doors.

30 "Assuredly, I say to you, this generation will by no means pass

---

34 Daniel 11:31; 12:11

35 Daniel 12:1   36 Isaiah 13:10
37 Isaiah 34:4   38 Daniel 7:13, 14

away till all these things take place.

31 "Heaven and earth will pass away, but My words will by no means pass away.

No One Knows the Day or Hour

32 "But of that day and hour no one knows, neither the angels who are in heaven, nor the Son, but only the Father.

33 "Take heed, watch and pray; for you do not know when the time is.

34 "It is like a man going to a far country, who left his house and gave authority to his servants, and to each his work, and commanded the doorkeeper to watch.

35 "Watch therefore, for you do not know when the master of the house is coming—in the evening, at midnight, at the crowing of the rooster, or in the morning—

36 "lest, coming suddenly, he find you sleeping.

37 "And what I say to you, I say to all: Watch!"

The Plot to Kill Yeshua

14 After two days it was the Passover and the Feast of Unleavened Bread. And the chief priests and the scribes sought how they might take Him by trickery and put Him to death.

2 But they said, "Not during the feast, lest there be an uproar of the people."

The Anointing at Bethany

3 And being in Bethany at the house of Simon the leper, as He sat at the table, a woman came having an alabaster flask of very costly oil of spikenard. And she broke the flask and poured it on His head.

4 And there were some who were indignant among themselves and said, "Why was this waste made of the fragrant oil?

5 "For it might have been sold for more than three hundred denarii and given to the poor." And they criticized her sharply.

6 But Yeshua said, "Let her alone. Why do you trouble her? She has done a good work for Me.

7 "For you have the poor with you always, and whenever you wish you may do them good; but Me you do not have always.

8 "She has done what she could. She has come beforehand to anoint My body for burial.

9 "Assuredly, I say to you, wherever this good news is preached throughout the whole world, what this woman has done will also be spoken of as a memorial to her."

Judas Agrees to Betray Yeshua

10 And Judas Iscariot, one of the twelve, went to the chief priests to betray Him to them.

11 And when they heard it, they were glad, and promised to give him money. And he sought how he might conveniently betray Him.

Yeshua Celebrates Passover with His Disciples

12 And on the first day of Unleavened Bread, when they killed the Passover lamb, His disciples said to Him, "Where do You want us to go and prepare, that You may eat the Passover?"

13 And He sent out two of His disciples and said to them, "Go

into the city, and a man will meet you carrying a pitcher of water; follow him.

14 "And wherever he goes in, say to the master of the house, 'The Rabbi says: Where is the guest room in which I may eat the Passover with My disciples?'

15 "And he will show you a large upper room, furnished and prepared; there make ready for us."

16 And His disciples went out, came into the city, and found it just as He had said to them; and they prepared the Passover.

17 And in the evening He came with the twelve.

18 And as they sat and ate, Yeshua said, "Assuredly, I say to you, one of you who eats with Me will betray Me." [39]

19 And they began to be sorrowful, and to say to Him one by one, "Is it I?" And another said, "Is it I?"

20 And He answered and said to them, "It is one of the twelve, who dips with Me in the dish.

21 "The Son of Man indeed goes just as it is written of Him, but woe to that man by whom the Son of Man is betrayed! It would have been good for that man if he had never been born."

22 And as they were eating, Yeshua took matzah, blessed it and broke it, and gave it to them and said, "Take, eat; this is My body."

23 And He took the cup, and when He had given thanks He gave it to them, and they all drank from it.

24 And He said to them, "This is My blood of the new covenant,[40] which is shed for many.

25 "Assuredly, I say to you, I will no longer drink of the fruit of the vine until that day when I drink it new in the kingdom of God."

26 And when they had sung a hymn,[41] they went out to the Mount of Olives.

Yeshua Predicts Peter's Denial

27 And Yeshua said to them, "All of you will be made to stumble because of Me this night, for it is written:

'I will strike the Shepherd,
And the sheep will be scat-
*   tered.'*[42]

28 "But after I have been raised, I will go before you to Galilee."

29 But Peter said to Him, "Even if all are made to stumble, yet I will not be."

30 And Yeshua said to him, "Assuredly, I say to you that today, even this night, before the rooster crows twice, you will deny Me three times."

31 But he spoke more vehemently, "If I have to die with You, I will not deny You!" And they all said likewise.

The Prayer in the Garden

32 And they came to a place which was named Gethsemane;

39 Psalm 41:9 (41:10 in some versions)

40 Jeremiah 31:31-34 (31:30-33 in some versions)

41 Psalm 118 is one of the hymns sung at Passover. See Psalm 118:22, which makes a prediction about the Messiah, calling Him "the Stone". 42 Zechariah 13:7

and He said to His disciples, "Sit here while I pray."

33 And He took Peter, James, and John with Him, and He began to be troubled and deeply distressed.

34 And He said to them, "My soul is exceedingly sorrowful, even to death. Stay here and watch."

35 And He went a little farther, fell on the ground, and prayed that, if it were possible, the hour might pass from Him.

36 And He said, "*Abba*, Father, all things are possible for You. Take this cup away from Me; nevertheless, not what I will, but what You will."

37 And He came and found them sleeping, and said to Peter, "Simon, are you sleeping? Could you not watch one hour?

38 "Watch and pray, lest you enter into temptation. The spirit truly is ready, but the flesh is weak."

39 And again He went away and prayed, and spoke the same words.

40 And when He returned, He found them asleep again, for their eyes were heavy; and they did not know what to answer Him.

41 And He came the third time and said to them, "Sleep on now and take your rest. It is enough; the hour has come; behold, the Son of Man is being betrayed into the hands of sinners.

42 "Rise up, let us go. See, he who betrays Me is at hand."

Betrayal and Arrest in Gethsemane

43 And immediately, while He was still speaking, Judas, one of the twelve, with a great multitude with swords and clubs, came from the chief priests, the scribes, and the elders.

44 And he who was betraying Him had given them a signal, saying, "Whomever I kiss, He is the One; take Him and lead Him away safely."

45 And as soon as He had come, immediately he went up to Him and said to Him, "Rabbi, Rabbi!" and kissed Him.

46 And they laid their hands on Him and took Him.

47 And one of those who stood by drew his sword and struck the servant of the high priest, and cut off his ear.

48 And Yeshua answered and said to them, "Have you come out, as against a robber, with swords and clubs to take Me?

49 "I was daily with you in the temple teaching, and you did not take Me. But the Scriptures must be fulfilled."

50 And they all forsook Him and fled.

A Young Man Flees Naked

51 And a certain young man followed Him, having a linen cloth thrown around his naked body. And the young men laid hold of him,

52 and he left the linen cloth and fled from them naked.

Yeshua Faces the Sanhedrin

53 And they led Yeshua away to the high priest; and with him were assembled all the chief priests, the elders, and the scribes.

54 And Peter followed Him at a distance, right into the courtyard of the high priest. And he sat with the servants and warmed himself at the fire.

55 And the chief priests and all the council sought testimony against Yeshua to put Him to death, and found none.

56 For many bore false witness against Him, but their testimonies did not agree.[43]

57 And some rose up and bore false witness against Him, saying,

58 "We heard Him say, 'I will destroy this temple that is made with hands, and within three days I will build another made without hands.' "

59 And not even then did their testimony agree.

60 And the high priest stood up in the midst and asked Yeshua, saying, "Do You answer nothing? What is it these men testify against You?"

61 But He kept silent and answered nothing. Again the high priest asked Him, saying to Him, "Are You the Messiah, the Son of the Blessed?"

62 And Yeshua said, "I am. And you will see the Son of Man sitting at the right hand of the Power,[44] and coming with the clouds of heaven." [45]

63 Then the high priest tore his clothes and said, "What further need do we have of witnesses?

64 "You have heard the blasphemy! What do you think?" And they all condemned Him to be guilty of death.

65 And some began to spit on Him, and to blindfold Him, and to beat Him, and to say to Him, "Prophesy!" And the officers struck Him with the palms of their hands.[46]

Peter Denies Yeshua—and Weeps Bitterly

66 And as Peter was below in the courtyard, one of the servant girls of the high priest came.

67 And when she saw Peter warming himself, she looked at him and said, "You also were with Yeshua of Nazareth."

68 But he denied it, saying, "I neither know nor understand what you are saying." And he went out on the porch, and a rooster crowed.

69 And the servant girl saw him again, and began to say to those who stood by, "This is one of them."

70 But he denied it again. And a little later, those who stood by said to Peter again, "Surely you are one of them; for you are a Galilean, and your speech shows it."

71 But he began to curse and swear, "I do not know this Man of whom you speak!"

72 And a second time the rooster crowed. And Peter called to mind the word that Yeshua said to him, "Before the rooster crows twice, you will deny Me three times." And when he thought about it, he wept.

Yeshua Faces Pilate

15 And right away, in the morning, the chief priests held a consultation with the elders and scribes and the whole council, and bound Yeshua, led Him

43 Psalm 35:11   44 Psalm 110:1
45 Daniel 7:13

46 Isaiah 50:6

away, and delivered Him to Pilate.[47]

2 And Pilate asked Him, "Are You the King of the Jews?" And He answered and said to him, "It is as you say."

3 And the chief priests accused Him of many things, but He answered nothing.

4 And Pilate asked Him again, saying, "Do You answer nothing? See how many things they testify against You!"

5 But Yeshua still answered nothing, so that Pilate marveled.[48]

Condemned in Our Place

6 Now at the feast he was accustomed to releasing one prisoner to them, whomever they requested.

7 And there was one named Barabbas, who was chained with his fellow insurrectionists, who had committed murder in the insurrection.

8 And the multitude, crying aloud, began to ask him to do just as he had always done for them.

9 But Pilate answered them, saying, "Do you want me to release to you the King of the Jews?"

10 For he knew that the chief priests had delivered Him because of envy.

11 But the chief priests stirred up the multitude, so that he should rather release Barabbas to them.

12 And Pilate answered and said to them again, "What then do you want me to do with Him whom you call the King of the Jews?"

13 And they cried out again, "Crucify Him!"

14 Then Pilate said to them, "Why, what evil has He done?" And they cried out more exceedingly, "Crucify Him!"

15 Then Pilate, wanting to gratify the crowd, released Barabbas to them; and he delivered Yeshua, after he had scourged Him,[49] to be crucified.

Bruised for Our Iniquities

16 And the soldiers led Him away into the hall called Praetorium, and they called together the whole band.

17 And they clothed Him with purple; and they twisted a crown of thorns, put it on His head,

18 and began to salute Him, "Hail, King of the Jews!"

19 And they struck Him on the head with a reed and spat on Him; and bowing the knee, they worshiped Him.[50]

20 And when they had mocked Him, they took the purple off Him, put His own clothes on Him, and led Him out to crucify Him.

Wounded for Our Transgressions

21 And they compelled a certain man, Simon a Cyrenian, the father of Alexander and Rufus, as he was coming out of the country and passing by, to bear His cross.

22 And they brought Him to the place *Golgotha,* which is translated, the Place of a Skull.

23 And they gave Him wine

47 Isaiah 53:8   48 Isaiah 53:7   49 Isaiah 53:5   50 Isaiah 50:6

mingled with myrrh to drink, but He did not take it.

24 And when they crucified Him, they divided His garments, casting lots for them to determine what every man should take.[51]

25 And it was the third hour,[52] and they crucified Him.[53]

26 And the inscription of His accusation was written above:

THE KING OF THE JEWS.

27 And with Him they crucified two robbers, one on His right and the other on His left.

28 And the Scripture was fulfilled which says, *And He was numbered with the transgressors.*[54]

29 And those who passed by blasphemed Him, wagging their heads and saying, "Aha! You who destroy the temple and build it in three days,

30 "save Yourself, and come down from the cross!"

31 Likewise the chief priests also, together with the scribes, mocked and said among themselves, "He saved others; Himself He cannot save.

32 "Let the Messiah, the King of Israel, descend now from the cross, that we may see and believe." And those who were crucified with Him reviled Him.

An Offering for Sin

33 And when the sixth hour had come,[55] there was darkness over the whole land until the ninth hour.[56]

34 And at the ninth hour Yeshua cried out with a loud voice, saying, *"Eloi, Eloi, lama sabachthani?"* which is translated, *"My God, My God, why have You forsaken Me?"*[57]

35 And some of those who stood by, when they heard it, said, "Look, He is calling for Elijah!"

36 And someone ran and filled a sponge full of sour wine, put it on a reed, and offered it to Him[58] to drink, saying, "Let Him alone; let us see if Elijah will come to take Him down."

37 And Yeshua cried out with a loud voice, and breathed His last.

38 And the curtain of the temple was torn in two from top to bottom.

39 And when the centurion, who stood opposite Him, saw that He cried out like this and breathed His last, he said, "Truly this Man was the Son of God!"

40 There were also women looking on from afar, among whom were Miriam of Magdala, Miriam the mother of James the Less and of Joses, and Salome,

41 who also followed Him and ministered to Him when He was in Galilee; and many other women who came up with Him to Jerusalem.

Yeshua Buried in Joseph's Tomb

42 And now when evening had come, because it was the Preparation Day, that is, the day before the Sabbath,

---

51 Psalm 22:18 (22:19 in some versions)
52 9 a.m.
53 Psalm 22:14–16 (22:15–17 in some versions) 54 Isaiah 53:12 55 Noon.

56 3 p.m.
57 Psalm 22:1 (22:2 in some versions)
58 Psalm 69:21 (69:22 in some versions)

43 Joseph of Arimathea, a prominent council member, who himself was waiting for the kingdom of God, coming and taking courage, went in to Pilate and asked for the body of Yeshua.

44 And Pilate marveled that He was already dead; and calling the centurion to him, he asked him if He had been dead for some time.

45 And when he found out from the centurion, he granted the body to Joseph.

46 And he bought fine linen, took Him down, and wrapped Him in the linen. And he laid Him in a tomb which had been hewn out of the rock, and rolled a stone against the door of the tomb.[59]

47 And Miriam of Magdala and Miriam the mother of Joses observed where He was laid.

He Is Risen

16 And when the Sabbath was past, Miriam of Magdala, Miriam the mother of James, and Salome bought spices that they might come and anoint Him.

2 And very early in the morning, on the first day of the week, they came to the tomb when the sun had risen.

3 And they said among themselves, "Who will roll away the stone from the door of the tomb for us?"

4 And when they looked up, they saw that the stone had been rolled away—for it was very large.

5 And entering the tomb, they saw a young man clothed in a long white robe sitting on the right side; and they were alarmed.

6 And he said to them, "Do not be alarmed. You seek Yeshua of Nazareth, who was crucified. He is risen! He is not here! See the place where they laid Him.[60]

7 "But go your way, tell His disciples—and Peter—that He is going before you into Galilee; there you will see Him as He said to you."

8 And they went out quickly and fled from the tomb, for they trembled and were amazed. And they said nothing to anyone, for they were afraid.

Miriam of Magdala Sees the Risen Messiah

9 Now when He had risen early on the first day of the week, He appeared first to Miriam of Magdala, out of whom He had cast seven demons.

10 She went and told those who had been with Him, as they mourned and wept.

11 And when they heard that He was alive and had been seen by her, they did not believe.

Yeshua Appears to Two Disciples

12 After that, He appeared in another form to two of them as they walked and went into the country.

13 And they went and told it to the rest; they did not believe them either.

The Great Commission

14 Afterward He appeared to the eleven as they sat at the table;

---

59 Isaiah 53:9

60 Psalm 16:10 (cf. Isaiah 53:9, 10)

and He rebuked their unbelief and hardness of heart, because they did not believe those who had seen Him after He had risen.

15 And He said to them, "Go into all the world and preach the good news to every creature.

16 "He who believes and is immersed will be saved; but he who does not believe will be condemned.

17 "And these signs will follow those who believe: In My name they will cast out demons; they will speak with new tongues;

18 "they will take up serpents; and if they drink anything deadly,

it shall not hurt them; they will lay hands on the sick, and they will recover."

The Messiah Ascends to God's Right Hand

19 So then, after the Lord had spoken to them, He was received up into heaven, and sat down at the right hand of God.[61]

20 And they went out and preached everywhere, the Lord working with them and confirming the word through the accompanying signs. Amen.

61 Psalm 110:1

The Good News According To

LUKE

INASMUCH as many have taken in hand to set in order a narrative of those things which are most surely believed among us,

2 just as those who from the beginning were eyewitnesses and servants of the word delivered them to us,

3 it seemed good to me also, having had perfect understanding of all things from the very first, to write to you an orderly account, most excellent Theophilus,

4 that you may know the certainty of those things in which you have been instructed.

John's Birth Announced to Zacharias

5 There was in the days of Herod, the king of Judea, a certain priest named Zacharias, of the division of Abijah. And his wife was of the daughters of Aaron,[1] and her name was Elizabeth.

6 And they were both righteous before God, walking in all the commandments and ordinances of the Lord blameless.

7 But they had no child, because Elizabeth was barren, and they were both well-advanced in years.

8 And it came to pass, that

while he was serving as priest before God in the order of his division,

9 according to the custom of the priesthood, his lot fell to burn incense when he went into the temple of the Lord.

10 And the whole multitude of the people was praying outside at the hour of incense.

11 And an angel of the Lord appeared to him, standing on the right side of the altar of incense.

12 And when Zacharias saw him, he was troubled, and fear fell upon him.

13 But the angel said to him, "Do not be afraid, Zacharias, for your prayer is heard; and your wife Elizabeth will bear you a son, and you shall call his name John.

14 "And you will have joy and gladness, and many will rejoice at his birth.

15 "For he will be great in the sight of the Lord, and shall drink neither wine nor strong drink. He will also be filled with the Holy Spirit, even from his mother's womb.

16 "And he will turn many of the children of Israel to the Lord their God.

17 "He will also go before Him in the spirit and power of Elijah, *'to turn the hearts of the fathers to*

---

1 That is, of priestly descent.

the children,'² and the disobedient to the wisdom of the just, to make ready a people prepared for the Lord."³

18 And Zacharias said to the angel, "How shall I know this? For I am an old man and my wife well-advanced in years."

19 And the angel answered and said to him, "I am Gabriel,⁴ who stands in the presence of God, and was sent to speak to you and bring you these glad tidings.

20 "And behold, you will be mute and not able to speak until the day these things take place, because you did not believe my words which will be fulfilled in their season."

21 And the people waited for Zacharias, and marveled that he tarried so long in the temple.

22 But when he came out, he could not speak to them; and they perceived that he had seen a vision in the temple, for he beckoned to them and remained speechless.

23 And it came to pass, as soon as the days of his service were completed, that he departed to his own house.

24 And after those days his wife Elizabeth conceived; and she hid herself five months, saying,

25 "Thus the Lord has dealt with me, in the days when He looked on me, to take away my reproach among men."

The Messiah's Birth Announced to Miriam

26 And in the sixth month the angel Gabriel was sent from God to a city of Galilee named Nazareth,

27 to a virgin betrothed to a man whose name was Joseph, of the house of David. And the virgin's name was Miriam.

28 And having come in, the angel said to her, "Hail, highly favored one, the Lord is with you; blessed are you among women!"

29 And when she saw him, she was troubled at his saying, and considered what manner of greeting this was.

30 And the angel said to her, "Do not be afraid, Miriam, for you have found favor with God.

31 "And behold, you will conceive in your womb and bring forth a Son, and shall call His name YESHUA.

32 "He will be great, and will be called the Son of the Highest; and the Lord God will give Him the throne of His father David.

33 "And He will reign over the house of Jacob forever, and of His kingdom there will be no end."⁵

34 Then Miriam said to the angel, "How can this be, since I do not know a man?"

35 And the angel answered and said to her, "The Holy Spirit will come upon you, and the power of the Highest will overshadow you;⁶ therefore, also, that Holy One who is to be born will be called the Son of God.

36 "And indeed, Elizabeth your relative has also conceived a son in her old age; and this is the sixth month for her who was called barren.

2 Malachi 4:5, 6 (3:23, 24 in some versions)
3 Isaiah 40:3   4 Daniel 8:16; 9:21

5 Isaiah 9:6, 7 (9:5, 6 in some versions)
6 Isaiah 7:14

37 "For with God nothing will be impossible."

38 And Miriam said, "Behold the maidservant of the Lord; let it be to me according to your word." And the angel departed from her.

Miriam Visits Elizabeth

39 And Miriam arose in those days and went into the hill country with haste, to a city of Judah,

40 and entered the house of Zacharias and greeted Elizabeth.

41 And it came to pass, when Elizabeth heard the greeting of Miriam, that the babe leaped in her womb; and Elizabeth was filled with the Holy Spirit.

42 And she spoke out with a loud voice and said, "Blessed are you among women, and blessed is the fruit of your womb!

43 "And why is this granted to me, that the mother of my Lord should come to me?

44 "For indeed, as soon as the voice of your greeting sounded in my ears, the babe leaped in my womb for joy.

45 "And blessed is she who believed, for there will be a fulfillment of those things which were told her from the Lord."

The Song of Miriam

46 And Miriam said:
"My soul magnifies the Lord,

47 And my spirit has rejoiced in God my Savior.

48 For He has regarded the lowly state of His maidservant;
For behold, from now on all generations will call me blessed.

49 For He who is mighty has done great things for me,

And holy is His name.

50 And His mercy is on those who fear Him
From generation to generation.

51 He has shown strength with His arm;
He has scattered the proud in the imagination of their hearts.

52 He has put down the mighty from their thrones,
And exalted the lowly.

53 He has filled the hungry with good things,
And the rich He has sent away empty.

54 He has helped His servant Israel,
In remembrance of His mercy,

55 As He spoke to our fathers,
To Abraham and to his seed forever."

56 And Miriam remained with her about three months, and returned to her own house.

Birth of John

57 Now Elizabeth's full time came that she should be delivered, and she brought forth a son.

58 And her neighbors and her relatives heard how the Lord had shown great mercy to her, and they rejoiced with her.

Circumcision of John

59 And it came to pass that on the eighth day they came to circumcise the child; and they would have called him by the name of his father, Zacharias.

60 And his mother answered and said, "No, but he shall be called John."

61 And they said to her, "There is no one among your relatives who is called by this name."

62 And they made signs to his father, what he would have him called.

63 And he asked for a writing tablet, and wrote, saying, "His name is John." And they all marveled.

64 And immediately his mouth was opened and his tongue loosed, and he spoke and praised God.

65 And fear came on all who dwelt around them; and all these sayings were discussed throughout all the hill country of Judea.

66 And all those who heard them laid them up in their hearts, saying, "What kind of child will this be?" And the hand of the Lord was with him.

Zacharias' Prophecy

67 And his father Zacharias was filled with the Holy Spirit, and prophesied, saying:

68 "Blessed is the Lord God of Israel,
For He has visited and redeemed His people,

69 And has raised up a horn of salvation for us
In the house of His servant David,[7]

70 As He spoke by the mouth of His holy prophets,
Who have been since the world began,

71 That we should be saved from our enemies
And from the hand of all who hate us,

72 To perform the mercy promised to our fathers
And to remember His holy covenant,

73 The oath which He swore to our father Abraham:

74 That He would grant to us that we, being delivered out of the hand of our enemies,
Might serve Him without fear,

75 In holiness and righteousness before Him all the days of our life.

76 And you, child, will be called the prophet of the Highest;
For you will go before the face of the Lord to prepare His ways,[8]

77 To give knowledge of salvation to His people
By the remission of their sins,

78 By the tender mercy of our God,
With which the Dayspring from on high has visited us;[9]

79 To give light to those who sit in darkness and the shadow of death,
To guide our feet into the way of peace."[10]

80 And the child grew and became strong in spirit, and was in the deserts till the day of his manifestation to Israel.

The Messiah Born of Miriam

2 And it came to pass in those days that a decree went out

---

7 Psalm 132:17; Jeremiah 23:5, 6; Ezekiel 29:21

8 Isaiah 40:3

9 Malachi 4:2 (3:20 in some versions)

10 Isaiah 9:2 (9:1 in some versions)

from Caesar Augustus that all the world[11] should be registered.

2 This census first took place while Quirinius was governing Syria.

3 And all went to be registered, everyone to his own city.

4 And Joseph also went up from Galilee, out of the city of Nazareth, into Judea, to the city of David, which is called Bethlehem, because he was of the house and lineage of David,

5 to be registered with Miriam, his betrothed wife, who was with child.

6 And so it was, that while they were there, the days were completed that she should be delivered.

7 And she brought forth her firstborn Son, and wrapped Him in swaddling cloths, and laid Him in a manger, because there was no room for them in the inn.

Glory in the Highest

8 And there were in the same country shepherds living out in the fields, keeping watch over their flock by night.

9 And behold, an angel of the Lord stood before them, and the glory of the Lord shone around them, and they were greatly afraid.

10 And the angel said to them, "Do not be afraid, for behold, I bring you good tidings of great joy which will be to all people.

11 "For there is born to you this day in the city of David a Savior, who is Messiah the Lord.[12]

12 "And this will be the sign to you: You will find a Babe wrapped in swaddling cloths, lying in a manger."

13 And suddenly there was with the angel a multitude of the heavenly host praising God and saying:

14 "Glory to God in the highest,
And on earth peace, good
will toward men!"

15 And so it was, when the angels had gone away from them into heaven, that the shepherds said to one another, "Let us now go to Bethlehem and see this thing that has come to pass, which the Lord has made known to us."

16 And they came with haste and found Miriam and Joseph, and the Babe lying in a manger.

17 And when they had seen it, they made widely known the saying which was told them concerning this Child.

18 And all those who heard it marveled at those things which were told them by the shepherds.

19 But Miriam kept all these things and pondered them in her heart.

20 And the shepherds returned, glorifying and praising God for all the things that they had heard and seen, as it was told to them.

Circumcision of Yeshua

21 And when eight days were completed for the circumcision of the Child, His name was called YESHUA, the name given by the angel before He was conceived in the womb.

Yeshua Presented in the Temple

22 And when the days of her purification according to the law of

---

11 That is, the Roman Empire.

12 Micah 5:2 (5:1 in some versions)

Moses were completed, they brought Him to Jerusalem to present Him to the Lord[13]

23 (as it is written in the law of the Lord, *"Every male who opens the womb shall be called holy to the LORD"*),[14]

24 and to offer a sacrifice according to what is said in the law of the Lord, *"A pair of turtledoves or two young pigeons."*[15]

Simeon Sees God's Salvation

25 And behold, there was a man in Jerusalem whose name was Simeon, and this man was just and devout, waiting for the Consolation of Israel, and the Holy Spirit was upon him.

26 And it was revealed to him by the Holy Spirit that he would not see death before he had seen the Lord's Messiah.

27 And he came by the Spirit into the temple. And when the parents brought in the Child Yeshua, to do for Him according to the custom of the law,

28 he took Him up in his arms and blessed God and said:

29 "Lord, now You are letting Your servant depart in peace,
According to Your word;

30 For my eyes have seen Your salvation

31 Which You have prepared before the face of all people,

32 A light to enlighten the Gentiles,
And the glory of Your people Israel." [16]

33 And Joseph and His mother marveled at those things which were spoken of Him.

34 And Simeon blessed them, and said to Miriam His mother, "Behold, this Child is destined for the fall and rising of many in Israel, and for a sign which will be spoken against [17]

35 (yes, a sword will pierce through your own soul also), that the thoughts of many hearts may be revealed."

Hannah Bears Witness to the Messiah

36 And there was one, Hannah, a prophetess, the daughter of Phanuel, of the tribe of Asher. She was of a great age, and had lived with a husband seven years from her virginity;

37 and she was a widow of about eighty-four years, who did not depart from the temple, but served God with fastings and prayers night and day.

38 And coming in that instant she gave thanks to the Lord, and spoke of Him to all those who looked for redemption in Jerusalem.

The Family Returns to Nazareth

39 And when they had performed all things according to the law of the Lord, they returned to Galilee, to their own city, Nazareth.

40 And the Child grew and became strong in spirit, filled with wisdom; and the grace of God was upon Him.

13 Leviticus 12:1–8

14 Exodus 13:2, 12, 15

15 Leviticus 12:8   16 Isaiah 49:6

17 Isaiah 8:14, 15

The Boy Yeshua Amazes the Rabbis

41 Now His parents went to Jerusalem every year at the Feast of the Passover.

42 And when He was twelve years old, they went up to Jerusalem according to the custom of the feast.

43 And when they had finished the days, as they returned, the Boy Yeshua tarried behind in Jerusalem. And Joseph and His mother did not know it;

44 but supposing Him to have been in the company, they went a day's journey, and sought Him among their relatives and acquaintances.

45 And when they did not find Him, they returned to Jerusalem, seeking Him.

46 And it came to pass that after three days they found Him in the temple, sitting in the midst of the Rabbis, both listening to them and asking them questions.

47 And all who heard Him were astonished at His understanding and answers.

48 And when they saw Him, they were amazed; and His mother said to Him, "Son, why have You done this to us? Look, Your father and I have sought You anxiously."

49 And He said to them, "How is it that you sought Me? Did you not know that I must be about My Father's business?"

50 And they did not understand the statement which He spoke to them.

*Yeshua Advances in Wisdom
and Favor*

51 And He went down with them and came to Nazareth, and was subject to them, but His mother kept all these things in her heart.

52 And Yeshua increased in wisdom and stature, and in favor with God and men.

John Prepares the Way

3 Now in the fifteenth year of the reign of Tiberius Caesar, Pontius Pilate being governor of Judea, Herod tetrarch of Galilee, his brother Philip tetrarch of Iturea and of the region of Trachonitis, and Lysanias tetrarch of Abilene,

2 Annas and Caiaphas being high priests, the word of God came to John the son of Zacharias in the wilderness.

3 And he went into all the region around the Jordan, preaching the immersion of repentance for the remission of sins,

4 as it is written in the book of the words of Isaiah the prophet, saying:

"The voice of one crying in
    the wilderness:
'Prepare the way of the
    LORD,
Make His paths straight.
5 Every valley will be filled
And every mountain and
    hill brought low;
And the crooked places will
    be made straight
And the rough ways made
    smooth;
6 And all flesh will see the salvation of God.' "18

John Exhorts the People

7 Then he said to the multitude that came out to be im-

18 Isaiah 40:3-5

mersed by him, "O brood of vipers! Who has warned you to flee from the wrath to come?

8 "Therefore bear fruits worthy of repentance, and do not begin to say to yourselves, 'We have Abraham as our father.' For I say to you that God is able to raise up children to Abraham from these stones.

9 "And even now the ax is laid to the root of the trees. Therefore every tree which does not bear good fruit is cut down and thrown into the fire."

10 And the people asked him, saying, "What shall we do then?"

11 He answered and said to them, "He who has two tunics, let him give to him who has none; and he who has food, let him do likewise."

12 Then tax collectors also came to be immersed, and said to him, "Rabbi, what shall we do?"

13 And he said to them, "Collect no more than what is appointed for you."

14 And likewise the soldiers asked him, saying, "And what shall we do?" And he said to them, "Do not intimidate anyone or accuse falsely, and be content with your wages."

15 And as the people were in expectation, and all reasoned in their hearts about John, whether he was the Messiah or not,

16 John answered, saying to them all, "I indeed immerse you in water; but One mightier than I is coming, whose sandal strap I am not worthy to loose. He will immerse you in the Holy Spirit and in fire.

17 "His winnowing fan is in His hand, and He will thoroughly purge His threshing floor, and gather the wheat into His barn; but the chaff He will burn with unquenchable fire."

18 And with many other exhortations he preached to the people.

19 But Herod the tetrarch, being rebuked by him concerning Herodias, his brother Philip's wife, and for all the evils which Herod had done,

20 also added this, above all, that he shut John up in prison.

John Immerses Yeshua

21 Now when all the people were immersed, it came to pass that Yeshua also was immersed; and while He prayed, the heaven was opened.

22 And the Holy Spirit descended in a bodily form like a dove upon Him, and a voice came from heaven which said, "You are My beloved Son; in You I am well pleased."

The Genealogy of Yeshua ha Mashiach

23 And Yeshua Himself was about thirty years of age, being (as was supposed), the son of Joseph, the son of Heli,[19]

24 the son of Matthat, the son of Levi, the son of Melchi, the son of Janna, the son of Joseph,

25 the son of Mattathiah, the son of Amos, the son of Nahum, the son of Esli, the son of Naggai,

26 the son of Maath, the son of Mattathiah, the son of Semei, the son of Joseph, the son of Judah,

19 This is the genealogy of Miriam the mother of Yeshua. Heli was Miriam's father, and Joseph's father-in-law.
Joseph's genealogy is found in Matthew 1.

27 the son of Joannas, the son of Rhesa, the son of Zerubbabel, the son of Shealtiel, the son of Neri,

28 the son of Melchi, the son of Addi, the son of Cosam, the son of Elmodam, the son of Er,

29 the son of Jose, the son of Eliezer, the son of Jorim, the son of Matthat, the son of Levi,

30 the son of Simeon, the son of Judah, the son of Joseph, the son of Jonan, the son of Eliakim,

31 the son of Melea, the son of Menan, the son of Mattathah, the son of Nathan, the son of David,

32 the son of Jesse, the son of Obed, the son of Boaz, the son of Salmon, the son of Nahshon,

33 the son of Amminadab, the son of Ram, the son of Hezron, the son of Perez, the son of Judah,

34 the son of Jacob, the son of Isaac, the son of Abraham, the son of Terah, the son of Nahor,

35 the son of Serug, the son of Reu, the son of Peleg, the son of Eber, the son of Shelah,

36 the son of Cainan, the son of Arphaxad, the son of Shem, the son of Noah, the son of Lamech,

37 the son of Methuselah, the son of Enoch, the son of Jared, the son of Mahalalel, the son of Cainan,

38 the son of Enos, the son of Seth, the son of Adam, the son of God.

Satan Tempts Yeshua

4 And Yeshua, being filled with the Holy Spirit, returned from the Jordan and was led by the Spirit into the wilderness,

2 being tempted for forty days by the devil. And in those days He ate nothing, and afterward, when they had ended, He was hungry.

3 And the devil said to Him, "If You are the Son of God, command this stone to become bread."

4 And Yeshua answered him, saying, "It is written, 'Man shall not live by bread alone, but by every word of God.'" [20]

5 And the devil, taking Him up on a high mountain, showed Him all the kingdoms of the world in a moment of time.

6 And the devil said to Him, "All this authority I will give You, and their glory; for that has been delivered to me, and I give it to whomever I wish.

7 "Therefore, if You will worship before me, all will be Yours."

8 And Yeshua answered and said to him, "Get behind Me, Satan! For it is written, 'You shall worship the LORD your God, and Him only you shall serve.'" [21]

9 And he brought Him to Jerusalem, set Him on the pinnacle of the temple, and said to Him, "If You are the Son of God, throw Yourself down from here.

10 "For it is written:
'He will give His angels
     charge over You,
     To keep You,'

11 "and,
'In their hands they will bear
     You up,
Lest You dash Your foot
     against a stone.'" [22]

12 And Yeshua answered and said to him, "It is said, 'You shall not tempt the LORD your God.'" [23]

[20] Deuteronomy 8:3
[21] Deuteronomy 6:13; cf. Deuteronomy 10:20   [22] Psalm 91:11, 12
[23] Deuteronomy 6:16

13 And when the devil had ended every temptation, he departed from Him until an opportune time.

Yeshua Begins at Galilee

14 And Yeshua returned in the power of the Spirit to Galilee, and news of Him went out through all the surrounding region.

15 And He taught in their synagogues, being glorified by all.

Yeshua Rejected at Nazareth

16 And He came to Nazareth, where He had been brought up. And as His custom was, He went into the synagogue on the Sabbath day, and stood up to read.

17 And He was handed the book of the prophet Isaiah. And when He had opened the book, He found the place where it was written:

18 *"The Spirit of the LORD is*
   upon Me,
   Because He has anointed
   Me to preach the good
   news to the poor.
   He has sent Me to heal the
   brokenhearted,
   To preach deliverance to the
   captives
   And recovery of sight to the
   blind,
   To set at liberty those who
   are oppressed,

19 *To preach the acceptable*
   year of the LORD." [24]

20 And He closed the book, and He gave it back to the attendant and sat down. And the eyes of all who were in the synagogue were fixed on Him.

21 And He began to say to them, "Today this Scripture is fulfilled in your ears."

22 And all bore witness to Him, and marveled at the gracious words which proceeded out of His mouth. And they said, "Is this not Joseph's son?"

23 And He said to them, "You will surely say this proverb to Me, 'Physician, heal yourself. Whatever we have heard done in Capernaum, do also here in your country.' "

24 And He said, "Assuredly, I say to you, no prophet is accepted in his own country.

25 "But I tell you truly, many widows were in Israel in the days of Elijah, when the heaven was shut up three years and six months, and a great famine was throughout all the land;

26 "but to none of them was Elijah sent except to Zarephath, in the region of Sidon, to a woman who was a widow. [25]

27 "And many lepers were in Israel in the time of Elisha the prophet; and none of them was cleansed except Naaman the Syrian." [26]

28 Then all those in the synagogue, when they heard these things, were filled with wrath,

29 and rose up and thrust Him out of the city; and they led Him to the brow of the hill on which their city was built, that they might throw Him down over the cliff.

30 But passing through the midst of them, He went His way.

---

24 Isaiah 61:1, 2   25 1 Kings 17   26 2 Kings 5

Yeshua Casts Out an Unclean Spirit

31 And He went down to Capernaum, a city of Galilee, and was teaching them on the Sabbaths.

32 And they were astonished at His teaching, for His word was with authority.

33 And in the synagogue there was a man who had a spirit of an unclean demon. And he cried out with a loud voice,

34 saying, "Let us alone! What have we to do with You, Yeshua of Nazareth? Have You come to destroy us? I know You, who You are—the Holy One of God!"

35 And Yeshua rebuked him, saying, "Be quiet, and come out of him!" And when the demon had thrown him in their midst, it came out of him and did not hurt him.

36 And they were all amazed and spoke among themselves, saying, "What a word this is! For with authority and power He commands the unclean spirits, and they come out."

37 And the report about Him went out into every place in the surrounding region.

Peter's Mother-in-Law Healed

38 And He arose from the synagogue and entered Simon's house. And Simon's wife's mother was sick with a high fever, and they made request of Him concerning her.

39 And He stood over her and rebuked the fever, and it left her. And immediately she arose and served them.

Many Healed After Sabbath Sunset

40 Now when the sun was setting, all those who had anyone sick with various diseases brought them to Him; and He laid His hands on every one of them and healed them.

41 And demons also came out of many, crying out and saying, "You are the Messiah, the Son of God!" And He, rebuking them, did not allow them to speak, for they knew that He was the Messiah.

42 And when it was day, He departed and went into a deserted place. And the people sought Him and came to Him, and tried to keep Him from leaving them;

43 but He said to them, "I must preach the kingdom of God to the other cities also, because for this purpose I have been sent."

44 And He was preaching in the synagogues of Galilee.

Four Fishermen Called as Disciples

5 And it came to pass, as the multitude pressed about Him to hear the word of God, He stood by the Lake of Gennesaret,

2 and saw two boats standing by the lake; but the fishermen had gone from them and were washing their nets.

3 And He got into one of the boats, which was Simon's, and asked him to put out a little from the land. And He sat down and taught the multitudes from the boat.

4 Now when He had stopped speaking, He said to Simon, "Launch out into the deep and let down your nets for a catch."

5 And Simon answered and said to Him, "Master, we have toiled all night and taken nothing; nevertheless at Your word I will let down the net."

6 And when they had done

this, they caught a great number of fish, and their net was breaking.

7 And they signaled to their partners, who were in the other boat, that they should come and help them. And they came and filled both the boats, so that they began to sink.

8 When Simon Peter saw it, he fell down at the knees of Yeshua, saying, "Depart from me, for I am a sinful man, O Lord!"

9 For he and all who were with him were astonished at the catch of fish which they had taken;

10 and so also were James and John, the sons of Zebedee, who were partners with Simon. And Yeshua said to Simon, "Do not be afraid. From now on you will catch men."

11 And when they had brought their boats to land, they forsook all and followed Him.

Yeshua Cleanses a Leper

12 And it came to pass when He was in a certain city, behold, a man full of leprosy who, seeing Yeshua, fell on his face and implored Him, saying, "Lord, if You are willing, You can make me clean."

13 And He put out His hand and touched him, saying, "I am willing; be cleansed." And immediately the leprosy left him.

14 And He charged him to tell no one, "But go and show yourself to the priest, and make an offering for your cleansing, as a testimony to them, just as Moses commanded."27

15 But the report went around concerning Him all the more; and great multitudes came together to hear, and to be healed by Him of their infirmities.

16 And He Himself often withdrew into the wilderness and prayed.

Yeshua Forgives and Heals a Paralytic

17 And it happened on a certain day, as He was teaching, that there were Pharisees and teachers of the Torah sitting by, who had come out of every town of Galilee, Judea, and Jerusalem. And the power of the Lord was present to heal them.

18 And behold, men brought on a bed a man who was paralyzed. And they sought means to bring him in and lay him before Him.

19 And when they could not find how they might bring him in, because of the crowd, they went up on the housetop and let him down through the tiling with his bed into the midst before Yeshua.

20 And when He saw their faith, He said to him, "Man, your sins are forgiven you."

21 And the scribes and the Pharisees began to reason, saying, "Who is this who speaks blasphemies? Who can forgive sins but God alone?"

22 But when Yeshua perceived their thoughts, He answered and said to them, "Why are you reasoning in your hearts?

23 "Which is easier, to say, 'Your sins are forgiven you,' or to say, 'Rise up and walk'?

24 "But that you may know that the Son of Man has power on earth to forgive sins"—He said to the man who was paralyzed, "I say to you, arise, take up your bed, and go to your house."

27 Leviticus 14:1-32

25 And immediately he rose up before them, took up what he had been lying on, and departed to his own house, glorifying God.

26 And they were all amazed, and they glorified God and were filled with fear, saying, "We have seen strange things today!"

Matthew the Tax Collector

27 And after these things He went out and saw a tax collector named Levi, sitting at the tax office. And He said to him, "Follow Me."

28 And he left all, rose up, and followed Him.

29 And Levi gave Him a great feast in his own house. And there were a great number of tax collectors and others who sat down with them.

30 But their scribes and the Pharisees murmured against His disciples, saying, "Why do You eat and drink with tax collectors and sinners?"

31 And Yeshua answered and said to them, "Those who are well do not need a physician, but those who are sick.

32 "I have not come to call the righteous, but sinners, to repentance."

Yeshua Is Questioned About Fasting

33 And they said to Him, "Why do the disciples of John fast often and make prayers, and likewise the disciples of the Pharisees, but Yours eat and drink?"

34 And He said to them, "Can you make the friends of the bridegroom fast while the bridegroom is with them?

35 "But the days will come when the bridegroom will be taken away from them; then they will fast in those days."

36 And He also spoke a parable to them: "No one puts a piece from a new garment on an old one; otherwise the new makes a tear, and also the piece that was taken out of the new does not match the old.

37 "And no one puts new wine into old wineskins; or else the new wine will burst the wineskins and be spilled, and the wineskins will be ruined.

38 "But new wine must be put into new wineskins, and both are preserved.

39 "And no one, having drunk old wine, immediately desires new; for he says, 'The old is better.' "

Yeshua Teaches Concerning the Sabbath

6 And it happened on the second Sabbath after the first that He went through the grainfields. And His disciples plucked the heads of grain and ate them, rubbing them in their hands.

2 And some of the Pharisees said to them, "Why are you doing what is not lawful to do on the Sabbath?"

3 And Yeshua, answering them, said, "Have you not even read this, what David did when he was hungry, he and those who were with him:

4 "how he went into the house of God, took and ate the showbread, and also gave some to those who were with him, which is not lawful but for the priests only to eat?" [28]

28 1 Samuel 21:3-6

5 And He said to them, "The Son of Man is also Lord of the Sabbath."

A Man with a Withered Hand Healed on the Sabbath

6 And it happened on another Sabbath, also, that He entered the synagogue and taught. And a man was there whose right hand was withered.

7 And the scribes and Pharisees watched Him closely whether He would heal on the Sabbath, that they might find an accusation against Him.

8 But He knew their thoughts, and He said to the man who had the withered hand, "Rise up and stand in the midst." And he arose and stood.

9 Then Yeshua said to them, "I will ask you one thing: Is it lawful on the Sabbath to do good or to do evil, to save life or to destroy it?"

10 And looking around at them all, He said to the man, "Stretch out your hand." And he did so, and his hand was restored as whole as the other.

11 And they were filled with rage, and discussed with one another what they might do to Yeshua.

The Twelve

12 And it came to pass in those days that He went out to the mountain to pray, and continued all night in prayer to God.

13 And when it was day, He called His disciples to Him; and from them He chose twelve whom He also named apostles:

14 Simon, whom He also named Peter, and Andrew his brother; James and John; Philip and Bartholomew;

15 Matthew and Thomas; James the son of Alphaeus, and Simon called the Zealot;

16 Judas the son of James, and also Judas Iscariot who became a traitor.

Yeshua Heals a Great Multitude

17 And He came down with them and stood on a level place with a crowd of His disciples and a great multitude of people from all Judea and Jerusalem, and from the seacoast of Tyre and Sidon, who came to hear Him and be healed of their diseases,

18 as well as those who were tormented with unclean spirits. And they were healed.

19 And the whole multitude sought to touch Him, for power went out from Him and healed them all.

The Blessings

20 And He lifted up His eyes toward His disciples, and said:
"Blessed are you poor,
For yours is the kingdom of God.
21 Blessed are you who hunger now,
For you shall be filled.
Blessed are you who weep now,
For you shall laugh.
22 Blessed are you when men hate you,
And when they exclude you,
And revile you, and cast out your name as evil,
For the Son of Man's sake.
23 Rejoice in that day and leap for joy,

For indeed your reward is
great in heaven;
For in like manner their fathers did to the prophets.

Yeshua Pronounces Woes

24 But woe to you who are
rich!
For you have received your
consolation.
25 Woe to you who are full!
For you shall hunger.
Woe to you who laugh now!
For you shall mourn and
weep.
26 Woe to you when all men
speak well of you!
For so did their fathers to
the false prophets.

Love Your Enemies

27 "But I say to you who hear:
Love your enemies, do good to
those who hate you,
28 "bless those who curse you,
and pray for those who spitefully
use you.
29 "And to him who strikes you
on the one cheek, offer the other
also. And from him who takes
away your cloak, do not withhold
your tunic either.
30 "Give to everyone who asks
from you. And from him who
takes away your goods do not ask
them back.
31 "And just as you want men to
do to you, you also do to them
likewise.
32 "For if you love those who
love you, what credit is that to
you? For sinners also love those
who love them.
33 "And if you do good to those
who do good to you, what credit is

that to you? For even sinners do
the same.
34 "And if you lend to those
from whom you hope to receive
back, what credit is that to you?
For sinners also lend to sinners to
receive as much back.
35 "But love your enemies, do
good, and lend, hoping for nothing
in return; and your reward will be
great, and you will be sons of the
Highest. For He is kind to the
unthankful and evil.
36 "Therefore be merciful, just
as your Father also is merciful.

Do Not Judge

37 "Judge not, and you shall not
be judged. Condemn not, and
you shall not be condemned. Forgive, and you will be forgiven.
38 "Give, and it will be given to
you: good measure, pressed down,
shaken together, and running over
will be put into your bosom. For
with the same measure that you
use, it will be measured back to
you."
39 And He spoke a parable to
them: "Can the blind lead the
blind? Will they not both fall
into the ditch?
40 "A disciple is not above his
teacher, but everyone who is perfectly trained will be like his
teacher.
41 "And why do you look at the
speck that is in your brother's eye,
but do not perceive the plank that
is in your own eye?
42 "Or how can you say to your
brother, 'Brother, let me take out
the speck that is in your eye,'
when you yourself do not see the
plank that is in your own eye?
You hypocrite! First remove the
plank from your own eye, and

then you will see clearly to take
out the speck that is in your brother's eye.

A Tree Is Known by Its Fruits

43 "For a good tree does not
bear bad fruit, nor does a bad tree
bear good fruit.

44 "For every tree is known by
its own fruit. For men do not
gather figs from thorns, nor do
they gather grapes from a bramble
bush.

45 "A good man out of the good
treasure of his heart brings forth
what is good; and an evil man out
of the evil treasure of his heart
brings forth what is evil. For out
of the abundance of the heart his
mouth speaks.

Build on the Rock

46 "And why do you call Me
'Lord, Lord,' and do not do the
things which I say?

47 "Whoever comes to Me, and
hears My sayings and does them, I
will show you whom he is like:

48 "He is like a man building a
house, who dug deep and laid the
foundation on the rock. And
when the flood arose, the stream
beat vehemently against that
house, and could not shake it, for
it was founded on the rock.

49 "But he who heard and did
nothing is like a man who built a
house on the earth without a foundation, against which the stream
beat vehemently; and immediately it fell. And the ruin of that
house was great."

Yeshua Heals a Centurion's Servant

7 Now when He had ended all
His sayings in the hearing of
the people, He entered Capernaum.

2 And a certain centurion's servant, who was dear to him, was
sick and ready to die.

3 And when he heard about
Yeshua, he sent elders of the Jews
to Him, pleading with Him to
come and heal his servant.

4 And when they came to
Yeshua, they begged Him earnestly, saying that the one for
whom He should do this was worthy,

5 "for he loves our nation, and
he has built us a synagogue."

6 Then Yeshua went with
them. And when He was already
not far from the house, the centurion sent friends to Him, saying to
Him, "Lord, do not trouble Yourself, for I am not worthy that You
should enter under my roof.

7 "Therefore I did not even
think myself worthy to come to
You. But say the word, and my
servant will be healed.

8 "For I also am a man placed
under authority, having soldiers
under me. And I say to one, 'Go,'
and he goes; and to another,
'Come,' and he comes; and to my
servant, 'Do this,' and he does it."

9 When Yeshua heard these
things, He marveled at him, and
turned around and said to the
crowd that followed Him, "I say to
you, I have not found such great
faith, not even in Israel!"

10 And those who were sent, returning to the house, found the
servant well who had been sick.

Yeshua Raises the Son of the Widow of Nain

11 And it happened, the day after, that He went into a city called

Nain; and many of His disciples went with Him, and a large crowd.

12 Now when He came near the gate of the city, behold, a dead man was being carried out, the only son of his mother; and she was a widow. And a large crowd from the city was with her.

13 And when the Lord saw her, He had compassion on her and said to her, "Do not weep."

14 And He came and touched the open coffin, and those who carried him stood still. And He said, "Young man, I say to you, arise."

15 And he who was dead sat up and began to speak. And He presented him to his mother.

16 And fear came upon all, and they glorified God, saying, "A great prophet has risen up among us"; and, "God has visited His people."

17 And this report about Him went throughout all Judea and all the surrounding region.

John Sends Messengers to Yeshua

18 And the disciples of John reported to him concerning all these things.

19 And John, calling two of his disciples to him, sent them to Yeshua, saying, "Are You the Coming One, or do we look for another?"

20 When the men had come to Him, they said, "John the Baptizer has sent us to You, saying, 'Are You the Coming One, or do we look for another?'"

21 And in that same hour He cured many people of their infirmities, afflictions, and evil spirits; and to many who were blind He gave sight.

22 Then Yeshua answered and said to them, "Go your way and tell John the things you have seen and heard: that the blind see, the lame walk, the lepers are cleansed, the deaf hear, the dead are raised, the poor have the good news preached to them.[29]

23 "And blessed is he who is not offended because of Me."

24 And when the messengers of John had departed, He began to speak to the multitudes concerning John: "What did you go out into the wilderness to see? A reed shaken by the wind?

25 "But what did you go out to see? A man clothed in soft garments? Indeed, those who are gorgeously appareled and live in luxury are in kings' courts.

26 "But what did you go out to see? A prophet? Yes, I say to you, and more than a prophet.

27 "This is he of whom it is written:

> 'Behold, I send My messenger before Your face,
> Who will prepare Your way before You.'[30]

28 "For I say to you, among those born of women there is not a greater prophet than John the Baptizer; but he who is least in the kingdom of God is greater than he."

29 And when all the people heard Him, even the tax collectors justified God, having been immersed with the immersion of John.

---

29 Isaiah 35:5, 6; 61:1   30 Malachi 3:1

30 But the Pharisees and lawyers[31] rejected the counsel of God for themselves, not having been immersed by him.

31 And the Lord said, "To what then shall I liken the men of this generation, and what are they like?

32 "They are like children sitting in the marketplace and calling to one another, saying:

'We played the flute for you,
    And you did not dance;
We mourned to you,
    And you did not weep.'

33 "For John the Baptizer came neither eating bread nor drinking wine, and you say, 'He has a demon.'

34 "The Son of Man has come eating and drinking, and you say, 'Look, a glutton and a winebibber, a friend of tax collectors and sinners!'

35 "But wisdom is justified by all her children."

A Sinful Woman Forgiven

36 And one of the Pharisees asked Him to eat with him. And He went to the Pharisee's house, and sat down to eat.

37 And behold, a woman in the city who was a sinner, when she knew that Yeshua sat at the table in the Pharisee's house, brought an alabaster flask of fragrant oil,

38 and stood at His feet behind Him weeping; and she began to wash His feet with her tears, and wiped them with the hair of her head; and she kissed His feet and anointed them with the fragrant oil.

39 Now when the Pharisee who had invited Him saw this, he spoke to himself, saying, "This man, if He were a prophet, would have known who and what manner of woman this is who is touching Him, for she is a sinner."

40 And Yeshua answered and said to him, "Simon, I have something to say to you." And he said, "Rabbi, say it."

41 "There was a certain creditor who had two debtors. One owed five hundred denarii, and the other fifty.

42 "And when they had nothing with which to repay, he freely forgave them both. Tell me, therefore, which of them will love him more?"

43 Simon answered and said, "I suppose the one whom he forgave more." And He said to him, "You have rightly judged."

44 And He turned to the woman and said to Simon, "Do you see this woman? I entered your house; you gave Me no water for My feet, but she has washed My feet with her tears and wiped them with the hair of her head.

45 "You gave Me no kiss, but this woman has not ceased to kiss My feet since the time I came in.

46 "You did not anoint My head with oil, but this woman has anointed My feet with fragrant oil.

47 "Therefore, I say to you, her sins which are many are forgiven, for she loved much. But to whom little is forgiven, the same loves little."

48 And He said to her, "Your sins are forgiven."

49 And those who sat at the table with Him began to say to

---

31 Experts in Torah and its legal implications.

themselves, "Who is this who even forgives sins?"

50 And He said to the woman, "Your faith has saved you. Go in peace."

Many Women Follow Yeshua

8 And it came to pass, afterward, that He went through every city and village preaching and bringing the glad tidings of the kingdom of God. And the twelve were with Him,

2 and certain women who had been healed of evil spirits and infirmities: Miriam called Magdalene, out of whom had come seven demons,

3 and Joanna the wife of Chuza, Herod's steward, and Susanna, and many others who provided for Him from their substance.

The Parable of the Sower

4 And when a great multitude had gathered together, and had come to Him from every city, He spoke by a parable:

5 "A sower went out to sow his seed. And as he sowed, some fell by the wayside; and it was trampled down, and the birds of the air devoured it.

6 "And some fell on rock; and as soon as it sprang up, it withered away because it lacked moisture.

7 "And some fell among thorns, and the thorns sprang up with it and choked it.

8 "And others fell on good ground, sprang up, and yielded a crop a hundredfold." And when He had said these things He cried, "He who has ears to hear, let him hear!"

The Purpose of Parables

9 And His disciples asked Him, saying, "What might this parable mean?"

10 And He said, "To you it has been given to know the mysteries of the kingdom of God, but to the rest in parables, that

'Seeing they may not see,
And hearing they may not
understand.'[32]

The Parable of the Sower Explained

11 "Now the parable is this: The seed is the word of God.

12 "Those by the wayside are those who hear; then the devil comes and takes away the word out of their hearts, lest they should believe and be saved.

13 "But the ones on the rock are those who, when they hear, receive the word with joy; and these have no root, who believe for a while and in time of temptation fall away.

14 "And what fell among thorns are those who, when they have heard, go out and are choked with cares, riches, and pleasures of this life, and bring no fruit to maturity.

15 "But what fell on the good ground are those who, having heard the word with a noble and good heart, keep it and bear fruit with patience.

The Parable of the Unhidden Light

16 "No one, when he has lit a lamp, covers it with a vessel or puts it under a bed, but sets it on a lampstand, that those who enter may see the light.

17 "For nothing is secret that

32 Isaiah 6:9

will not be revealed, nor anything hidden that will not be known and come to light.

18 "Therefore take heed how you hear. For whoever has, to him will be given; and whoever does not have, even what he seems to have will be taken from him."

Yeshua's Mother and Brothers Come to Him

19 Then His mother and His brothers came to Him, and could not get to Him because of the crowd.

20 And it was told Him by some who said, "Your mother and Your brothers are standing outside, desiring to see You."

21 And He answered and said to them, "My mother and My brothers are these who hear the word of God and do it."

Wind and Wave Obey Yeshua

22 Now it happened, on a certain day, that He got into a boat with His disciples. And He said to them, "Let us go over to the other side of the lake." And they launched out.

23 But as they sailed He fell asleep. And a windstorm came down on the lake, and they were filling with water, and were in jeopardy.

24 And they came to Him and awoke Him, saying, "Master, Master, we are perishing!" Then He arose and rebuked the wind and the raging of the water. And they ceased, and there was a calm.

25 And He said to them, "Where is your faith?" And they were afraid and marveled, saying to one another, "What kind of Man is this? For He commands even the winds and water, and they obey Him!"

A Demon-Possessed Man Healed

26 And they arrived at the country of the Gadarenes, which is opposite Galilee.

27 And when He stepped out on the land, there met Him a certain man from the city who had demons for a long time. And he wore no clothes, nor did he live in a house but in the tombs.

28 When he saw Yeshua, he cried out, fell down before Him, and with a loud voice said, "What have I to do with You, Yeshua, Son of the Most High God? I beg You, do not torment me!"

29 For He had commanded the unclean spirit to come out of the man. For it had often seized him, and he was kept under guard, bound with chains and shackles; and he broke the bonds and was driven by the demon into the wilderness.

30 And Yeshua asked him, saying, "What is your name?" And he said, "Legion," because many demons had entered him.

31 And they begged Him that He would not command them to go out into the abyss.

32 And a herd of many swine was feeding there on the mountain. And they begged Him that He would permit them to enter them. And He permitted them.

33 Then the demons went out of the man and entered the swine, and the herd ran violently down the steep place into the lake and drowned.

34 When those who fed them saw what had happened, they fled

and told it in the city and in the country.

35 Then they went out to see what had happened, and came to Yeshua, and found the man from whom the demons had departed, sitting at the feet of Yeshua, clothed and in his right mind. And they were afraid.

36 They also who had seen it told them by what means he who had been demon-possessed was healed.

37 Then the whole multitude of the surrounding region of the Gadarenes asked Him to depart from them, for they were seized with great fear. And He got into the boat and returned.

38 Now the man out of whom the demons had departed begged Him that he might be with Him. But Yeshua sent him away, saying,

39 "Return to your own house, and tell what great things God has done for you." And he went his way and proclaimed throughout the whole city what great things Yeshua had done for him.

A Girl Restored to Life and a Woman Healed

40 And it came to pass, when Yeshua returned, that the multitude gladly received Him, for they were all waiting for Him.

41 And behold, there came a man named Jairus, and he was a ruler of the synagogue. And he fell down at the feet of Yeshua and begged Him to come to his house,

42 for he had an only daughter about twelve years of age, and she was dying. But as He went, the multitudes thronged Him.

43 And a woman, having a flow

of blood for twelve years, who had spent all her livelihood on physicians and could not be healed by any,

44 came behind Him and touched the border of His garment.[33] And immediately her flow of blood stopped.

45 And Yeshua said, "Who touched Me?" When all denied it, Peter and those who were with him said, "Master, the multitudes throng You and press You, and You say, 'Who touched Me?' "

46 And Yeshua said, "Somebody has touched Me, for I perceive that power has gone out from Me."

47 And when the woman saw that she was not hidden, she came trembling; and falling down before Him, she declared to Him in the presence of all the people the reason she had touched Him and how she was healed immediately.

48 And He said to her, "Daughter, be of good cheer; your faith has made you well. Go in peace."

49 While He was still speaking, someone came from the ruler of the synagogue's house, saying to him, "Your daughter is dead. Do not trouble the Rabbi."

50 But when Yeshua heard it, He answered him, saying, "Do not be afraid; only believe, and she will be made well."

51 And when He came into the house, He permitted no one to go in except Peter, James, and John, and the father and mother of the girl.

52 And all wept and mourned for her; but He said, "Do not

33 Tzitzit (cf. Numbers 15:37-41).

weep; she is not dead but sleeping."

53 And they laughed Him to scorn, knowing that she was dead.

54 But He put them all out, took her by the hand and called, saying, "Child, arise."

55 And her spirit came back, and she arose immediately. And He commanded them to give her something to eat.

56 And her parents were astonished, but He charged them to tell no one what had happened.

Sending Out the Twelve

9 Then He called His twelve disciples together and gave them power and authority over all demons, and to cure diseases.

2 And He sent them to preach the kingdom of God and to heal the sick.

3 And He said to them, "Take nothing for your journey, neither staffs, bag, bread, nor money; and do not have two tunics apiece.

4 "And whatever house you enter, stay there, and from there depart.

5 "And whoever will not receive you, when you go out of that city, shake off the very dust from your feet as a testimony against them."

6 And they departed and went through the towns, preaching the good news and healing everywhere.

John Beheaded

7 Now Herod the tetrarch heard of all that was done by Him; and he was perplexed, because it was said by some that John had risen from the dead,

8 and by some that Elijah had appeared, and by others that one of the old prophets had risen again.

9 And Herod said, "John I have beheaded, but who is this of whom I hear such things?" And he sought to see Him.

Feeding the Five Thousand

10 And the apostles, when they had returned, told Him all that they had done. And He took them and went aside privately into a deserted place belonging to the city called Bethsaida.

11 And when the multitudes knew it, they followed Him; and He received them and spoke to them about the kingdom of God, and healed those who had need of healing.

12 And when the day began to wear away, the twelve came and said to Him, "Send the multitude away, that they may go into the surrounding towns and country, and lodge and get provisions; for we are in a deserted place here."

13 But He said to them, "You give them something to eat." And they said, "We have no more than five loaves and two fish, unless we go and buy food for all these people."

14 For there were about five thousand men. And He said to His disciples, "Make them sit down in groups of fifty."

15 And they did so, and made them all sit down.

16 Then He took the five loaves and the two fish, and looking up to heaven, He blessed and broke them, and gave them to the disciples to set before the multitude.

17 And they all ate and were filled, and twelve baskets of the remaining fragments were taken up by them.

Peter Confesses Yeshua as the Messiah

18 And it came to pass, as He was alone praying, His disciples were with Him, and He asked them, saying, "Who do the crowds say that I am?"

19 And they answered and said, "John the Baptizer, but some say Elijah; [34] and others say that one of the old prophets has risen again."

20 He said to them, "But who do you say that I am?" Peter answered and said, "The Messiah of God."

Yeshua Predicts His Death and Resurrection

21 And He strictly warned them and commanded them to tell this to no one,

22 saying, "The Son of Man must suffer many things, and be rejected by the elders and chief priests and scribes, and be killed, and be raised the third day."

Deny Yourself and Follow Him

23 And He said to them all, "If anyone desires to come after Me, let him deny himself, take up his cross daily, and follow Me.

24 "For whoever desires to save his life will lose it, but whoever loses his life for My sake will save it.

25 "For what advantage is it to a man if he gains the whole world, and loses himself or is cast away?

26 "For whoever is ashamed of Me and My words, of him the Son of Man[35] will be ashamed when He comes in His own glory, and in His Father's, and of the holy angels.

27 "But I tell you truly, there are some standing here who shall not taste death till they see the kingdom of God."

Yeshua Transfigured on the Mount

28 And it came to pass, about eight days after these sayings, that He took Peter, John, and James and went up on the mountain to pray.

29 And as He prayed, the appearance of His face was altered, and His robe became white and glistening.

30 And behold, two men talked with Him, who were Moses and Elijah,

31 who appeared in glory and spoke of His decease, which He was about to accomplish at Jerusalem.

32 But Peter and those who were with him were heavy with sleep; and when they were fully awake, they saw His glory and the two men who stood with Him.

33 And it came to pass, as they departed from Him, that Peter said to Yeshua, "Master, it is good for us to be here; and let us make three tabernacles: [36] one for You, one for Moses, and one for Elijah—" not knowing what he said.

34 While he was saying this, a cloud came and overshadowed

---

34 Cf. Malachi 4:5 (3:23 in some versions)

35 A Messianic title (see Daniel 7:13, 14).

36 Hebrew: Sukkot (Leviticus 23:33f.; cf. Zechariah 14:1-9, 16-19).

them; and they were fearful as they entered the cloud.

35 And a voice came out of the cloud, saying, "This is My beloved Son. Hear Him!"

36 And when the voice had ceased, Yeshua was found alone. And they kept it quiet and told no one in those days any of the things they had seen.

A Boy Is Healed

37 And it came to pass, the next day, when they had come down from the mountain, that a great multitude met Him.

38 And suddenly a man from the multitude cried out, saying, "Rabbi, I beg You, look on my son, for he is my only child.

39 "And behold, a spirit seizes him, and he suddenly cries out; and it convulses him so that he foams at the mouth, and bruising him, departs from him with great difficulty.

40 "And I implored Your disciples to cast it out, and they could not."

41 And Yeshua answered and said, "O faithless and perverse generation, how long shall I be with you and bear with you? Bring your son here."

42 And as he was still coming, the demon threw him down and convulsed him. And Yeshua rebuked the unclean spirit, healed the child, and presented him again to his father.

Yeshua Again Predicts His Death

43 And they were all amazed at the majesty of God. But while everyone marveled at all the things which Yeshua did, He said to His disciples,

44 "Let these words sink down into your ears, for the Son of Man is about to be delivered into the hands of men."

45 But they did not understand this saying, and it was hidden from them so that they did not perceive it; and they were afraid to ask Him about that saying.

Who Is the Greatest?

46 Then a dispute arose among them, which of them would be greatest.

47 And Yeshua, perceiving the thought of their heart, took a little child and set him by Him,

48 and said to them, "Whoever receives this little child in My name receives Me; and whoever receives Me receives Him who sent Me. For he who is least among you all will be great."

Yeshua Emphasizes Unity

49 And John answered and said, "Master, we saw someone casting out demons in Your name, and we forbade him because he does not follow with us."

50 And Yeshua said to him, "Do not forbid him, for he who is not against us is for us."

A Samaritan Village Rejects the Messiah

51 And it came to pass, when the time had come that He should be received up, He steadfastly set His face to go to Jerusalem,

52 and sent messengers before His face. And as they went, they entered a village of the Samaritans, to prepare for Him.

53 And they did not receive Him, because His face was set as though He would go to Jerusalem.

54 And when His disciples James and John saw this, they said, "Lord, do You want us to command fire to come down from heaven and consume them, just as Elijah did?" [37]

55 But He turned and rebuked them, and said, "You do not know what manner of spirit you are of.

56 "For the Son of Man has not come to destroy men's lives but to save them." And they went to another village.

The Cost of Discipleship

57 And it came to pass, as they went on the road, a certain man said to Him, "Lord, I will follow You wherever You go."

58 And Yeshua said to him, "Foxes have holes and birds of the air have nests, but the Son of Man has nowhere to lay His head."

59 And He said to another, "Follow Me." But he said, "Lord, let me first go and bury my father."

60 Yeshua said to him, "Let the dead bury their own dead, but you go and preach the kingdom of God."

61 And another also said, "Lord, I will follow You, but let me first go bid them farewell who are at my house."

62 And Yeshua said to him, "No one, having put his hand to the plow, and looking back, is fit for the kingdom of God."

The Seventy Sent Out

10 After these things the Lord appointed seventy others also, and sent them two by two before His face into every city and place where He Himself was about to go.

2 Then He said to them, "The harvest truly is great, but the laborers are few; therefore pray the Lord of the harvest that He would send out laborers into His harvest.

3 "Go your way; behold, I send you out as lambs among wolves.

4 "Carry neither money bag, sack, nor sandals; and greet no one along the road.

5 "And whatever house you enter, first say, 'Peace be to this house.'

6 "And if a son of peace is there, your peace will rest on it; if not, it will return to you.

7 "And remain in the same house, eating and drinking such things as they give, for the laborer is worthy of his wages. Do not go from house to house.

8 "And whatever city you enter, and they receive you, eat such things as are set before you.

9 "And heal the sick who are there, and say to them, 'The kingdom of God has come near to you.'

10 "But whatever city you enter, and they do not receive you, go out into its streets and say,

11 'Even the very dust of your city which clings to us we wipe off against you. Nevertheless know this, that the kingdom of God has come near to you.'

12 "But I say to you that it will be more tolerable in that Day for Sodom than for that city.

Woe to the Impenitent Cities

13 "Woe to you, Chorazin! Woe to you, Bethsaida! For if the mighty works which have been done in you had been done in Tyre and Sidon, they would have

repented a great while ago, sitting in sackcloth and ashes.

14 "But it will be more tolerable for Tyre and Sidon at the judgment than for you.

15 "And you, Capernaum, who are exalted to heaven, will be thrust down to Hades.

16 "He who hears you hears Me, he who rejects you rejects Me, and he who rejects Me rejects Him who sent Me."

The Seventy Return with Joy

17 And the seventy returned with joy, saying, "Lord, even the demons are subject to us through Your name."

18 And He said to them, "I saw Satan fall from heaven like lightning.

19 "Behold, I give you authority to trample on serpents and scorpions, and over all the power of the enemy, and nothing shall by any means hurt you.

20 "Nevertheless do not rejoice in this, that the spirits are subject to you, but rather rejoice because your names are written in heaven."

Yeshua Rejoices in Spirit

21 In that hour Yeshua rejoiced in the Spirit and said, "I thank You, O Father, Lord of heaven and earth, that You have hidden these things from the wise and prudent and revealed them to babes. Even so, Father, for so it seemed good in Your sight.

22 "All things have been delivered to Me by My Father, and no one knows who the Son is but the Father, and who the Father is but the Son, and he to whom the Son wills to reveal Him."

23 And He turned to His disciples and said privately, "Blessed are the eyes which see the things that you see;

24 "for I tell you that many prophets and kings have desired to see those things which you see, and have not seen them, and to hear those things which you hear, and have not heard them."

The Parable of the Good Samaritan

25 And behold, a certain lawyer stood up and tested Him, saying, "Rabbi, what shall I do to inherit eternal life?"

26 He said to him, "What is written in the Torah? How do you read?"

27 And he answered and said, " *'You shall love the LORD your God with all your heart, with all your soul, with all your strength, and with all your mind,'* [38] and *your neighbor as yourself.'* " [39]

28 And He said to him, "You have answered right; do this and you will live."

29 But he, wanting to justify himself, said to Yeshua, "And who is my neighbor?"

30 And Yeshua answered and said, "A certain man went down from Jerusalem to Jericho, and fell among thieves, who stripped him of his clothing, wounded him, and departed, leaving him half dead.

31 "And by chance a certain priest came down that road. And when he saw him, he passed by on the other side.

32 "And likewise a Levite, when he was at the place, came and

38 Deuteronomy 6:5   39 Leviticus 19:18

looked at him, and passed by on the other side.

33 "But a certain Samaritan, as he journeyed, came where he was. And when he saw him, he had compassion on him,

34 "and went to him and bandaged his wounds, pouring on oil and wine; and he set him on his own donkey, brought him to an inn, and took care of him.

35 "And the next day, when he departed, he took out two denarii, gave them to the innkeeper, and said to him, 'Take care of him; and whatever more you spend, when I come again, I will repay you.'

36 "Now which of these three do you think was neighbor to him who fell among the thieves?"

37 And he said, "He who showed mercy on him." Then Yeshua said to him, "Go and do likewise."

Miriam and Martha Worship and Serve

38 Now it came to pass, as they went, that He entered a certain village. And a certain woman named Martha received Him into her house.

39 And she had a sister called Miriam, who also sat at the feet of Yeshua and heard His word.

40 But Martha was distracted with much serving, and she came to Him and said, "Lord, do You not care that my sister has left me to serve alone? Therefore tell her to help me."

41 And Yeshua answered and said to her, "Martha, Martha, you are worried and troubled about many things.

42 "But one thing is needed, and Miriam has chosen that good part, which will not be taken away from her."

The Model Prayer

11 And it came to pass, as He was praying in a certain place, when He ceased, one of His disciples said to Him, "Lord, teach us to pray, as John also taught his disciples."

2 And He said to them, "When you pray, say:
Our Father in heaven,
Hallowed be Your name.
Your kingdom come.
Your will be done,
As in heaven, so on earth.

3 Give us day by day our daily bread.

4 And forgive us our sins,
For we also forgive everyone who is indebted to us.
And do not lead us into temptation,
But deliver us from the evil one."

A Friend Comes at Midnight

5 And He said to them, "Which of you shall have a friend, and shall go to him at midnight and say to him, 'Friend, lend me three loaves;

6 'for a friend of mine has come to me on his journey, and I have nothing to set before him';

7 "and he will answer from within and say, 'Do not trouble me; the door is now shut, and my children are with me in bed; I cannot rise and give to you'?

8 "I say to you, though he will not rise and give to him because he is his friend, yet because of his persistence he will rise and give him as many as he needs.

Keep Asking, Seeking, Knocking

9 "And I say to you, ask, and it will be given to you; seek, and you will find; knock, and it will be opened to you.

10 "For everyone who asks receives, and he who seeks finds, and to him who knocks it will be opened.

11 "If a son asks for bread from any of you who is a father, will he give him a stone? Or if he asks for a fish, will he give him a serpent instead of a fish?

12 "Or if he asks for an egg, will he offer him a scorpion?

13 "If you then, being evil, know how to give good gifts to your children, how much more will your heavenly Father give the Holy Spirit to those who ask Him!"

A House Divided Cannot Stand

14 And He was casting out a demon, and it was mute. And it came to pass, when the demon had gone out, that the mute spoke; and the multitudes marveled.

15 But some of them said, "He casts out demons by Beelzebub, the ruler of the demons."

16 And others, testing Him, sought from Him a sign from heaven.

17 But He, knowing their thoughts, said to them: "Every kingdom divided against itself is brought to desolation, and a house divided against a house falls.

18 "If Satan also is divided against himself, how will his kingdom stand? Because you say I cast out demons by Beelzebub.

19 "And if I cast out demons by Beelzebub, by whom do your sons cast them out? Therefore they will be your judges.

20 "But if I cast out demons with the finger of God, no doubt the kingdom of God has come upon you.

21 "When a strong man, fully armed, guards his own palace, his goods are in peace.

22 "But when a stronger than he comes upon him and overcomes him, he takes from him all his armor in which he trusted, and divides his spoils.

23 "He who is not with Me is against Me, and he who does not gather with Me scatters.

An Unclean Spirit Returns

24 "When an unclean spirit goes out of a man, he goes through dry places, seeking rest; and finding none, he says, 'I will return to my house from which I came.'

25 "And when he comes, he finds it swept and put in order.

26 "Then he goes and takes with him seven other spirits more wicked than himself, and they enter and dwell there; and the last state of that man is worse than the first."

Keeping the Word

27 And it came to pass, as He spoke these things, that a certain woman from the crowd raised her voice and said to Him, "Blessed is the womb that bore You, and the breasts which nursed You!"

28 But He said, "More than that, blessed are those who hear the word of God and keep it!"

Seeking a Sign

29 And while the crowds were thickly gathered together, He began to say, "This is an evil generation. It seeks a sign, and no sign will be given to it except the sign of Jonah the prophet.

30 "For as Jonah was a sign to the Ninevites, so also the Son of Man will be to this generation.[40]

31 "The queen of the South will rise up in the judgment with the men of this generation and condemn them, for she came from the ends of the earth to hear the wisdom of Solomon;[41] and indeed a greater than Solomon is here.

32 "The men of Nineveh will rise up in the judgment with this generation and condemn it, for they repented at the preaching of Jonah;[42] and indeed a greater than Jonah is here.

The Lamp of the Body

33 "No one, when he has lit a lamp, puts it in a secret place or under a basket, but on a lampstand, that those who come in may see the light.

34 "The lamp of the body is the eye. Therefore, when your eye is good, your whole body also is full of light. But when your eye is bad, your body also is full of darkness.

35 "Therefore take heed that the light which is in you not be darkness.

36 "If then your whole body is full of light, having no part dark, the whole body will be full of light, as when the bright shining of a lamp gives you light."

Woe to the Pharisees and Lawyers

37 And as He spoke, a certain Pharisee asked Him to dine with him. And He went in and sat down to eat.

38 And when the Pharisee saw it, he marveled that He had not first washed before dinner.

39 And the Lord said to him, "Now you Pharisees make the outside of the cup and the dish clean, but your inward part is full of greed and wickedness.

40 "Foolish ones! Did not He who made what is outside make what is inside also?

41 "But rather give alms of such things as you have; and indeed, all things are clean to you.

42 "But woe to you Pharisees! For you tithe mint and rue and all manner of herbs, and pass by justice and the love of God. These you ought to have done, without leaving the others undone.

43 "Woe to you Pharisees! For you love the best seats in the synagogues and greetings in the marketplaces.

44 "Woe to you, scribes and Pharisees, hypocrites! For you are like graves which are not seen, and the men who walk over them are not aware of them."

45 Then one of the lawyers[43] answered and said to Him, "Rabbi, by saying these things You reproach us also."

46 And He said, "Woe to you also, you lawyers! For you load men with burdens hard to bear, and you yourselves do not touch

---

40 Jonah 1:17 (2:1 in some versions)
41 1 Kings 10:1-13   42 Jonah 3

43 Masters of Torah studies.

the burdens with one of your fingers.

47 "Woe to you! For you build the tombs of the prophets, and your fathers killed them.

48 "In fact, you bear witness that you approve the deeds of your fathers; for they indeed killed them, and you build their tombs.

49 "Therefore, also, the wisdom of God said, 'I will send them prophets and apostles, and some of them they will kill and persecute,'

50 "that the blood of all the prophets which was shed from the foundation of the world may be required of this generation,

51 "from the blood of Abel to the blood of Zechariah who perished between the altar and the temple. Yes, I say to you, it shall be required of this generation.

52 "Woe to you lawyers! For you have taken away the key of knowledge. You did not enter in yourselves, and those who were entering in you hindered."

53 And as He said these things to them, the scribes and the Pharisees began to assail Him vehemently, and to provoke Him to speak of many things,

54 lying in wait for Him, and seeking to catch Him in something He might say, that they might accuse Him.

Beware of Hypocrisy

12 In the meantime, when an innumerable multitude of people had gathered together, so that they trampled one another, He began to say to His disciples first of all, "Beware of the leaven of the Pharisees, which is hypocrisy.

2 "For there is nothing covered that will not be revealed, nor hidden that will not be known.

3 "Therefore whatever you have spoken in darkness will be heard in the light, and what you have spoken in the ear in inner rooms will be proclaimed on the housetops.

Yeshua Teaches the Fear of God

4 "And I say to you, My friends, do not be afraid of those who kill the body, and after that have no more that they can do.

5 "But I will warn you whom you should fear: Fear Him who, after He has killed, has power to cast into hell; yes, I say to you, fear Him!

6 "Are not five sparrows sold for two copper coins? And not one of them is forgotten before God.

7 "But even the very hairs of your head are all numbered. Do not fear therefore; you are of more value than many sparrows.

Proclaim the Messiah Before Men

8 "Also I say to you, whoever confesses Me before men, him the Son of Man will also confess before the angels of God.

9 "But he who denies Me before men will be denied before the angels of God.

10 "And whoever will speak a word against the Son of Man, it will be forgiven him; but to him who blasphemes against the Holy Spirit, it will not be forgiven.

11 "And when they bring you to the synagogues and to magistrates and authorities, do not worry about how or what you will answer, or what you will say.

12 "For the Holy Spirit will teach you in the same hour what you ought to say."

The Parable of the Rich Fool

13 And one from the crowd said to Him, "Rabbi, tell my brother to divide the inheritance with me."

14 And He said to him, "Man, who made Me a judge or an arbitrator over you?"

15 And He said to them, "Take heed and beware of covetousness, for a man's life does not consist in the abundance of the things he possesses."

16 And He spoke a parable to them, saying: "The ground of a certain rich man yielded plentifully.

17 "And he thought within himself, saying, 'What shall I do, since I have no room to store my crops?'

18 "And he said, 'I will do this: I will pull down my barns and build greater, and there I will store all my crops and my goods.

19 'And I will say to my soul: Soul, you have many goods laid up for many years; take your ease; eat, drink, and be merry.'

20 "But God said to him, 'You fool! This night your soul will be required of you; then whose will those things be which you have provided?'

21 "So is he who lays up treasure for himself, and is not rich toward God."

Do Not Be Anxious

22 And He said to His disciples, "Therefore I say to you, do not worry about your life, what you will eat; nor about the body, what you will put on.

23 "The life is more than food, and the body is more than clothing.

24 "Consider the ravens, for they neither sow nor reap, which have neither storehouse nor barn; and God feeds them. Of how much more value are you than the birds?

25 "And which of you by worrying can add one cubit[44] to his stature?

26 "If you then are not able to do that thing which is least, why are you anxious for the rest?

27 "Consider the lilies, how they grow: they neither toil nor spin; and yet I say to you, even Solomon in all his glory was not arrayed like one of these.

28 "If then God so clothes the grass, which today is in the field and tomorrow is thrown into the oven, how much more will He clothe you, O you of little faith?

29 "And do not seek what you should eat or what you should drink, nor have an anxious mind.

30 "For all these things the nations of the world seek after, and your Father knows that you need these things.

31 "But rather seek the kingdom of God, and all these things will be added to you.

32 "Do not fear, little flock, for it is your Father's good pleasure to give you the kingdom.

33 "Sell what you have and give alms; provide yourselves money bags which do not grow old, a treasure in the heavens that does not fail, where no thief approaches nor moth destroys.

44 A unit of measure equal to almost 18 inches, or nearly one-half meter.

34 "For where your treasure is, there your heart will be also.

The Faithful Servant
and the Bad Servant

35 "Let your waist be girded about and your lamps burning;

36 "and you yourselves be like men who wait for their master, when he will return from the wedding, that when he comes and knocks they may open to him immediately.

37 "Blessed are those servants whom the master, when he comes, will find watching. Assuredly, I say to you that he will gird himself and have them sit down to eat, and will come and serve them.

38 "And if he should come in the second watch,[45] or come in the third watch,[46] and find them so, blessed are those servants.

39 "But know this, that if the master of the house had known what hour the thief would come, he would have watched and not allowed his house to be broken into.

40 "Therefore you also be ready, for the Son of Man is coming at an hour you do not expect."

41 Then Peter said to Him, "Lord, do You speak this parable only to us, or to all people?"

42 And the Lord said, "Who then is that faithful and wise steward, whom his master will make ruler over his household, to give them their portion of food in due season?

43 "Blessed is that servant whom his master will find so doing when he comes.

44 "Truly, I say to you that he will make him ruler over all that he has.

45 "But if that servant says in his heart, 'My master is delaying his coming,' and begins to beat the menservants and maidservants, and to eat and drink and be drunk,

46 "the master of that servant will come on a day when he is not looking for him, and at an hour when he is not aware; and he will cut him in two and appoint him his portion with the unbelievers.

47 "And that servant who knew his master's will and did not prepare himself, nor do according to his will, shall be beaten with many stripes.

48 "But he who did not know, and committed things worthy of stripes, shall be beaten with few. For everyone to whom much is given, from him much will be required; and to whom men have committed much, of him they will ask the more.

The Messiah Brings Division

49 "I have come to send fire on the earth, and how I wish it were already kindled!

50 "But I have a baptism[47] to be baptized with, and how distressed I am till it is accomplished!

51 "Do you suppose that I have come to give peace on earth? I tell you, not at all, but rather division.

52 "For from now on five in one house will be divided: three against two, and two against three.

---

45 9 p.m. to midnight.
46 Midnight to 3 a.m.

47 Yeshua is referring to His coming death to atone for our sins.

53 "The father will be divided against the son and the son against the father, the mother against the daughter and the daughter against the mother, the mother-in-law against her daughter-in-law and the daughter-in-law against her mother-in-law."

Discern the Time

54 And He also said to the multitudes, "When you see a cloud rise out of the west, immediately you say, 'A shower is coming'; and so it is.

55 "And when you see the south wind blow, you say, 'There will be heat'; and there is.

56 "Hypocrites! You can discern the face of the sky and of the earth, but how is it you do not discern this time?

Make Peace with Your Adversary

57 "Yes, and why, even of yourselves, do you not judge what is right?

58 "When you go with your adversary to the magistrate, as you are on the way, make every effort that you may be released from him, lest he drag you to the judge, the judge deliver you to the officer, and the officer throw you into prison.

59 "I tell you, you shall not depart from there till you have paid the very last mite."

Repent or Perish

13 There were present at that season some who told Him about the Galileans whose blood Pilate had mingled with their sacrifices.

2 And Yeshua answered and said to them, "Do you suppose that these Galileans were worse sinners than all the Galileans, because they suffered such things?

3 "I tell you, no; but unless you repent you will all likewise perish!

4 "Or those eighteen on whom the tower in Siloam fell and killed them, do you think that they were worse sinners than all men who dwelt in Jerusalem?

5 "I tell you, no; but unless you repent you will all likewise perish!"

The Parable of the Barren Fig Tree

6 He also spoke this parable: "A certain man had a fig tree planted in his vineyard, and he came seeking fruit on it and found none.

7 "Then he said to the keeper of his vineyard, 'Look, these three years I have come seeking fruit on this fig tree and find none. Cut it down; why does it use up the ground?'

8 "And he answered and said to him, 'Sir, let it alone this year also, until I dig around it and fertilize it.

9 'And if it bears fruit, well. But if not, after that you shall cut it down.' "

A Spirit of Infirmity

10 And He was teaching in one of the synagogues on the Sabbath.

11 And behold, there was a woman who had a spirit of infirmity eighteen years, and was bent over and could in no way raise herself up.

12 But when Yeshua saw her, He called her to Him and said to

her, "Woman, you are loosed from your infirmity."

13 And He laid His hands on her, and immediately she was made straight, and glorified God.

14 And the ruler of the synagogue answered with indignation, because Yeshua had healed on the Sabbath; and he said to the people, "There are six days in which men ought to work; therefore come and be healed in them, and not on the Sabbath day."

15 The Lord then answered him and said, "You hypocrite! Does not each one of you on the Sabbath loose his ox or his donkey from the stall, and lead it away to water it?

16 "And ought not this woman, being a daughter of Abraham, whom Satan has bound these eighteen years, be loosed from this bond on the Sabbath?"

17 And when He had said these things, all His adversaries were put to shame; and all the multitude rejoiced for all the glorious things that were done by Him.

The Parable of the Mustard Seed

18 Then He said, "What is the kingdom of God like? And to what shall I compare it?

19 "It is like a mustard seed, which a man took and planted in his garden; and it grew and became a large tree, and the birds of the air nested in its branches."

The Parable of the Leaven

20 And again He said, "To what shall I liken the kingdom of God?

21 "It is like leaven, which a woman took and hid in three measures of meal till it was all leavened."

The Narrow Way

22 And He went through the cities and villages, teaching, and journeying toward Jerusalem.

23 Then one said to Him, "Lord, are there few who are saved?" And He said to them,

24 "Strive to enter in at the narrow gate, for many, I say to you, will seek to enter in and will not be able.

25 "When once the Master of the house has risen up and shut the door, and you begin to stand outside and knock at the door, saying, 'Lord, Lord, open for us,' and He will answer and say to you, 'I do not know you, where you are from,'

26 "then you will begin to say, 'We have eaten and drunk in Your presence, and You have taught in our streets.'

27 "But He will say, 'I tell you I do not know you, where you are from. Depart from Me, all you workers of iniquity.'

28 "There will be weeping and gnashing of teeth, when you see Abraham and Isaac and Jacob and all the prophets in the kingdom of God, and you yourselves thrust out.

29 "And they will come from the east and from the west and from the north and from the south, and sit down in the kingdom of God.

30 "And indeed there are last who will be first, and there are first who will be last."

31 On the same day some of the Pharisees came, saying to Him, "Get out and depart from here, for Herod wants to kill You."

32 And He said to them, "Go, tell that fox, 'Behold, I cast out demons and perform cures today and tomorrow, and the third day I shall be perfected.'

33 "Nevertheless I must journey today, tomorrow, and the day following; for it cannot be that a prophet perish outside of Jerusalem.

Yeshua Laments over Jerusalem

34 "O Jerusalem, Jerusalem, the one who kills the prophets and stones those wno are sent to her! How often I wanted to gather your children together, as a hen gathers her brood under her wings, and you were not willing!

35 "See! Your house is left to you desolate; and assuredly, I say to you, you shall not see Me until the time comes when you say, *'Blessed is He who comes in the name of the LORD!'* " [48]

A Man with Dropsy Healed on the Sabbath

14 And it happened, as He went into the house of one of the rulers of the Pharisees to eat bread on the Sabbath, that they watched Him closely.

2 And behold, there was a certain man before Him who had dropsy.

3 And Yeshua, answering, spoke to the lawyers and Pharisees, saying, "Is it lawful to heal on the Sabbath?"

4 And they kept silent. And He took him, healed him, and let him go.

5 And He answered them, saying, "Which of you, having a donkey or an ox that has fallen into a pit, will not immediately pull him out on the Sabbath day?"

6 And they could not answer Him regarding these things.

Take the Lowly Place

7 And He told a parable to those who were invited, when He noted how they chose the best places, saying to them:

8 "When you are invited by anyone to a wedding, do not sit down in the best place, lest a more honorable man than you be invited by him;

9 "and he who invited you and him come and say to you, 'Give place to this man,' and then you begin with shame to take the lowest place.

10 "But when you are invited, go and sit down in the lowest place, so that when he who invited you comes he may say to you, 'Friend, go up higher.' Then you will have glory in the presence of those who sit at the table with you.

11 "For whoever exalts himself will be abased, and he who humbles himself will be exalted."

12 Then He also said to him who invited Him, "When you give a dinner or a supper, do not ask your friends, your brothers, your relatives, nor your rich neighbors, lest they also invite you back, and you be repaid.

13 "But when you give a feast, invite the poor, the maimed, the lame, the blind.

14 "And you will be blessed, because they cannot repay you; for you shall be repaid at the resurrection of the just."

[48] Psalm 118:26

The Parable of the Great Supper

15 And when one of those who sat at the table with Him heard these things, he said to Him, "Blessed is he who shall eat bread in the kingdom of God!"

16 Then He said to him, "A certain man gave a great supper and invited many,

17 "and sent his servant at supper time to say to those who were invited, 'Come, for all things are now ready.'

18 "And they all with one accord began to make excuses. The first said to him, 'I have bought a piece of ground, and I must go and see it. I ask you to have me excused.'

19 "And another said, 'I have bought five yoke of oxen, and I am going to test them. I ask you to have me excused.'

20 "And another said, 'I have married a wife, and therefore I cannot come.'

21 "So that servant came and reported these things to his master. Then the master of the house, being angry, said to his servant, 'Go out quickly into the streets and lanes of the city, and bring in here the poor and the maimed and the lame and the blind.'

22 "And the servant said, 'Master, it is done as you have commanded, and still there is room.'

23 "And the master said to the servant, 'Go out into the highways and hedges, and compel them to come in, that my house may be filled.

24 'For I say to you that none of those men who were invited shall taste my supper.' "

Leaving All to Follow the Messiah

25 And there went great multitudes with Him. And He turned and said to them,

26 "If anyone comes to Me and does not hate his father and mother, wife and children, brothers and sisters, yes, and his own life also, he cannot be My disciple.

27 "And whoever does not bear his cross and come after Me cannot be My disciple.

28 "For which of you, intending to build a tower, does not sit down first and count the cost, whether he has enough to finish it—

29 "lest, after he has laid the foundation, and is not able to finish it, all who see it begin to mock him,

30 "saying, 'This man began to build and was not able to finish.'

31 "Or what king, going to make war against another king, does not sit down first and consider whether he is able with ten thousand to meet him who comes against him with twenty thousand?

32 "Or else, while the other is still a great way off, he sends a delegation and asks conditions of peace.

33 "So likewise, whoever of you does not forsake all that he has, he cannot be My disciple.

Tasteless Salt Is Worthless

34 "Salt is good; but if the salt has lost its flavor, how shall it be seasoned?

35 "It is neither fit for the land nor for the dung hill, but men throw it out. He who has ears to hear, let him hear!"

The Parable of the Lost Sheep

15 Then all the tax collectors and sinners drew near to Him to hear Him.

2 And the Pharisees and scribes murmured, saying, "This man receives sinners and eats with them."

3 And He spoke this parable to them, saying:

4 "What man of you, having a hundred sheep, if he loses one of them, does not leave the ninety-nine in the wilderness, and go after the one which is lost until he finds it?

5 "And when he has found it, he lays it on his shoulders, rejoicing.

6 "And when he comes home, he calls together his friends and neighbors, saying to them, 'Rejoice with me, for I have found my sheep which was lost!'

7 "I say to you that likewise there will be more joy in heaven over one sinner who repents than over ninety-nine just persons who need no repentance.

The Parable of the Lost Coin

8 "Or what woman having ten pieces of silver, if she loses one piece, does not light a lamp, sweep the house, and seek diligently until she finds it?

9 "And when she has found it, she calls her friends and her neighbors together, saying, 'Rejoice with me, for I have found the piece which I had lost!'

10 "Likewise, I say to you, there is joy in the presence of the angels of God over one sinner who repents."

The Parable of the Lost Son

11 And He said: "A certain man had two sons.

12 "And the younger of them said to his father, 'Father, give me the portion of goods that falls to me.' And he divided to them his livelihood.

13 "And not many days after, the younger son gathered all together, journeyed to a far country, and there wasted his possessions with prodigal living.

14 "But when he had spent all, there arose a mighty famine in that land, and he began to be in want.

15 "And he went and joined himself to a citizen of that country, and he sent him into his fields to feed swine.

16 "And he would gladly have filled his stomach with the pods that the swine ate, and no one gave him anything.

17 "And when he came to himself, he said, 'How many of my father's hired servants have bread enough and to spare, and I perish with hunger!

18 'I will arise and go to my father, and will say to him: Father, I have sinned against heaven and before you,

19 and I am no longer worthy to be called your son. Make me like one of your hired servants.'

20 "And he arose and came to his father. But when he was still a great way off, his father saw him and had compassion, and ran and fell on his neck and kissed him.

21 "And the son said to him, 'Father, I have sinned against heaven and in your sight, and am no longer worthy to be called your son.'

22 "But the father said to his servants, 'Bring out the best robe and put it on him, and put a ring on his hand and sandals on his feet.

23 'And bring the fattened calf here and kill it, and let us eat and be merry;

24 'for this my son was dead and is alive again; he was lost and is found.' And they began to be merry.

25 "Now his older son was in the field. And as he came and drew near to the house, he heard music and dancing.

26 "And he called one of the servants and asked what these things meant.

27 "And he said to him, 'Your brother has come, and because he has received him safe and sound, your father has killed the fattened calf.'

28 "And he was angry and would not go in. Therefore his father came out and pleaded with him.

29 "But he answered and said to his father, 'Lo these many years I have been serving you; I never transgressed your commandment at any time, and yet you never gave me a young goat, that I might make merry with my friends.

30 'But as soon as this son of yours came, who has devoured your livelihood with harlots, you killed the fattened calf for him.'

31 "And he said to him, 'Son, you are always with me, and all that I have is yours.

32 'It was right that we should make merry and be glad, for your brother was dead and is alive again, and was lost and is found.' "

The Parable of the Unjust Steward

16 And He also said to His disciples: "There was a certain rich man who had a steward, and an accusation was brought to him that this man was wasting his goods.

2 "And he called him and said to him, 'What is this I hear about you? Give an account of your stewardship, for you may no longer be steward.'

3 "Then the steward said within himself, 'What shall I do? For my master is taking the stewardship away from me. I cannot dig; I am ashamed to beg.

4 'I have resolved what to do, that when I am put out of the stewardship, they may receive me into their houses.'

5 "So he called every one of his master's debtors to him, and said to the first, 'How much do you owe my master?'

6 "And he said, 'A hundred measures of oil.' And he said to him, 'Take your bill, and sit down quickly and write fifty.'

7 "Then he said to another, 'And how much do you owe?' And he said, 'A hundred measures of wheat.' And he said to him, 'Take your bill, and write eighty.'

8 "And the master commended the unjust steward because he had dealt shrewdly. For the sons of this world are shrewder in their generation than the sons of light.

9 "And I say to you, make friends for yourselves by unrighteous mammon, that when you fail, they may receive you into everlasting habitations.

10 "He who is faithful in what is

least is faithful also in much; and he who is unjust in the least is unjust also in much.

11 "Therefore if you have not been faithful in the unrighteous mammon, who will commit to your trust the true riches?

12 "And if you have not been faithful in what is another man's, who will give you what is your own?

13 "No servant can serve two masters; for either he will hate the one and love the other, or else he will hold to the one and despise the other. You cannot serve God and mammon."

The Torah, the Prophets, and the Kingdom

14 And the Pharisees, who were lovers of money, also heard all these things, and they derided Him.

15 And He said to them, "You are those who justify yourselves before men, but God knows your hearts. For what is highly esteemed among men is an abomination in the sight of God.

16 "The Torah and the prophets were until John. Since that time the kingdom of God is preached, and everyone is pressing into it.

17 "And it is easier for heaven and earth to pass away than one mark[49] of the Torah to fail.

18 "Whoever divorces his wife and marries another commits adultery; and whoever marries her who is divorced from her husband commits adultery.

49 Hebrew: *tag,* an elaboration, functional or ornamental, of a line or stroke in a Hebrew letter.

The Rich Man and Lazarus

19 "There was a certain rich man who was clothed in purple and fine linen and fared sumptuously every day.

20 "But there was a certain beggar named Lazarus, full of sores, who was laid at his gate,

21 "desiring to be fed with the crumbs which fell from the rich man's table. Moreover the dogs came and licked his sores.

22 "And it came to pass that the beggar died and was carried by the angels to Abraham's bosom. The rich man also died and was buried.

23 "And being in torments in Hades, he lifted up his eyes and saw Abraham afar off, and Lazarus in his bosom.

24 "And he cried and said, 'Father Abraham, have mercy on me, and send Lazarus that he may dip the tip of his finger in water and cool my tongue; for I am tormented in this flame.'

25 "But Abraham said, 'Son, remember that in your lifetime you received your good things, and likewise Lazarus evil things; but now he is comforted and you are tormented.

26 'And besides all this, between us and you there is a great gulf fixed, so that those who want to pass from here to you cannot, nor can those who want to come from there pass to us.'

27 "Then he said, 'I beg you therefore, father, that you would send him to my father's house,

28 'for I have five brothers, that he may testify to them, lest they also come to this place of torment.'

29 "Abraham said to him, 'They

have Moses and the prophets; let them hear them.'

30 "And he said, 'No, father Abraham; but if one goes to them from the dead, they will repent.'

31 "And he said to him, 'If they do not hear Moses and the prophets, neither will they be persuaded though one rise from the dead.' "

Yeshua Warns of Offenses

17 Then He said to the disciples, "It is impossible that no offenses should come, but woe to him through whom they do come!

2 "It would be better for him if a millstone were hung around his neck, and he were thrown into the sea, than that he should offend one of these little ones.

3 "Take heed to yourselves. If your brother sins against you, rebuke him; and if he repents, forgive him.

4 "And if he sins against you seven times in a day, and seven times in a day returns to you, saying, 'I repent,' you shall forgive him."

Faith and Duty

5 And the apostles said to the Lord, "Increase our faith."

6 And the Lord said, "If you had faith as a mustard seed, you might say to this mulberry tree, 'Be pulled up by the roots and be planted in the sea,' and it would obey you.

7 "And which of you, having a servant plowing or tending sheep, will say to him when he has come in from the field, 'Come at once and sit down to eat'?

8 "But will he not rather say to him, 'Prepare something for my supper, and gird yourself and serve me till I have eaten and drunk, and afterward you will eat and drink'?

9 "Does he thank that servant because he did the things that were commanded him? I think not.

10 "So likewise you, when you have done all those things which you are commanded, say, 'We are unprofitable servants. We have done what was our duty to do.' "

Ten Lepers Cleansed

11 And it came to pass, as He went to Jerusalem, that He passed through the midst of Samaria and Galilee.

12 And as He entered a certain village, there met Him ten men who were lepers, who stood afar off.

13 And they lifted up their voices and said, "Yeshua, Master, have mercy on us!"

14 And when He saw them, He said to them, "Go, show yourselves to the priests." And it came to pass, that as they went, they were cleansed.

15 And one of them, when he saw that he was healed, returned, and with a loud voice glorified God,

16 and fell down on his face at His feet, giving Him thanks. And he was a Samaritan.

17 And Yeshua answered and said, "Were there not ten cleansed? But where are the nine?

18 "Were there not any found who returned to give glory to God except this foreigner?"

19 And He said to him, "Arise, go your way. Your faith has made you well."

The Coming of the Kingdom

20 And when He was asked by the Pharisees when the kingdom of God would come, He answered them and said, "The kingdom of God does not come with observation;

21 "nor will they say, 'See here!' or, 'See there!' For, indeed, the kingdom of God is within you."

22 And He said to the disciples, "The days will come when you will desire to see one of the days of the Son of Man, and you will not see it.

23 "And they will say to you, 'Look here!' or, 'Look there!' Do not go after them nor follow them.

24 "For as the lightning that flashes out of one part under heaven shines to the other part under heaven, so also the Son of Man will be in His day.

25 "But first He must suffer many things and be rejected by this generation.

26 "And as it was in the days of Noah, so it will be also in the days of the Son of Man:

27 "They ate, they drank, they married wives, they were given in marriage, until the day that Noah entered the ark, and the flood came and destroyed them all.[50]

28 "Likewise also as it was in the days of Lot: They ate, they drank, they bought, they sold, they planted, they built;

29 "but the same day that Lot went out of Sodom it rained fire

and brimstone from heaven and destroyed them all.[51]

30 "Even so will it be in the day when the Son of Man is revealed.

31 "In that day, he who is on the housetop, and his goods in the house, let him not come down to take them away. And he who is in the field, likewise let him not turn back.

32 "Remember Lot's wife.[51]

33 "Whoever seeks to save his life will lose it, and whoever loses his life will preserve it.

34 "I tell you, in that night there will be two men in one bed: the one will be taken and the other will be left.

35 "Two women will be grinding together: the one will be taken and the other left.

36 "Two men will be in the field: the one will be taken and the other left."

37 And they answered and said to Him, "Where, Lord?" And He said to them, "Wherever the body is, there the eagles will be gathered together."

The Parable of the Persistent Widow

18 And He spoke a parable to them for this purpose, that men always ought to pray and not lose heart,

2 saying: "There was in a certain city a judge who did not fear God nor regard man.

3 "And there was a widow in that city; and she came to him, saying, 'Avenge me of my adversary.'

4 "And he would not for a

---

50 Genesis 6 and 7   51 Genesis 19:24-26

while; but afterward he said within himself, 'Though I do not fear God nor regard man,

5 'yet because this widow troubles me I will avenge her, lest by her continual coming she weary me.' "

6 And the Lord said, "Hear what the unjust judge said.

7 "And shall God not avenge His own elect who cry out day and night to Him, though He bears long with them?

8 "I tell you that He will avenge them speedily. Nevertheless, when the Son of Man comes, will He find faith on the earth?"

The Parable of the Pharisee and the Tax Collector

9 And He spoke this parable to some who trusted in themselves that they were righteous, and despised others:

10 "Two men went up to the temple to pray, the one a Pharisee and the other a tax collector.

11 "The Pharisee stood and prayed thus with himself, 'God, I thank You that I am not like other men—extortioners, unjust, adulterers, or even as this tax collector.

12 'I fast twice a week; I give tithes of all that I possess.'

13 "And the tax collector, standing afar off, would not so much as raise his eyes to heaven, but beat his breast, saying, 'God be merciful to me a sinner!'

14 "I tell you, this man went down to his house justified rather than the other; for everyone who exalts himself will be abased, and he who humbles himself will be exalted."

Yeshua Blesses Little Children

15 And they also brought infants to Him that He might touch them; but when His disciples saw it, they rebuked them.

16 But Yeshua called them to Him and said, "Let the little children come to Me, and do not forbid them; for of such is the kingdom of God.

17 "Assuredly, I say to you, whoever does not receive the kingdom of God as a little child will by no means enter it."

Yeshua Counsels the Rich Young Ruler

18 And a certain ruler asked Him, saying, "Good Rabbi, what shall I do to inherit eternal life?"

19 And Yeshua said to him, "Why do you call Me good? No one is good but One, that is, God.

20 "You know the commandments: *'Do not commit adultery,' 'Do not murder,' 'Do not steal,' 'Do not bear false witness,' 'Honor your father and your mother.'* " [52]

21 And he said, "All these I have kept from my youth."

22 Now when Yeshua heard these things, He said to him, "You still lack one thing. Sell all that you have and distribute to the poor, and you will have treasure in heaven; and come, follow Me."

23 And when he heard this, he became very sorrowful, for he was very rich.

With God All Things Are Possible

24 And when Yeshua saw that he became very sorrowful, He

52 Exodus 20:12-16; Deuteronomy 5:16-20 (5:16, 17 in some versions)

said, "How hard it is for those who have riches to enter the kingdom of God!

25 "For it is easier for a camel to go through a needle's eye than for a rich man to enter the kingdom of God."

26 And those who heard it said, "Who then can be saved?"

27 And He said, "The things which are impossible with men are possible with God."

28 Then Peter said, "See, we have left all and followed You."

29 And He said to them, "Assuredly, I say to you, there is no one who has left house or parents or brothers or wife or children, for the sake of the kingdom of God,

30 "who shall not receive many times more in this present time, and in the age to come everlasting life."

Yeshua a Third Time Predicts His Death and Resurrection

31 Then He took the twelve aside and said to them, "Behold, we are going up to Jerusalem, and all things that are written by the prophets concerning the Son of Man will be accomplished.[53]

32 "For He will be delivered to the Gentiles and will be mocked and insulted and spit upon.[54]

33 "And they will scourge Him and put Him to death. And the third day He will rise again."[55]

34 And they understood none of these things; this saying was hidden from them, and they did not know the things which were spoken.

A Blind Man Receives His Sight

35 And it came to pass, that as He was coming near Jericho, a certain blind man sat by the road begging.

36 And hearing the multitude passing by, he asked what it meant.

37 And they told him that Yeshua of Nazareth was passing by.

38 And he cried out, saying, "Yeshua, Son of David,[56] have mercy on me!"

39 And those who went before warned him that he should be quiet; but he cried out all the more, "Son of David, have mercy on me!"

40 And Yeshua stood still and commanded him to be brought to Him. And when he had come near, He asked him,

41 saying, "What do you want Me to do for you?" And he said, "Lord, I want to receive my sight."

42 And Yeshua said to him, "Receive your sight; your faith has saved you."

43 And immediately he received his sight, and followed Him, glorifying God. And all the people, when they saw it, gave praise to God.

Yeshua Comes to Zacchaeus' House

19 And Yeshua entered and passed through Jericho.

2 And behold, there was a man named Zacchaeus who was a chief tax collector, and he was rich.

3 And he sought to see who Yeshua was, but could not for the

---

53 Isaiah 52:13—53:12   54 Isaiah 50:6
55 Psalm 16:10 (cf. Isaiah 53:10)

56 A title of Messiah (Jeremiah 23:5, 6).

crowd, because he was of short stature.

4 And he ran ahead and climbed up into a sycamore tree to see Him, for He was going to pass that way.

5 And when Yeshua came to the place, He looked up and saw him, and said to him, "Zacchaeus, make haste and come down, for today I must stay at your house."

6 And he made haste and came down, and received Him joyfully.

7 And when they saw it, they all murmured, saying, "He has gone to be a guest with a man who is a sinner."

8 And Zacchaeus stood and said to the Lord, "Look, Lord, I give half of my goods to the poor; and if I have taken anything from anyone by false accusation, I restore to him fourfold."

9 And Yeshua said to him, "Today salvation has come to this house, because he also is a son of Abraham;

10 "for the Son of Man has come to seek and to save that which was lost."

The Parable of the Minas

11 And as they heard these things, He added and spoke a parable, because He was near Jerusalem and because they thought the kingdom of God would appear immediately.

12 Therefore He said: "A certain nobleman went into a far country to receive for himself a kingdom and to return.

13 "And he called his ten servants, delivered to them ten minas,[57] and said to them, 'Do business till I come.'

14 "But his citizens hated him, and sent a delegation after him, saying, 'We will not have this man to reign over us.'

15 "And it came to pass that when he returned, having received the kingdom, he then commanded these servants, to whom he had given the money, to be called to him, that he might know how much every man had gained by trading.

16 "Then came the first, saying, 'Master, your mina has earned ten minas.'

17 "And he said to him, 'Well done, good servant; because you have been faithful in a very little, have authority over ten cities.'

18 "And the second came, saying, 'Master, your mina has earned five minas.'

19 "And he said likewise to him, 'You also be over five cities.'

20 "And another came, saying, 'Master, look, here is your mina, which I have kept put away in a handkerchief.

21 'For I feared you, because you are an austere man. You collect what you did not deposit, and reap what you did not sow.'

22 "And he said to him, 'Out of your own mouth I will judge you, you wicked servant. You knew that I was an austere man, collecting what I did not deposit and reaping what I did not sow.

23 'Why then did you not put my money in the bank, that at my coming I might have collected my own with interest?'

24 "And he said to those who

---

57 A mina equalled about $375.00.

stood by, 'Take the mina from him, and give it to him who has ten minas.'

25 ("And they said to him, 'Master, he has ten minas.')

26 'For I say to you, that to everyone who has will be given; and from him who does not have, even what he has will be taken away from him.

27 'But bring here those enemies of mine, who did not want me to reign over them, and slay them before me.' "

The Triumphal Entry

28 And when He had said this, He went on ahead, going up to Jerusalem.

29 And it came to pass, when He came near to Bethphage and Bethany, at the mountain called the Mount of Olives, that He sent two of His disciples,

30 saying, "Go into the village opposite you, in which as you enter you will find a colt tied, on which no one has ever sat. Loose him and bring him here.

31 "And if anyone asks you, 'Why are you loosing him?' thus you shall say to him, 'Because the Lord has need of him.' "

32 And those who were sent departed and found just as He had said to them.

33 But as they were loosing the colt, the owners of it said to them, "Why are you loosing the colt?"

34 And they said, "The Lord has need of him."

35 And they brought him to Yeshua. And they threw their garments on the colt, and they set Yeshua on him.[58]

36 And as He went, they spread their clothes on the road.

37 And as He was now drawing near the descent of the Mount of Olives, the whole multitude of the disciples began to rejoice and praise God with a loud voice for all the mighty works they had seen,

38 saying:

" 'Blessed is the King who comes in the name of the LORD!'[59]

Peace in heaven and glory in the highest!"

39 And some of the Pharisees in the multitude said to Him, "Rabbi, rebuke Your disciples."

40 And He answered and said to them, "I tell you that if these should keep silent, the stones would immediately cry out."

Yeshua Weeps over Jerusalem

41 And when He had come near, He saw the city and wept over it,

42 saying, "If you had known, even you, especially in this your day, the things which belong to your peace! But now they are hidden from your eyes.

43 "For the days will come upon you when your enemies will build an embankment around you, surround you and close you in on every side,

44 "and level you, and your children within you, to the ground; and they will not leave in you one stone upon another, because you did not know the time of your visitation."

58 Zechariah 9:9   59 Psalm 118:26

Yeshua Cleanses the Temple

45 And He went into the temple and began to drive out those who bought and sold in it,

46 saying to them, "It is written, *'My house is a house of prayer,'*[60] but you have made it a *'den of thieves.'* " [61]

47 And He taught daily in the temple. But the chief priests, the scribes, and the leaders of the people sought to destroy Him,

48 and could not find anything they might do; for all the people were very attentive to hear Him.

Authority of Yeshua Questioned

20 And it came to pass on one of those days, as He taught the people in the temple and preached the good news, that the chief priests and the scribes came with the elders

2 and spoke to Him, saying, "Tell us, by what authority are You doing these things? Or who is he who gave You this authority?"

3 And He answered and said to them, "I will also ask you one thing, and answer Me:

4 "The immersion of John— was it from heaven or from men?"

5 And they reasoned among themselves, saying, "If we say, 'From heaven,' He will say, 'Why then did you not believe him?'

6 "But if we say, 'From men,' all the people will stone us, for they are persuaded that John was a prophet."

7 And they answered that they did not know where it was from.

8 And Yeshua said to them,

"Neither will I tell you by what authority I do these things."

The Parable of the Wicked Vinedressers

9 Then He began to speak to the people this parable: "A certain man planted a vineyard, leased it to vinedressers, and went into a far country for a long time.

10 "And at harvesttime he sent a servant to the vinedressers, that they might give him some of the fruit of the vineyard. But the vinedressers beat him and sent him away empty-handed.

11 "And again he sent another servant; and they beat him also, treated him shamefully, and sent him away empty-handed.

12 "And again he sent a third; and they wounded him also and cast him out.

13 "Then the owner of the vineyard said, 'What shall I do? I will send my beloved son. It may be they will respect him when they see him.'

14 "But when the vinedressers saw him, they reasoned among themselves, saying, 'This is the heir. Come, let us kill him, that the inheritance may be ours.'

15 "So they cast him out of the vineyard and killed him. Therefore what will the owner of the vineyard do to them?

16 "He will come and destroy those vinedressers and give the vineyard to others." And when they heard it they said, "Certainly not!"

17 And He looked at them and said, "What then is this that is written:

'The stone which the builders rejected

60 Isaiah 56:7   *61* Jeremiah 7:11

*Has become the chief corner-
stone'?* [62]

18 "Whoever falls on that stone
will be broken; [63] but on whomever it falls, it will grind him to
powder." [64]

19 And the chief priests and the
scribes the same hour sought to lay
hands on Him, but they feared the
people; for they perceived that He
had spoken this parable against
them.

The Pharisees: Is It Lawful to Pay Taxes to Caesar?

20 And they watched Him, and
sent spies who pretended to be
righteous men, that they might
seize on His words, in order to deliver Him to the power and the
authority of the governor.

21 And they asked Him, saying,
"Rabbi, we know that You say
and teach rightly, and You do not
show personal favoritism, but
teach the way of God truly:

22 "Is it lawful for us to pay
taxes to Caesar or not?"

23 But He perceived their craftiness, and said to them, "Why do
you test Me?

24 "Show Me a denarius.
Whose image and inscription does
it have?" They answered and
said, "Caesar's."

25 And He said to them, "Render therefore to Caesar the things
that are Caesar's, and to God the
things that are God's."

26 And they could not catch
Him in His words in the presence
of the people. And they marveled
at His answer and kept silent.

The Sadducees: What About the Resurrection?

27 Then some of the Sadducees,
who deny that there is any resurrection, came to Him and asked
Him,

28 saying: "Rabbi, Moses wrote
to us that if a man's brother dies,
having a wife, and he dies without
children, his brother should take
his wife and raise up offspring for
his brother. [65]

29 "Now there were seven
brothers. And the first took a
wife, and died without children.

30 "And the second took her as
wife, and he died childless.

31 "And the third took her, and
in like manner the seven also; and
they left no children, and died.

32 "Last of all the woman died
also.

33 "Therefore, in the resurrection, whose wife does she become?
For all seven had her as wife."

34 And Yeshua answered and
said to them, "The sons of this age
marry and are given in marriage.

35 "But those who are counted
worthy to attain that age, and the
resurrection from the dead, neither marry nor are given in marriage;

36 "nor can they die anymore,
for they are equal to the angels
and are the sons of God, being the
sons of the resurrection.

37 "Now even Moses showed in
the burning bush passage that the
dead are raised, when he called
the Lord *'the God of Abraham,
the God of Isaac, and the God of
Jacob.'* [66]

62 Psalm 118:22
63 Isaiah 8:14, 15   64 Daniel 2:34, 35
65 Deuteronomy 25:5, 6
66 Exodus 3:6, 15

38 "For He is not the God of the dead but of the living, for all live to Him."

39 Then some of the scribes answered and said, "Rabbi, You have spoken well."

40 And after that they dared not ask Him any question at all.

Yeshua: How Can David Call His Descendant Lord?

41 And He said to them, "How can they say that the Messiah is David's Son?

42 "And David himself said in the Book of Psalms,

'The LORD said to my Lord,
"Sit at My right hand,
43 Till I make Your enemies
    Your footstool." '[67]

44 "David therefore calls Him 'Lord'; how is He then his Son?"

Beware of the Scribes

45 Then, in the hearing of all the people, He said to His disciples,

46 "Beware of the scribes, who desire to walk in long robes, love greetings in the marketplaces, the best seats in the synagogues, and the best places at feasts,

47 "who devour widows' houses, and for a pretense make long prayers. These will receive greater condemnation."

The Widow's Two Mites

21 And He looked up and saw the rich putting their gifts into the treasury,

2 and He saw also a certain poor widow putting in two mites.

3 And He said, "Truly I say to you that this poor widow has put in more than all;

4 "for all these out of their abundance have given offerings for God, but she out of her poverty has put in all the livelihood that she had."

Yeshua Predicts the Destruction of the Temple

5 And as some spoke of the temple, how it was adorned with beautiful stones and gifts, He said,

6 "As for these things which you see, the days will come in which not one stone shall be left upon another that shall not be thrown down."

The Signs of the Times and the End of the Age

7 And they asked Him, saying, "Rabbi, but when will these things be? And what sign will there be when these things are about to take place?"

8 And He said: "Take heed that you not be deceived. For many will come in My name, saying, 'I am He, and the time has drawn near.' Therefore do not go after them.

9 "But when you hear of wars and commotions, do not be terrified; for these things must come to pass first, but the end is not immediate."

10 Then He said to them, "Nation will rise against nation, and kingdom against kingdom.

11 "And there will be great earthquakes in various places, and famines and pestilences; and there will be fearful sights and great signs from heaven.

12 "But before all these things, they will lay their hands on you

67 Psalm 110:1

and persecute you, delivering you up to the synagogues and prisons, and you will be brought before kings and rulers for My name's sake.

13 "And it will turn out for you as an occasion for testimony.

14 "Therefore settle it in your hearts not to meditate beforehand on what you will answer;

15 "for I will give you a mouth and wisdom which all your adversaries will not be able to contradict nor resist.

16 "And you will be betrayed both by parents and brothers, relatives and friends; and they will cause some of you to be put to death.

17 "And you will be hated by all for My name's sake.

18 "But not a hair of your head shall be lost.

19 "In your patience possess your souls.

The Great Tribulation

20 "And when you see Jerusalem surrounded by armies, then know that its desolation is near.

21 "Then let those in Judea flee to the mountains, let those who are in the midst of her depart, and let not those who are in the country enter her.

22 "For these are the days of vengeance, that all things which are written may be fulfilled.

23 "But woe to those who are pregnant and to those who are nursing babies in those days! For there will be great distress in the land and wrath upon this people.

24 "And they will fall by the edge of the sword, and be led away captive into all nations. And Jerusalem will be trampled by the Gentiles until the times of the Gentiles are fulfilled.

The Second Coming of the Messiah

25 "And there will be signs in the sun, in the moon, and in the stars; and on the earth distress of nations, with perplexity, the sea and the waves roaring;

26 "men's hearts failing them from fear and the expectation of those things which are coming on the earth, for the powers of heaven will be shaken.

27 "And then they will see the Son of Man coming in a cloud with power and great glory.[68]

28 "Now when these things begin to happen, look up and lift up your heads, because your redemption draws near."

The Parable of the Fig Tree

29 And He spoke to them a parable: "Look at the fig tree, and all the trees.

30 "When they are already budding, you see and know for yourselves that summer is now near.

31 "So you, likewise, when you see these things coming to pass, know that the kingdom of God is near.

32 "Assuredly, I say to you, this generation will by no means pass away till all things are fulfilled.

33 "Heaven and earth will pass away, but My words will by no means pass away.

The Importance of Watching

34 "But take heed to yourselves, lest your hearts be weighed down

68 Daniel 7:13, 14

with carousing, drunkenness, and cares of this life, and that Day come on you unexpectedly.

35 "For it will come as a snare on all those who dwell on the face of the whole earth.

36 "Watch therefore, and pray always that you may be counted worthy to escape all these things that will come to pass, and to stand before the Son of Man."

37 And in the daytime He was teaching in the temple, but at night He went out and stayed on the mountain that is called the Mount of Olives.

38 And early in the morning all the people came to Him in the temple to hear Him.

The Plot to Kill Yeshua

22 Now the Feast of Unleavened Bread drew near, which is called Passover.

2 And the chief priests and the scribes sought how they might kill Him, for they feared the people.

3 Then Satan entered Judas surnamed Iscariot, who was numbered among the twelve.

4 And he went his way and conferred with the chief priests and captains, how he might betray Him to them.

5 And they were glad, and agreed to give him money.

6 And he promised and sought opportunity to betray Him to them in the absence of the multitude.

Yeshua and His Disciples Prepare the Passover

7 Then came the Day of Unleavened Bread, when the Passover must be killed.

8 And He sent Peter and John, saying, "Go and prepare the Passover for us, that we may eat."

9 And they said to Him, "Where do You want us to prepare?"

10 And He said to them, "Behold, when you have entered the city, a man will meet you carrying a pitcher of water; follow him into the house which he enters.

11 "And you shall say to the master of the house, 'The Rabbi says to you: Where is the guest room in which I may eat the Passover with My disciples?'

12 "And he will show you a large, furnished upper room; there make ready."

13 And they went and found it as He had said to them, and they prepared the Passover.

14 And when the hour had come, He sat down, and the twelve apostles with Him.

15 And He said to them, "With desire I have desired to eat this Passover with you before I suffer;

16 "for I say to you, I will no longer eat of it until it is fulfilled in the kingdom of God."

17 And He took the cup, and gave thanks, and said, "Take this and divide it among yourselves;

18 "for I say to you, I will not drink of the fruit of the vine until the kingdom of God comes."

19 And He took matzah, gave thanks and broke it, and gave it to them, saying, "This is My body which is given for you; do this in remembrance of Me."

20 Likewise also He took the cup after supper, saying, "This cup is

the new covenant[69] in My blood, which is shed for you.

21 "But behold, the hand of the one who betrays Me is with Me on the table.[70]

22 "And truly the Son of Man goes as it has been determined, but woe to that man by whom He is betrayed!"

23 And they began to question among themselves, which of them it was who would do this thing.

The Disciples Argue about Greatness

24 But there was also strife among them, which of them should be considered the greatest.

25 And He said to them, "The kings of the Gentiles exercise lordship over them, and those who exercise authority over them are called 'benefactors.'

26 "But not so you; on the contrary, he who is greatest among you, let him be as the younger, and he who is chief as he who serves.

27 "For who is greater, he who sits at the table, or he who serves? Is it not he who sits at the table? But I am among you as the One who serves.

28 "You are those who have continued with Me in My trials.

29 "And I appoint for you a kingdom, as My Father has appointed for Me,

30 "that you may eat and drink at My table in My kingdom, and sit on thrones judging the twelve tribes of Israel."

Yeshua Predicts Peter's Denial

31 And the Lord said, "Simon, Simon! Indeed, Satan has asked to have you, that he may sift you as wheat.

32 "But I have prayed for you, that your faith should not fail; and when you have turned again, strengthen your brethren."

33 And he said to Him, "Lord, I am ready to go with You, both to prison and to death."

34 And He said, "I tell you, Peter, the rooster will not crow this day before you will deny three times that you know Me."

Wallet, Bag, and Sword

35 And He said to them, "When I sent you without money bag, sack, and sandals, did you lack anything?" And they said, "Nothing."

36 Then He said to them, "But now, he who has a money bag, let him take it, and likewise his sack; and he who has no sword, let him sell his garment and buy one.

37 "For I say to you that this which is written must still be accomplished in Me: 'And He was numbered with the transgressors.'[71] For the things concerning Me have a goal."

38 And they said, "Lord, look, here are two swords." And He said to them, "It is enough."

The Prayer in the Garden

39 And coming out, He went to the Mount of Olives, as He was accustomed, and His disciples also followed Him.

---

69 Jeremiah 31:31–34 (31:30–33 in some versions)

70 Psalm 41:9 (41:10 in some versions)

71 Isaiah 53:12

40 And when He came to the place, He said to them, "Pray that you not enter into temptation."

41 And He was withdrawn from them about a stone's throw, and He knelt down and prayed,

42 saying, "Father, if it is Your will, remove this cup from Me; nevertheless not My will, but Yours, be done."

43 And there appeared an angel to Him from heaven, strengthening Him.

44 And being in agony, He prayed more earnestly. And His sweat became like great drops of blood falling down to the ground.

45 And when He rose up from prayer, and had come to His disciples, He found them sleeping from sorrow.

46 And He said to them, "Why do you sleep? Rise and pray, lest you enter into temptation."

Betrayal and Arrest in Gethsemane

47 And while He was still speaking, behold, a multitude; and he who was called Judas, one of the twelve, went before them and drew near to Yeshua to kiss Him.

48 But Yeshua said to him, "Judas, are you betraying the Son of Man with a kiss?"

49 When those around Him saw what was going to happen, they said to him, "Lord, shall we strike with the sword?"

50 And one of them struck the servant of the high priest and cut off his right ear.

51 And Yeshua answered and said, "Permit even this." And He touched his ear and healed him.

52 Then Yeshua said to the chief priests, captains of the temple, and the elders who had come to Him, "Have you come out, as against a robber, with swords and clubs?

53 "When I was with you daily in the temple, you did not lay hands on Me. But this is your hour, and the power of darkness."

Peter Denies Yeshua—and Weeps Bitterly

54 Then, having arrested Him, they led Him and brought Him into the high priest's house. And Peter followed at a distance.

55 And when they had kindled a fire in the midst of the courtyard and sat down together, Peter sat among them.

56 But a certain servant girl, seeing him as he sat by the fire, looked intently at him and said, "This man was also with Him."

57 And he denied Him, saying, "Woman, I do not know Him."

58 And after a little while another saw him and said, "You are also of them." And Peter said, "Man, I am not!"

59 And after about the space of one hour another confidently affirmed, saying, "Surely this fellow also was with Him, for he is a Galilean."

60 And Peter said, "Man, I do not know what you are saying!" And immediately, while he was still speaking, the rooster crowed.

61 And the Lord turned and looked at Peter. And Peter remembered the word of the Lord, how He had said to him, "Before the rooster crows, you will deny Me three times."

62 And Peter went out and wept bitterly.

Bruised for Our Inquities

63 And the men who held Yeshua mocked Him and beat Him.

64 And when they had blind-
folded Him, they struck Him on
the face and asked Him, saying,
"Prophesy! Who is it that struck
You?"

65 And many other things they
blasphemously spoke against Him.

Yeshua and the Sanhedrin

66 And as soon as it was day, the
elders of the people, both chief
priests and scribes, came together
and led Him into their council,
saying,

67 "Are You the Messiah? Tell
us." And He said to them, "If I
tell you, you will by no means believe.

68 "And if I also ask you, you
will by no means answer Me or let
Me go.

69 "Hereafter the Son of Man
will sit on the right hand of the
power of God." [72]

70 Then they all said, "Are You
then the Son of God?" And He
said to them, "You rightly say that
I am."

71 And they said, "What further
testimony do we need? For we
ourselves have heard it from His
own mouth."

Yeshua Led to Pilate

23 Then the whole multitude
of them arose and led Him
to Pilate.

2 And they began to accuse
Him, saying, "We found this fellow perverting the nation, and forbidding to pay taxes to Caesar,
saying that He Himself is the Messiah, a King."

Yeshua and Pilate

3 And Pilate asked Him, saying, "Are You the King of the
Jews?" And He answered him
and said, "It is as you say."

4 Then Pilate said to the chief
priests and to the people, "I find
no fault in this Man."

5 But they were the more
fierce, saying, "He stirs up the
people, teaching throughout all
Judea, beginning from Galilee to
this place."

Yeshua and Herod

6 When Pilate heard of Galilee,
he asked if the Man were a Galilean.

7 And as soon as he knew that
He belonged to Herod's jurisdic-
tion, he sent Him to Herod, who
himself also was in Jerusalem at
that time.

8 And when Herod saw Ye-
shua, he was exceedingly glad; for
he had desired for a long time to
see Him, because he had heard
many things about Him, and he
hoped to see some miracle done by
Him.

9 Then he questioned Him
with many words, but He answered him nothing.[73]

10 And the chief priests and
scribes stood and vehemently accused Him.

11 And Herod, with his men of
war, treated Him with contempt
and mocked Him, arrayed Him in
a gorgeous robe, and sent Him
back to Pilate.[74]

---

72 Psalm 110:1

73 Isaiah 53:7   74 Isaiah 53:8

12 And the same day Pilate and Herod became mutual friends, for before they had been at enmity between themselves.

Condemned in Our Place

13 And Pilate, when he had called together the chief priests, the rulers, and the people,

14 said to them, "You have brought this Man to me, as one who misleads the people. And indeed, having examined Him in your presence, I have found no fault in this Man concerning those things of which you accuse Him;

15 "no, nor did Herod, for I sent you back to him; and indeed nothing worthy of death has been done by Him.

16 "I will therefore chastise Him and release Him"

17 (for it was necessary for him to release one to them at the feast).

18 And they all cried out at once, saying, "Away with this Man, and release to us Barabbas"—

19 who had been thrown into prison for a certain insurrection made in the city, and for murder.

20 Pilate, therefore, wishing to release Yeshua, spoke again to them.

21 But they shouted, saying, "Crucify Him, crucify Him!"

22 And he said to them the third time, "Why, what evil has He done? I have found no reason for death in Him. I will therefore chastise Him and let Him go."

23 But they were insistent, demanding with loud voices that He be crucified. And the voices of these men and of the chief priests prevailed.

24 And Pilate gave sentence that it should be as they requested.

25 And he released to them the one they requested, who for insurrection and murder had been thrown into prison; but he delivered Yeshua to their will.

Wounded for Our Transgressions

26 And as they led Him away, they laid hold on a certain man, Simon a Cyrenian, who was coming out of the country, and on him they laid the cross that he might bear it after Yeshua.

27 And a great multitude of the people followed Him, and women who also mourned and lamented Him.

28 But Yeshua, turning to them, said, "Daughters of Jerusalem, do not weep for Me, but weep for yourselves and for your children.

29 "For, indeed, the days are coming in which they will say, 'Blessed are the barren, the wombs that never bore, and the breasts which never nursed.'

30 "Then they will begin *'to say to the mountains: Fall on us! and to the hills: Cover us!'*[75]

31 "For if they do these things in the green wood, what will be done in the dry?"

32 And there were also two others, criminals, led with Him to be put to death.

33 And when they had come to the place which is called Calvary, there they crucified Him, and the criminals, one on the right hand and the other on the left.[76]

34 Then Yeshua said, "Father, forgive them, for they do not know

75 Hosea 10:8   76 Isaiah 53:9-12

what they do." And they divided His garments and cast lots.[77]

35 And the people stood looking on. And even the rulers with them derided Him, saying, "He saved others; let Him save Himself if He is the Messiah, the chosen of God."

36 And the soldiers also mocked Him, coming and offering Him sour wine,[78]

37 and saying, "If You are the King of the Jews, save Yourself."

38 And also an inscription was written over Him in letters of Greek, Latin, and Hebrew:

THIS IS
THE KING OF THE JEWS.

39 And one of the criminals who were hanged blasphemed Him, saying, "If You are the Messiah, save Yourself and us."

40 But the other, answering, rebuked him, saying, "Do you not fear God, seeing you are under the same condemnation?

41 "And we indeed justly, for we receive the due reward of our deeds; but this Man has done nothing wrong."

42 And he said to Yeshua, "Lord, remember me when You come into Your kingdom."

43 And Yeshua said to him, "Assuredly, I say to you, today you will be with Me in Paradise."

An Offering for Sin

44 And it was about the sixth hour,[79] and there was darkness over all the earth until the ninth hour.[80]

45 And the sun was darkened, and the curtain of the temple was torn in two.

46 And when Yeshua had cried out with a loud voice, He said, "Father, *'into Your hands I commend My spirit.'"* [81] And having said this, He breathed His last.

47 Now when the centurion saw what had happened, he glorified God, saying, "Certainly this was a righteous Man!"

48 And all the multitude who came together to that sight, seeing the things which were done, beat their breasts and returned.

49 And all His acquaintances, and the women who followed Him from Galilee, stood at a distance, watching these things.

Yeshua Buried in Joseph's Tomb

50 And behold, there was a man named Joseph, a council member, who was a good and just man.

51 He had not consented to their counsel and deed. He was from Arimathea, a city of Judah, who himself was also waiting for the kingdom of God.

52 This man went to Pilate and asked for the body of Yeshua.

53 And he took it down, wrapped it in linen, and laid it in a tomb that was hewn out of the rock, where no one had ever lain before.[82]

54 And that day was the Preparation, and the Sabbath drew near.

---

77 Psalm 22:18 (22:19 in some versions)
78 Psalm 69:21 (69:22 in some versions)
79 Noon.

80 3 p.m.
81 Psalm 31:5 (31:6 in some versions)
82 Isaiah 53:9

55 And the women who came with Him from Galilee followed after, and they observed the tomb and how His body was laid.

56 And they returned and prepared spices and fragrant oils, and rested on the Sabbath according to the commandment.

He Is Risen

24 Now on the first day of the week, very early in the morning, they, and certain other women with them, came to the tomb bringing the spices which they had prepared.

2 And they found the stone rolled away from the tomb.

3 And they went in and did not find the body of the Lord Yeshua.

4 And it came to pass, as they were greatly perplexed about this, behold, two men stood by them in shining garments.

5 And as they were afraid and bowed their faces to the earth, they said to them, "Why do you seek the living among the dead?

6 "He is not here, but is risen! Remember how He spoke to you when He was still in Galilee,

7 "saying, 'The Son of Man must be delivered into the hands of sinful men, and be crucified, and the third day rise again.' "[83]

8 And they remembered His words.

9 And they returned from the tomb and told all these things to the eleven and to all the rest.

10 It was Miriam of Magdala, Joanna, Miriam the mother of James, and the other women who were with them who told these things to the apostles.

11 And their words seemed to them like idle tales, and they did not believe them.

12 But Peter arose and ran to the tomb; and stooping down, he saw the linen cloths lying by themselves; and he departed, marveling to himself at what had happened.

The Road to Emmaus

13 And behold, two of them went that same day to a village called Emmaus, which was about seven miles from Jerusalem.

14 And they talked together of all these things which had happened.

15 And so it was, while they conversed together and reasoned, that Yeshua Himself drew near and went with them.

16 But their eyes were restrained, so that they did not know Him.

17 And He said to them, "What manner of conversation is this that you have with one another as you walk and are sad?"

18 And the one whose name was Cleopas answered and said to Him, "Are You the only stranger in Jerusalem, and have You not known the things which have happened there in these days?"

19 And He said to them, "What things?" And they said to Him, "Concerning Yeshua of Nazareth, who was a Prophet mighty in deed and word before God and all the people,

20 "and how the chief priests and our rulers delivered Him to be condemned to death, and have crucified Him.

83 Psalm 16:10 (cf. Isaiah 53:9, 10)

21 "But we were hoping that it was He who was going to redeem Israel. And besides all this, today is the third day since these things happened.

22 "Yes, and certain women of our company, who were at the tomb early, astonished us.

23 "And when they did not find His body, they came saying that they had also seen a vision of angels who said He was alive.

24 "And certain of those who were with us went to the tomb and found it just as the women had said; but Him they did not see."

25 Then He said to them, "O foolish ones, and slow of heart to believe all that the prophets have spoken!

26 "Ought not the Messiah to have suffered these things and to enter into His glory?" [84]

27 And beginning at Moses and all the Prophets, He expounded to them in all the Scriptures the things concerning Himself.

The Disciples' Eyes Opened

28 And they drew near to the village where they were going, and He indicated that He would have gone farther.

29 But they constrained Him, saying, "Abide with us, for it is toward evening, and the day is far spent." And He went in to stay with them.

30 And it came to pass, as He sat at the table with them, that He took bread, blessed and broke it, and gave it to them.

31 And their eyes were opened and they knew Him; and He vanished from their sight.

32 And they said to one another, "Did not our heart burn within us while He talked with us on the road, and while He opened the Scriptures to us?"

33 And they rose up the same hour and returned to Jerusalem, and found the eleven and those who were with them gathered together,

34 saying, "The Lord is risen indeed, and has appeared to Simon!"

35 And they told about the things that had happened on the road, and how He was known to them in the breaking of bread.

Yeshua Appears to His Disciples

36 And as they said these things, Yeshua Himself stood in the midst of them, and said to them, "Peace be with you."

37 But they were terrified and frightened, and supposed they had seen a spirit.

38 And He said to them, "Why are you troubled? And why do doubts arise in your hearts?

39 "Behold My hands and My feet, that it is I Myself. Handle Me and see, for a spirit does not have flesh and bones as you see I have."

40 And when He had said this, He showed them His hands and His feet.

41 But while they still did not believe for joy, and marveled, He said to them, "Have you any food here?"

42 And they gave Him a piece of a broiled fish and some honeycomb.

43 And He took it and ate in their presence.

84 Cf. Isaiah 53:10

The Scriptures Opened

44 And He said to them, "These are the words which I spoke to you while I was still with you, that all things must be fulfilled which were written in the Torah of Moses and the Prophets and the Psalms concerning Me."

45 Then He opened their understanding, that they might understand the Scriptures.

46 And He said to them, "Thus it is written, and thus it was necessary for the Messiah to suffer and to rise from the dead the third day,[85]

47 "and that repentance and remission of sins should be preached in His name to all nations, beginning at Jerusalem.

48 "And you are witnesses of these things.

49 "And behold, I send the Promise of My Father upon you;[86] but tarry in the city of Jerusalem until you are endued with power from on high."

The Ascension

50 And He led them out as far as Bethany, and He lifted up His hands and blessed them.

51 And it came to pass, while He blessed them, that He was parted from them and carried up into heaven.

52 And they worshiped Him, and returned to Jerusalem with great joy,

53 and were continually in the temple praising and blessing God. Amen.

85 Isaiah 52:13—53:12

86 Ezekiel 36:27

The Good News According To

JOHN

The Eternal Word

IN the beginning was the Word, and the Word was with God, and the Word was God.

2 He was in the beginning with God.

3 All things were made by Him, and without Him nothing was made that was made.

4 In Him was life, and the life was the light of men.

5 And the light shines in the darkness, and the darkness did not comprehend it.

John's Witness: The True Light

6 There was a man sent from God, whose name was John.

7 This man came for a witness, to bear witness of the Light, that all through him might believe.

8 He was not that Light, but was sent to bear witness of that Light.

9 That was the true Light which gives light to every man who comes into the world.

10 He was in the world, and the world was made by Him, and the world did not know Him.

11 He came to His own, and His own did not receive Him.

12 But as many as received Him, to them He gave the right to become children of God, even to those who believe in His name:

13 who were born, not of blood, nor of the will of the flesh, nor of the will of man, but of God.

The Word Becomes Flesh

14 And the Word became flesh and dwelt among us, and we beheld His glory, the glory as of the only begotten of the Father, full of grace and truth.

15 John bore witness of Him and cried out, saying, "This was He of whom I said, 'He who comes after me is preferred before me, for He was before me.' "

16 And of His fullness we have all received, and grace for grace.

17 For the law was given by Moses, but grace and truth came by Yeshua ha Mashiach.

18 No one has seen God at any time. The only begotten Son, who is in the bosom of the Father, He has declared Him.

A Voice in the Wilderness

19 And this is the testimony of John, when the Judeans[1] sent priests and Levites from Jerusalem to ask him, "Who are you?"

1 In John, "Judeans" may refer to the temple authorities, the political leadership of the Pharisees, or some other expression of the authority structure of Judea at that time.

20 And he confessed, and did not deny, but confessed, "I am not the Messiah."

21 And they asked him, "What then? Are you Elijah?" [2] And he said, "I am not." "Are you the Prophet?" And he answered, "No."

22 Then they said to him, "Who are you, that we may give an answer to those who sent us? What do you say about yourself?"

23 He said:

"I am the voice of one crying in the wilderness:

'Make straight the way of the LORD,'[3]

as the prophet Isaiah said."

24 And those who were sent were from the Pharisees.

25 And they asked him, saying, "Why then do you immerse if you are not the Messiah, nor Elijah, nor the Prophet?"[4]

26 John answered them, saying, "I immerse in water, but there stands One among you whom you do not know.

27 "It is He who, coming after me, is preferred before me, whose sandal strap I am not worthy to loose."

28 These things were done in Bethabara beyond the Jordan, where John was immersing.

The Lamb of God

29 The next day John saw Yeshua coming toward him, and said, "Behold! The Lamb of God who takes away the sin of the world![5]

30 "This is He of whom I said, 'After me comes a Man who is preferred before me, for He was before me.'

31 "And I did not know Him; but that He should be revealed to Israel, therefore I came immersing in water."

32 And John bore witness, saying, "I saw the Spirit descending from heaven like a dove, and He remained upon Him.

33 "And I did not know Him, but He who sent me to immerse in water said to me, 'Upon whom you see the Spirit descending, and remaining on Him, this is He who immerses in the Holy Spirit.'

34 "And I have seen and testified that this is the Son of God."

The First Disciples

35 Again, the next day John stood with two of his disciples.

36 And looking at Yeshua as He walked, he said, "Behold the Lamb of God!"

37 And the two disciples heard him speak, and they followed Yeshua.

38 Then Yeshua turned, and seeing them following, said to them, "What do you seek?" They said to Him, "Rabbi" (which is to say, when translated,

---

2 See Malachi 4:5 (3:23 in some versions). Elijah was to announce the coming of Messiah.

3 Isaiah 40:3   4 Deuteronomy 18:15–18

5 Yeshua's forthcoming sacrificial death fulfills the Messianic meaning of Passover (see Exodus 12). As God gave Israel deliverance from physical death, so He now gives deliverance from spiritual death. The phrase John uses is taken from temple passover liturgy.

Teacher), "where are You staying?"

39 He said to them, "Come and see." They came and saw where He was staying, and remained with Him that day; for it was about the tenth hour.[6]

40 One of the two who heard John speak, and followed Him, was Andrew, Simon Peter's brother.

41 He first found his own brother Simon, and said to him, "We have found the Messiah" (which is translated, the Anointed).

42 And he brought him to Yeshua. And when Yeshua looked at him, He said, "You are Simon the son of Jonah. You shall be called Cephas" (which is translated, A Stone).

Philip and Nathanael

43 The following day Yeshua wanted to go to Galilee, and He found Philip and said to him, "Follow Me."

44 Now Philip was from Bethsaida, the city of Andrew and Peter.

45 Philip found Nathanael and said to him, "We have found Him of whom Moses in the Torah, and also the prophets, wrote—Yeshua of Nazareth, the son of Joseph."

46 And Nathanael said to him, "Can anything good come out of Nazareth?" Philip said to him, "Come and see."

47 Yeshua saw Nathanael coming toward Him, and said of him, "Behold, an Israelite indeed, in whom is no guile!"

48 Nathanael said to Him, "How do You know me?" Ye-shua answered and said to him, "Before Philip called you, when you were under the fig tree, I saw you."

49 Nathanael answered and said to Him, "Rabbi, You are the Son of God! You are the King of Israel!"

50 Yeshua answered and said to him, "Because I said to you, 'I saw you under the fig tree,' do you believe? You will see greater things than these."

51 And He said to him, "Most assuredly, I say to you, hereafter you will see heaven open, and the angels of God ascending and descending upon the Son of Man." [7]

Water Turned to Wine

2 And the third day there was a wedding in Cana of Galilee, and the mother of Yeshua was there.

2 And both Yeshua and His disciples were invited to the wedding.

3 And when they ran out of wine, the mother of Yeshua said to Him, "They have no wine."

4 Yeshua said to her, "Woman, what does your concern have to do with Me? My hour has not yet come."

5 His mother said to the servants, "Whatever He says to you, do it."

6 And there were set there six waterpots of stone, according to the manner of purification of the Jews, containing twenty or thirty gallons apiece.

7 Yeshua said to them, "Fill the waterpots with water." And they filled them up to the brim.

---

6 4 p.m.

7 A title of Messiah (Daniel 7:13, 14).

8 And He said to them, "Draw some out now, and take it to the master of the feast." And they took it.

9 When the master of the feast had tasted the water that was made wine, and did not know where it came from (but the servants who drew the water knew), the master of the feast called the bridegroom.

10 And he said to him, "Every man at the beginning sets out the good wine, and when men have well drunk, then that which is inferior; but you have kept the good wine until now."

11 This beginning of signs Yeshua did in Cana of Galilee, and manifested His glory; and His disciples believed in Him.

12 After this He went down to Capernaum, He, His mother, His brothers, and His disciples; and they did not stay there many days.

Yeshua Cleanses the Temple

13 And the Passover of the Jews was at hand, and Yeshua went up to Jerusalem.

14 And He found in the temple those who sold oxen and sheep and doves, and the moneychangers doing business.

15 And when He had made a whip of cords, He drove them all out of the temple, with the sheep and the oxen, and poured out the changers' money and overturned the tables.

16 And He said to those who sold doves, "Take these things away! Do not make My Father's house a house of merchandise!"

17 And His disciples remembered that it was written, "Zeal for Your house has eaten Me up."[8]

18 Then the Judeans answered and said to Him, "What sign do You show to us, seeing that You do these things?"

19 Yeshua answered and said to them, "Destroy this temple, and in three days I will raise it up."

20 Then the Judeans said, "It has taken forty-six years to build this temple, and will You raise it up in three days?"

21 But He was speaking of the temple of His body.

22 Therefore, when He had risen from the dead, His disciples remembered that He had said this to them; and they believed the Scripture[9] and the word which Yeshua had said.

The Discerner of Hearts

23 Now when He was in Jerusalem at the Passover, during the feast, many believed in His name when they saw the signs which He did.

24 But Yeshua did not commit Himself to them, because He knew all men,

25 and did not need that anyone should testify of man, for He knew what was in man.

The New Birth

3 There was a man of the Pharisees named Nicodemus, a ruler of the Judeans.

2 This man came to Yeshua by night and said to Him, "Rabbi, we know that You are a teacher come

8 Psalm 69:9 (69:10 in some versions)
9 Psalm 16:10

from God; for no one can do these signs that You do unless God is with him."

3 Yeshua answered and said to him, "Most assuredly, I say to you, unless one is born again, he cannot see the kingdom of God."

4 Nicodemus said to Him, "How can a man be born when he is old? Can he enter a second time into his mother's womb and be born?"

5 Yeshua answered, "Most assuredly, I say to you, unless one is born of water and the Spirit, he cannot enter the kingdom of God.[10]

6 "That which is born of the flesh is flesh, and that which is born of the Spirit is spirit.

7 "Do not marvel that I said to you, 'You must be born again.'

8 "The wind blows where it wishes, and you hear the sound of it, but cannot tell where it comes from and where it goes. So is everyone who is born of the Spirit."

9 Nicodemus answered and said to Him, "How can these things be?"

10 Yeshua answered and said to him, "Are you the teacher of Israel, and do not know these things?

11 "Most assuredly, I say to you, We speak what We know and testify what We have seen, and you do not receive Our witness.

12 "If I have told you earthly things and you do not believe, how will you believe if I tell you heavenly things?

13 "And no one has ascended to heaven but He who came down from heaven, even the Son of Man who is in heaven.

14 "And as Moses lifted up the serpent in the wilderness, even so must the Son of Man be lifted up,[11]

15 "that whoever believes in Him should not perish but have eternal life.

16 "For God so loved the world that He gave His only begotten Son, that whoever believes in Him should not perish but have everlasting life.

17 "For God did not send His Son into the world to condemn the world, but that the world through Him might be saved.

18 "He who believes in Him is not condemned; but he who does not believe is condemned already, because he has not believed in the name of the only begotten Son of God.

19 "And this is the condemnation, that light has come into the world, and men loved darkness rather than light, because their deeds were evil.

20 "For everyone who does evil hates the light and does not come to the light, lest his deeds should be exposed.

21 "But he who does the truth comes to the light, that his deeds may be clearly seen, that they are done in God."

He Must Increase. . .I Must Decrease

22 After these things Yeshua and His disciples came into the land of Judea, and there He remained with them and immersed.

23 And John also was immersing

10 Ezekiel 36:25–27

11 Numbers 21:9

in Aenon near Salim, because there was much water there. And they came and were immersed.

24 For John had not yet been thrown into prison.

25 Then there arose a dispute between some of John's disciples and the Judeans about purification.

26 And they came to John and said to him, "Rabbi, He who was with you beyond the Jordan, to whom you bore witness—behold, He is immersing, and all are coming to Him!"

27 John answered and said, "A man can receive nothing unless it has been given to him from heaven.

28 "You yourselves bear me witness, that I said, 'I am not the Messiah,' but, 'I have been sent before Him.'

29 "He who has the bride is the bridegroom; but the friend of the bridegroom, who stands and hears him, rejoices greatly because of the bridegroom's voice. Therefore this joy of mine is fulfilled.

30 "He must increase, but I must decrease.

31 "He who comes from above is above all; he who is of the earth is earthly and speaks of the earth. He who comes from heaven is above all.

32 "And what He has seen and heard, that He testifies; and no one receives His testimony.

33 "He who has received His testimony has certified that God is true.

34 "For He whom God has sent speaks the words of God,[12] for God does not give the Spirit by measure.

35 "The Father loves the Son, and has given all things into His hand.

36 "He who believes in the Son has everlasting life; and he who does not believe the Son will not see life, but the wrath of God abides on him."

A Samaritan Woman Meets Her Messiah

4 Therefore, when the Lord knew that the Pharisees had heard that Yeshua made and immersed more disciples than John

2 (though Yeshua Himself did not immerse, but His disciples),

3 He left Judea and departed again to Galilee.

4 But He needed to go through Samaria.

5 So He came to a city of Samaria which is called Sychar, near the plot of ground that Jacob gave to his son Joseph.

6 Now Jacob's well was there. Yeshua therefore, being wearied from His journey, sat thus by the well. It was about the sixth hour.[13]

7 A woman of Samaria came to draw water. Yeshua said to her, "Give Me a drink."

8 For His disciples had gone away into the city to buy food.

9 Then the woman of Samaria said to Him, "How is it that You, being a Jew, ask a drink from me, a Samaritan woman?" For Jews have no dealings with Samaritans.

10 Yeshua answered and said to her, "If you knew the gift of God, and who it is who says to you,

12 Deuteronomy 18:18

13 Noon.

'Give Me a drink,' you would have asked Him, and He would have given you living water."

11 The woman said to Him, "Sir, You have nothing to draw with, and the well is deep. Where then do You get that living water?

12 "Are You greater than our father Jacob, who gave us the well, and drank from it himself, as well as his sons and his livestock?"

13 Yeshua answered and said to her, "Whoever drinks of this water will thirst again,

14 "but whoever drinks of the water that I shall give him will never thirst. But the water that I shall give him will become in him a well of water springing up into everlasting life." [14]

15 The woman said to Him, "Sir, give me this water, that I may not thirst, nor come here to draw."

16 Yeshua said to her, "Go, call your husband, and come here."

17 The woman answered and said, "I have no husband." Yeshua said to her, "You have well said, 'I have no husband,'

18 "for you have had five husbands, and the one whom you now have is not your husband; in that you spoke truly."

19 The woman said to Him, "Sir, I perceive that You are a prophet.

20 "Our fathers worshiped on this mountain, and you say that in Jerusalem is the place where one ought to worship."

21 Yeshua said to her, "Woman, believe Me, the hour is coming when you will neither on this mountain, nor in Jerusalem, worship the Father.

22 "You worship what you do not know; we know what we worship, for salvation is of the Jews.

23 "But the hour is coming, and now is, when the true worshipers will worship the Father in spirit and truth; for the Father is seeking such to worship Him.

24 "God is Spirit, and those who worship Him must worship Him in spirit and truth."

25 The woman said to Him, "I know that the Messiah is coming" (who is called Anointed). "When He comes, He will tell us all things."

26 Yeshua said to her, "I who speak to you am He."

The Whitened Harvest

27 And at this point His disciples came, and they marveled that He talked with a woman; yet no one said, "What do You seek?" or, "Why are You talking with her?"

28 The woman then left her waterpot, went her way into the city, and said to the men,

29 "Come, see a Man who told me all things that I ever did. Could this be the Messiah?"

30 Then they went out of the city and came to Him.

31 In the meantime His disciples urged Him, saying, "Rabbi, eat."

32 But He said to them, "I have food to eat of which you do not know."

33 Therefore the disciples said to one another, "Has anyone brought Him anything to eat?"

34 Yeshua said to them, "My food is to do the will of Him who sent Me, and to finish His work.

14 Isaiah 12:2, 3; Jeremiah 2:13

35 "Do you not say, 'There are still four months and then comes the harvest'? Behold, I say to you, lift up your eyes and look at the fields, for they are already white for harvest!

36 "And he who reaps receives wages, and gathers fruit for eternal life, that both he who sows and he who reaps may rejoice together.

37 "For in this the saying is true: 'One sows and another reaps.'

38 "I sent you to reap that for which you have not labored; other men have labored, and you have entered into their labors."

The Messiah Is the Savior of the World

39 And many of the Samaritans of that city believed in Him because of the word of the woman who testified, "He told me all that I ever did."

40 So when the Samaritans had come to Him, they urged Him to stay with them; and He stayed there two days.

41 And many more believed because of His own word.

42 And they said to the woman, "Now we believe, not because of what you said, for we have heard for ourselves and know that this is indeed the Messiah, the Savior of the world."

Welcome at Galilee

43 Now after the two days He departed from there and went to Galilee.

44 For Yeshua Himself testified that a prophet has no honor in his own country.

45 Then, when He came to Galilee, the Galileans received Him, having seen all the things He did in Jerusalem at the feast; for they also had gone to the feast.

A Nobleman's Son Healed

46 So Yeshua came again to Cana of Galilee where He had made the water wine. And there was a certain nobleman whose son was sick at Capernaum.

47 When he heard that Yeshua had come out of Judea into Galilee, he went to Him and begged Him to come down and heal his son, for he was at the point of death.

48 Then Yeshua said to him, "Unless you see signs and wonders, you will by no means believe."

49 The nobleman said to Him, "Sir, come down before my child dies!"

50 Yeshua said to him, "Go your way; your son lives." And the man believed the word that Yeshua spoke to him, and he went his way.

51 And as he was now going down, his servants met him and told him, saying, "Your son lives!"

52 Then he inquired of them the hour when he got better. And they said to him, "Yesterday at the seventh hour the fever left him."

53 So the father knew that it was at the same hour in which Yeshua said to him, "Your son lives." And he himself believed, and his whole household.

54 This again is the second sign that Yeshua did when He had come out of Judea into Galilee.

A Man Healed at the Pool of Bethesda

5 After this there was a feast of the Jews, and Yeshua went up to Jerusalem.

2 Now there is in Jerusalem by the Sheep Gate a pool, which is called in Hebrew, *Bethesda,* having five porches.

3 In these lay a great multitude of sick people, blind, lame, paralyzed, waiting for the moving of the water.

4 For an angel went down at a certain time into the pool and stirred up the water; then whoever stepped in first, after the stirring of the water, was made well of whatever disease he had.

5 And a certain man was there who had an infirmity thirty-eight years.

6 When Yeshua saw him lying there, and knew that he already had been in that condition a long time, He said to him, "Do you want to be made well?"

7 The sick man answered Him, "Sir, I have no man to put me into the pool when the water is stirred up; but while I am coming, another steps down before me."

8 Yeshua said to him, "Rise, take up your bed and walk."

9 And immediately the man was made well, took up his bed, and walked. And that day was the Sabbath.

10 The Judeans therefore said to him who was cured, "It is the Sabbath; it is not lawful for you to carry your bed."

11 He answered them, "He who made me well said to me, 'Take up your bed and walk.' "

12 Then they asked him, "Who is the Man who said to you, 'Take up your bed and walk?' "

13 And the one who was healed did not know who it was, for Yeshua had withdrawn, a multitude being in that place.

14 Afterward Yeshua found him in the temple, and said to him, "See, you have been made well. Sin no more, lest a worse thing come upon you."

15 The man departed and told the Judeans that it was Yeshua who had made him well.

16 And therefore the Judeans persecuted Yeshua, and sought to kill Him, because He had done these things on the Sabbath.

17 But Yeshua answered them, "My Father has been working until now, and I have been working."

18 Therefore the Judeans sought all the more to kill Him, because He not only broke the Sabbath, but also said that God was His Father, making Himself equal with God.[15]

19 Then Yeshua answered and said to them, "Most assuredly, I say to you, the Son can do nothing of Himself, but what He sees the Father do; for whatever He does, the Son also does in like manner.

20 "For the Father loves the Son, and shows Him all things that He Himself does; and He will show Him greater works than these, that you may marvel.

21 "For as the Father raises the dead and gives life to them, even so the Son gives life to whom He will.

22 "For the Father judges no one, but has committed all judgment to the Son,

15 Psalm 2:7-9; Proverbs 30:4

23 "that all should honor the Son just as they honor the Father. He who does not honor the Son does not honor the Father who sent Him.

24 "Most assuredly, I say to you, he who hears My word and believes in Him who sent Me has everlasting life, and shall not come into judgment, but has passed from death into life.

25 "Most assuredly, I say to you, the hour is coming, and now is, when the dead will hear the voice of the Son of God; and those who hear will live.

26 "For as the Father has life in Himself, so He has given to the Son to have life in Himself,

27 "and has given Him authority to execute judgment also, because He is the Son of Man.

28 "Do not marvel at this; for the hour is coming in which all who are in the graves will hear His voice

29 "and come forth—those who have done good, to the resurrection of life, and those who have done evil, to the resurrection of condemnation.[16]

30 "I can of Myself do nothing. As I hear, I judge; and My judgment is righteous, because I do not seek My own will but the will of the Father who sent Me.

31 "If I bear witness of Myself, My witness is not true.

32 "There is another who bears witness of Me, and I know that the witness which He witnesses of Me is true.

33 "You sent to John, and he bore witness to the truth.

34 "Yet I do not receive testimony from man, but I say these things that you may be saved.

35 "He was the burning and shining lamp, and you were willing for a time to rejoice in his light.

36 "But I have a greater witness than John's; for the works which the Father has given Me to finish—the very works that I do—bear witness of Me, that the Father has sent Me.

37 "And the Father Himself, who sent Me, has testified of Me. You have neither heard His voice at any time, nor seen His form.

38 "And you do not have His word abiding in you, because whom He sent, Him you do not believe.

39 "You search the Scriptures, for in them you think you have eternal life; and these are they which testify of Me.

40 "And you are not willing to come to Me that you may have life.

41 "I do not receive honor from men.

42 "But I know you, that you do not have the love of God in you.

43 "I have come in My Father's name, and you do not receive Me; if another comes in his own name, him you will receive.

44 "How can you believe, who receive honor from one another, and do not seek the honor that comes from the only God?

45 "Do not think that I shall accuse you to the Father; there is one who accuses you—Moses, in whom you trust.

46 "For if you believed Moses, you would believe Me; for he wrote about Me.

16 Daniel 12:2

47 "But if you do not believe his writings, how will you believe My words?"

Feeding the Five Thousand

6 After these things Yeshua went over the Sea of Galilee, which is the Sea of Tiberias.

2 And a great multitude followed Him, because they saw His signs which He performed on those who were diseased.

3 And Yeshua went up on a mountain, and there He sat with His disciples.

4 And the Passover, a feast of the Jews, was near.

5 Then Yeshua lifted up His eyes, and seeing a great multitude coming toward Him, He said to Philip, "Where shall we buy bread, that these may eat?"

6 And this He said to test him, for He Himself knew what He would do.

7 Philip answered Him, "Two hundred denarii worth of bread is not sufficient for them, that every one of them may get a little."

8 One of His disciples, Andrew, Simon Peter's brother, said to Him,

9 "There is a lad here who has five barley loaves and two small fish, but what are they among so many?"

10 And Yeshua said, "Make the people sit down." Now there was much grass in the place. So the men sat down, in number about five thousand.

11 And Yeshua took the loaves, and when He had given thanks He distributed them to the disciples, and the disciples to those sitting down; and likewise of the fish, as much as they wanted.

12 And when they were filled, He said to His disciples, "Gather up the fragments that remain, so that nothing is lost."

13 Therefore they gathered them up, and filled twelve baskets with the fragments of the five barley loaves which were left over by those who had eaten.

14 Then those men, when they had seen the sign that Yeshua did, said, "This is truly the Prophet who is to come into the world." 17

Yeshua Walks on the Sea

15 Therefore when Yeshua perceived that they were about to come and take Him by force to make Him king, He departed again to a mountain by Himself alone.

16 And when evening came, His disciples went down to the sea,

17 got into the boat, and went over the sea toward Capernaum. And it was now dark, and Yeshua had not come to them.

18 And the sea arose because a great wind was blowing.

19 So when they had rowed about three or four miles, they saw Yeshua walking on the sea and drawing near the boat; and they were afraid.

20 But He said to them, "It is I; do not be afraid."

21 Then they willingly received Him into the boat, and immediately the boat was at the land where they were going.

The Bread from Heaven

22 The following day, when the people who stood on the other side

17 Deuteronomy 18:15–18

of the sea saw that there was no other boat there, except that one which His disciples had entered, and that Yeshua had not entered the boat with His disciples, but His disciples had gone away alone—

23 however, other boats came from Tiberias, near the place where they ate bread after the Lord had given thanks—

24 when the people therefore saw that Yeshua was not there, nor His disciples, they also got into boats and came to Capernaum, seeking Yeshua.

25 And when they had found Him on the other side of the sea, they said to Him, "Rabbi, when did You come here?"

26 Yeshua answered them and said, "Most assuredly, I say to you, you seek Me, not because you saw the signs, but because you ate of the loaves and were filled.

27 "Do not labor for the food which perishes, but for the food which endures to everlasting life, which the Son of Man will give you, because God the Father has set His seal on Him."

28 Then they said to Him, "What shall we do, that we may work the works of God?"

29 Yeshua answered and said to them, "This is the work of God, that you believe in Him whom He sent."

30 Therefore they said to Him, "What sign will You perform then, that we may see it and believe You? What work will You do?

31 "Our fathers ate the manna in the desert; as it is written, 'He gave them bread from heaven to eat.'" [18]

32 Then Yeshua said to them, "Most assuredly, I say to you, Moses did not give you the bread from heaven, but My Father gives you the true bread from heaven.

33 "For the bread of God is He who comes down from heaven and gives life to the world."

34 Then they said to Him, "Lord, always give us this bread."

35 And Yeshua said to them, "I am the bread of life. He who comes to Me shall never hunger, and he who believes in Me shall never thirst.

36 "But I said to you that you also have seen Me and do not believe.

37 "All that the Father gives Me will come to Me, and the one who comes to Me I will by no means cast out.

38 "For I came down from heaven, not to do My own will, but the will of Him who sent Me.

39 "And this is the will of the Father who sent Me, that of all He has given Me I should lose nothing, but should raise it up at the last day.

40 "And this is the will of Him who sent Me, that everyone who sees the Son and believes in Him may have everlasting life; and I will raise him up at the last day."

Despised and Rejected by Men [19]

41 The Judeans then murmured against Him, because He said, "I am the bread which came down from heaven."

18 Exodus 16:4; Nehemiah 9:15; Psalm 78:24   19 Isaiah 53:3

42 And they said, "Is not this Yeshua, the son of Joseph, whose father and mother we know? How is it then that He says, 'I came down from heaven'?"

43 Yeshua therefore answered and said to them, "Do not murmur among yourselves.

44 "No one can come to Me unless the Father who sent Me draws him; and I will raise him up at the last day.

45 "It is written in the prophets, *'And they will all be taught by God.'*[20] Therefore everyone who has heard and learned from the Father comes to Me.

46 "Not that anyone has seen the Father, except He who is from God; He has seen the Father.

47 "Most assuredly, I say to you, he who believes in Me has everlasting life.

48 "I am the bread of life.

49 "Your fathers ate the manna in the wilderness, and are dead.

50 "This is the bread which comes down from heaven, that a man may eat of it and not die.

51 "I am the living bread which came down from heaven. If anyone eats of this bread, he will live forever; and the bread that I shall give is My flesh, which I shall give for the life of the world."

52 The Judeans therefore quarreled among themselves, saying, "How can this Man give us His flesh to eat?"

53 Then Yeshua said to them, "Most assuredly, I say to you, unless you eat the flesh of the Son of Man and drink His blood, you have no life in you.

54 "Whoever eats My flesh and drinks My blood has eternal life, and I will raise him up at the last day.

55 "For My flesh is food indeed, and My blood is drink indeed.

56 "He who eats My flesh and drinks My blood dwells in Me, and I in him.

57 "As the living Father sent Me, and I live because of the Father, so he who feeds on Me will live because of Me.

58 "This is the bread which came down from heaven, not as your fathers ate the manna, and are dead. He who eats this bread will live forever."

59 These things He said in the synagogue as He taught in Capernaum.

60 Therefore many of His disciples, when they heard this, said, "This is a hard saying; who can understand it?"

61 When Yeshua knew in Himself that His disciples murmured about this, He said to them, "Does this offend you?

62 "What then if you should see the Son of Man ascend where He was before?

63 "It is the Spirit who gives life; the flesh profits nothing. The words that I speak to you are spirit, and they are life.

64 "But there are some of you who do not believe." For Yeshua knew from the beginning who they were who did not believe, and who would betray Him.

65 And He said, "Therefore I said to you that no one can come to Me unless it has been given to him from My Father."

66 From that time many of His

20 Isaiah 54:13

disciples went back and walked with Him no more.

67 Then Yeshua said to the twelve, "Do you also want to go away?"

68 Then Simon Peter answered Him, "Lord, to whom shall we go? You have the words of eternal life."

69 "And we believe and are sure that You are the Messiah, the Son of the living God."

70 Yeshua answered them, "Have I not chosen you, the twelve, and one of you is a devil?"

71 He spoke of Judas Iscariot, the son of Simon, for it was he who would betray Him, being one of the twelve.

The Brothers of Yeshua Disbelieve

7 After these things Yeshua walked in Galilee; for He did not want to walk in Judea, because the Judeans sought to kill Him.

2 Now the Jewish Feast of Sukkot was at hand.

3 His brothers therefore said to Him, "Depart from here and go into Judea, that Your disciples also may see the works that You are doing.

4 "For no one does anything in secret while he himself seeks to be known openly. If You do these things, show Yourself to the world."

5 For not even His brothers believed in Him.

6 Then Yeshua said to them, "My time has not yet come, but your time is always ready.

7 "The world cannot hate you, but it hates Me because I testify of it that its works are evil.

8 "You go up to this feast. I am not yet going up to this feast, for My time has not yet fully come."

9 When He had said these words to them, He remained in Galilee.

The Heavenly Sage

10 But when His brothers had gone up, then He also went up to the feast, not openly, but as it were in secret.

11 Then the Judeans sought Him at the feast, and said, "Where is He?"

12 And there was much murmuring among the people concerning Him, for some said, "He is a good Man"; others said, "No, on the contrary, He deceives the people."

13 However, no one spoke openly of Him for fear of the Judeans.

14 Now about the middle of the feast Yeshua went up into the temple and taught.

15 And the Judeans marveled, saying, "How does this Man know letters, never having studied?"

16 Yeshua answered them and said, "My doctrine is not Mine, but His who sent Me.

17 "If anyone wants to do His will, he shall know concerning the doctrine, whether it is from God or whether I speak of Myself.

18 "He who speaks from himself seeks his own glory; but He who seeks the glory of the One who sent Him is true, and no unrighteousness is in Him.

19 "Did not Moses give you the Torah, and yet none of you keeps the Torah? Why do you seek to kill Me?"

20 The people answered and

said, "You have a demon. Who is seeking to kill You?"

21 Yeshua answered and said to them, "I have done one work, and you all marvel.

22 "Moses therefore gave you circumcision (not that it is from Moses, but from the fathers), and you circumcise a man on the Sabbath.

23 "If a man receives circumcision on the Sabbath, that the Torah of Moses should not be broken, are you angry with Me because I have made a man completely well on the Sabbath?

24 "Do not judge according to appearance, but judge with righteous judgment."

Could This Be the Messiah?

25 Then some of them from Jerusalem said, "Is this not He whom they seek to kill?

26 "But look! He speaks boldly, and they say nothing to Him. Do the rulers know indeed that this is truly the Messiah?

27 "However, we know where this Man is from; but when the Messiah comes, no one knows where He is from."

28 Then Yeshua cried out, as He taught in the temple, saying, "You both know Me, and you know where I am from; and I have not come of Myself, but He who sent Me is true, whom you do not know.

29 "But I know Him, for I am from Him, and He has sent Me."

30 Then they sought to take Him; but no one laid hands on Him, because His hour had not yet come.

31 And many of the people believed in Him, and said, "When the Messiah comes, will He do more signs than these which this Man has done?"

Yeshua and the Religious Leaders

32 The Pharisees heard that the people murmured such things concerning Him, and the Pharisees and the chief priests sent officers to take Him.

33 Then Yeshua said to them, "I shall be with you a little while longer, and then I go to Him who sent Me.

34 "You will seek Me and not find Me, and where I am you cannot come."

35 Then the Judeans said among themselves, "Where does He intend to go that we shall not find Him? Does He intend to go to the Dispersion among the Greeks and teach the Greeks?

36 "What is this thing that He said, 'You will seek Me and not find Me, and where I am you cannot come'?"

The Promise of the Holy Spirit

37 On the last day, that great day of the feast,[21] Yeshua stood and cried out, saying, "If anyone thirsts, let him come to Me and drink.

38 "He who believes in Me, as the Scripture has said, out of his heart will flow rivers of living water." [22]

39 But this He spoke concerning the Spirit, whom those who believe in Him would receive; [23] for

21 Hoshanah Rabbah.
22 Isaiah 12:2, 3; Jeremiah 2:13
23 Ezekiel 36:25-27; Isaiah 44:3; Joel 2:28 (3:1 in some versions)

the Holy Spirit was not yet given, because Yeshua was not yet glorified.

Who Is He?

40 Therefore many from the crowd, when they heard this saying, said, "Truly this is the Prophet." [24]

41 Others said, "This is the Messiah," but some said, "Will the Messiah come out of Galilee?

42 "Has not the Scripture said that the Messiah comes from the seed of David and from the town of Bethlehem, where David was?" [25]

43 So there was a division among the people because of Him.

44 And some of them wanted to take Him, but no one laid hands on Him.

Rejected by the Authorities

45 Then the officers came to the chief priests and Pharisees, who said to them, "Why have you not brought Him?"

46 The officers answered, "No man ever spoke like this Man!"

47 Then the Pharisees answered them, "Are you also deceived?

48 "Have any of the rulers or the Pharisees believed in Him?

49 "But this crowd that does not know the Torah is accursed."

50 Nicodemus (he who came to Yeshua by night, being one of them) said to them,

51 "Does our Torah judge a man before it hears him and knows what he is doing?"

52 They answered and said to him, "Are you also from Galilee? Search and look, for no prophet has arisen out of Galilee."

An Adulteress Before the Light of the World

53 And everyone went to his own house.

8 But Yeshua went to the Mount of Olives.

2 And early in the morning He came again into the temple, and all the people came to Him; and He sat down and taught them.

3 And the scribes and Pharisees brought to Him a woman caught in adultery. And when they had set her in the midst,

4 they said to Him, "Rabbi, this woman was caught in adultery, in the very act.

5 "Now Moses, in the Torah, commanded us that such should be stoned. But what do You say?" [26]

6 This they said, testing Him, that they might have something of which to accuse Him. But Yeshua stooped down and wrote on the ground with His finger, as though He did not hear.

7 So when they continued asking Him, He raised Himself up and said to them, "He who is without sin among you, let him throw a stone at her first."

8 And again He stooped down and wrote on the ground.

9 And those who heard it, being convicted by their own conscience, went out one by one, beginning with the oldest even to the last. And Yeshua was left alone, and the woman standing in the midst.

24 Deuteronomy 18:15–18
25 Micah 5:2 (5:1 in some versions)
26 Deuteronomy 22:22–24

10 When Yeshua had raised Himself up and saw no one but the woman, He said to her, "Woman, where are those accusers of yours? Has no one condemned you?"

11 She said, "No one, Lord." And Yeshua said to her, "Neither do I condemn you; go and sin no more."

12 Then Yeshua spoke to them again, saying, "I am the light of the world. He who follows Me shall not walk in darkness, but have the light of life."

Yeshua Defends His Self-Witness

13 The Pharisees therefore said to Him, "You bear witness of Yourself; Your witness is not true."

14 Yeshua answered and said to them, "Even if I bear witness of Myself, My witness is true, for I know where I came from and where I am going; but you do not know where I come from and where I am going.

15 "You judge according to the flesh; I judge no one.

16 "And yet if I do judge, My judgment is true; for I am not alone, but I and the Father who sent Me.

17 "It is also written in your Torah that the testimony of two men is true.[27]

18 "I am One who bears witness of Myself, and the Father who sent Me bears witness of Me."

19 Then they said to Him, "Where is Your Father?" Yeshua answered, "You know neither Me nor My Father. If you had known Me, you would have known My Father also."

20 These words Yeshua spoke in the treasury, as He taught in the temple; and no one laid hands on Him, for His hour had not yet come.

Yeshua Predicts His Departure

21 Then Yeshua said to them again, "I am going away, and you will seek Me, and will die in your sin. Where I go you cannot come."

22 Then the Judeans said, "Will He kill Himself, because He says, 'Where I go you cannot come'?"

23 And He said to them, "You are from beneath; I am from above. You are of this world; I am not of the world.

24 "Therefore I said to you that you will die in your sins; for if you do not believe that I am He, you will die in your sins."

25 Then they said to Him, "Who are You?" And Yeshua said to them, "Just what I have been saying to you from the beginning.

26 "I have many things to say and to judge concerning you, but He who sent Me is true; and I speak to the world those things which I have heard from Him."

27 They did not understand that He spoke to them of the Father.

28 Then Yeshua said to them, "When you have lifted up the Son of Man, then you will know that I am He, and that I do nothing of Myself; but as My Father has taught Me, I speak these things.

29 "And He who sent Me is with Me. The Father has not left Me

27 Deuteronomy 19:15

alone, for I always do those things that please Him."

The Truth Shall Make You Free

30 As He spoke these words, many believed in Him.

31 Then Yeshua said to those Judeans who believed Him, "If you continue in My word, then you are My disciples indeed.

32 "And you shall know the truth, and the truth shall make you free."

33 They answered Him, "We are Abraham's descendants, and were never in bondage to anyone. How is it that you say, 'You will be made free'?"

34 Yeshua answered them, "Most assuredly, I say to you, whoever commits sin is a slave of sin.

35 "And a slave does not abide in the house forever, but a son abides forever.

36 "Therefore if the Son makes you free, you shall be free indeed.

Abraham's Seed and Satan's

37 "I know that you are Abraham's descendants, but you seek to kill Me, because My word has no place in you.

38 "I speak what I have seen with My Father, and you do what you have seen with your father."

39 They answered and said to Him, "Abraham is our father." Yeshua said to them, "If you were Abraham's children, you would do the works of Abraham.

40 "But now you seek to kill Me, a Man who has told you the truth which I have heard from God. Abraham did not do this.

41 "You do the deeds of your father." Then they said to Him, "We were not born of fornication; we have one Father—God."

42 Yeshua said to them, "If God were your Father, you would love Me, for I proceeded forth and came from God; nor did I come of Myself, but He sent Me.

43 "Why do you not understand My speech? Because you are not able to listen to My word.

44 "You are of your father the devil, and the desires of your father you want to do. He was a murderer from the beginning, and does not stand in the truth, because there is no truth in him. When he speaks a lie, he speaks from his own resources, for he is a liar and the father of it.

45 "And because I tell you the truth, you do not believe Me.

46 "Which of you convicts Me of sin? And if I tell the truth, why do you not believe Me?

47 "He who is of God hears God's words; therefore you do not hear them, because you are not of God."

Before Abraham Was, I AM

48 Then the Judeans answered and said to Him, "Do we not say rightly that You are a Samaritan and have a demon?"

49 Yeshua answered, "I do not have a demon; but I honor My Father, and you dishonor Me.

50 "And I do not seek My own glory; there is One who seeks and judges.

51 "Most assuredly, I say to you, if anyone keeps My word he shall never see death."

52 Then the Judeans said to

Him, "Now we know that You have a demon! Abraham is dead, and the prophets; and You say, 'If anyone keeps My word he shall never taste death.'

53 "Are You greater than our father Abraham, who is dead? And the prophets are dead. Whom do You make Yourself out to be?"

54 Yeshua answered, "If I honor Myself, My honor is nothing. It is My Father who honors Me, of whom you say that He is your God.

55 "Yet you have not known Him, but I know Him. And if I say, 'I do not know Him,' I shall be a liar like you; but I do know Him and keep His word.

56 "Your father Abraham rejoiced to see My day, and he saw it and was glad."

57 Then the Judeans said to Him, "You are not yet fifty years old, and have You seen Abraham?"

58 Yeshua said to them, "Most assuredly, I say to you, before Abraham was, I AM." [28]

59 Then they took up stones to throw at Him; but Yeshua hid Himself and went out of the temple, going through the midst of them, and so passed by.

A Man Born Blind Receives Sight

9 And as Yeshua passed by, He saw a man who was blind from birth.

2 And His disciples asked Him, saying, "Rabbi, who sinned, this man or his parents, that he was born blind?"

3 Yeshua answered, "Neither this man nor his parents sinned, but that the works of God should be revealed in him.

4 "I must work the works of Him who sent Me while it is day; the night is coming when no one can work.

5 "As long as I am in the world, I am the light of the world."

6 When He had said these things, He spat on the ground and made clay with the saliva; and He anointed the eyes of the blind man with the clay.

7 And He said to him, "Go, wash in the pool of Siloam" (which is translated, Sent). So he went his way and washed, and came back seeing.

8 Therefore the neighbors and those who previously had seen that he was blind said, "Is not this he who sat and begged?"

9 Some said, "This is he." Others said, "He is like him." He said, "I am he."

10 Therefore they said to him, "How were your eyes opened?"

11 He answered and said, "A Man called Yeshua made clay and anointed my eyes and said to me, 'Go to the pool of Siloam and wash.' And I went and washed, and I received sight."

12 Then they said to him, "Where is He?" He said, "I do not know."

The Pharisees Question the Healed Man

13 They brought him who formerly was blind to the Pharisees.

14 And it was a Sabbath when Yeshua made the clay and opened his eyes.

28 Cf. Exodus 3:14; Micah 5:2 (5:1 in some versions)

15 Then the Pharisees also asked him again how he had received his sight. He said to them, "He put clay on my eyes, and I washed, and I see."

16 Therefore some of the Pharisees said, "This Man is not from God, because He does not keep the Sabbath." Others said, "How can a man who is a sinner do such miracles?" And there was a division among them.

17 They said to the blind man again, "What do you say about Him because He opened your eyes?" He said, "He is a prophet."

18 But the Judeans did not believe concerning him, that he had been blind and received his sight, until they called the parents of him who had received his sight.

19 And they asked them, saying, "Is this your son, who you say was born blind? How then does he now see?"

20 His parents answered them and said, "We know that this is our son, and that he was born blind;

21 "but by what means he now sees we do not know, or who opened his eyes we do not know. He is of age; ask him. He shall speak for himself."

22 His parents spoke these words because they feared the Judeans, for the Judeans had agreed already that if anyone confessed that He was the Messiah, he would be put out of the synagogue.

23 Therefore his parents said, "He is of age; ask him."

24 Then they again called the man who was blind, and said to him, "Give God the praise! We know that this Man is a sinner."

25 He answered and said, "Whether He is a sinner or not I do not know. One thing I know: that though I was blind, now I see."

26 Then they said to him again, "What did He do to you? How did He open your eyes?"

27 He answered them, "I have told you already, and you did not listen. Why do you want to hear it again? Do you also want to become His disciples?"

28 Then they reviled him and said, "You are His disciple, but we are Moses' disciples.

29 "We know that God spoke to Moses; as for this fellow, we do not know where He is from."

30 The man answered and said to them, "Why, this is a marvelous thing, that you do not know where He is from, and yet He has opened my eyes!

31 "Now we know that God does not hear sinners; but if anyone is a worshiper of God and does His will, He hears him.

32 "Since the world began it has been unheard of that anyone opened the eyes of one who was born blind.

33 "If this Man were not from God, He could do nothing."

34 They answered and said to him, "You were completely born in sins, and are you teaching us?" And they cast him out.

True Vision and True Blindness

35 Yeshua heard that they had cast him out; and when He had found him, He said to him, "Do you believe in the Son of God?"

36 He answered and said, "Who is He, Lord, that I may believe in Him?"

37 And Yeshua said to him, "You have both seen Him and it is He who is talking with you."

38 And he said, "Lord, I believe!" And he worshiped Him.

39 And Yeshua said, "For judgment I have come into this world, that those who do not see may see, and that those who see may be made blind."

40 And some of the Pharisees who were with Him heard these words, and said to Him, "Are we blind also?"

41 Yeshua said to them, "If you were blind, you would have no sin; but now you say, 'We see.' Therefore your sin remains.

Yeshua the True Shepherd

10 "Most assuredly, I say to you, he who does not enter the sheepfold by the door, but climbs up some other way, the same is a thief and a robber.

2 "But he who enters by the door is the shepherd of the sheep.

3 "To him the doorkeeper opens, and the sheep hear his voice; and he calls his own sheep by name and leads them out.

4 "And when he brings out his own sheep, he goes before them; and the sheep follow him, for they know his voice.

5 "And a stranger they will by no means follow, but will flee from him, for they do not know the voice of strangers."

6 Yeshua used this illustration, but they did not understand the things which He spoke to them.

Yeshua the Good Shepherd

7 Then Yeshua said to them again, "Most assuredly, I say to you, I am the door of the sheep.

8 "All who ever came before Me are thieves and robbers, but the sheep did not hear them.

9 "I am the door. If anyone enters by Me, he will be saved, and will go in and out and find pasture.

10 "The thief does not come except to steal, and to kill, and to destroy. I have come that they may have life, and that they may have it more abundantly.

11 "I am the good shepherd. The good shepherd gives His life for the sheep.

12 "But he who is a hireling and not the shepherd, one who does not own the sheep, sees the wolf coming, leaves the sheep, and flees; and the wolf catches the sheep and scatters them.

13 "The hireling flees because he is a hireling and does not care about the sheep.

14 "I am the good shepherd; and I know My sheep, and am known by My own.

15 "As the Father knows Me, even so I know the Father; and I lay down My life for the sheep.

16 "And other sheep I have which are not of this fold; them also I must bring, and they will hear My voice; and there will be one flock and one shepherd.[29]

17 "Therefore My Father loves Me, because I lay down My life that I may take it again.

18 "No one takes it from Me, but I lay it down of Myself. I have power to lay it down, and I

29 Ezekiel 34:23

have power to take it again. This command I have received from My Father."

19 Therefore there was a division again among the Judeans because of these sayings.

20 And many of them said, "He has a demon and is mad. Why do you listen to Him?"

21 Others said, "These are not the words of one who has a demon. Can a demon open the eyes of the blind?"

Hanukkah in Jerusalem

22 Now it was the Feast of Hanukkah in Jerusalem, and it was winter.

23 And Yeshua walked in the temple, in Solomon's porch.

24 Then the Judeans surrounded Him and said to Him, "How long do You make us doubt? If You are the Messiah, tell us plainly."

25 Yeshua answered them, "I told you, and you do not believe. The works that I do in My Father's name, they bear witness of Me.

26 "But you do not believe, because you are not of My sheep, as I said to you.

27 "My sheep hear My voice, and I know them, and they follow Me.

28 "And I give them eternal life, and they shall never perish; neither shall anyone snatch them out of My hand.

29 "My Father, who gave them to Me, is greater than all; and no one is able to snatch them out of My Father's hand.

30 "I and My Father are one."

Renewed Efforts to Stone Yeshua

31 Then the Judeans took up stones again to stone Him.

32 Yeshua answered them, "Many good works I have shown you from My Father. For which of those works do you stone Me?"

33 The Judeans answered Him, saying, "For a good work we do not stone You, but for blasphemy, and because You, being a Man, make Yourself God."

34 Yeshua answered them, "Is it not written in your Torah, *'I said, you are gods'*? [30]

35 "If He called them gods, to whom the word of God came (and the Scripture cannot be broken),

36 "do you say of Him whom the Father sanctified and sent into the world, 'You are blaspheming,' because I said, 'I am the Son of God'?

37 "If I do not do the works of My Father, do not believe Me;

38 "but if I do, though you do not believe Me, believe the works, that you may know and believe that the Father is in Me, and I in Him."

39 Therefore they sought again to seize Him, but He escaped out of their hand.

The Believers Beyond Jordan

40 And He went away again beyond the Jordan to the place where John was immersing at first, and there He stayed.

41 And many came to Him and said, "John performed no sign, but all the things that John spoke about this Man were true."

42 And many believed in Him there.

30 Psalm 82:6

The Death of Lazarus

11 Now a certain man was sick, Lazarus of Bethany, the town of Miriam and her sister Martha.

2 It was that Miriam who anointed the Lord with fragrant oil and wiped His feet with her hair, whose brother Lazarus was sick.

3 Therefore his sisters sent to Him, saying, "Lord, behold, he whom You love is sick."

4 When Yeshua heard that, He said, "This sickness is not to death, but for the glory of God, that the Son of God may be glorified through it."

5 Now Yeshua loved Martha and her sister and Lazarus.

6 So, when He heard that he was sick, He stayed two more days in the place where He was.

7 Then after this He said to His disciples, "Let us go to Judea again."

8 His disciples said to Him, "Rabbi, lately the Judeans sought to stone You, and are You going there again?"

9 Yeshua answered, "Are there not twelve hours in the day? If anyone walks in the day, he does not stumble, because he sees the light of this world.

10 "But if one walks in the night, he stumbles, because there is no light in him."

11 These things He said, and after that He said to them, "Our friend Lazarus sleeps, but I go that I may wake him out of sleep."

12 Then His disciples said, "Lord, if he sleeps he will get well."

13 However, Yeshua spoke of his death, but they thought that He was speaking about taking rest in sleep.

14 Then Yeshua said to them plainly, "Lazarus is dead.

15 "And I am glad for your sakes that I was not there, that you may believe. Nevertheless let us go to him."

16 Then Thomas, who is called Didymus, said to his fellow disciples, "Let us also go, that we may die with Him."

I Am the Resurrection and the Life

17 Then, when Yeshua came, He found that he had already been in the tomb four days.

18 Now Bethany was near Jerusalem, about two miles away.

19 And many of the Judeans came to Martha and Miriam to comfort them concerning their brother.

20 Then Martha, as soon as she heard that Yeshua was coming, went and met Him, but Miriam was sitting in the house.

21 Then Martha said to Yeshua, "Lord, if You had been here, my brother would not have died.

22 "But I know that even now, whatever You ask of God, God will give You."

23 Yeshua said to her, "Your brother will rise again."

24 Martha said to Him, "I know that he will rise again in the resurrection at the last day." [31]

25 Yeshua said to her, "I am the resurrection and the life. He who believes in Me, though he may die, he shall live.

31 Daniel 12:2

26 "And whoever lives and believes in Me shall never die. Do you believe this?"

27 She said to Him, "Yes, Lord, I believe that You are the Messiah, the Son of God, who is to come into the world."

Yeshua and Death, the Last Enemy

28 And when she had said these things, she went her way and called Miriam her sister secretly, saying, "The Rabbi has come and is calling for you."

29 As soon as she heard that, she arose quickly and came to Him.

30 Now Yeshua had not yet come into the town, but was in the place where Martha met Him.

31 Then the Judeans who were with her in the house, and comforting her, when they saw that Miriam rose up quickly and went out, followed her, saying, "She is going to the tomb to weep there."

32 Then, when Miriam came where Yeshua was, and saw Him, she fell down at His feet, saying to Him, "Lord, if You had been here, my brother would not have died."

33 Therefore, when Yeshua saw her weeping, and the Judeans who came with her also weeping, He groaned in the spirit and was troubled.

34 And He said, "Where have you laid him?" They said to Him, "Lord, come and see."

35 Yeshua wept.

36 Then the Judeans said, "See how He loved him!"

37 And some of them said, "Could not this Man, who opened the eyes of the blind, also have kept this man from dying?"

Lazarus Raised from the Dead

38 Then Yeshua, again groaning in Himself, came to the tomb. It was a cave, and a stone lay against it.

39 Yeshua said, "Take away the stone." Martha, the sister of him who was dead, said to Him, "Lord, by this time there is a stench, for he has been dead four days."

40 Yeshua said to her, "Did I not say to you that if you would believe you would see the glory of God?"

41 Then they took away the stone from the place where the dead man was lying. And Yeshua lifted up His eyes and said, "Father, I thank You that You have heard Me.

42 "And I know that You always hear Me, but because of the people who are standing by I said this, that they may believe that You sent Me."

43 And when He had said these things, He cried with a loud voice, "Lazarus, come forth!"

44 And he who had died came out bound hand and foot with graveclothes, and his face was wrapped with a cloth. Yeshua said to them, "Loose him, and let him go."

The Plot to Kill Yeshua

45 Then many of the Judeans who had come to Miriam, and had seen the things Yeshua did, believed in Him.

46 But some of them went their way to the Pharisees and told them the things Yeshua did.

47 Then the chief priests and the

Pharisees gathered a council and said, "What shall we do? For this Man works many signs.

48 "If we let Him alone like this, everyone will believe in Him, and the Romans will come and take away both our place and nation."

49 And one of them, Caiaphas, being high priest that year, said to them, "You know nothing at all,

50 "nor do you consider that it is expedient for us that one man should die for the people, and not that the whole nation should perish."

51 And this he did not say on his own authority; but being high priest that year, he prophesied that Yeshua would die for the nation,[32]

52 and not for that nation only, but also that He would gather together in one the children of God who were scattered abroad.[33]

53 Then from that day on they plotted to put Him to death.

54 Therefore Yeshua no longer walked openly among the Judeans, but went from there into the country near the wilderness, to a city called Ephraim, and there remained with His disciples.

55 And the Passover of the Jews was near, and many went from the country up to Jerusalem before the Passover, to purify themselves.

56 Then they sought Yeshua, and spoke among themselves as they stood in the temple, "What do you think—that He will not come to the feast?"

57 Now both the chief priests and the Pharisees had given a command, that if anyone knew where He was, he should report it, that they might seize Him.

The Anointing at Bethany

12 Then, six days before the Passover, Yeshua came to Bethany, where Lazarus was who had been dead, whom He raised from the dead.

2 There they made Him a supper; and Martha served, but Lazarus was one of those who sat at the table with Him.

3 Then Miriam took a pound of very costly oil of spikenard, anointed the feet of Yeshua, and wiped His feet with her hair. And the house was filled with the fragrance of the oil.

4 Then one of His disciples, Judas Iscariot, Simon's son, who would betray Him, said,

5 "Why was this fragrant oil not sold for three hundred denarii[34] and given to the poor?"

6 This he said, not that he cared for the poor, but because he was a thief, and had the money box, and used to take what was put in it.

7 Then Yeshua said, "Let her alone; she has kept this for the day of My burial.[35]

8 "For the poor you have with you always, but Me you do not have always."

The Plot to Kill Lazarus

9 Then a great many of the Judeans knew that He was there;

32 Isaiah 53:8   33 Isaiah 11:10–12; 49:6
34 About one year's wages for a worker.
35 I.e., the custom of anointing for burial.

and they came, not for the sake of Yeshua only, but that they might also see Lazarus, whom He had raised from the dead.

10 But the chief priests took counsel that they might also put Lazarus to death,

11 because on account of him many of the Judeans went away and believed in Yeshua.

The Triumphal Entry

12 The next day a great multitude that had come to the feast, when they heard that Yeshua was coming to Jerusalem,

13 took branches of palm trees, went out to meet Him, and cried out:

"Hosanna!
'Blessed is He who comes in the name of the LORD!' [36]
The King of Israel!"

14 And Yeshua, when He had found a young donkey, sat on it; as it is written:

15 "Fear not, daughter of Zion;
Behold, your King is coming,
Sitting on a donkey's colt." [37]

16 His disciples did not understand these things at first; but when Yeshua was glorified, then they remembered that these things were written about Him and that they had done these things to Him.

17 Therefore the people, who were with Him when He called Lazarus out of his tomb and raised him from the dead, bore witness.

18 For this reason the people also met Him, because they heard that He had done this sign.

19 The Pharisees therefore said among themselves, "You see that you are accomplishing nothing. Look, the world has gone after Him!"

The Fruitful Grain of Wheat

20 And there were certain Greeks among those who came up to worship at the feast.

21 Then they came to Philip, who was from Bethsaida of Galilee, and asked him, saying, "Sir, we wish to see Yeshua."

22 Philip came and told Andrew, and again Andrew and Philip told Yeshua.

23 And Yeshua answered them, saying, "The hour has come that the Son of Man should be glorified.

24 "Most assuredly, I say to you, unless a grain of wheat falls into the ground and dies, it remains alone; but if it dies, it produces much grain.

25 "He who loves his life will lose it, and he who hates his life in this world will keep it to eternal life.

26 "If anyone serves Me, let him follow Me; and where I am, there My servant will be also. If anyone serves Me, him My Father will honor.

Yeshua Predicts His Death

27 "Now My soul is troubled, and what shall I say? 'Father, save Me from this hour'? But for this purpose I came to this hour.

28 "Father, glorify Your name." Then a voice came from heaven,

36 Psalm 118:25, 26   37 Zechariah 9:9

saying, "I have both glorified it and will glorify it again."

29 Therefore the people who stood by and heard it said that it thundered. Others said, "An angel spoke to Him."

30 Yeshua answered and said, "This voice did not come because of Me, but for your sake.

31 "Now is the judgment of this world; now the ruler of this world will be cast out.

32 "And I, if I am lifted up from the earth, will draw all men to Myself."

33 This He said, signifying by what death He would die.

34 The people answered Him, "We have heard from the Torah that the Messiah remains forever; and how is it You say, 'The Son of Man must be lifted up'? Who is this Son of Man?"

35 Then Yeshua said to them, "A little while longer the light is with you. Walk while you have the light, lest darkness overtake you, for he who walks in darkness does not know where he is going.

36 "While you have the light, believe in the light, that you may become sons of light." These things Yeshua spoke, and departed, and was hidden from them.

Who Has Believed Our Report?

37 But though He had done so many signs before them, they did not believe in Him,

38 that the word of Isaiah the prophet might be fulfilled, which he spoke:

*"Lord, who has believed our
    report?*

*And to whom has the arm of
    the Lord been re-
    vealed?"38*

39 Therefore they could not believe, because Isaiah said again:

40*"He has blinded their eyes
    and hardened their heart,
That they should not see
    with their eyes,
Nor understand with their
    heart,
And turn again, and I
    should heal them."39*

41 These things Isaiah said when he saw His glory and spoke of Him.

Walk in the Light

42 Nevertheless even among the rulers many believed in Him, but because of the Pharisees they did not confess Him, lest they be put out of the synagogue;

43 for they loved the praise of men more than the praise of God.

44 Then Yeshua cried out and said, "He who believes in Me, believes not in Me but in Him who sent Me.

45 "And he who sees Me sees Him who sent Me.

46 "I have come as a light into the world, that whoever believes in Me should not abide in darkness.

47 "And if anyone hears My words, and does not believe, I do not judge him; for I did not come to judge the world but to save the world.

48 "He who rejects Me, and does not receive My words, has that which judges him—the word

38 Isaiah 53:1
39 Isaiah 6:10; see also 6:1-9

that I have spoken will judge him in the last day.

49 "For I have not spoken on My own authority; but the Father who sent Me gave Me a command, what I should say and what I should speak.[40]

50 "And I know that His command is everlasting life. Therefore, whatever I speak, just as the Father said to Me, so I speak."

The Rabbi Becomes a Servant

13 Now before the feast of the Passover, when Yeshua knew that His hour had come that He should depart out of this world to the Father, having loved His own who were in the world, He loved them to the end.

2 And supper being ended, the devil having already put it into the heart of Judas Iscariot, Simon's son, to betray Him,

3 Yeshua, knowing that the Father had given all things into His hands, and that He had come from God and was going to God,

4 rose from supper, laid aside His garments, took a towel, and girded Himself.

5 After that, He poured water into a basin and began to wash the disciples' feet, and to wipe them with the towel with which He was girded.

6 Then He came to Simon Peter. And Peter said to Him, "Lord, are You washing my feet?"

7 Yeshua answered and said to him, "What I am doing you do not understand now, but you will know after this."

8 Peter said to Him, "You shall never wash my feet!" Yeshua answered him, "If I do not wash you, you have no part with Me."

9 Simon Peter said to Him, "Lord, not my feet only, but also my hands and my head!"

10 Yeshua said to him, "He who is bathed needs only to wash his feet, but is completely clean; and you are clean, but not all of you."

11 For He knew who would betray Him; therefore He said, "You are not all clean."

We Must Also Serve

12 So when He had washed their feet, taken His garments, and sat down again, He said to them, "Do you know what I have done to you?

13 "You call me Rabbi and Lord, and you say well, for so I am.

14 "If I then, your Lord and Rabbi, have washed your feet, you also ought to wash one another's feet.

15 "For I have given you an example, that you should do as I have done to you.

16 "Most assuredly, I say to you, a servant is not greater than his master; nor is he who is sent greater than he who sent him.

17 "If you know these things, happy are you if you do them.

18 "I do not speak concerning all of you. I know whom I have chosen; but that the Scripture may be fulfilled, 'He who eats bread with Me has lifted up his heel against Me.'[41]

19 "Now I tell you before it comes, that when it comes to pass, you may believe that I am He.

20 "Most assuredly, I say to you,

---

40 Deuteronomy 18:18, 19; Isaiah 61:1-4

41 Psalm 41:9 (41:10 in some versions)

he who receives whomever I send receives Me; and he who receives Me receives Him who sent Me."

21 When Yeshua had said these things, He was troubled in spirit, and testified and said, "Most assuredly, I say to you, one of you will betray Me."

22 Then the disciples looked at one another, perplexed about whom He spoke.

23 Now there was leaning on the bosom of Yeshua one of His disciples, whom Yeshua loved.

24 Simon Peter therefore nodded to him, that he should ask who it was of whom He spoke.

25 Then, leaning back on the chest of Yeshua, he said to Him, "Lord, who is it?"

26 Yeshua answered, "It is he to whom I shall give a morsel when I have dipped it." And having dipped the morsel, He gave it to Judas Iscariot, the son of Simon.

27 And after the morsel, Satan entered him. Then Yeshua said to him, "What you do, do quickly."

28 Now no one at the table knew for what reason He said this to him.

29 For some of them thought, because Judas had the money box, that Yeshua had said to him, "Buy those things we need for the feast," or that he should give something to the poor.

30 Having received the morsel, he then went out immediately. And it was night.

The New Commandment

31 Then, when he had gone out, Yeshua said, "Now the Son of Man is glorified, and God is glorified in Him.

32 "If God is glorified in Him, God will also glorify Him in Himself, and glorify Him immediately.

33 "Little children, I shall be with you a little while longer. You will seek Me; and as I said to the Judeans, 'Where I am going, you cannot come,' so now I say to you.

34 "A new commandment I give to you, that you love one another; as I have loved you, that you also love one another.

35 "By this all will know that you are My disciples, if you have love for one another."

Yeshua Predicts Peter's Denial

36 Simon Peter said to Him, "Lord, where are You going?" Yeshua answered him, "Where I am going you cannot follow Me now, but you shall follow Me afterward."

37 Peter said to Him, "Lord, why can I not follow You now? I will lay down my life for Your sake."

38 Yeshua answered him, "Will you lay down your life for My sake? Most assuredly, I say to you, the rooster shall not crow till you have denied Me three times.

The Way, the Truth, and the Life

14 "Let not your heart be troubled; you believe in God, believe also in Me.

2 "In My Father's house are many dwelling places; if it were not so, I would have told you. I go to prepare a place for you.

3 "And if I go and prepare a place for you, I will come again and receive you to Myself; that

where I am, there you may be also.

4 "And where I go you know, and the way you know."

5 Thomas said to Him, "Lord, we do not know where You are going, and how can we know the way?"

6 Yeshua said to him, "I am the way, the truth, and the life. No one comes to the Father except through Me.

7 "If you had known Me, you would have known My Father also; and from now on you know Him and have seen Him."

8 Philip said to Him, "Lord, show us the Father, and it is sufficient for us."

9 Yeshua said to him, "Have I been with you so long, and yet you have not known Me, Philip? He who has seen Me has seen the Father; so how can you say, 'Show us the Father'?

10 "Do you not believe that I am in the Father, and the Father in Me? The words that I speak to you I do not speak on My own authority; but the Father who dwells in Me does the works.

11 "Believe Me that I am in the Father and the Father in Me, or else believe Me for the sake of the works themselves.

The Answered Prayer

12 "Most assuredly, I say to you, he who believes in Me, the works that I do he will do also; and greater works than these he will do, because I go to My Father.

13 "And whatever you ask in My name, that I will do, that the Father may be glorified in the Son.

14 "If you ask anything in My name, I will do it.

Yeshua Promises Another Helper

15 "If you love Me, keep My commandments.

16 "And I will pray the Father, and He will give you another Helper, that He may abide with you forever,

17 "even the Spirit of truth, whom the world cannot receive, because it neither sees Him nor knows Him; but you know Him, for He dwells with you and will be in you.[42]

18 "I will not leave you orphans; I will come to you.

Indwelling Presence of God

19 "A little while longer and the world will see Me no more, but you will see Me. Because I live, you will live also.

20 "At that day you will know that I am in My Father, and you in Me, and I in you.

21 "He who has My commandments and keeps them, it is he who loves Me. And he who loves Me will be loved by My Father, and I will love him and manifest Myself to him."

22 Judas (not Iscariot) said to Him, "Lord, how is it that You will manifest Yourself to us, and not to the world?"

23 Yeshua answered and said to him, "If anyone loves Me, he will keep My word; and My Father will love him, and We will come to him and make Our home with him.

42 Ezekiel 36:25-27; Isaiah 44:3; Joel 2:28 (3:1 in some versions)

24 "He who does not love Me does not keep My words; and the word which you hear is not Mine but the Father's who sent Me.

The Gift of His Peace

25 "These things I have spoken to you while being present with you.

26 "But the Helper, the Holy Spirit, whom the Father will send in My name, He will teach you all things, and bring to your remembrance all things that I said to you.

27 "Peace I leave with you, My peace I give to you; not as the world gives do I give to you. Let not your heart be troubled, neither let it be afraid.

28 "You have heard how I said to you, 'I am going away and coming back to you.' If you loved Me, you would rejoice because I said, 'I am going to the Father,' for My Father is greater than I.

29 "And now I have told you before it comes to pass, that when it comes to pass, you may believe.

30 "I will no longer talk much with you, for the ruler of this world is coming, and he has nothing in Me.

31 "But that the world may know that I love the Father, and as the Father gave Me commandment, so I do. Arise, let us go from here.

The True Vine

15 "I am the true vine, and My Father is the vine-dresser.

2 "Every branch in Me that does not bear fruit He takes away; and every branch that bears fruit He prunes, that it may bear more fruit.

3 "You are already clean because of the word which I have spoken to you.

4 "Abide in Me, and I in you. As the branch cannot bear fruit of itself, unless it abides in the vine, neither can you, unless you abide in Me.

5 "I am the vine, you are the branches. He who abides in Me, and I in him, bears much fruit; for without Me you can do nothing.

6 "If anyone does not abide in Me, he is cast out as a branch and is withered; and they gather them and throw them into the fire, and they are burned.

7 "If you abide in Me, and My words abide in you, you shall ask what you desire, and it shall be done for you.

8 "By this My Father is glorified, that you bear much fruit; so you will be My disciples.

Love and Joy Perfected

9 "As the Father loved Me, I also have loved you; continue in My love.

10 "If you keep My commandments, you will abide in My love, just as I have kept My Father's commandments and abide in His love.

11 "These things I have spoken to you that My joy may remain in you, and that your joy may be full.

12 "This is My commandment, that you love one another as I have loved you.

13 "Greater love has no one than this, that he lay down his life for his friends.

14 "You are My friends if you do whatever I command you.

15 "No longer do I call you servants, for a servant does not know what his master is doing; but I have called you friends, for all things that I have heard from My Father I have made known to you.

16 "You have not chosen Me, but I have chosen you and appointed you that you should go and bear fruit, and that your fruit should remain, that whatever you ask the Father in My name He may give you.

17 "These things I command you, that you love one another.

The World's Hatred

18 "If the world hates you, you know that it hated Me before it hated you.

19 "If you were of the world, the world would love its own. Yet because you are not of the world, but I have chosen you out of the world, therefore the world hates you.

20 "Remember the word that I said to you, 'A servant is not greater than his master.' If they have persecuted Me, they will also persecute you. If they have kept My word, they will keep yours also.

21 "But all these things they will do to you for My name's sake, because they do not know Him who sent Me.

22 "If I had not come and spoken to them, they would have no sin, but now they have no excuse for their sin.

23 "He who hates Me hates My Father also.

24 "If I had not done among them the works which no one else has done, they would have no sin; but now they have seen and also hated both Me and My Father.

25 "But this happened that the word might be fulfilled which is written in their law, *'They hated Me without a cause.'*[43]

The Coming Rejection

26 "But when the Helper comes, whom I shall send to you from the Father, the Spirit of truth who proceeds from the Father, He will testify of Me.

27 "And you also will bear witness, because you have been with Me from the beginning.

16 "These things I have spoken to you, that you should not be made to stumble.

2 "They will put you out of the synagogues; yes, the time is coming that whoever kills you will think that he offers God service.

3 "And these things they will do to you because they have not known the Father nor Me.

4 "But these things I have told you, that when the time comes, you may remember that I told you of them. And these things I did not say to you at the beginning, because I was with you.

The Work of the Holy Spirit

5 "But now I go away to Him who sent Me, and none of you asks Me, 'Where are You going?'

6 "But because I have said these things to you, sorrow has filled your heart.

7 "Nevertheless I tell you the truth. It is to your advantage that I go away; for if I do not go

43 Psalm 69:4 (69:5 in some versions)

away, the Helper will not come to you; but if I depart, I will send Him to you.

8 "And when He has come, He will convict the world of sin, and of righteousness, and of judgment:

9 "of sin, because they do not believe in Me;

10 "of righteousness, because I go to My Father and you see Me no more;

11 "of judgment, because the ruler of this world is judged.

12 "I still have many things to say to you, but you cannot bear them now.

13 "However, when He, the Spirit of truth, has come, He will guide you into all truth; for He will not speak on His own authority, but whatever He hears He will speak; and He will tell you things to come.

14 "He will glorify Me, for He will take of what is Mine and declare it to you.

15 "All things that the Father has are Mine. Therefore I said that He will take of Mine and declare it to you.

Sorrow Will Turn to Joy

16 "A little while, and you will not see Me; and again a little while, and you will see Me, because I go to the Father."

17 Then some of His disciples said among themselves, "What is this that He says to us, 'A little while, and you will not see Me; and again a little while, and you will see Me'; and, 'because I go to the Father'?"

18 They said therefore, "What is this that He says, 'A little while'? We do not know what He is saying."

19 Now Yeshua knew that they desired to ask Him, and He said to them, "Are you inquiring among yourselves about what I said, 'A little while and you will not see Me, and again a little while and you will see Me'?

20 "Most assuredly, I say to you that you will weep and lament, but the world will rejoice; and you will be sorrowful, but your sorrow will be turned into joy.

21 "A woman, when she is in labor, has sorrow because her hour has come; but as soon as she has given birth to the child, she no longer remembers the anguish, for joy that a human being has been born into the world.

22 "And therefore you now have sorrow; but I will see you again and your heart will rejoice, and your joy no one will take from you.

23 "And in that day you will ask Me nothing. Most assuredly, I say to you, whatever you ask the Father in My name He will give you.

24 "Until now you have asked nothing in My name. Ask and you will receive, that your joy may be full.

Yeshua ha Mashiach Has Overcome the World

25 "These things I have spoken to you in figurative language; but the time is coming when I will no longer speak to you in figurative language, but I will tell you plainly about the Father.

26 "In that day you will ask in My name, and I do not say to you

that I shall pray the Father for you;

27 "for the Father Himself loves you, because you have loved Me, and have believed that I came forth from God.

28 "I came forth from the Father and have come into the world. Again, I leave the world and go to the Father."

29 His disciples said to Him, "See, now You are speaking plainly, and using no figure of speech!

30 "Now we are sure that You know all things, and do not need that anyone question You. By this we believe that You came forth from God."

31 Yeshua answered them, "Do you now believe?

32 "Indeed, the hour is coming, yes, has now come, that you will be scattered, each to his own, and will leave Me alone. And yet I am not alone, because the Father is with Me.

33 "These things I have spoken to you, that in Me you may have peace. In the world you will have tribulation; but be of good cheer, I have overcome the world."

The Prayer of Yeshua for Himself

17 Yeshua spoke these words, lifted up His eyes to heaven, and said, "Father, the hour has come. Glorify Your Son, that Your Son also may glorify You,

2 "as You have given Him authority over all flesh, that He should give eternal life to as many as You have given Him.

3 "And this is eternal life, that they may know You, the only true God, and Yeshua ha Mashiach whom You have sent.

4 "I have glorified You on the earth. I have finished the work which You have given Me to do.

5 "And now, O Father, glorify Me together with Yourself, with the glory which I had with You before the world was.

Prayer of Yeshua for His Disciples

6 "I have manifested Your name to the men whom You gave Me out of the world. They were Yours, You gave them to Me, and they have kept Your word.

7 "Now they have known that all things which You have given Me are from You.

8 "For I have given to them the words which You gave Me; and they have received them, and have known surely that I came forth from You; and they have believed that You sent Me.

9 "I pray for them. I do not pray for the world but for those whom You have given Me, for they are Yours.

10 "And all Mine are Yours, and Yours are Mine, and I am glorified in them.

11 "And now I am no longer in the world, but these are in the world, and I come to You. Holy Father, keep through Your name those whom You have given Me, that they may be one as We are.

12 "While I was with them in the world, I kept them in Your name. Those whom You gave Me I have kept; and none of them is lost except the son of perdition, that the Scripture might be fulfilled.

13 "But now I come to You, and these things I speak in the world, that they may have My joy fulfilled in themselves.

14 "I have given them Your word; and the world has hated them because they are not of the world, just as I am not of the world.

15 "I do not pray that You take them out of the world, but that You keep them from the evil one.

16 "They are not of the world, just as I am not of the world.

17 "Sanctify them by Your truth. Your word is truth.

18 "As You have sent Me into the world, I also have sent them into the world.

19 "And for their sakes I sanctify Myself, that they also may be sanctified by the truth.

Prayer of Yeshua for All Believers

20 "I do not pray for these alone, but also for those who will believe in Me through their word;

21 "that they all may be one, as You, Father, are in Me, and I in You; that they also may be one in Us, that the world may believe that You have sent Me.

22 "And the glory which You gave Me I have given them, that they may be one just as We are one:

23 "I in them, and You in Me; that they may be made perfect in one, and that the world may know that You have sent Me, and have loved them as You have loved Me.

24 "Father, I desire that they also whom You have given Me may be with Me where I am, that they may behold My glory which

You have given Me; for You loved Me before the foundation of the world.

25 "O righteous Father! The world has not known You, but I have known You; and these have known that You have sent Me.

26 "And I have declared to them Your name, and will declare it, that the love with which You have loved Me may be in them, and I in them."

Betrayal and Arrest in Gethsemane

18 When Yeshua had spoken these words, He went out with His disciples over the Brook Kidron, where there was a garden, which He and His disciples entered.

2 And Judas, who betrayed Him, also knew the place; for Yeshua often met there with His disciples.

3 Then Judas, having received a band of soldiers, and officers from the chief priests and Pharisees, came there with lanterns, torches, and weapons.

4 Yeshua therefore, knowing all things that would come upon Him, went forward and said to them, "Whom are you seeking?"

5 They answered Him, "Yeshua of Nazareth." Yeshua said to them, "I am He." And Judas, who betrayed Him, also stood with them.

6 Then, as soon as He had said to them, "I am He," they drew back and fell to the ground.

7 Then He asked them again, "Whom are you seeking?" And they said, "Yeshua of Nazareth."

8 Yeshua answered, "I have

told you that I am He. Therefore, if you seek Me, let these go their way,"

9 that the saying might be fulfilled which He spoke, "Of those whom You gave Me I have lost none."

10 Then Simon Peter, having a sword, drew it and struck the high priest's servant, and cut off his right ear. The servant's name was Malchus.

11 Then Yeshua said to Peter, "Put your sword into the sheath. Shall I not drink the cup which My Father has given Me?"

Before Caiaphas

12 Then the band of soldiers and their captain and the officers of the Judeans arrested Yeshua and bound Him.

13 And they led Him away to Annas first, for he was the father-in-law of Caiaphas who was high priest that year.

14 Now Caiaphas was he who gave counsel to the Judeans that it was expedient that one man should die for the people.

15 And Simon Peter followed Yeshua, and so did another disciple. That disciple was known to the high priest, and went with Yeshua into the courtyard of the high priest.

16 But Peter stood at the door outside. Then that other disciple, who was known to the high priest, went out and spoke to her who kept the door, and brought Peter in.

17 Then the servant girl who kept the door said to Peter, "You are not also one of this Man's disciples, are you?" He said, "I am not."

18 And the servants and officers who had made a fire of coals stood there, for it was cold, and they warmed themselves. And Peter stood with them and warmed himself.

19 The high priest then asked Yeshua about His disciples and His doctrine.

20 Yeshua answered him, "I spoke openly to the world. I always taught in the synagogues and in the temple, where the Judeans always meet, and in secret I have said nothing.

21 "Why do you ask Me? Ask those who heard Me what I have said to them. Indeed they know what I said."

22 And when He had said these things, one of the officers who stood by struck Yeshua with the palm of his hand, saying, "Do You answer the high priest like that?"

23 Yeshua answered him, "If I have spoken evil, bear witness of the evil; but if well, why do you strike Me?"

24 Then Annas sent Him bound to Caiaphas the high priest.

Peter Denies Twice More

25 And Simon Peter stood and warmed himself. Therefore they said to him, "You are not also one of His disciples, are you?" He denied it and said, "I am not!"

26 One of the servants of the high priest, a relative of him whose ear Peter cut off, said, "Did I not see you in the garden with Him?"

27 Peter then denied again; and immediately a rooster crowed.

In Pilate's Court

28 Then they led Yeshua from Caiaphas to the Praetorium,[44] and it was early morning. And they themselves did not go into the Praetorium, lest they should be defiled, but that they might eat the Passover.

29 Pilate then went out to them and said, "What accusation do you bring against this Man?"

30 They answered and said to him, "If He were not an evildoer, we would not have delivered Him up to you."

31 Then Pilate said to them, "You take Him and judge Him according to your law." Therefore the Judeans said to him, "It is not lawful for us to put anyone to death,"

32 that the saying of Yeshua might be fulfilled which He spoke, signifying by what death He would die.

33 Then Pilate entered the Praetorium again, called Yeshua, and said to Him, "Are You the King of the Jews?"

34 Yeshua answered him, "Are you speaking for yourself, or did others tell you this about Me?"

35 Pilate answered, "Am I a Jew? Your own nation and the chief priests have delivered You to me. What have You done?"

36 Yeshua answered, "My kingdom is not of this world. If My kingdom were of this world, then My servants would fight, so that I should not be delivered to the Judeans; but now My kingdom is not from here."

37 Pilate therefore said to Him,

"Are You a king then?" Yeshua answered, "You say rightly that I am a king. For this cause I was born, and for this cause I came into the world, that I should bear witness to the truth. Everyone who is of the truth hears My voice."

38 Pilate said to Him, "What is truth?" And when he had said this, he went out again to the Judeans, and said to them, "I find no fault in Him at all.

Condemned in Our Place

39 "But you have a custom that I should release someone to you at the Passover. Do you therefore want me to release to you the King of the Jews?"

40 Then they all cried again, saying, "Not this Man, but Barabbas!" Now Barabbas was a robber.

Bruised for Our Iniquities

19 So Pilate then took Yeshua and scourged Him.

2 And the soldiers twisted a crown out of thorns and put it on His head, and they put on Him a purple robe.

3 And they said, "Hail, King of the Jews!" And they struck Him with their hands.[45]

4 Pilate then went out again, and said to them, "Look, I am bringing Him out to you, that you may know that I find no fault in Him."

Pilate's Decision

5 Then Yeshua came out, wearing the crown of thorns and

44 Governor's official residence. This was also the place of the military barracks.

45 Isaiah 53:3, 5, 7

the purple robe. And Pilate said to them, "Behold the Man!"

6 Therefore, when the chief priests and officers saw Him, they cried out, saying, "Crucify Him, crucify Him!" Pilate said to them, "You take Him and crucify Him, for I find no fault in Him."

7 The Judeans answered Him, "We have a Torah, and by our Torah He ought to die, because He made Himself the Son of God."

8 Therefore, when Pilate heard that saying, he was the more afraid,

9 and went again into the Praetorium, and said to Yeshua, "Where are You from?" But Yeshua gave him no answer.

10 Then Pilate said to Him, "Are You not speaking to me? Do You not know that I have power to crucify You, and power to release You?"

11 Yeshua answered, "You could have no power at all against Me unless it had been given you from above. Therefore the one who delivered Me to you has the greater sin."

12 From then on Pilate sought to release Him, but the Judeans cried out, saying, "If you let this Man go, you are not Caesar's friend. Whoever makes himself a king speaks against Caesar."

13 When Pilate therefore heard that saying, he brought Yeshua out and sat down in the judgment seat in a place that is called The Pavement, but in Hebrew, Gabbatha.

14 And it was the Preparation Day of the Passover, and about the sixth hour.[46] And he said to the Judeans, "Behold your King!"

15 But they cried out, "Away with Him, away with Him! Crucify Him!" Pilate said to them, "Shall I crucify your King?" The chief priests answered, "We have no king but Caesar!"

16 So then he delivered Him to them to be crucified. And they took Yeshua and led Him away.

Wounded for Our Transgressions

17 And He, bearing His cross, went out to a place called the Place of a Skull, which is called in Hebrew, Golgotha,

18 where they crucified Him, and two others with Him, one on either side, and Yeshua in the center.[47]

19 And Pilate wrote a title and put it on the cross. And the writing was:

YESHUA OF NAZARETH,
THE KING OF THE JEWS.

20 Then many of the Judeans read this title, for the place where Yeshua was crucified was near the city; and it was written in Hebrew, Greek, and Latin.

21 Then the chief priests of the Judeans said to Pilate, "Do not write, 'The King of the Jews,' but, 'He said: I am King of the Jews.' "

22 Pilate answered, "What I have written, I have written."

23 Then the soldiers, when they had crucified Yeshua, took His garments and made four parts, to each soldier a part, and also His tunic. Now the tunic was without seam, woven from the top in one piece.

46 Noon.   47 Isaiah 53:12

24 They said therefore among themselves, "Let us not tear it, but cast lots for it, whose it shall be," that the Scripture might be fulfilled which says:

"They divided My garments among them,
And for My clothing they cast lots."[48]

Therefore the soldiers did these things.

25 Now there stood by the cross of Yeshua His mother, and His mother's sister, Miriam the wife of Clopas, and Miriam of Magdala.

26 When Yeshua therefore saw His mother, and the disciple whom He loved standing by, He said to His mother, "Woman, behold your son!"

27 Then He said to the disciple, "Behold your mother!" And from that hour that disciple took her to his own home.

An Offering for Sin

28 After this, Yeshua, knowing that all things were now accomplished, that the Scripture might be fulfilled, said, "I thirst!"

29 Now a vessel full of sour wine was sitting there; and they filled a sponge with sour wine, put it on hyssop, and put it to His mouth.[49]

30 So when Yeshua had received the sour wine, He said, "It is finished!" And He bowed His head, and gave up His spirit.

Piercing the Side of Yeshua

31 Therefore, because it was the Preparation Day, that the bodies should not remain on the cross on the Sabbath (for that Sabbath was a high day), the Judeans asked Pilate that their legs might be broken, and that they might be taken away.

32 Then the soldiers came and broke the legs of the first and of the other who was crucified with Him.

33 But when they came to Yeshua and saw that He was already dead, they did not break His legs.

34 But one of the soldiers pierced His side with a spear, and immediately blood and water came out.

35 And he who saw it bore witness, and his witness is true; and he knows that he is telling the truth, that you may believe.

36 For these things were done that the Scripture should be fulfilled, "Not one of His bones shall be broken."[50]

37 And again another Scripture says, "They will look on Him whom they pierced."[51]

Yeshua Buried in Joseph's Tomb

38 And after this, Joseph of Arimathea, being a disciple of Yeshua , but secretly, for fear of the Judeans, asked Pilate that he might take away the body of Yeshua; and Pilate gave him permission. So he came and took the body of Yeshua.

39 And Nicodemus, who at first came to Yeshua by night, also came; and he brought a mixture of myrrh and aloes, about a hundred pounds.

40 Then they took the body of Yeshua, and bound it in strips of linen with the spices, as the custom of the Jews is to bury.

48 Psalm 22:18 (22:19 in some versions)
49 Psalm 69:21 (69:22 in some versions)
50 Exodus 12:46; Numbers 9:12; Psalm 34:20 (34:21 in some versions)
51 Zechariah 12:10

188

41 Now in the place where He was crucified there was a garden, and in the garden a new tomb in which no one had yet been laid.[52]

42 So there they laid Yeshua, because of the Jews' Preparation Day, for the tomb was nearby.

The Empty Tomb

20 The first day of the week Miriam of Magdala came to the tomb early, while it was still dark, and saw the stone had been taken away from the tomb.

2 Then she ran and came to Simon Peter, and to the other disciple, whom Yeshua loved, and said to them, "They have taken away the Lord out of the tomb, and we do not know where they have laid Him."

3 Peter therefore went out, and the other disciple, and came to the tomb.

4 So they both ran together, and the other disciple outran Peter and came to the tomb first.

5 And he, stooping down and looking in, saw the linen cloths lying there; yet he did not go in.

6 Then Simon Peter came, following him, and went into the tomb; and he saw the linen cloths lying there,

7 and the handkerchief that had been around His head, not lying with the linen cloths, but folded together in a place by itself.

8 Then the other disciple, who came to the tomb first, went in also; and he saw and believed.

9 For as yet they did not know the Scripture, that He must rise again from the dead.[53]

10 Then the disciples went away again to their own homes.

Miriam of Magdala Sees the Risen Lord

11 But Miriam stood outside by the tomb weeping, and as she wept she stooped down and looked into the tomb.

12 And she saw two angels in white sitting, one at the head and the other at the feet, where the body of Yeshua had lain.

13 And they said to her, "Woman, why are you weeping?" She said to them, "Because they have taken away my Lord, and I do not know where they have laid Him."

14 And when she had said this, she turned around and saw Yeshua standing there, and did not know that it was Yeshua.

15 Yeshua said to her, "Woman, why are you weeping? Whom are you seeking?" She, supposing Him to be the gardener, said to Him, "Sir, if You have carried Him away, tell me where You have laid Him, and I will take Him away."

16 Yeshua said to her, "Miriam!" She turned and said to Him, *"Rabboni!"* (which is to say, Teacher).

17 Yeshua said to her, "Do not cling to Me, for I have not yet ascended to My Father; but go to My brethren and say to them, 'I am ascending to My Father and your Father, and to My God and your God.' "

18 Miriam of Magdala came and told the disciples that she had

seen the Lord, and that He had spoken these things to her.

The Disciples Commissioned

19 Then, the same day at evening, being the first day of the week, when the doors were shut where the disciples were assembled, for fear of the Judeans, Yeshua came and stood in the midst, and said to them, "Peace be with you."

20 And when He had said this, He showed them His hands and His side. Then the disciples were glad when they saw the Lord.

21 Then Yeshua said to them again, "Peace be with you. As My Father has sent Me, I also send you."

22 And when He had said this, He breathed on them, and said to them, "Receive the Holy Spirit.

23 "If you forgive the sins of any, they are forgiven them; and if you retain the sins of any, they are retained."

Seeing and Believing

24 But Thomas, called Didymus, one of the twelve, was not with them when Yeshua came.

25 The other disciples therefore said to him, "We have seen the Lord." But he said to them, "Unless I see in His hands the print of the nails, put my finger into the print of the nails, and put my hand into His side, I will not believe."

26 And after eight days His disciples were again inside, and Thomas with them. Yeshua came, the doors being shut, and stood in the midst, and said, "Peace be with you."

27 Then He said to Thomas, "Reach your finger here, and look at My hands; and reach your hand here, and put it into My side. And do not be unbelieving, but believing."

28 And Thomas answered and said to Him, "My Lord and my God!"

29 Yeshua said to him, "Thomas, because you have seen Me, you have believed. Blessed are those who have not seen and yet have believed."

That You May Believe

30 And truly Yeshua did many other signs in the presence of His disciples, which are not written in this book;

31 but these are written that you may believe that Yeshua is the Messiah, the Son of God, and that believing you may have life in His name.[54]

Breakfast at Galilee

21 After these things Yeshua showed Himself again to the disciples at the Sea of Tiberias, and in this way He showed Himself:

2 Simon Peter, Thomas called Didymus, Nathanael of Cana in Galilee, the sons of Zebedee, and two others of His disciples were together.

3 Simon Peter said to them, "I am going fishing." They said to him, "We are going with you also." They went out and imme-

54 Psalm 2:7, 12

diately got into the boat, and that night they caught nothing.

4 But when the morning had now come, Yeshua stood on the shore; yet the disciples did not know that it was Yeshua.

5 Then Yeshua said to them, "Children, have you any food?" They answered Him, "No."

6 And He said to them, "Cast the net on the right side of the boat, and you will find some." So they cast, and now they were not able to draw it in because of the multitude of fish.

7 Therefore that disciple whom Yeshua loved said to Peter, "It is the Lord!" Now when Simon Peter heard that it was the Lord, he put on his outer garment (for he was wearing only an undergarment), and plunged into the sea.

8 And the other disciples came in the little boat (for they were not far from land, but about two hundred cubits), dragging the net with fish.

9 Then, as soon as they had come to land, they saw a fire of coals there, and fish laid on it, and bread.

10 Yeshua said to them, "Bring some of the fish which you have just caught."

11 Simon Peter went up and dragged the net to land, full of large fish, one hundred and fifty-three; and although there were so many, the net was not broken.

12 Yeshua said to them, "Come and eat breakfast." And none of the disciples dared ask Him, "Who are You?"—knowing that it was the Lord.

13 Yeshua then came and took the bread and gave it to them, and likewise the fish.

14 This is now the third time Yeshua showed Himself to His disciples after He was raised from the dead.

Yeshua Restores Peter

15 So when they had eaten breakfast, Yeshua said to Simon Peter, "Simon, son of Jonah, do you love Me more than these?" He said to Him, "Yes, Lord; You know that I love You." He said to him, "Feed My lambs."

16 He said to him again a second time, "Simon, son of Jonah, do you love Me?" He said to Him, "Yes, Lord; You know that I love You." He said to him, "Tend My sheep."

17 He said to him the third time, "Simon, son of Jonah, do you love Me?" Peter was grieved because He said to him the third time, "Do you love Me?" And he said to Him, "Lord, You know all things; You know that I love You." Yeshua said to him, "Feed My sheep.

18 "Most assuredly, I say to you, when you were younger, you girded yourself and walked where you wished; but when you are old, you will stretch out your hands, and another will gird you and carry you where you do not wish."

19 This He spoke, signifying by what death he would glorify God. And when He had spoken this, He said to him, "Follow Me."

You Follow Me

20 Then Peter, turning around, saw the disciple whom Yeshua loved following, who also had

leaned on His chest at the supper, and had said, "Lord, who is the one who betrays You?"

21 Peter, seeing him, said to Yeshua, "Lord, and what will this man do?"

22 Yeshua said to him, "If I will that he remain till I come, what is that to you? You follow Me."

23 Then this saying went out among the brethren that this disciple would not die. Yet Yeshua did not say to him that he would not die, but, "If I will that he remain till I come, what is that to you?"

24 This is the disciple who testifies of these things, and wrote these things; and we know that his testimony is true.

25 And there are also many other things that Yeshua did, which if they were written one by one, I suppose that even the world itself could not contain the books that would be written. Amen.

ACTS

Prologue

THE former account[1] I made, O Theophilus, of all that Yeshua began both to do and teach,

2 until the day in which He was taken up, after He through the Holy Spirit had given commandments to the apostles whom He had chosen,

3 to whom He also presented Himself alive after His suffering by many infallible proofs, being seen by them forty days and speaking of the things pertaining to the kingdom of God.

The Holy Spirit Promised

4 And being assembled together with them, He commanded them that they should not depart from Jerusalem, but wait for the Promise of the Father,[2] "which," He said, "you have heard from Me;

5 "for John truly immersed in water, but you will be immersed in the Holy Spirit not many days from now."

6 Therefore, when they had come together, they asked Him, saying, "Lord, will You at this time restore the kingdom[3] to Israel?"

7 And He said to them, "It is not for you to know times or seasons which the Father has put in His own authority.

8 "But you will receive power when the Holy Spirit has come upon you; and you will be witnesses to Me in Jerusalem, and in all Judea and Samaria, and to the end of the earth."

Yeshua Ascends to Heaven

9 And when He had spoken these things, while they watched, He was taken up, and a cloud received Him out of their sight.

10 And while they looked steadfastly toward heaven as He went up, behold, two men stood by them in white apparel,

11 who also said, "Men of Galilee, why do you stand gazing up into heaven? This same Yeshua, who was taken up from you into heaven, will so come in like manner as you have seen Him go into heaven."

The Upper Room

12 Then they returned to Jerusalem from the Mount called Olivet, which is near Jerusalem, a Sabbath day's journey.

13 And when they had entered, they went up into the upper room where they were staying: Peter, James, John, and Andrew; Philip and Thomas; Bartholomew and Matthew; James the son of Alphaeus and Simon the Zealot; and Judas the son of James.

1 That is, the Good News According to Luke (p. 91 above).
2 Ezekiel 36:25–27; Isaiah 44:3
3 A reference to the kingdom over which Messiah will rule; see Jeremiah 23:5, 6; Isaiah 9:6, 7 (9:5, 6 in some versions).

14 These all continued with one accord in prayer and supplication, with the women and Miriam the mother of Yeshua, and with His brothers.

Matthias Chosen

15 And in those days Peter stood up in the midst of the disciples (altogether the number of names was about a hundred and twenty), and said,

16 "Men and brethren, this Scripture had to be fulfilled, which the Holy Spirit spoke before by the mouth of David concerning Judas, who became a guide to those who arrested Yeshua;[4]

17 "for he was numbered with us and obtained a part in this ministry."

18 (Now this man purchased a field with the wages of iniquity; and falling headlong, he burst open in the middle and all his entrails gushed out.

19 And it became known to all those dwelling in Jerusalem; so that field is called in their own language, *Chakál-Demá,* that is, Field of Blood.)

20 "For it is written in the book of Psalms:

'Let his habitation be desolate,
And let no one live in it';[5]

and,

'His office let another take.'[6]

21 "Therefore, of these men who have accompanied us all the time that the Lord Yeshua went in and out among us,

22 "beginning from the immersion of John to that day when He was taken up from us, one of these must become a witness with us of His resurrection."

23 And they proposed two: Joseph called Barsabas, who was also named Justus, and Matthias.

24 And they prayed and said, "You, O Lord, who know the hearts of all men, show which of these two You have chosen,

25 "that he may take part in this ministry and apostleship from which Judas by transgression fell, that he might go to his own place."

26 And they cast their lots, and the lot fell on Matthias. And he was numbered with the eleven apostles.

Coming of the Holy Spirit

2 And when the day of Shavuot had fully come, they were all with one accord in one place.

2 And suddenly there came a sound from heaven, as of a rushing mighty wind, and it filled the whole house where they were sitting.

3 And there appeared to them divided tongues, as of fire, and it sat upon each of them.

4 And they were all filled with the Holy Spirit and began to speak with other tongues, as the Spirit gave them utterance.

The Crowd's Response

5 And there were dwelling in Jerusalem Jews, devout men, from every nation under heaven.

---

4 Psalm 41:9 (41:10 in some versions)
5 Psalm 69:25 (69:26 in some versions)
6 Psalm 109:8

6 Now when this sound occurred, the multitude came together; and they were astonished, because everyone heard them speak in his own language.

7 And they were all amazed and marveled, saying to one another, "Look, are not all these who speak Galileans?

8 "And how is it we hear, each in our own language in which we were born?

9 "Parthians, Medes, and Elamites; those dwelling in Mesopotamia, Judea, and Cappadocia, Pontus and Asia,

10 "Phrygia and Pamphylia, Egypt and the parts of Libya adjoining Cyrene, visitors from Rome, both Jews and proselytes,[7]

11 "Cretans and Arabs—we hear them speaking in our tongues the wonderful works of God."

12 And they were all amazed and perplexed, saying to one another, "What does this mean?"

13 Others mocking said, "They are full of new wine."

Peter's Sermon

14 But Peter, standing up with the eleven, raised his voice and said to them, "Men of Judea and all who dwell in Jerusalem, let this be known to you, and heed my words.

15 "For these are not drunk, as you suppose, seeing it is only the third hour of the day.[8]

16 "But this is what was spoken by the prophet Joel:

17 'And it will come to pass in the last days, says God,

I will pour out of My Spirit
  on all flesh;
And your sons and your
  daughters will prophesy,
And your young men will
  see visions,
And your old men will
  dream dreams.

18 And on My menservants
  and on My maidservants
I will pour out in those days
  of My Spirit;
And they will prophesy.

19 And I will show wonders in
  heaven above
And signs in the earth beneath:
Blood, fire, and vapor of
  smoke.

20 The sun will be turned into
  darkness,
And the moon into blood,
Before the coming of the
  great and notable day of
  the LORD.

21 And it will come to pass that
  whoever calls on the name
  of the LORD will be
  saved.'[9]

22 "Men of Israel, hear these words: Yeshua of Nazareth, a Man attested by God to you by miracles, wonders, and signs which God did through Him in your midst, as you yourselves also know—

23 "Him, being delivered by the determined counsel and foreknowledge of God, you have taken by lawless hands, have crucified, and put to death;

24 "whom God raised up, having loosed the pains of death, because it was not possible that He should be held by it.

7 Gentile converts to Judaism.
8 9 a.m.

9 Joel 2:28-32 (3:1-5 in some versions)

25 "For David says concerning Him:
> 'I foresaw the LORD always before my face,
> For He is at my right hand, that I may not be shaken;
26 Therefore my heart rejoiced, and my tongue was glad;
> Moreover my flesh will also rest in hope,
27 Because You will not leave my soul in Hades,
> Nor will You allow Your Holy One to see corruption.
28 You have made known to me the ways of life;
> You will make me full of joy in Your presence.' [10]

29 "Men and brethren, let me speak freely to you of the patriarch David, that he is both dead and buried, and his tomb is with us to this day.

30 "Therefore, being a prophet, and knowing that God had sworn with an oath to him that of the fruit of his body, according to the flesh, He would raise up the Messiah to sit on his throne,[11]

31 "he, foreseeing this, spoke concerning the resurrection of the Messiah, that His soul was not left in Hades, nor did His flesh see corruption.

32 "This Yeshua God has raised up, of which we are all witnesses.

33 "Therefore being exalted to the right hand of God, and having received from the Father the promise of the Holy Spirit, He poured out this which you now see and hear.

34 "For David did not ascend into the heavens, but he says himself:
> 'The LORD said to my Lord, "Sit at My right hand,
35 Till I make Your enemies Your footstool." ' [12]

36 "Therefore let all the house of Israel know assuredly that God has made this Yeshua, whom you have crucified, both Lord and Messiah."

37 Now when they heard this, they were cut to the heart, and said to Peter and to the rest of the apostles, "Men and brethren, what shall we do?"

38 Then Peter said to them, "Repent, and let every one of you be immersed in the name of Yeshua ha Mashiach for the remission of sins; and you will receive the gift of the Holy Spirit.

39 "For the promise is to you and to your children, and to all who are afar off, as many as the Lord our God will call."

A Vital Congregation Grows

40 And with many other words he testified and exhorted them, saying, "Be saved from this perverse generation."

41 Then those who gladly received his word were immersed; and the same day about three thousand souls[13] were added to them.

42 And they continued steadfastly in the apostles' doctrine and fellowship, in the breaking of bread, and in prayers.

43 And fear came upon every

10 Psalm 16:8-11

11 Psalm 89:3, 4, 35, 36 (89:4, 5, 36, 37 in some versions)

12 Psalm 110:1   13 Persons.

soul, and many wonders and signs were done by the apostles.

44 And all who believed were together, and had all things in common,

45 and sold their possessions and goods, and divided them among all, as anyone had need.

46 And continuing daily with one accord in the temple, and breaking bread from house to house, they ate their food with gladness and simplicity of heart,

47 praising God and having favor with all the people. And the Lord added to the congregation daily those who were being saved.

A Lame Man Healed

3 Now Peter and John went up together to the temple at the hour of prayer, the ninth hour.[14]

2 And a certain man lame from his mother's womb was carried, whom they laid daily at the gate of the temple which is called Beautiful, to ask alms from those who entered the temple;

3 who, seeing Peter and John about to go into the temple, asked for alms.

4 And fixing his eyes on him, with John, Peter said, "Look at us."

5 And he gave them his attention, expecting to receive something from them.

6 Then Peter said, "Silver and gold I do not have, but what I do have I give you: In the name of Yeshua ha Mashiach of Nazareth, rise up and walk."

7 And he took him by the right hand and lifted him up, and immediately his feet and ankle bones received strength.

8 And he, leaping up, stood and walked and entered the temple with them—walking, leaping, and praising God.

9 And all the people saw him walking and praising God.

10 And they knew that it was he who sat begging alms at the Beautiful Gate of the temple; and they were filled with wonder and amazement at what had happened to him.

Solomon's Porch

11 And as the lame man who was healed held on to Peter and John, all the people ran together to them in the porch which is called Solomon's, greatly amazed.

12 And when Peter saw it, he responded to the people: "Men of Israel, why do you marvel at this? Or why look so intently at us, as though by our own power or godliness we had made this man walk?

13 "The God of Abraham, Isaac, and Jacob, the God of our fathers, glorified His Servant Yeshua, whom you delivered up and denied in the presence of Pilate, when he was determined to let Him go.

14 "But you denied the Holy One and the Just, and asked for a murderer to be granted to you,

15 "and killed the Prince of life, whom God has raised from the dead, of which we are witnesses.

16 "And His name, through faith in His name, has made this man strong, whom you see and know. Yes, the faith which comes through Him has given him this perfect soundness in the presence of you all.

14 3 p.m.

17 "And now, brethren, I know that you did it through ignorance, as did also your rulers.

18 "But those things which God foretold by the mouth of all His prophets, that the Messiah would suffer, He has thus fulfilled.[15]

19 "Repent therefore and be turned to God, that your sins may be blotted out, so that times of refreshing may come from the presence of the Lord,

20 "and that He may send Yeshua ha Mashiach, who was preached to you before,

21 "whom heaven must receive until the times of restoration of all things, which God has spoken by the mouth of all His holy prophets since the world began.

22 "For Moses truly said to the fathers, *'The LORD your God will raise up for you a Prophet like me from your brethren. Him you shall hear in all things, whatever He says to you.*

23 *'And it will come to pass that every soul who will not hear that Prophet will be utterly destroyed from among the people.'*[16]

24 "Yes, and all the prophets, from Samuel and those who follow, as many as have spoken, have likewise foretold these days.

25 "You are sons of the prophets, and of the covenant which God made with our fathers, saying to Abraham, *'And in your seed all the families of the earth will be blessed.'*[17]

26 "To you first, God, having raised up His Servant Yeshua, sent Him to bless you, in turning

away every one of you from your iniquities."

Peter and John Arrested

4 And as they spoke to the people, the priests, the captain of the temple, and the Sadducees came upon them,

2 being greatly disturbed that they taught the people and preached through Yeshua the resurrection from the dead.

3 And they laid hands on them, and put them in custody until the next day, for it was already evening.

4 However, many of those who heard the word believed; and the number of the men came to be about five thousand.

Addressing the Sanhedrin

5 And it came to pass, on the next day, that their rulers, elders, and scribes,

6 as well as Annas the high priest, Caiaphas, John, and Alexander, and as many as were of the family of the high priest, were gathered together at Jerusalem.

7 And when they had set them in the midst, they asked, "By what power or by what name have you done this?"

8 Then Peter, filled with the Holy Spirit, said to them, "Rulers of the people and elders of Israel:

9 "If we this day are judged for a good deed done to the helpless man, by what means he has been made well,

10 "let it be known to you all, and to all the people of Israel, that by the name of Yeshua ha Mashiach of Nazareth, whom you crucified, whom God raised from the

15 Isaiah 53

16 Deuteronomy 18:15, 18, 19

17 Genesis 22:18; 26:4; 28:14

dead, by Him this man stands here before you whole.

11 "This is the *'stone which was rejected by you builders, which has become the chief cornerstone.'* [18]

12 "Nor is there salvation in any other, for there is no other name under heaven given among men by which we must be saved."

The Name of Yeshua Forbidden

13 Now when they saw the boldness of Peter and John, and perceived that they were uneducated and untrained men, they marveled. And they realized that they had been with Yeshua.

14 And seeing the man who had been healed standing with them, they could say nothing against it.

15 But when they had commanded them to go aside out of the council, they conferred among themselves,

16 saying, "What shall we do to these men? For, indeed, that a notable miracle has been done by them is evident to all who dwell in Jerusalem, and we cannot deny it.

17 "But so that it spreads no further among the people, let us severely threaten them, that from now on they speak to no man in this name."

18 And they called them and commanded them not to speak at all nor teach in the name of Yeshua.

19 But Peter and John answered and said to them, "Whether it is right in the sight of God to listen to you more than to God, you judge.

20 "For we cannot but speak the things which we have seen and heard."

21 So when they had further threatened them, they let them go, finding no way of punishing them, because of the people, since they all glorified God for what had been done.

22 For the man was over forty years old on whom this miracle of healing had been performed.

Prayer for Boldness

23 And being let go, they went to their own companions and reported all that the chief priests and elders had said to them.

24 And when they heard that, they raised their voice to God with one accord and said: "Lord, You are God, who made heaven and earth and the sea, and all that is in them,

25 "who by the mouth of Your servant David have said:
   'Why did the nations rage,
   And the people plot vain
      things?
26 *The kings of the earth took*
      their stand,
   And the rulers were gathered together
   Against the LORD and
      against His Messiah.' [19]

27 "For truly against Your holy Servant Yeshua, whom You have anointed, both Herod and Pontius Pilate, with the Gentiles and the people of Israel, were gathered together

28 "to do whatever Your hand and Your purpose determined before to be done.

18 Psalm 118:22   *19* Psalm 2:1, 2

29 "And now, Lord, look on their threats, and grant to Your servants that with all boldness they may speak Your word,

30 "by stretching out Your hand to heal, and that signs and wonders may be done by the name of Your holy Servant Yeshua."

31 And when they had prayed, the place was shaken where they were assembled together; and they were all filled with the Holy Spirit, and they spoke the word of God with boldness.

Sharing in All Things

32 And the multitude of those who had believed were of one heart and of one soul; neither did anyone say that any of the things he possessed was his own, but they had all things in common.

33 And with great power the apostles gave witness to the resurrection of the Lord Yeshua. And great grace was upon them all.

34 Nor was there anyone among them who lacked; for all who were possessors of lands or houses sold them, and brought the proceeds of the things that were sold,

35 and laid them at the apostles' feet; and they distributed to each as he had need.

36 And Joses, who was also named Barnabas by the apostles (which is translated Son of Encouragement), a Levite of the country of Cyprus,

37 having land, sold it, and brought the money and laid it at the apostles' feet.

Lying to the Holy Spirit

5 But a certain man named Ananias, with Sapphira his wife, sold a possession.

2 And he kept back part of the proceeds, his wife also being aware of it, and brought a certain part and laid it at the apostles' feet.

3 But Peter said, "Ananias, why has Satan filled your heart to lie to the Holy Spirit and keep back part of the price of the land for yourself?

4 "While it remained, was it not your own? And after it was sold, was it not in your own control? Why have you conceived this thing in your heart? You have not lied to men but to God."

5 And Ananias, hearing these words, fell down and breathed his last. And great fear came on all those who heard these things.

6 And the young men arose and wrapped him up, carried him out, and buried him.

7 And it was about three hours later when his wife came in, not knowing what had happened.

8 And Peter answered her, "Tell me whether you sold the land for so much?" And she said, "Yes, for so much."

9 Then Peter said to her, "How is it that you have agreed together to test the Spirit of the Lord? Look, the feet of those who have buried your husband are at the door, and they will carry you out."

10 Then immediately she fell down at his feet and breathed her last. And the young men came in and found her dead, and carrying her out, buried her by her husband.

11 And great fear came on all the congregation and on all who heard these things.

Continuing Power in the Body of Believers

12 And by the hands of the apostles many signs and wonders were done among the people. And they were all with one accord in Solomon's Porch.

13 And none of the rest dared join them, but the people esteemed them highly.

14 And believers were increasingly added to the Lord, multitudes of both men and women,

15 so that they brought the sick out into the streets and laid them on beds and couches, that at least the shadow of Peter passing by might fall on some of them.

16 Also a multitude came out of the surrounding cities to Jerusalem, bringing sick people and those who were tormented by unclean spirits, and they were all healed.

Imprisoned Apostles Freed

17 Then the high priest rose up, and all those who were with him (which is the sect of the Sadducees), and they were filled with indignation,

18 and laid their hands on the apostles and put them in the common prison.

19 But at night an angel of the Lord opened the prison doors and brought them out, and said,

20 "Go, stand and speak to the people in the temple all the words of this life."

21 And when they heard that, they entered the temple early in the morning and taught. But the high priest and those who were with him came and called the council together, with all the elders of the children of Israel, and sent to the prison to have them brought.

Apostles on Trial Again

22 But when the officers came and did not find them in the prison, they returned and reported,

23 saying, "Indeed we found the prison shut securely, the guards standing outside before the doors; but when we opened them, we found no one inside!"

24 Now when the high priest, the captain of the temple, and the chief priests heard these things, they wondered what the outcome would be.

25 Then one came and told them, saying, "Look, the men whom you put in prison are standing in the temple and teaching the people!"

26 Then the captain went with the officers and brought them without violence, for they feared the people, lest they should be stoned.

27 And when they had brought them, they set them before the council. And the high priest asked them,

28 saying, "Did we not strictly command you that you should not teach in this name? And indeed you have filled Jerusalem with your doctrine, and intend to bring this Man's blood on us!"

29 Then Peter and the other apostles answered and said: "We ought to obey God rather than men.

30 "The God of our fathers raised up Yeshua whom you killed by hanging on a tree.

31 "Him God has exalted with His right hand to be Prince and Savior,[20] to give repentance to Israel and forgiveness of sins.

32 "And we are His witnesses to these things, and so also is the Holy Spirit whom God has given to those who obey Him."

Gamaliel's Advice

33 When they heard this, they were furious and took counsel to kill them.

34 Then one in the council stood up, a Pharisee named Gamaliel, a teacher of the law held in respect by all the people, and commanded them to put the apostles outside for a little while.

35 And he said to them: "Men of Israel, take heed to yourselves what you intend to do regarding these men.

36 "For some time ago Theudas rose up, claiming to be somebody. A number of men, about four hundred, joined him. He was killed, and all who obeyed him were scattered and brought to nothing.

37 "After this man, Judas of Galilee rose up in the days of the census, and drew away many people after him. He also perished, and all who obeyed him were dispersed.

38 "And now I say to you, keep away from these men and let them alone; for if this plan or this work is of men, it will come to nothing;

39 "but if it is of God, you cannot overthrow it—lest you be found to fight even against God."

40 And they agreed with him, and when they had called for the apostles and beaten them, they commanded that they should not speak in the name of Yeshua, and let them go.

41 And they departed from the presence of the council, rejoicing that they were counted worthy to suffer shame for His name.

42 And daily in the temple, and in every house, they did not cease teaching and preaching Yeshua as the Messiah.

Seven Chosen to Serve

6 And in those days, when the number of the disciples was multiplying, there arose a murmuring against the Hebrews by the Hellenists,[21] because their widows were neglected in the daily distribution.

2 Then the twelve called the multitude of the disciples to them and said, "It is not desirable that we should leave the word of God and serve tables.

3 "Therefore, brethren, seek out from among you seven men of good reputation, full of the Holy Spirit and wisdom, whom we may appoint over this business;

4 "but we will give ourselves continually to prayer and to the ministry of the word."

5 And the saying pleased the whole multitude. And they chose Stephen, a man full of faith and the Holy Spirit, and Philip, Prochorus, Nicanor, Timon, Parmenas, and Nicolas, a proselyte[22] from Antioch,

---

20 Psalm 110:1

21 People of Israel who lived outside of Israel and normally spoke Greek.

22 A Gentile convert to Judaism, now a believer.

6 whom they set before the apostles; and when they had prayed, they laid hands on them.

7 And the word of God spread, and the number of the disciples multiplied greatly in Jerusalem, and a great many of the priests were obedient to the faith.

Stephen Accused of Blasphemy

8 And Stephen, full of faith and power, did great wonders and miracles among the people.

9 Then there arose some from what is called the Synagogue of the Freedmen, the Cyrenians, the Alexandrians, and those from Cilicia and Asia, disputing with Stephen.

10 And they were not able to resist the wisdom and the Spirit by which he spoke.

11 Then they secretly induced men to say, "We have heard him speak blasphemous words against Moses and God."

12 And they stirred up the people, the elders, and the scribes; and they came upon him, seized him, and brought him to the council.

13 They also set up false witnesses who said, "This man does not cease to speak blasphemous words against this holy place and the Torah;

14 "for we have heard him say that this Yeshua of Nazareth will destroy this place and change the customs which Moses delivered to us."

15 And all who sat in the council, looking steadfastly at him, saw his face as the face of an angel.

Stephen's Address: The Call of Abraham

7 Then the high priest said, "Are these things so?"

2 And he said, "Men and brethren and fathers, listen: The God of glory appeared to our father Abraham when he was in Mesopotamia, before he dwelt in Haran,

3 "and said to him, 'Get out of your country and from your relatives, and come to the land which I will show you.' [23]

4 "Then he came out of the land of the Chaldeans and dwelt in Haran. And from there, when his father was dead, He moved him to this land in which you now dwell. [24]

5 "And He gave him no inheritance in it, not even enough to set his foot on. Yet He promised that He would give it to him for a possession, and to his descendants after him, when as yet he had no child.

6 "And God spoke in this way, that his descendants would sojourn in a foreign land, and that they would bring them into bondage and oppress them four hundred years.

7 'And the nation to whom they will be in bondage I will judge,' [25] said God, 'and after that they shall come out and serve Me in this place.' [26]

8 "And He gave him the covenant of circumcision; and so Abraham begot Isaac and circumcised him the eighth day; and

---

23 Genesis 12:1   24 Genesis 11:31
25 Genesis 15:13, 14   26 Exodus 3:12

Isaac begot Jacob, and Jacob begot the twelve patriarchs.

The Patriarchs in Egypt

9 "And the patriarchs, becoming envious, sold Joseph into Egypt. But God was with him

10 "and delivered him out of all his troubles, and gave him favor and wisdom in the presence of Pharaoh, king of Egypt; and he made him governor over Egypt and all his house.

11 "Now a famine and great trouble came over all the land of Egypt and Canaan, and our fathers found no sustenance.

12 "But when Jacob heard there was grain in Egypt, he sent out our fathers first.

13 "And the second time Joseph was made known to his brothers, and Joseph's family became known to the Pharaoh.

14 "Then Joseph sent and called his father Jacob and all his relatives to him, seventy-five people.

15 "So Jacob went down to Egypt and died, he and our fathers.

16 "And they were carried back to Shechem and laid in the tomb that Abraham bought for a sum of money from the sons of Hamor, the father of Shechem.

God Delivers Israel by Moses

17 "But when the time of the promise drew near which God had sworn to Abraham, the people grew and multiplied in Egypt

18 "till another king arose who did not know Joseph.[27]

19 "He dealt treacherously with our people, and oppressed our forefathers, so that they put out their young children that they might not live.

20 "At this time Moses was born, and was well-pleasing to God; and he was brought up in his father's house for three months.

21 "And when he was set out, Pharaoh's daughter took him away and brought him up as her own son.

22 "And Moses was learned in all the wisdom of the Egyptians, and was mighty in words and deeds.

23 "But when he was forty years old, it came into his heart to visit his brethren, the children of Israel.

24 "And seeing one of them suffer wrong, he defended and avenged him who was oppressed, and struck down the Egyptian.

25 "For he supposed his brethren would have understood that God would deliver them by his hand, but they did not understand.

26 "And the next day he appeared to two of them as they were fighting, and tried to reconcile them, saying, 'Men, you are brethren; why do you wrong one another?'

27 "But he who did his neighbor wrong pushed him away, saying, '*Who made you a ruler and a judge over us?*

28 '*Do you want to kill me as you did the Egyptian yesterday?*'[28]

29 "Then, at this saying, Moses fled and became a sojourner in the land of Midian, where he begot two sons.

30 "And when forty years had

27 Exodus 1:8   28 Exodus 2:14

passed, an Angel of the Lord appeared to him in a flame of fire in a bush, in the wilderness of Mount Sinai.

31 "When Moses saw it, he marveled at the sight; and as he drew near to observe it, the voice of the Lord came to him,

32 "saying, *'I am the God of your fathers—the God of Abraham, the God of Isaac, and the God of Jacob.'* [29] And Moses trembled and dared not look.

33 *'Then the LORD said to him: Take your sandals off your feet, for the place where you stand is holy ground.*

34 *I have certainly seen the oppression of my people who are in Egypt; I have heard their groaning and have come down to deliver them. And now come, I will send you to Egypt.'* [30]

35 "This Moses whom they rejected, saying, *'Who made you a ruler and a judge?'* [31] is the one God sent to be a ruler and a deliverer by the hand of the Angel who appeared to him in the bush.

36 "He brought them out, after he had shown wonders and signs in the land of Egypt, and in the Red Sea, and in the wilderness forty years.

A Rebellious Generation

37 "This is that Moses who said to the children of Israel, *'The LORD your God will raise up for you a Prophet like me from your brethren. Him you shall hear.'* [32]

38 "This is he who was in the congregation in the wilderness with the Angel who spoke to him on Mount Sinai, and with our fathers, the one who received the living oracles to give to us,

39 "whom our fathers would not obey, but rejected. And in their hearts they turned back to Egypt,

40 "saying to Aaron, *'Make us gods to go before us; as for this Moses who brought us out of the land of Egypt, we do not know what has become of him.'* [33]

41 "And they made a calf in those days, offered sacrifices to the idol, and rejoiced in the works of their own hands.

42 "Then God turned and gave them up to worship the host of heaven, as it is written in the book of the Prophets:

> *'Have you offered to Me slaughtered animals and sacrifices during forty years in the wilderness,*
> *O house of Israel?*
> 43 *Yes, you took up the tabernacle of Moloch,*
> *And the star of your god Remphan,*
> *Images which you made to worship;*
> *And I will carry you away beyond Babylon.'* [34]

The Tabernacle of Witness

44 "Our fathers had the tabernacle of witness in the wilderness, as He appointed, saying to Moses that he should make it according to the pattern that he had seen,

45 "which our fathers, having received it in succession, also brought with Joshua into the land possessed by the Gentiles, whom God drove out before the face of

29 Exodus 3:6, 15   30 Exodus 3:2-10
31 Exodus 2:14
32 Deuteronomy 18:15, 18

33 Exodus 32:1, 23   34 Amos 5:25-27

our fathers until the days of David,

46 "who found favor before God and asked to find a dwelling for the God of Jacob.

47 "But Solomon built Him a house.

48 "However, the Most High does not dwell in temples made with hands, as the prophet says:

49 'Heaven is My throne,
   And earth is My footstool.
   What house will you build
      for Me? says the LORD,
   Or what is the place of My
      rest?

50 Has My hand not made all
   these things?'[35]

Those Who Were Uncircumcised in Heart

51 "You stiffnecked and uncircumcised in heart and ears! You always resist the Holy Spirit; as your fathers did, so do you.

52 "Which of the prophets have your fathers not persecuted? And they have killed those who foretold the coming of the Just One, of whom you now have become the betrayers and murderers,

53 "who have received the Torah by the direction of angels and have not kept it."

The Stoning of Stephen

54 When they heard these things they were cut to the heart, and they gnashed at him with their teeth.

55 But he, being full of the Holy Spirit, gazed into heaven and saw the glory of God, and Yeshua standing at the right hand of God,[36]

56 and said, "Look! I see the heavens opened and the Son of Man standing at the right hand of God!" [37]

57 Then they cried out with a loud voice, stopped their ears, and ran at him with one accord;

58 and they cast him out of the city and stoned him. And the witnesses laid down their clothes at the feet of a young man whose name was Saul.

59 And they stoned Stephen as he was calling on God and saying, "Lord Yeshua, receive my spirit."

60 And he knelt down and cried out with a loud voice, "Lord, do not charge them with this sin." And when he had said this, he fell asleep.

Saul Persecutes the Body of Believers

8 And Saul was consenting to his death. And at that time a great persecution arose against the congregation which was at Jerusalem; and they were all scattered throughout the regions of Judea and Samaria, except the apostles.

2 And devout men carried Stephen to his burial, and made great lamentation over him.

3 As for Saul, he made havoc of the congregation, entering every house, and dragging off men and women, committing them to prison.

The Messiah Is Proclaimed in Samaria

4 Therefore those who were scattered went everywhere preaching the word.

5 Then Philip went down to the city of Samaria and preached the Messiah to them.

---

35 Isaiah 66:1, 2   36 Psalm 110:1   37 Cf. Daniel 7:13, 14

6 And the multitudes with one accord heeded those things which Philip spoke, hearing and seeing the miracles which he did.

7 For unclean spirits, crying with a loud voice, came out of many who were possessed; and many who were paralyzed and lame were healed.

8 And there was great joy in that city.

The Sorcerer's Profession of Faith

9 But there was a certain man called Simon, who previously practiced sorcery in the same city and astonished the people of Samaria, claiming that he was someone great,

10 to whom they all gave heed, from the least to the greatest, saying, "This man is the great power of God."

11 And they heeded him because he had astonished them with his sorceries for a long time.

12 But when they believed Philip as he preached the things concerning the kingdom of God and the name of Yeshua ha Mashiach, both men and women were immersed.

13 Then Simon himself also believed; and when he was immersed he continued with Philip, and was amazed, seeing the miracles and signs which were done.

The Sorcerer's Sin

14 Now when the apostles who were at Jerusalem heard that Samaria had received the word of God, they sent Peter and John to them,

15 who, when they had come down, prayed for them that they might receive the Holy Spirit.

16 For as yet He had fallen upon none of them. They had only been immersed in the name of the Lord Yeshua.

17 Then they laid hands on them, and they received the Holy Spirit.

18 And when Simon saw that through the laying on of the apostles' hands the Holy Spirit was given, he offered them money,

19 saying, "Give me this power also, that on whomever I lay hands he may receive the Holy Spirit."

20 But Peter said to him, "Your money perish with you, because you have thought that the gift of God may be purchased with money!

21 "You have neither part nor portion in this matter, for your heart is not right in the sight of God.

22 "Repent therefore of this your wickedness, and pray God if perhaps the thought of your heart may be forgiven you.

23 "For I perceive that you are poisoned by bitterness and bound by iniquity."

24 Then Simon answered and said, "Pray to the Lord for me that none of the things which you have spoken may come upon me."

25 Then, when they had testified and preached the word of the Lord, they returned to Jerusalem, preaching the good news in many villages of the Samaritans.

Messiah Is Proclaimed to an Ethiopian

26 And an angel of the Lord spoke to Philip, saying, "Arise and go toward the south to the road which goes down from Jerusalem to Gaza." This is desert.

27 And he arose and went. And behold, a man of Ethiopia, a eunuch of great authority under Candace the queen of the Ethiopians, who had charge of all her treasury, and had come to Jerusalem to worship,

28 was returning. And sitting in his chariot, he was reading Isaiah the prophet.

29 Then the Spirit said to Philip, "Go near and overtake this chariot."

30 And Philip ran to him, and heard him reading the prophet Isaiah, and said, "Do you understand what you are reading?"

31 And he said, "How can I, unless someone guides me?" And he asked Philip to come up and sit with him.

32 The place in the Scripture which he read was this:

"He was led as a sheep to the
     slaughter;
And like a lamb silent before
     its shearer,
So He did not open His
     mouth.

33 In His humiliation His justice was taken away.
And who will declare His
     generation?
For His life is taken from the
     earth." [38]

34 And the eunuch answered Philip and said, "I ask you, of whom does the prophet say this, of himself or of some other man?"

35 Then Philip opened his mouth, and beginning at this Scripture, preached Yeshua to him.

36 And as they went down the road, they came to some water. And the eunuch said, "See, here is water. What hinders me from being immersed?"

37 And Philip said, "If you believe with all your heart, you may." And he answered and said, "I believe that Yeshua ha Mashiach is the Son of God."

38 And he commanded the chariot to stand still. And both Philip and the eunuch went down into the water, and he immersed him.

39 And when they had come up out of the water, the Spirit of the Lord caught Philip away, so that the eunuch saw him no more; and he went on his way rejoicing.

40 But Philip was found at Azotus. And passing through, he preached in all the cities till he came to Caesarea.

Saul Meets Yeshua on the Damascus Road

9 And Saul, still breathing threats and murder against the disciples of the Lord, went to the high priest

2 and asked letters from him to the synagogues of Damascus, so that if he found any who were of the Way, whether men or women, he might bring them bound to Jerusalem.

3 And as he journeyed he came near Damascus, and suddenly a light shone around him from heaven.

4 And he fell to the ground, and heard a voice saying to him, "Saul, Saul, why are you persecuting Me?"

5 And he said, "Who are You, Lord?" And the Lord said, "I am Yeshua, whom you are persecut-

38 Isaiah 53:7, 8

ing. It is hard for you to kick against the goads."

6 And he, trembling and astonished, said, "Lord, what do You want me to do?" And the Lord said to him, "Arise and go into the city, and you will be told what you must do."

7 And the men who journeyed with him stood speechless, hearing a voice but seeing no one.

8 And Saul arose from the ground, and when his eyes were opened he saw no one. But they led him by the hand and brought him into Damascus.

9 And he was three days without sight, and neither ate nor drank.

Ananias Immerses Saul

10 Now there was a certain disciple at Damascus named Ananias; and to him the Lord said in a vision, "Ananias." And he said, "Here I am, Lord."

11 And the Lord said to him, "Arise and go to the street called Straight, and inquire in the house of Judas for one called Saul of Tarsus, for behold, he is praying.

12 "And in a vision he has seen a man named Ananias coming in and putting his hand on him, so that he might receive his sight."

13 Then Ananias answered, "Lord, I have heard from many about this man, how much harm he has done to Your followers in Jerusalem.

14 "And here he has authority from the chief priests to bind all who call on Your name."

15 But the Lord said to him, "Go your way, for he is a chosen vessel of Mine to bear My name before Gentiles, kings, and the children of Israel.

16 "For I will show him what great things he must suffer for My name's sake."

17 And Ananias went his way and entered the house. And laying his hands on him he said, "Brother Saul, the Lord Yeshua, who appeared to you on the road as you came, has sent me that you may receive your sight and be filled with the Holy Spirit."

18 And immediately there fell from his eyes something like scales, and he received his sight at once; and he arose and was immersed.

19 And when he had received food, he was strengthened. Then Saul spent some days with the disciples who were at Damascus.

Saul Shares the Messiah

20 And immediately he preached the Messiah in the synagogues, that He is the Son of God.[39]

21 But all who heard him were amazed, and said, "Is this not he who destroyed those who called on this name in Jerusalem, and came here for that purpose, so that he might bring them bound to the chief priests?"

22 But Saul increased all the more in strength, and confounded the Judeans who dwelt in Damascus, proving that this is indeed the Messiah.

Saul Escapes Death

23 And after many days were past, the Judeans plotted to kill him.

24 But their plot became known

39 Psalm 2:2, 7; Proverbs 30:4

to Saul. And they watched the gates day and night, to kill him.

25 Then the disciples took him by night and let him down through the wall in a large basket.

Saul at Jerusalem

26 And when Saul had come to Jerusalem, he tried to join the disciples; but they were all afraid of him, and did not believe that he was a disciple.

27 But Barnabas took him and brought him to the apostles. And he declared to them how he had seen the Lord on the road, and that He had spoken to him, and how he had preached boldly at Damascus in the name of Yeshua.

28 And he was with them at Jerusalem, coming in and going out.

29 And he spoke boldly in the name of the Lord Yeshua and disputed against the Hellenists, but they attempted to kill him.

30 When the brethren found out, they brought him down to Caesarea and sent him out to Tarsus.

The Congregation Prospers

31 Then the congregations throughout all Judea, Galilee, and Samaria had peace and were edified. And walking in the fear of the Lord and in the comfort of the Holy Spirit, they were multiplied.

Aeneas Healed

32 And it came to pass, as Peter passed through all parts of the country, that he also came down to the believers who dwelt in Lydda.

33 And there he found a certain man named Aeneas, who had been bedridden eight years and was paralyzed.

34 And Peter said to him, "Aeneas, Yeshua the Messiah heals you. Arise and make your bed." And he arose immediately.

35 And all who dwelt at Lydda and Sharon saw him and turned to the Lord.

Dorcas Restored to Life

36 Now there was at Joppa a certain disciple named Tabitha, which is translated Dorcas. This woman was full of good works and charitable deeds which she did.

37 But it happened in those days that she became sick and died. When they had washed her, they laid her in an upper room.

38 And since Lydda was near Joppa, and the disciples had heard that Peter was there, they sent two men to him, imploring him that he would not delay in coming to them.

39 Then Peter arose and went with them. When he had come, they brought him to the upper room. And all the widows stood by him weeping, showing the tunics and garments which Dorcas had made while she was with them.

40 But Peter put them all out, knelt down, and prayed. And turning to the body he said, "Tabitha, arise." And she opened her eyes, and when she saw Peter she sat up.

41 And he gave her his hand and lifted her up; and when he had called the believers and widows, he presented her alive.

42 And it became known throughout all Joppa, and many believed on the Lord.

43 And it came to pass that he stayed many days in Joppa with Simon, a tanner.

Cornelius Sends a Delegation

10 There was a certain man in Caesarea called Cornelius, a centurion of what was called the Italian Regiment,

2 a devout man and one who feared God with all his household, who gave alms generously to the people, and prayed to God always.

3 About the ninth hour [40] of the day he saw clearly in a vision an angel of God coming in and saying to him, "Cornelius."

4 And when he observed him, he was afraid, and said, "What is it, lord?" And he said to him, "Your prayers and your alms have come up for a memorial before God.

5 "And now send men to Joppa, and call for Simon whose surname is Peter.

6 "He is lodging with Simon, a tanner, whose house is by the seaside. He will tell you what you must do."

7 And when the angel who spoke to him had departed, Cornelius called two of his household servants and a devout soldier from among those who waited on him continually.

8 And when he had explained all these things to them, he sent them to Joppa.

Peter's Vision

9 The next day, as they went on their journey and drew near the city, Peter went up on the housetop to pray, about the sixth [41] hour.

10 And he became very hungry and wanted to eat; but while they made ready, he fell into a trance

11 and saw heaven opened and an object like a great sheet bound at the four corners, descending to him, and let down to the earth.

12 In it were all kinds of four-footed animals of the earth, wild beasts, creeping things, and birds of the air.

13 And a voice came to him, "Rise, Peter; kill and eat."

14 But Peter said, "Not so, Lord! For I have never eaten anything that is common or unclean."

15 And a voice spoke to him again the second time, "What God has cleansed you must not call common."

16 This was done three times. And the object was taken up into heaven again.

Summoned to Caesarea

17 Now while Peter wondered within himself what this vision which he had seen meant, behold, the men who had been sent from Cornelius had made inquiry for Simon's house, and stood before the gate.

18 And they called and asked whether Simon, who was also named Peter, was lodging there.

19 While Peter thought about the vision, the Spirit said to him, "Behold, three men are seeking you.

20 "Arise therefore, go down and go with them, doubting nothing; for I have sent them."

---

40 3 p.m., the time of the offering of the evening sacrifice at the temple.

41 Noon.

21 Then Peter went down to the men who were sent to him from Cornelius and said, "Yes, I am he whom you seek. For what reason have you come?"

22 And they said, "Cornelius the centurion, a just man, one who fears God and has a good reputation among all the nation of the Judeans, was divinely instructed by a holy angel to send for you to come to his house, and to hear words from you."

23 Then he invited them in and lodged them. And the next day Peter went away with them, and some brethren from Joppa accompanied him.

Peter Meets Cornelius

24 And the following day they entered Caesarea. And Cornelius was waiting for them, and he had called together his relatives and close friends.

25 And as Peter was coming in, Cornelius met him and fell down at his feet and worshiped him.

26 But Peter lifted him up, saying, "Stand up; I myself am also a man."

27 And as he talked with him, he went in and found many who had come together.

28 And he said to them, "You know how it is an unlawful thing for a man who is a Jew to keep company with or go to one of another nation. But God has shown me that I should not call any man common or unclean.

29 "Therefore I came to you without objection as soon as I was sent for. I ask, then, for what reason have you sent for me?"

30 And Cornelius said, "Four days ago I was fasting until this

hour; and at the ninth hour [42] I prayed in my house, and behold, a man stood before me in bright clothing,

31 "and said, 'Cornelius, your prayer has been heard, and your alms are remembered in the sight of God.

32 'Send therefore to Joppa and call Simon here, whose surname is Peter. He is lodging in the house of Simon, a tanner, by the seaside. When he comes, he will speak to you.'

33 "So I sent to you immediately, and you have done well to come. Now therefore, we are all present before God, to hear all the things commanded you by God."

The Good News Proclaimed to Cornelius' Household

34 Then Peter opened his mouth and said: "In truth I perceive that God shows no partiality.

35 "But in every nation whoever fears Him and works righteousness is accepted by Him.

36 "The word which God sent to the children of Israel, preaching peace by Yeshua ha Mashiach— He is Lord of all—

37 "that word you know, which was proclaimed throughout all Judea, and began from Galilee after the immersion which John preached:

38 "how God anointed Yeshua of Nazareth with the Holy Spirit and with power, who went about doing good and healing all who were oppressed by the devil, for God was with Him.

39 "And we are witnesses of all things which He did both in the

42 3 p.m.

land of the Judeans and in Jerusalem, whom they killed by hanging on a tree.

40 "Him God raised up on the third day, and showed Him openly,

41 "not to all the people, but to witnesses chosen before by God, even to us who ate and drank with Him after He arose from the dead.

42 "And He commanded us to preach to the people, and to testify that it is He who was ordained by God to be Judge of the living and the dead.

43 "To Him all the prophets witness that, through His name, whoever believes in Him will receive forgiveness of sins."

The Holy Spirit Falls on the Gentiles

44 While Peter was still speaking these words, the Holy Spirit fell on all those who heard the word.

45 And those of the circumcision who believed were astonished, as many as came with Peter, because the gift of the Holy Spirit had been poured out on the Gentiles also.

46 For they heard them speak with tongues and magnify God. Then Peter answered,

47 "Can anyone forbid water, that these should not be immersed who have received the Holy Spirit just as we?"

48 And he commanded them to be immersed in the name of the Lord. Then they asked him to stay a few days.

Peter Defends God's Grace

11 And the apostles and brethren who were in Judea heard that the Gentiles had also received the word of God.

2 And when Peter came up to Jerusalem, those of the circumcision contended with him,

3 saying, "You went in to uncircumcised men and ate with them!"

4 But Peter explained it to them in order from the beginning, saying:

5 "I was in the city of Joppa praying; and in a trance I saw a vision, an object descending like a great sheet, let down from heaven by four corners; and it came to me.

6 "When I observed it intently and considered, I saw four-footed animals of the earth, wild beasts, creeping things, and birds of the air.

7 "And I heard a voice saying to me, 'Rise, Peter; kill and eat.'

8 "But I said, 'Not so, Lord! For nothing common or unclean has at any time entered my mouth.'

9 "But the voice answered me again from heaven, 'What God has cleansed you must not call common.'

10 "And this was done three times, and all were drawn up again into heaven.

11 "And behold, immediately three men sent to me from Caesarea came to the house where I was.

12 "And the Spirit told me to go with them, doubting nothing. Moreover these six brethren accompanied me, and we entered the man's house.

13 "And he told us how he had seen an angel in his house, who stood and said to him, 'Send men to Joppa, and call for Simon whose surname is Peter,

14 'who will tell you words by which you and all your household will be saved.'

15 "And as I began to speak, the Holy Spirit fell on them, as on us at the beginning.

16 "Then I remembered the word of the Lord, how He said, 'John indeed immersed with water, but you will be immersed in the Holy Spirit.'

17 "If then God gave them the same gift as He gave us who believed on the Lord Yeshua ha Mashiach, who was I that I could withstand God?"

18 When they heard these things they became silent; and they glorified God, saying, "Then God has also granted to the Gentiles repentance to life."

Barnabas and Saul at Antioch

19 Now those who were scattered after the persecution that arose over Stephen traveled as far as Phoenicia, Cyprus, and Antioch, preaching the word to no one but the Jews only.

20 And some of them were men from Cyprus and Cyrene, who, when they had come to Antioch, spoke to the Hellenists, preaching the Lord Yeshua.

21 And the hand of the Lord was with them, and a great number believed and turned to the Lord.

22 Then news of these things came to the ears of the congregation in Jerusalem, and they sent out Barnabas to go as far as Antioch.

23 When he came and had seen the grace of God, he was glad, and encouraged them all that with

purpose of heart they should continue with the Lord.

24 For he was a good man, full of the Holy Spirit and of faith. And many people were added to the Lord.

25 Then Barnabas departed for Tarsus to seek Saul.

26 And when he had found him, he brought him to Antioch. And it came to pass that for a whole year they assembled with the congregation and taught many people. And the disciples were first called Christians [43] in Antioch.

Relief to Judea

27 And in these days prophets came from Jerusalem to Antioch.

28 And one of them, named Agabus, stood up and showed by the Spirit that there was going to be a great famine throughout all the world, which also came to pass in the days of Claudius Caesar.

29 Then the disciples, each according to his ability, determined to send relief to the brethren dwelling in Judea.

30 This they also did, and sent it to the elders by the hands of Barnabas and Saul.

Herod's Violence

12 Now about that time Herod the king stretched out his hand to harass some from the congregation.

2 And he killed James the brother of John with the sword.

3 And because he saw it pleased the Judeans, he proceeded

43 This is the anglicized form of the Greek *Christianoi:* Messianists, followers of the Messiah.

further to seize Peter also. Now it was during the Days of Unleavened Bread.

4 And when he had apprehended him, he put him in prison, and delivered him to four squads of soldiers to keep him, intending to bring him before the people after Passover.

Peter Freed from Prison

5 Peter therefore was kept in prison, but prayer for him was made to God without ceasing by the congregation.

6 And when Herod was about to bring him out, that night Peter, bound with two chains, was sleeping between two soldiers; and the guards before the door were keeping the prison.

7 And behold, an angel of the Lord stood by him, and a light shone in the prison; and he struck Peter on the side and raised him up, saying, "Arise quickly!" And his chains fell off his hands.

8 And the angel said to him, "Gird yourself and tie on your sandals." And so he did. And he said to him, "Put on your garment and follow me."

9 And he went out and followed him, and did not know that what was done by the angel was real, but thought he was seeing a vision.

10 When they were past the first and the second guard posts, they came to the iron gate that leads to the city, which opened to them of its own accord; and they went out and went down one street, and immediately the angel departed from him.

11 And when Peter had come to himself, he said, "Now I know for certain that the Lord has sent His angel, and has delivered me out of the hand of Herod and from all the expectation of the Judean people."

12 And when he had considered this, he came to the house of Miriam, the mother of John whose surname was Mark, where many were gathered together praying.

13 And as Peter knocked at the door in the gate, a girl named Rhoda came to answer.

14 And when she recognized Peter's voice, she did not open the gate for gladness, but ran in and announced that Peter stood before the gate.

15 And they said to her, "You are beside yourself!" But she kept insisting that it was so. Then they said, "It is his angel."

16 But Peter continued knocking; and when they opened the door and saw him, they were astonished.

17 But motioning to them with his hand to keep silent, he declared to them how the Lord had brought him out of the prison. And he said, "Go, tell these things to James and to the brethren." And he departed and went to another place.

18 Now as soon as it was day, there was no small stir among the soldiers about what had become of Peter.

19 And when Herod had searched for him and not found him, he examined the guards and commanded that they should be put to death. And he went down from Judea to Caesarea, and stayed there.

Herod's Violent Death

20 Now Herod had been very angry with the people of Tyre and Sidon; but they came to him with one accord, and having made Blastus the king's chamberlain their friend, they asked for peace, because their country was supplied with food by the king's country.

21 And on a set day Herod, arrayed in royal apparel, sat on his throne and gave an oration to them.

22 And the people kept shouting, "The voice of a god and not of a man!"

23 And immediately an angel of the Lord struck him, because he did not give glory to God. And he was eaten by worms and died.

24 But the word of God grew and multiplied.

Barnabas and Saul Appointed

25 And Barnabas and Saul returned from Jerusalem when they had fulfilled their ministry, and they also took with them John whose surname was Mark.

13 Now in the congregation that was at Antioch there were certain prophets and teachers: Barnabas, Simeon who was called Niger, Lucius of Cyrene, Manaen who had been brought up with Herod the tetrarch, and Saul.

2 As they ministered to the Lord and fasted, the Holy Spirit said, "Separate to Me Barnabas and Saul for the work to which I have called them."

3 And when they had fasted and prayed, and laid hands on them, they sent them away.

A False Prophet

4 So, being sent out by the Holy Spirit, they departed to Seleucia, and from there they sailed to Cyprus.

5 And when they arrived in Salamis, they preached the word of God in the synagogues of the Jews. And they also had John as their assistant.

6 And when they had gone through the island to Paphos, they found a certain sorcerer, a false prophet, a Jew whose name was Bar-Yeshua,

7 who was with the proconsul of the country, Sergius Paulus, an intelligent man. He called for Barnabas and Saul and desired to hear the word of God.

8 But Elymas the sorcerer (for so his name is translated) withstood them, seeking to turn the proconsul away from the faith.

9 Then Saul, who also is called Paul, filled with the Holy Spirit, looked intently at him

10 and said, "O full of all deceit and all fraud, you son of the devil, you enemy of all righteousness, will you not cease perverting the straight ways of the Lord?

11 "And now, indeed, the hand of the Lord is upon you, and you will be blind, not seeing the sun for a time." And immediately there fell on him a mist and a darkness, and he went around seeking someone to lead him by the hand.

12 Then the proconsul believed, when he saw what had been done, being astonished at the teaching of the Lord.

At Antioch in Pisidia

13 Now when Paul and his party set sail from Paphos, they came to Perga in Pamphylia; and John, departing from them, returned to Jerusalem.

14 But when they departed from Perga, they came to Antioch in Pisidia, and went into the synagogue on the Sabbath day and sat down.

15 And after the reading of the Torah and the Prophets, the rulers of the synagogue sent to them, saying, "Men and brethren, if you have any word of exhortation for the people, say on."

16 Then Paul stood up, and motioning with his hand said, "Men of Israel, and you who fear God, listen:

17 "The God of this people of Israel chose our fathers, and exalted the people when they dwelt as strangers in the land of Egypt, and with an uplifted arm He brought them out of it.

18 "And for a time of about forty years He put up with their ways in the wilderness.

19 "And when He had destroyed seven nations in the land of Canaan, He distributed their land to them by allotment.

20 "And after that He gave them judges for about four hundred and fifty years, until Samuel the prophet.

21 "And afterward they asked for a king. And God gave them Saul the son of Kish, a man of the tribe of Benjamin, for forty years.

22 "And when He had removed him, He raised up David for them to be their king, to whom also He gave testimony and said, 'I have found David[44] the son of Jesse, a man after My own heart, who will do all My will.' [45]

23 "From this man's seed, God, according to His promise, has raised up for Israel a Savior—Yeshua—

24 "after John first preached, before His coming, the immersion of repentance to all the people of Israel.

25 "And as John was finishing his course, he said, 'Who do you think I am? I am not He. But behold, there comes One after me, the sandals of whose feet I am not worthy to loose.'

26 "Men and brethren, sons of the family of Abraham, and those among you who fear God, to you is the word of this salvation sent.

27 "For those who dwell in Jerusalem, and their rulers, because they did not know Him, nor even the voices of the Prophets which are read every Sabbath, have fulfilled them in condemning Him.

28 "And though they found no cause for death in Him, yet they asked Pilate that He should be put to death.

29 "And when they had fulfilled all that was written concerning Him, they took Him down from the tree and laid Him in a tomb.

30 "But God raised Him from the dead.

31 "And He was seen many days by those who came up with Him from Galilee to Jerusalem, who are His witnesses to the people.

32 "And we declare to you glad tidings—that promise which was made to the fathers.

44 Psalm 89:20   45 1 Samuel 13:14

33 "God has fulfilled this for us their children, in that He has raised up Yeshua. As it is also written in the second Psalm:

'You are My Son,
Today I have begotten
You.'⁴⁶

34 "And that He raised Him from the dead, no more to return to corruption, He has spoken thus:

'I will give you the sure mercies of David.'⁴⁷

35 "Therefore He also says in another Psalm:

'You will not allow Your Holy One to see corruption.'⁴⁸

36 "For David, after he had served his own generation by the will of God, fell asleep, was buried with his fathers, and saw corruption;

37 "but He whom God raised up saw no corruption.

38 "Therefore let it be known to you, brethren, that through this Man is preached to you the forgiveness of sins;

39 "and by Him everyone who believes is justified from all things from which you could not be justified by the Torah of Moses.

40 "Beware therefore, lest that come upon you which is spoken of in the prophets:

41 'Behold, you despisers,
Marvel and perish;
For I work a work in your days,
A work which you will by no means believe,
Though someone declare it to you.'"⁴⁹

Blessing and Conflict at Antioch

42 And when the Jews went out of the synagogue, the Gentiles begged that these words might be preached to them the next Sabbath.

43 Now when the synagogue had broken up, many of the Jews and devout proselytes followed Paul and Barnabas who, speaking to them, persuaded them to continue in the grace of God.

44 And the next Sabbath almost the whole city came together to hear the word of God.

45 But when the Jews saw the multitudes, they were filled with envy; and contradicting and blaspheming, they opposed the things spoken by Paul.

46 Then Paul and Barnabas grew bold and said, "It was necessary that the word of God should be spoken to you first; but seeing you reject it, and judge yourselves unworthy of everlasting life, behold, we turn to the Gentiles.⁵⁰

47 "For so the Lord has commanded us:

'I have set you to be a light to the Gentiles,
That you should be for salvation to the ends of the earth.'"⁵¹

48 And when the Gentiles heard

---

46 Psalm 2:7   *47* Isaiah 55:3
48 Psalm 16:10   *49* Habakkuk 1:5

50 Paul made this statement to a specific group of Jewish people. In no way do we understand this as a general truth. Paul always went to the synagogue whenever he entered a new city. God intends for the good news always to be shared with His people Israel. Paul's heart's desire was to reach his own people with the good news (Romans 10:1).   *51* Isaiah 49:6

this, they were glad and glorified the word of the Lord. And as many as had been appointed to eternal life believed.

49 And the word of the Lord was being spread throughout all the region.

50 But the Jews stirred up the devout and prominent women and the chief men of the city, raised up persecution against Paul and Barnabas, and expelled them from their region.

51 But they shook off the dust from their feet against them, and came to Iconium.

52 And the disciples were filled with joy and with the Holy Spirit.

At Iconium

14 Now it came to pass in Iconium that they went together to the synagogue of the Jews, and so spoke that a great multitude both of the Jews and of the Greeks believed.

2 But the unbelieving Jews stirred up the Gentiles and poisoned their minds against the brethren.

3 Therefore they stayed there a long time, speaking boldly in the Lord, who was bearing witness to the word of His grace, granting signs and wonders to be done by their hands.

4 But the multitude of the city was divided: part sided with the Jews, and part with the apostles.

5 And when an attempt was made by both the Gentiles and Jews, with their rulers, to abuse and stone them,

6 they became aware of it and fled to Lystra and Derbe, cities of Lycaonia, and to the surrounding region.

7 And they were preaching the good news there.

Idolatry at Lystra

8 And in Lystra a certain man without strength in his feet was sitting, a cripple from his mother's womb, who had never walked.

9 He heard Paul speaking. And Paul, observing him intently and perceiving that he had faith to be healed,

10 said with a loud voice, "Stand up straight on your feet!" And he leaped and walked.

11 And when the people saw what Paul had done, they raised their voices, saying in the language of Lycaonia, "The gods have come down to us in the likeness of men!"

12 And Barnabas they called Zeus, and Paul, Hermes, because he was the chief speaker.

13 Then the priest of Zeus, whose temple was in front of their city, brought oxen and garlands to the gates, intending to sacrifice with the multitudes.

14 When the apostles, Barnabas and Paul heard this, they tore their clothes and ran in among the multitude, crying out

15 and saying, "Men, why are you doing these things? We also are men with the same nature as you, and preach to you that you should turn from these vain things to the living God, who made the heaven, the earth, the sea, and all things that are in them,

16 "who in times past allowed all nations to walk in their own ways.

17 "Nevertheless He did not

leave Himself without witness, in that He did good, gave us rain from heaven and fruitful seasons, filling our hearts with food and gladness."

18 And with these sayings they could scarcely restrain the multitudes from sacrificing to them.

Stoning, Escape to Derbe

19 And Jews from Antioch and Iconium came there and persuaded the multitudes; and having stoned Paul, they dragged him out of the city, supposing him to be dead.

20 However, when the disciples gathered around him, he rose up and went into the city. And the next day he departed with Barnabas to Derbe.

Strengthening the Believers

21 And when they had preached the good news to that city and made many disciples, they returned to Lystra, Iconium, and Antioch,

22 strengthening the souls of the disciples, exhorting them to continue in the faith, and saying, "We must through many tribulations enter the kingdom of God."

23 And when they had appointed elders in every congregation, and prayed with fasting, they commended them to the Lord in whom they believed.

24 And after they had passed through Pisidia, they came to Pamphylia.

25 And when they had preached the word in Perga, they went down to Attalia.

26 And from there they sailed to Antioch, where they had been commended to the grace of God for the work which they had completed.

27 And when they had come and gathered the congregation together, they reported all that God had done with them, and how He had opened the door of faith to the Gentiles.

28 And they stayed there a long time with the disciples.

Conflict over Circumcision

15 And certain men came down from Judea and taught the brethren, "Unless you are circumcised according to the custom of Moses, you cannot be saved."

2 Therefore, when Paul and Barnabas had no small dissension and dispute with them, they determined that Paul and Barnabas and certain others of them should go up to Jerusalem, to the apostles and elders, about this question.

3 And so, being sent on their way by the congregation, they passed through Phoenicia and Samaria, describing the conversion of the Gentiles; and they caused great joy to all the brethren.

4 And when they had come to Jerusalem, they were received by the congregation, the apostles, and elders; and they reported all things that God had done with them.

5 But some of the sect of the Pharisees who believed rose up, saying, "It is necessary to circumcise them, and to command them to keep the Torah of Moses."

The Jerusalem Council

6 And the apostles and elders came together to consider this matter.

7 And when there had been much dispute, Peter rose up and said to them: "Men and brethren, you know that a good while ago God chose among us, that by my mouth the Gentiles should hear the word of the good news and believe.

8 "And God, who knows the heart, acknowledged them, giving them the Holy Spirit just as He did to us,

9 "and made no distinction between us and them, purifying their hearts by faith.

10 "Now therefore why do you test God by putting a yoke on the neck of the disciples which neither our fathers nor we were able to bear?

11 "But we believe that through the grace of the Lord Yeshua ha Mashiach we shall be saved in the same manner as they."

12 Then all the multitude kept silent and listened to Barnabas and Paul declaring what miracles and wonders God had worked among the Gentiles by them.

13 And after they had become silent, James answered, saying, "Men and brethren, listen to me:

14 "Simon has declared how God at the first visited the Gentiles to take out of them a people for His name.

15 "And with this the words of the prophets agree, just as it is written:

16 'After this I will return
And will rebuild the tabernacle of David which has fallen down.
I will rebuild its ruins,
And I will set it up,

17 So that the rest of mankind may seek the LORD,

Even all the Gentiles upon whom My name is called,
Says the LORD who does all these things.

18 Known to God are all His works from the beginning of the world.'[52]

19 "Therefore I judge that we should not trouble those from the Gentiles who are turning to God,

20 "but that we write to them to abstain from things polluted by idols, from sexual immorality, from things strangled, and from blood.

21 "For Moses of old time has in every city those who preach him, being read in the synagogues every Sabbath."

The Jerusalem Decree

22 Then it pleased the apostles and elders, with the whole congregation, to send chosen men of their own company to Antioch with Paul and Barnabas, namely, Judas who was also named Barsabas, and Silas, leading men among the brethren.

23 And they wrote this letter by them:

"The apostles, the elders, and the brethren,

To the brethren who are of the Gentiles in Antioch, Syria, and Cilicia:

Greetings.

24 Since we have heard that some who went out from us have troubled you with their words, unsettling your souls, saying, 'You must be circumcised and keep the Torah'—

52 Amos 9:11, 12

to whom we gave no such commandment—

25 it seemed good to us, being assembled with one accord, to send chosen men to you with our beloved Barnabas and Paul,

26 men who have risked their lives for the name of our Lord Yeshua ha Mashiach.

27 We have therefore sent Judas and Silas, who will also tell you the same things by word of mouth.

28 For it seemed good to the Holy Spirit, and to us, to lay upon you no greater burden than these necessary things:

29 that you abstain from things offered to idols, from blood, from things strangled, and from sexual immorality; if you keep yourselves from these, you will do well.

Farewell."

Continuing Service in Syria

30 So when they were sent off, they came to Antioch; and when they had gathered the multitude together, they delivered the letter.

31 When they had read it, they rejoiced over its encouragement.

32 Now Judas and Silas, themselves being prophets also, exhorted the brethren with many words and strengthened them.

33 And after they had stayed there for a time, they were sent back with greetings from the brethren to the apostles.

34 However, it seemed good to Silas to remain there.

35 Paul and Barnabas also remained in Antioch, teaching and preaching the word of the Lord, with many others also.

Division over John Mark

36 And after some days Paul said to Barnabas, "Let us go back and visit our brethren in every city where we have preached the word of the Lord, and see how they are doing."

37 And Barnabas determined to take with them John called Mark.

38 But Paul insisted they not take with them the one who had departed from them in Pamphylia, and had not gone with them to the work.

39 Then the contention became so sharp between them that they parted from one another. And so Barnabas took Mark and sailed to Cyprus;

40 but Paul chose Silas and departed, being commended by the brethren to the grace of God.

41 And he went through Syria and Cilicia, strengthening the congregations.

Timothy Joins Paul and Silas

16 Then he came to Derbe and Lystra. And behold, a certain disciple was there, named Timothy, the son of a certain Jewish woman who believed, but his father was a Greek.

2 He was well spoken of by the brethren who were at Lystra and Iconium.

3 Paul wanted to have him go on with him. And he took and circumcised him because of the Jews who were in that region, for they all knew that his father was a Greek.

4 And as they went through the cities, they delivered to them the decrees to keep, which were determined by the apostles and elders at Jerusalem.

5 And so the congregations were strengthened in the faith, and increased in number daily.

The Macedonian Call

6 Now when they had gone through Phrygia and the region of Galatia, they were forbidden by the Holy Spirit to preach the word in Asia.

7 After they had come to Mysia, they tried to go into Bithynia, but the Spirit did not permit them.

8 And passing by Mysia, they came down to Troas.

9 And a vision appeared to Paul in the night. A man of Macedonia stood and pleaded with him, saying, "Come over to Macedonia and help us."

10 And after he had seen the vision, immediately we sought to go to Macedonia, concluding that the Lord had called us to preach the good news to them.

Lydia Immersed at Philippi

11 Therefore, sailing from Troas, we ran a straight course to Samothrace, and the next day came to Neapolis,

12 and from there to Philippi, which is the chief city of that part of Macedonia, and a colony. And we were staying in that city for some days.

13 And on the Sabbath day we went out of the city to the riverside, where prayer was customarily made; and we sat down and spoke to the women who met there.

14 And a certain woman named Lydia, a seller of purple from the city of Thyatira, who worshiped God, heard us. The Lord opened her heart so that she heeded the things which were spoken by Paul.

15 And when she and her household were immersed, she begged us, saying, "If you have judged me to be faithful to the Lord, come to my house and stay." And she constrained us.

Paul and Silas Imprisoned

16 Now it happened, as we went to prayer, that a certain slave girl possessed with a spirit of divination met us, who brought her masters much profit by fortunetelling.

17 She followed Paul and us, and cried out, saying, "These men are the servants of the Most High God, who proclaim to us the way of salvation."

18 And this she did many days. But Paul, greatly annoyed, turned and said to the spirit, "I command you in the name of Yeshua ha Mashiach to come out of her." And he came out that very hour.

19 And when her masters saw that their hope of profit was gone, they seized Paul and Silas and dragged them into the marketplace to the authorities.

20 And they brought them to the magistrates, saying, "These men, being Jews, exceedingly trouble our city;

21 "and they teach customs which are not lawful for us, being Romans, to receive or observe."

22 And the multitude rose up together against them; and the mag-

istrates tore off their clothes and commanded them to be beaten with rods.

23 And when they had laid many stripes on them, they threw them into prison, commanding the jailer to keep them safely.

24 Having received such a charge, he put them into the inner prison and fastened their feet in the stocks.

The Philippian Jailer Believes

25 And at midnight Paul and Silas were praying and singing hymns to God, and the prisoners were listening to them.

26 And suddenly there was a great earthquake, so that the foundations of the prison were shaken; and immediately all the doors were opened and everyone's chains were loosed.

27 And the keeper of the prison, awaking from sleep and seeing the prison doors open, drew his sword and would have killed himself, supposing the prisoners had fled;

28 but Paul cried with a loud voice, saying, "Do yourself no harm, for we are all here."

29 Then he called for a light, ran in, and fell down trembling before Paul and Silas.

30 And he brought them out and said, "Sirs, what must I do to be saved?"

31 And they said, "Believe on the Lord Yeshua ha Mashiach, and you will be saved, you and your household."

32 And they spoke the word of the Lord to him and to all who were in his house.

33 And he took them the same hour of the night and washed their stripes. And immediately he and all his family were immersed.

34 And when he had brought them into his house, he set food before them; and he rejoiced, believing in God with all his household.

Paul Refuses to Depart Secretly

35 And when it was day, the magistrates sent the officers, saying, "Let those men go."

36 And the keeper of the prison reported this to Paul, saying, "The magistrates have sent to let you go. Now therefore depart, and go in peace."

37 But Paul said to them, "They have beaten us openly, uncondemned Romans, and have thrown us into prison. And now do they put us out secretly? No indeed! Let them come themselves and get us out."

38 And the officers told these words to the magistrates, and they were afraid when they heard that they were Romans.

39 And they came and pleaded with them, brought them out, and asked them to depart from the city.

40 And they went out of the prison and entered the house of Lydia; and when they had seen the brethren, they encouraged them and departed.

Proclaiming the Messiah at Thessalonica

17 Now when they had passed through Amphipolis and Apollonia, they came to Thessalonica, where there was a synagogue of the Jews.

2 And Paul, as his custom was, went in to them, and for three Sabbaths reasoned with them from the Scriptures,

3 explaining and demonstrating that the Messiah had to suffer and rise again from the dead, and saying, "This Yeshua whom I preach to you is the Messiah."

4 And some of them believed; and a great multitude of the devout Greeks, and not a few of the leading women, joined Paul and Silas.

Assault on Jason's House

5 But the Jews who did not believe, becoming envious, took some of the evil men from the marketplace, and gathering a mob, set all the city in an uproar, attacked the house of Jason, and sought to bring them out to the people.

6 But when they did not find them, they dragged Jason and some brethren to the rulers of the city, crying out, "These who have turned the world upside down have come here too.

7 "Jason has received them, and these are all acting contrary to the decrees of Caesar, saying there is another king—Yeshua."

8 And they troubled the people and the rulers of the city when they heard these things.

9 And when they had taken security from Jason and the rest, they let them go.

Serving at Berea

10 And the brethren immediately sent Paul and Silas away by night to Berea. Arriving there, they went into the synagogue of the Jews.

11 These were more noble-minded than those in Thessalonica, in that they received the word with all readiness of mind, and searched the Scriptures daily to find out whether these things were so.

12 Therefore many of them believed, and also not a few of the Greeks, prominent women as well as men.

13 But when the Jews from Thessalonica learned that the word of God was preached by Paul at Berea, they came there also and stirred up the people.

14 And then immediately the brethren sent Paul away, to go to the sea; but both Silas and Timothy remained there.

15 And those who conducted Paul brought him to Athens; and receiving a command for Silas and Timothy to come to him with all speed, they departed.

The Philosophers at Athens

16 Now while Paul waited for them at Athens, his spirit was provoked within him when he saw that the city was given over to idols.

17 Therefore he reasoned in the synagogue with the Jews and with the Gentile worshipers, and in the marketplace daily with those who happened to be there.

18 Then certain philosophers of the Epicureans and the Stoics encountered him. And some said, "What does this babbler want to say?" Others said, "He seems to be a proclaimer of foreign gods," because he preached to them Yeshua and the resurrection.

19 And they took him and brought him to the Areopagus, saying, "May we know what this new doctrine is of which you speak?

20 "For you are bringing some strange things to our ears. Therefore we want to know what these things mean."

21 For all the Athenians and the foreigners who were there spent their time in nothing else but either to tell or to hear some new thing.

Addressing the Areopagus

22 Then Paul stood in the midst of the Areopagus and said, "Men of Athens, I perceive that in all things you are very religious;

23 "for as I was passing through and considering the objects of your worship, I found an altar with this inscription:

'TO THE UNKNOWN GOD.'

Therefore, the One whom you worship without knowing, Him I proclaim to you:

24 "God, who made the world and everything in it, seeing He is Lord of heaven and earth, does not dwell in temples made with hands.

25 "Nor is He worshiped with men's hands, as though He needed anything, seeing He gives to all life, breath, and all things.

26 "And He has made from one blood every nation of men to dwell on all the face of the earth, and has determined their preappointed times and the boundaries of their habitation,

27 "so that they should seek the Lord, in the hope that they might grope for Him and find Him, though He is not far from each one of us;

28 "for in Him we live and move and have our being, as also some of your own poets have said, 'For we are also His offspring.'

29 "Therefore, since we are the offspring of God, we ought not to think that the Divine Nature is like gold or silver or stone, something shaped by art and man's devising.

30 "And these times of ignorance God overlooked, but now commands all men everywhere to repent,

31 "because He has appointed a day on which He will judge the world in righteousness by the Man whom He has ordained. He has given assurance of this to all, in that He has raised Him from the dead."

32 And when they heard of the resurrection of the dead, some mocked, while others said, "We will hear you again on this matter."

33 So Paul departed from among them.

34 However, some men joined him and believed, among them Dionysius the Areopagite, and a woman named Damaris, and others with them.

Serving at Corinth

18 After these things Paul departed from Athens and went to Corinth.

2 And he found a certain Jew named Aquila, born in Pontus, who had recently come from Italy with his wife Priscilla (because Claudius had commanded all

Jews to depart from Rome); and he came to them.

3 And because he was of the same trade, he stayed with them and worked; for by occupation they were tentmakers.

4 And he reasoned in the synagogue every Sabbath, and persuaded both Jews and Greeks.

5 And when Silas and Timothy had come from Macedonia, Paul was constrained by the Spirit, and testified to the Jews that Yeshua is the Messiah.

6 And when they opposed him and blasphemed, he shook his garments and said to them, "Your blood be upon your own heads; I am clean. From now on I will go to the Gentiles." [53]

7 And he departed from there and entered the house of a certain man named Justus, one who worshiped God, whose house was next door to the synagogue.

8 And Crispus, the ruler of the synagogue, believed on the Lord with all his household. And many of the Corinthians, hearing, believed and were immersed.

9 Then the Lord spoke to Paul in the night by a vision, "Do not be afraid, but speak, and do not keep silent;

10 "for I am with you, and no one will attack you to hurt you; for I have many people in this city."

11 And he continued there a year and six months, teaching the word of God among them.

12 And when Gallio was proconsul of Achaia, the Jews with one accord rose up against Paul and brought him to the judgment seat,

13 saying, "This fellow persuades men to worship God contrary to the Torah."

14 And when Paul was about to open his mouth, Gallio said to the Jews, "If it were a matter of wrongdoing or wicked crimes, O Jews, there would be reason why I should bear with you.

15 "But if it is a question of words and names and your own law, look to it yourselves; for I do not want to be a judge of such matters."

16 And he drove them from the judgment seat.

17 Then all the Greeks took Sosthenes, the ruler of the synagogue, and beat him before the judgment seat. And Gallio took no notice of these things.

Paul Returns to Antioch

18 And Paul still remained a good while. And he took leave of the brethren and sailed for Syria, and Priscilla and Aquila were with him. He had his hair cut off at Cenchrea, for he had taken a vow.

19 And he came to Ephesus, and left them there; but he himself entered the synagogue and reasoned with the Jews.

20 When they asked him to stay a longer time with them, he did not consent,

21 but took leave of them, saying, "I must by all means keep this coming feast in Jerusalem; but I will return again to you, God willing." And he sailed from Ephesus.

53 See footnote to Acts 13:46 and see Acts 18:19.

22 And when he had landed at Caesarea, and gone up and greeted the congregation, he went down to Antioch.

23 And after he had spent some time there, he departed and went over all the region of Galatia and Phrygia in order, strengthening all the disciples.

Apollos

24 And a certain Jew named Apollos, born at Alexandria, an eloquent man and mighty in the Scriptures, came to Ephesus.

25 This man had been instructed in the way of the Lord; and being fervent in his spirit, he spoke and taught accurately the things of the Lord, though he knew only the immersion of John.

26 And he began to speak boldly in the synagogue. When Aquila and Priscilla heard him, they took him aside and explained to him the way of God more accurately.

27 And when he desired to cross to Achaia, the brethren wrote, exhorting the disciples to receive him; and when he arrived, he greatly helped those who had believed through grace;

28 for he vigorously refuted the Jews publicly, showing by the Scriptures that Yeshua is the Messiah.

Paul at Ephesus

19 And it came to pass, while Apollos was at Corinth, that Paul, having passed through the upper regions, came to Ephesus. And finding some disciples

2 he said to them, "Did you receive the Holy Spirit when you believed?" And they said to him,

"We have not so much as heard whether there is a Holy Spirit."

3 And he said to them, "Into what then were you immersed?" and they said, "Into John's immersion."

4 Then Paul said, "John indeed immersed with the immersion of repentance, saying to the people that they should believe on Him who would come after him, that is, on Messiah Yeshua."

5 When they heard this, they were immersed in the name of the Lord Yeshua.

6 And when Paul had laid his hands on them, the Holy Spirit came upon them, and they spoke with tongues and prophesied.

7 And the men were about twelve in all.

8 And he went into the synagogue and spoke boldly for three months, reasoning and persuading concerning the things of the kingdom of God.

9 But when some were hardened and did not believe, but spoke evil of the Way before the multitude, he departed from them and withdrew the disciples, reasoning daily in the school of Tyrannus.

10 And this continued for two years, so that all who dwelt in Asia heard the word of the Lord Yeshua, both Jews and Greeks.

Miracles Glorify the Messiah

11 And God worked special miracles by the hands of Paul,

12 so that handkerchiefs or aprons were brought from his body to the sick, and the diseases left them and the evil spirits went out of them.

13 Then some of the itinerant Jewish exorcists took it upon themselves to call the name of the Lord Yeshua over those who had evil spirits, saying, "We adjure you by the Yeshua whom Paul preaches."

14 And there were seven sons of Sceva, a Jew and a chief priest, who did so.

15 And the evil spirit answered and said, "Yeshua I know, and Paul I know; but who are you?"

16 And the man in whom the evil spirit was leaped on them, overpowered them, and prevailed against them, so that they fled out of that house naked and wounded.

17 And this became known both to all Jews and Greeks dwelling in Ephesus; and fear fell on them all, and the name of the Lord Yeshua was magnified.

18 And many who believed came confessing and telling their deeds.

19 Also, many of those who practiced magic brought their books together and burned them in the sight of all. And they counted up the value of them, and it totaled fifty thousand pieces of silver.

20 So the word of the Lord grew mightily and prevailed.

The Ephesian Riot

21 After these things were ended, Paul purposed in the Spirit, when he had passed through Macedonia and Achaia, to go to Jerusalem, saying, "After I have been there, I must also see Rome."

22 So he sent into Macedonia two of those who ministered to him, Timothy and Erastus, but he himself stayed in Asia for a time.

23 And about that time there arose no small stir about the Way.

24 For a certain man named Demetrius, a silversmith, who made silver shrines of Artemis, brought no small profit to the craftsmen.

25 He called them together with the workers of similar occupation, and said: "Men, you know that we have our prosperity by this trade.

26 "Moreover you see and hear that not only at Ephesus, but throughout almost all Asia, this Paul has persuaded and turned away many people, saying that they are not gods which are made with hands;

27 "so that not only this trade of ours is in danger of falling into disrepute, but also the temple of the great goddess Artemis may be despised and her magnificence destroyed, whom all Asia and the world worship."

28 And when they heard this, they were full of wrath and cried out, saying, "Great is Artemis of the Ephesians!"

29 And the whole city was filled with confusion, and rushed into the theater with one accord, having seized Gaius and Aristarchus, men of Macedonia, Paul's travel companions.

30 And when Paul wanted to go in to the people, the disciples would not allow him.

31 And some of the officials of Asia, who were his friends, sent to him pleading that he would not venture into the theater.

32 Some therefore cried one thing and some another, for the

assembly was confused, and most of them did not know why they had come together.

33 And they drew Alexander out of the multitude, the Jews putting him forward. And Alexander motioned with his hand, and wanted to make his defense to the people.

34 But when they found out that he was a Jew, all with one voice cried out for about two hours, "Great is Artemis of the Ephesians!"

35 And when the city clerk had quieted the crowd, he said: "Men of Ephesus, what man is there who does not know that the city of the Ephesians is temple guardian of the great goddess Artemis, and of the image which fell down from heaven?

36 "Seeing then that these things cannot be denied, you ought to be quiet and do nothing rashly.

37 "For you have brought these men here who are neither robbers of temples nor blasphemers of your goddess.

38 "Therefore if Demetrius and the craftsmen who are with him have a case against anyone, the courts are open and there are proconsuls. Let them bring charges against one another.

39 "But if you have any other inquiry to make, it shall be determined in the lawful assembly.

40 "For we are in danger of being called in question for today's uproar, there being no reason which we may give to account for this disorderly gathering."

41 And when he had said these things, he dismissed the assembly.

Journeys in Greece

20 And after the uproar had ceased, Paul called the disciples to him, embraced them, and departed to go to Macedonia.

2 And when he had gone over that region and given them much encouragement, he came to Greece,

3 and stayed there three months. And when the Jews plotted against him as he was about to sail to Syria, he decided to return through Macedonia.

4 And Sopater of Berea accompanied him to Asia—also Aristarchus and Secundus of the Thessalonians, and Gaius of Derbe, and Timothy, and Tychicus and Trophimus of Asia.

5 These, going ahead, waited for us at Troas.

6 And we sailed away from Philippi after the Days of Unleavened Bread,[54] and in five days joined them at Troas, where we stayed seven days.

Serving at Troas

7 And on the first day of the week, when the disciples came together to break bread, Paul, ready to depart the next day, spoke to them and continued his message until midnight.

8 And there were many lamps in the upper room where they were gathered together.

9 And in a window sat a certain young man named Eutychus, who was sinking into a deep sleep. He was overcome by sleep, and as Paul continued speaking, he fell

54 Passover.

down from the third story and was taken up dead.

10 And Paul went down, fell on him, and embracing him said, "Do not trouble yourselves, for his life is in him."

11 Now when he had come up again, had broken bread and eaten, and talked a long while, even till daybreak, he departed.

12 And they brought the young man in alive, and they were not a little comforted.

From Troas to Miletus

13 And we went ahead to the ship and sailed to Assos, there intending to take Paul on board; for so he had given orders, himself intending to go on foot.

14 And when he met us at Assos, we took him on board and came to Mitylene.

15 And we sailed from there, and the next day came opposite Chios; the following day we arrived at Samos and stayed at Trogyllium; and the next day we came to Miletus.

16 For Paul had decided to sail past Ephesus, so that he would not have to spend time in Asia; for he was hurrying to be at Jerusalem, if possible, on the Day of Shavuot.

The Ephesian Elders Exhorted

17 And from Miletus he sent to Ephesus and called for the elders of the congregation.

18 And when they had come to him, he said to them: "You know, from the first day that I came to Asia, in what manner I always lived among you,

19 "serving the Lord with all humility, with many tears and trials

which happened to me by the plotting of the Jews;

20 "and how I kept back nothing that was helpful to you, but declared it to you, and taught you publicly and from house to house,

21 "testifying to Jews, and also to Greeks, repentance toward God and faith toward our Lord Yeshua ha Mashiach.

22 "And now, see, I go bound in the spirit to Jerusalem, not knowing the things that will happen to me there,

23 "except that the Holy Spirit testifies in every city, saying that chains and tribulations await me.

24 "But none of these things move me; nor do I count my life dear to myself, so that I may finish my race with joy, and the ministry which I have received from the Lord Yeshua, to testify to the good news of the grace of God.

25 "And indeed, now I know that you all, among whom I have gone preaching the kingdom of God, will see my face no more.

26 "Therefore I testify to you this day that I am innocent of the blood of all men.

27 "For I have not shunned to declare to you all the counsel of God.

28 "Therefore take heed to yourselves and to all the flock, over which the Holy Spirit has made you overseers, to shepherd the called-out ones of God whom He purchased with His own blood.

29 "For I know this, that after my departure savage wolves will come in among you, not sparing the flock.

30 "Also from among yourselves

men will rise up, speaking perverse things, to draw away disciples after themselves.

31 "Therefore watch, and remember that for three years I did not cease to warn everyone night and day with tears.

32 "And now, brethren, I commend you to God and to the word of His grace, which is able to build you up and give you an inheritance among all those who are sanctified.

33 "I have coveted no one's silver or gold or apparel.

34 "Yes, you yourselves know that these hands have provided for my necessities, and for those who were with me.

35 "I have shown you in every way, by laboring like this, that you must support the weak. And remember the words of the Lord Yeshua, how He said, 'It is more blessed to give than to receive.' "

36 And when he had said these things, he knelt down and prayed with them all.

37 And they all wept greatly, and fell on Paul's neck and kissed him,

38 sorrowing most of all for the words which he spoke, that they would see his face no more. And they accompanied him to the ship.

Warnings on the Journey to Jerusalem

21 And it came to pass, that when we had departed from them and set sail, running a straight course we came to Cos, the following day to Rhodes, and from there to Patara.

2 And finding a ship sailing over to Phoenicia, we went aboard and set sail.

3 Now when we had sighted Cyprus, we passed it on the left, sailed to Syria, and landed at Tyre; for there the ship was to unload her cargo.

4 And finding disciples, we stayed there seven days. They said to Paul through the Spirit that he should not go up to Jerusalem.

5 And when we had come to the end of those days, we departed and went on our way; and they all accompanied us, with wives and children, till we were out of the city. And we knelt down on the shore and prayed.

6 And when we had taken our leave of one another, we boarded the ship, and they returned home.

7 And when we had finished our voyage from Tyre, we came to Ptolemais, greeted the brethren, and stayed with them one day.

8 And the next day we who were Paul's companions departed and came to Caesarea, and entered the house of Philip the evangelist, who was one of the seven, and stayed with him.

9 Now this man had four virgin daughters who prophesied.

10 And as we stayed there many days, a certain prophet named Agabus came down from Judea.

11 And when he had come to us, he took Paul's belt, bound his own hands and feet, and said, "Thus says the Holy Spirit, 'So shall the Judeans at Jerusalem bind the man who owns this belt, and deliver him into the hands of the Gentiles.' "

12 And when we heard these things, both we and those from that place pleaded with him not to go up to Jerusalem.

13 Then Paul answered, "What do you mean by weeping and breaking my heart? For I am ready not only to be bound, but also to die at Jerusalem for the name of the Lord Yeshua."

14 And when he would not be persuaded, we ceased, saying, "The will of the Lord be done."

Paul Urged to Make Peace

15 And after those days we packed and went up to Jerusalem.

16 Also some of the disciples from Caesarea went with us and brought with them one Mnason of Cyprus, an early disciple, with whom we were to lodge.

17 And when we had come to Jerusalem, the brethren received us gladly.

18 And the following day Paul went in with us to James, and all the elders were present.

19 And when he had greeted them, he told in detail those things which God had done among the Gentiles by his ministry.

20 And when they heard it, they glorified the Lord. And they said to him, "You see, brother, how many thousands of Jews there are who believe, and they are all zealous for the Torah;

21 "but they have been informed about you that you teach all the Jews who are among the Gentiles to forsake Moses, saying that they ought not to circumcise their children nor to walk according to the customs.

22 "What then? The assembly must certainly meet, for they will hear that you have come.

23 "Therefore do what we tell you: We have four men who have taken a vow.

24 "Take them and be purified with them, and pay their expenses so that they may shave their heads, and that all may know that those things of which they have been informed concerning you are nothing, but that you yourself also walk orderly and keep the Torah.

25 "But concerning the Gentiles who believe, we have written and decided that they observe no such thing, except that they keep themselves from things offered to idols, from blood, from things strangled, and from sexual immorality."

Arrested in the Temple

26 Then Paul took the men, and the next day, having been purified with them, entered the temple to announce the completion of the days of purification, at which time an offering should be made for each one of them.

27 And when the seven days were almost ended, the Jews who were from Asia, seeing him in the temple, stirred up all the people and laid hands on him,

28 crying out, "Men of Israel, help! This is the man who teaches all men everywhere against the people, the Torah, and this place; and furthermore he also brought Greeks into the temple and has defiled this holy place."

29 (For they had previously seen Trophimus the Ephesian with him in the city, whom they supposed Paul had brought into the temple.)

30 And all the city was disturbed; and the people ran together, seized Paul, and dragged him out of the temple; and immediately the doors were shut.

31 And as they were seeking to kill him, news came to the commander[55] of the band of soldiers that all Jerusalem was in an uproar.

32 He immediately took soldiers and centurions, and ran down to them. And when they saw the commander and the soldiers, they stopped beating Paul.

33 Then the commander came near and took him, and commanded him to be bound with two chains; and he asked who he was and what he had done.

34 And some among the multitude cried one thing and some another. And when he could not ascertain the truth because of the tumult, he commanded him to be taken into the barracks.

35 And when he reached the stairs, he had to be carried by the soldiers because of the violence of the people.

36 For the multitude of the people followed after, crying out, "Away with him!"

Addressing the Jerusalem Mob

37 And as Paul was about to be led into the barracks, he said to the commander, "May I speak to you?" He replied, "Can you speak Greek?

38 "Are you not the Egyptian who some time ago raised an insurrection and led four thousand assassins out into the wilderness?"

39 But Paul said, "I am a Jew from Tarsus, a city in Cilicia, a citizen of no mean city; and I implore you, permit me to speak to the people."

---

55 Lit. *Chiliarch*, commander of 1,000 soldiers.

40 And when he had given him permission, Paul stood on the stairs and motioned with his hand to the people. And when there was a great silence, he spoke to them in the Hebrew language, saying,

22 "Men, brethren, and fathers, hear my defense to you now."

2 And when they heard that he spoke to them in the Hebrew language, they kept all the more silent. And he said:

3 "I am indeed a Jew, born in Tarsus, a city of Cilicia, but brought up in this city at the feet of Gamaliel, taught according to the strictness of our fathers' Torah, and was zealous toward God as you all are today.

4 "And I persecuted this Way to the death, binding and delivering into prisons both men and women,

5 "as also the high priest bears me witness, and all the council of the elders, from whom I also received letters to the brethren, and went to Damascus to bring even those who were there in chains to Jerusalem to be punished.

6 "And it came to pass, as I made my journey and came near to Damascus, about noon suddenly a great light from heaven shone around me.

7 "And I fell to the ground and heard a voice saying to me, 'Saul, Saul, why are you persecuting Me?'

8 "And I answered, 'Who are You, Lord?' And He said to me, 'I am Yeshua of Nazareth, whom you are persecuting.'

9 "And those who were with me indeed saw the light, and were

afraid, but they did not hear the voice of Him who spoke to me.

10 "And I said, 'What shall I do, Lord?' And the Lord said to me, 'Arise and go into Damascus, and there you will be told all things which are appointed for you to do.'

11 "And since I could not see for the glory of that light, being led by the hand of those who were with me, I came into Damascus.

12 "And one Ananias, a devout man according to the Torah, having a good testimony with all the Judeans who dwelt there,

13 "came to me; and he stood and said to me, 'Brother Saul, receive your sight.' And at that same hour I looked up at him.

14 "And he said, 'The God of our fathers has chosen you that you should know His will, and see the Just One, and hear the voice of His mouth.

15 'For you will be His witness to all men of what you have seen and heard.

16 'And now why are you waiting? Arise and be immersed, and wash away your sins, calling on the name of the Lord.'

17 "And it came to pass, when I returned to Jerusalem and was praying in the temple, that I was in a trance

18 "and saw Him saying to me, 'Make haste and get out of Jerusalem quickly, for they will not receive your testimony concerning Me.'

19 "And I said, 'Lord, they know that in every synagogue I imprisoned and beat those who believed on You.

20 'And when the blood of Your martyr Stephen was shed, I also was standing by, consenting to his death, and keeping the clothes of those who were killing him.'

21 "And He said to me, 'Depart, for I will send you far from here to the Gentiles.' "

Paul's Roman Citizenship

22 And they listened to him until this word, and then they raised their voices and said, "Away with such a fellow from the earth, for it is not fitting that he should live!"

23 And as they cried out, tore off their clothes, and threw dust into the air,

24 the commander ordered him to be brought into the barracks, and said that he should be examined under scourging, so that he might know why they shouted so against him.

25 And as they bound him with thongs, Paul said to the centurion who stood by, "Is it lawful for you to scourge a man who is a Roman, and uncondemned?"

26 When the centurion heard that, he went and told the commander, saying, "Take care what you do, for this man is a Roman."

27 Then the commander came and said to him, "Tell me, are you a Roman?" He said, "Yes."

28 And the commander answered, "With a large sum I obtained this citizenship." And Paul said, "But I was born a citizen."

29 Then immediately those who were about to examine him withdrew from him; and the commander was also afraid after he found out that he was a Roman, and because he had bound him.

The Sanhedrin Divided

30 The next day, because he wanted to know for certain why he was accused by the Judeans, he released him from his bonds, commanded the chief priests and all their council to appear, and brought Paul down and set him before them.

23 And Paul, looking earnestly at the council, said, "Men and brethren, I have lived in all good conscience before God until this day."

2 And the high priest Ananias commanded those who stood by him to strike him on the mouth.

3 Then Paul said to him, "God will strike you, you whitewashed wall! For you sit to judge me according to the Torah, and do you command me to be struck contrary to the Torah?"

4 And those who stood by said, "Do you revile God's high priest?"

5 Then Paul said, "I did not know, brethren, that he was the high priest; for it is written, *'You shall not speak evil of the ruler of your people.'*" [56]

6 But when Paul perceived that one part were Sadducees and the other Pharisees, he cried out in the council, "Men and brethren, I am a Pharisee, the son of a Pharisee; concerning the hope and resurrection of the dead I am being judged!"

7 And when he had said this, a dissension arose between the Pharisees and the Sadducees; and the assembly was divided.

8 For the Sadducees say that there is no resurrection—nor angel or spirit; but the Pharisees confess both.

9 And there arose a loud outcry. And the scribes who were of the Pharisees' party arose and protested, saying, "We find no evil in this man; but if a spirit or an angel has spoken to him, let us not fight against God."

10 And when there arose a great dissension, the commander, fearing lest Paul be pulled to pieces by them, commanded the soldiers to go down, take him by force from among them, and bring him into the barracks.

The Plot Against Paul

11 And the following night the Lord stood by him and said, "Be of good cheer, Paul; for as you have testified for Me in Jerusalem, so you must bear witness also at Rome."

12 And when it was day, some of the Judeans banded together and bound themselves under an oath, saying that they would neither eat nor drink till they had killed Paul.

13 And there were more than forty who had formed this conspiracy.

14 And they came to the chief priests and elders, and said, "We have bound ourselves under a great oath that we will eat nothing until we have killed Paul.

15 "Now therefore you, together with the council, suggest to the commander that he be brought down to you tomorrow, as though you were going to make further inquiries concerning him; but we are ready to kill him before he comes near."

16 And when Paul's sister's son

56 Exodus 22:28 (22:27 in some versions)

heard of their ambush, he went and entered the barracks and told Paul.

17 Then Paul called one of the centurions to him and said, "Take this young man to the commander, for he has something to tell him."

18 So he took him and brought him to the commander and said, "Paul the prisoner called me to him and asked me to bring you this young man who has something to say to you."

19 Then the commander took him by the hand, went aside privately with him, and asked him, "What is it you have to tell me?"

20 And he said, "The Judeans have agreed to ask that you bring Paul down to the council tomorrow, as though they were going to inquire more fully about him.

21 "But do not yield to them, for more than forty of them lie in wait for him, men who have bound themselves by an oath that they will neither eat nor drink till they have killed him; and now they are ready, waiting for the promise from you."

22 So the commander let the young man depart, and he commanded him, "Tell no one that you have revealed these things to me."

Sent to Felix

23 And he called for two centurions, saying, "Prepare two hundred soldiers, seventy horsemen, and two hundred spearmen to go to Caesarea at the third hour of the night;

24 "and provide mounts to set Paul on, and bring him safely to Felix the governor."

25 And he wrote a letter in the following manner:

26"Claudius Lysias,

To the most excellent governor Felix:

Greetings.

27 This man was seized by the Judeans and was about to be killed by them. Then I came with the troops and rescued him, having learned that he was a Roman.

28 And when I wanted to know the reason they accused him, I brought him before their council.

29 I found out that he was accused concerning questions of their law, but had nothing charged against him worthy of death or chains.

30 And when it was told me that the Judeans lay in wait for the man, I sent him immediately to you, and also commanded his accusers to state before you the charge they brought against him. Farewell."

31 Then the soldiers, as they were commanded, took Paul and brought him by night to Antipatris.

32 The next day they left the horsemen to go with him, and returned to the barracks.

33 When they came to Caesarea and had delivered the letter to the governor, they also presented Paul to him.

34 And when the governor had read the letter, he asked what province he was from. And when

he understood that he was from Cilicia,

35 he said, "I will hear you when your accusers have also come." And he commanded him to be kept in Herod's Praetorium.

Accused of Sedition

24 And after five days Ananias the high priest came down with the elders and a certain orator named Tertullus. These gave evidence to the governor against Paul.

2 And when he was called on, Tertullus began his accusation, saying: "Seeing that through you we enjoy great peace, and prosperity is being brought to this nation by your foresight,

3 "we accept it always and in all places, most noble Felix, with all thankfulness.

4 "Nevertheless, not to be tedious to you any further, I beg you to hear, by your courtesy, a few words from us.

5 "For we have found this man a plague, a creator of dissension among all the Jews throughout the world, and a ringleader of the sect of the Nazarenes.

6 "He even tried to profane the temple, and we seized him, and wanted to judge him according to our law.

7 "But the commander Lysias came by and with great violence took him out of our hands,

8 "commanding his accusers to come to you. By examining him yourself you may ascertain all these things of which we accuse him."

9 And the Judeans also assented, saying that these things were so.

The Defense Before Felix

10 Then Paul, after the governor had nodded to him to speak, answered: "Inasmuch as I know that you have been for many years a judge of this nation, I do the more cheerfully answer for myself,

11 "because you may ascertain that it is no more than twelve days since I went up to Jerusalem to worship.

12 "And they neither found me in the temple disputing with anyone nor inciting the people, neither in the synagogues nor in the city.

13 "Nor can they prove the things of which they now accuse me.

14 "But this I confess to you, that according to the Way which they call a sect, so I worship the God of my fathers, believing all things which are written in the Torah and in the Prophets.

15 "And I have hope in God, which they themselves also accept, that there will be a resurrection of the dead, both of the just and the unjust.

16 "And for this, I myself always strive to have a conscience without offense toward God and men.

17 "Now after many years I came to bring alms and offerings to my nation,

18 "in the midst of which some Jews from Asia found me purified in the temple, neither with a multitude nor with tumult.

19 "They ought to have been here before you to object if they had anything against me.

20 "Or else let those who are here themselves say if they have found any wrongdoing in me while I stood before the council,

21 "unless it is for this one statement which I cried out, standing among them, 'Concerning the resurrection of the dead I am being judged by you this day.'"

Felix Procrastinates

22 And when Felix heard these things, having more accurate knowledge of the Way, he adjourned the proceedings and said, "When Lysias the commander comes down, I will make a decision on your case."

23 And he commanded a centurion to keep Paul and to let him have liberty, and told him not to forbid any of his friends to provide for or visit him.

24 And after some days, when Felix came with his wife Drusilla, who was Jewish, he sent for Paul and heard him concerning the faith in the Messiah.

25 And as he reasoned about righteousness, self-control, and judgment to come, Felix was afraid and answered, "Go away for now; when I have a convenient time I will call for you."

26 Meanwhile he also hoped that money would be given him by Paul, that he might release him. Therefore he sent for him more often and conversed with him.

27 But after two years Porcius Festus succeeded Felix; and Felix, wanting to do the Judeans a favor, left Paul bound.

Appeal to Caesar

25 Now when Festus had come to the province, after three days he went up from Caesarea to Jerusalem.

2 Then the high priest and the chief men of the Judeans informed him against Paul; and they petitioned him,

3 asking a favor against him, that he would summon him to Jerusalem—while they lay in ambush along the road to kill him.

4 But Festus answered that Paul should be kept at Caesarea, and that he himself was going there shortly.

5 "Therefore," he said, "let those who have authority among you go down with me and accuse this man, to see if there is any fault in him."

6 And when he had remained among them more than ten days, he went down to Caesarea. And the next day, sitting on the judgment seat, he commanded Paul to be brought.

7 And when he had come, the Judeans who had come down from Jerusalem stood about and laid many serious complaints against Paul which they could not prove,

8 while he answered for himself, "Neither against the law of the Judeans, nor against the temple, nor against Caesar have I offended in anything at all."

9 But Festus, wanting to do the Judeans a favor, answered Paul and said, "Are you willing to go up to Jerusalem and there be judged before me concerning these things?"

10 Then Paul said, "I stand at Caesar's judgment seat, where I ought to be judged. To the Judeans I have done no wrong, as you very well know.

11 "For if I am an offender, or have committed anything worthy

of death, I do not refuse to die; but if there is nothing in these things of which these men accuse me, no one can deliver me to them. I appeal to Caesar."

12 Then Festus, when he had conferred with the council, answered, "You have appealed to Caesar? To Caesar you shall go!"

Paul Before Agrippa

13 And after some days King Agrippa and Bernice came to Caesarea to greet Festus.

14 And when they had been there many days, Festus laid Paul's case before the king, saying: "There is a certain man left a prisoner by Felix,

15 "about whom the chief priests and the elders of the Judeans informed me, when I was in Jerusalem, asking for a judgment against him.

16 "To them I answered, 'It is not the custom of the Romans to deliver any man to die before he who is accused meets the accusers face to face, and has opportunity to answer for himself concerning the charge laid against him.'

17 "Therefore when they had come together, without any delay, the next day I sat on the judgment seat and commanded the man to be brought in.

18 "When the accusers stood up, they brought no accusation against him of such things as I supposed,

19 "but had some questions against him about their own religion and about one Yeshua, who was dead, whom Paul affirmed to be alive.

20 "And because I was uncer-tain of such questions, I asked him whether he was willing to go to Jerusalem and there be judged concerning these matters.

21 "But when Paul had appealed to be reserved for the decision of Augustus,[57] I commanded him to be kept till I could send him to Caesar."

22 Then Agrippa said to Festus, "I also would like to hear the man myself." "Tomorrow," he said, "you shall hear him."

23 And the next day, when Agrippa and Bernice had come with great pomp, and had entered the auditorium with the commanders and prominent men of the city, at Festus' command Paul was brought in.

24 And Festus said: "King Agrippa and all the men who are here present with us, you see this man about whom the whole assembly of the Judeans petitioned me, both at Jerusalem and here, crying out that he ought not to live any longer.

25 "But when I found that he had committed nothing worthy of death, and that he himself had appealed to Augustus, I decided to send him.

26 "I have nothing certain to write to my lord concerning him. Therefore I have brought him out before you, and especially before you, King Agrippa, so that after the examination has taken place I may have something to write.

27 "For it seems to me unreasonable to send a prisoner and not to signify the charges against him."

57 Lit. "The Sebastos," or Emperor of Rome: at this time, Nero.

Paul's Early Life

26 Then Agrippa said to Paul, "You are permitted to speak for yourself." Then Paul stretched out his hand and answered for himself:

2 "I think myself happy, King Agrippa, because today I shall answer for myself before you concerning all the things of which I am accused by the Judeans,

3 "especially because you are expert in all customs and questions which have to do with the Judeans. Therefore I beg you to hear me patiently.

4 "My manner of life from my youth, which was spent from the beginning among my own nation at Jerusalem, all the Judeans know.

5 "They knew me from the first, if they were willing to testify, that according to the strictest sect of our religion I lived a Pharisee.

6 "And now I stand and am judged for the hope of the promise made by God to our fathers.

7 "To this promise our twelve tribes, earnestly serving God night and day, hope to attain. For this hope's sake, King Agrippa, I am accused by the Judeans.

8 "Why should it be thought incredible by you that God should raise the dead?

9 "Indeed, I myself thought I must do many things contrary to the name of Yeshua of Nazareth.

10 "This I also did in Jerusalem, and many of the believers I shut up in prison, having received authority from the chief priests; and when they were put to death, I cast my vote against them.

11 "And I punished them often in every synagogue and compelled them to blaspheme; and being exceedingly enraged against them, I persecuted them even to foreign cities.

Paul Tells His Story

12 "While thus occupied, as I journeyed to Damascus with authority and commission from the chief priests,

13 "at midday, O king, along the road I saw a light from heaven, brighter than the sun, shining around me and those who journeyed with me.

14 "And when we had all fallen to the ground, I heard a voice speaking to me and saying in the Hebrew language, 'Saul, Saul, why are you persecuting Me? It is hard for you to kick against the goads.'

15 "And I said, 'Who are You, Lord?' And He said, 'I am Yeshua, whom you are persecuting.

16 'But rise and stand on your feet; for I have appeared to you for this purpose, to make you a minister and a witness both of the things which you have seen and of the things which I will yet reveal to you.

17 'I will deliver you from the Jewish people, as well as from the Gentiles, to whom I now send you,

18 'to open their eyes and to turn them from darkness to light, and from the power of Satan to God, that they may receive forgiveness of sins and an inheritance among those who are sanctified by faith in Me.'

19 "Therefore, King Agrippa, I was not disobedient to the heavenly vision,

20 "but declared first to those in Damascus and in Jerusalem, and throughout all the region of Judea, and then to the Gentiles, that they should repent, turn to God, and do works suitable to repentance.

21 "For these reasons the Judeans seized me in the temple and tried to kill me.

22 "Having therefore obtained help from God, I continue to this day, witnessing both to small and great, saying no other things than those which the prophets and Moses said would come—

23 "that the Messiah would suffer, that He would be the first to rise from the dead, and would proclaim light to the Jewish people and to the Gentiles."

Agrippa Parries Paul's Challenge

24 And as he thus made his defense, Festus said with a loud voice, "Paul, you are beside yourself! Much learning is driving you mad!"

25 But he said, "I am not mad, most noble Festus, but speak the words of truth and reason.

26 "For the king, before whom I also speak freely, knows these things; for I am convinced that none of these things escapes his attention, since this thing was not done in a corner.

27 "King Agrippa, do you believe the prophets? I know that you do believe."

28 Then Agrippa said to Paul, "You almost persuade me to become a follower of the Messiah." [58]

29 And Paul said, "I would to God that not only you, but also all who hear me today, might become

58 Greek: *Christianos*, a follower of Yeshua.

both almost and altogether such as I am, except for these chains."

30 And when he had said these things, the king rose up, as well as the governor, Bernice, and those who sat with them;

31 and when they had gone aside, they talked among themselves, saying, "This man is doing nothing worthy of death or chains."

32 Then Agrippa said to Festus, "This man might have been set free if he had not appealed to Caesar."

The Voyage to Rome Begins

27 And when it was decided that we should sail to Italy, they delivered Paul and some other prisoners to one named Julius, a centurion of the Augustan Regiment.

2 And entering a ship of Adramyttium, we put to sea, meaning to sail along the coasts of Asia. Aristarchus, a Macedonian of Thessalonica, was with us.

3 And the next day we landed at Sidon. And Julius treated Paul kindly and gave him liberty to go to his friends and receive care.

4 When we had put to sea from there, we sailed under the shelter of Cyprus, because the winds were contrary.

5 And when we had sailed over the sea which is off Cilicia and Pamphylia, we came to Myra, a city of Lycia.

6 And there the centurion found an Alexandrian ship sailing to Italy, and he put us on board.

7 And when we had sailed slowly many days, and arrived with difficulty off Cnidus, the wind not permitting us to proceed,

we sailed under the shelter of Crete off Salmone.

8 And passing it with difficulty, we came to a place called Fair Havens, near the city of Lasea.

Paul's Warning Ignored

9 Now when much time had been spent, and sailing was now dangerous because the Fast[59] was already over, Paul advised them,

10 and said to them, "Men, I perceive that this voyage will end with disaster and much loss, not only of the cargo and ship, but also our lives."

11 Nevertheless the centurion believed the helmsman and the owner of the ship more than the things which were spoken by Paul.

12 And because the harbor was not suitable to winter in, the majority advised to set sail from there also, if by any means they could reach Phoenix, a harbor of Crete opening toward the southwest and northwest, and winter there.

In the Tempest

13 And when the south wind blew softly, supposing that they had obtained their purpose, putting out to sea, they sailed close by Crete.

14 But not long after, a tempestuous head wind arose, called Euroclydon.[60]

15 And when the ship was caught, and could not head into the wind, we let her drive.

16 And running under the shelter of an island called Clauda, we secured the skiff with difficulty.

17 When they had taken it on board, they used cables to undergird the ship; and fearing lest they should run aground on the Syrtis Sands, they struck sail and so were driven.

18 And we being exceedingly tempest-tossed, the next day they lightened the ship.

19 And the third day we threw the ship's tackle overboard with our own hands.

20 And when neither sun nor stars appeared for many days, and no small tempest beat on us, all hope that we would be saved was finally given up.

21 But when they had gone a long time without food, then Paul stood in the midst of them and said, "Men, you should have listened to me, and not have sailed from Crete and incurred this disaster and loss.

22 "And now I urge you to take heart, for there will be no loss of life among you, but only of the ship.

23 "For there stood by me this night an angel of the God to whom I belong and whom I serve,

24 "saying, 'Do not be afraid, Paul; you must be brought before Caesar; and indeed God has given you all those who sail with you.'

25 "Therefore take heart, men, for I believe God that it will be just as it was told me.

26 "However, we must run aground on a certain island."

27 But when the fourteenth night had come, as we were driven up and down in the Adriatic Sea, about midnight the sailors sensed that they were drawing near some land.

59 Yom Kippur.   60 A northeaster.

28 And they took soundings and found it to be twenty fathoms; and when they had gone a little farther, they took soundings again and found it to be fifteen fathoms.

29 Then, fearing lest we should run aground on the rocks, they dropped four anchors from the stern, and prayed for day to come.

30 And as the sailors were seeking to escape from the ship, when they had let down the skiff into the sea, under pretense of putting out anchors from the prow,

31 Paul said to the centurion and to the soldiers, "Unless these men stay in the ship, you cannot be saved."

32 Then the soldiers cut away the ropes of the skiff and let it fall off.

33 And as day was about to dawn, Paul begged them all to take food, saying, "Today is the fourteenth day you have waited and continued without food, and eaten nothing.

34 "Therefore I urge you to take some food, for this is for your survival, since not a hair will fall from the head of any of you."

35 And when he had said these things, he took bread and gave thanks to God in the presence of them all; and when he had broken it he began to eat.

36 Then they were all encouraged, and also took food themselves.

37 And in all we were two hundred and seventy-six persons on the ship.

38 And when they had eaten enough, they lightened the ship and threw out the wheat into the sea.

Shipwrecked at Malta

39 And when it was day, they did not recognize the land; but they observed a bay with a beach, onto which they planned to run the ship if possible.

40 And they let go the anchors and left them in the sea, meanwhile loosing the rudder ropes; and they hoisted the mainsail to the wind and made for shore.

41 And striking a place where two seas met, they ran the ship aground; and the prow stuck fast and remained immovable, but the stern was being broken up by the violence of the waves.

42 And the soldiers' plan was to kill the prisoners, lest any of them should swim away and escape.

43 But the centurion, wanting to save Paul, kept them from their purpose, and commanded that those who could swim should throw themselves into the sea first and get to land,

44 and the rest, some on boards and some on broken pieces of the ship. And so it was that they all escaped safely to land.

Honored by the Natives

28 And when they had escaped, they then found out that the island was called Malta.

2 And the natives showed us no little kindness; for they kindled a fire and made us all welcome, because of the rain that was falling and because of the cold.

3 And when Paul had gathered a bundle of sticks and laid them on the fire, a viper came out because of the heat, and fastened on his hand.

4 And when the natives saw the creature hanging on his hand, they said to one another, "No doubt this man is a murderer, whom, though he has escaped the sea, yet justice does not allow to live."

5 But he shook off the creature into the fire and suffered no harm.

6 However, they were expecting that he would swell up or suddenly fall down dead; but after they had looked for a long time and saw no harm come to him, they changed their minds and said that he was a god.

7 Now in that region there was an estate of the chief man of the island, whose name was Publius, who received us and entertained us courteously for three days.

8 And it happened that the father of Publius lay sick of a fever and dysentery. Paul went in to him and prayed, and he laid his hands on him and healed him.

9 So when this was done, the rest of those on the island who had diseases also came and were healed.

10 They also honored us in many ways; and when we departed, they provided us with such things as were necessary.

Arrival at Rome

11 And after three months we sailed in an Alexandrian ship whose figurehead was the Twin Brothers, which had wintered at the island.

12 And landing at Syracuse, we stayed there three days.

13 And from there we circled round and reached Rhegium. And after one day the south wind blew; and the next day we came to Puteoli,

14 where we found brethren, and were invited to stay with them seven days. And so we went toward Rome.

15 And from there, when the brethren heard about us, they came to meet us as far as Appii Forum and Three Inns. When Paul saw them, he thanked God and took courage.

16 And when we came to Rome, the centurion delivered the prisoners to the captain of the guard; but Paul was permitted to dwell by himself with the soldier who guarded him.

Paul at Rome

17 And it came to pass after three days that Paul called the leaders of the Jews together. And when they had come together, he said to them: "Men and brethren, though I have done nothing against our people or the customs of our fathers, yet I was delivered as a prisoner from Jerusalem into the hands of the Romans,

18 "who, when they had examined me, wanted to let me go, because there was no cause for putting me to death.

19 "But when the Judeans spoke against it, I was compelled to appeal to Caesar, not that I had anything of which to accuse my nation.

20 "For this reason therefore I have called for you, to see you and speak with you, because for the hope of Israel I am bound with this chain."

21 And they said to him, "We neither received letters from Judea concerning you, nor have any of

the brethren who came reported or spoken any evil of you.

22 "But we desire to hear from you what you think; for concerning this sect, we know that it is spoken against everywhere."

23 And when they had appointed him a day, many came to him at his lodging, to whom he explained and solemnly testified of the kingdom of God, persuading them concerning Yeshua from both the Torah of Moses and the Prophets, from morning till evening.

24 And some believed the things which were spoken, and some disbelieved.

25 And when they did not agree among themselves, they departed after Paul had said one word: "The Holy Spirit spoke rightly by Isaiah the prophet to our fathers,

26 "saying,

'Go to this people and say;
Hearing you will hear, and
   by no means understand;
And seeing you will see, and
   by no means perceive;

27 For the heart of this people
   has grown dull.
Their ears are hard of hearing,
And their eyes they have
   closed,
Lest they should see with
   their eyes,
And hear with their ears,
And understand with their
   heart,
And should turn again,
And I heal them.' [61]

28 "Therefore let it be known to you that the salvation of God has been sent to the Gentiles, and they will hear it!"

29 And when he had said these words, the Jews departed and had a great dispute among themselves.

30 And Paul dwelt two whole years in his own rented house, and received all who came to him,

31 preaching the kingdom of God and teaching the things which concern the Lord Yeshua ha Mashiach with all confidence, no one forbidding him.

61 Isaiah 6:9, 10

The Letter Of Paul To The
ROMANS

Greeting

PAUL, a servant of Yeshua ha Mashiach, called to be an apostle,[1] separated to the good news of God

2 which He promised before by His prophets in the Holy Scriptures,

3 concerning His Son Yeshua ha Mashiach our Lord, who was born of the seed of David according to the flesh,[2]

4 and declared to be the Son of God with power,[3] according to the Spirit of holiness, by the resurrection from the dead,

5 by whom we have received grace and apostleship for obedience to the faith among all nations for His name,

6 among whom you also are the called of Yeshua ha Mashiach;

7 To all who are in Rome, beloved of God, called to be believers:

Grace to you and peace from God our Father and the Lord Yeshua ha Mashiach.

1 Hebrew: "shaliach," an emissary or specially designated representative empowered to act on behalf of another. *2* Jeremiah 23:5, 6; 33:14-16 (cf. Isaiah 4:1-5) *3* Psalm 2:7; cf. Acts 2:32-36

Desire to Visit Rome

8 First, I thank my God through Yeshua ha Mashiach for you all, that your faith is spoken of throughout the whole world.

9 For God is my witness, whom I serve with my spirit in the good news of His Son, that without ceasing I make mention of you always in my prayers,

10 making request if, by some means, now at last I may find a way in the will of God to come to you.

11 For I long to see you, that I may impart to you some spiritual gift, so that you may be established—

12 that is, that I may be encouraged together with you by the mutual faith both of you and me.

13 Now I do not want you to be unaware, brethren, that I often planned to come to you (but was hindered until now), that I might have some fruit among you also, just as among the other Gentiles.

14 I am a debtor both to Greeks and to barbarians, both to wise and to unwise.

15 So, as much as is in me, I am ready to preach the good news to you who are in Rome also.

The Just Live by Faith

16 For I am not ashamed of the good news of the Messiah, for it is

the power of God to salvation for everyone who believes, for the Jew first and also for the Greek.

17 For in it the righteousness of God is revealed from faith to faith; as it is written, *"The just shall live by faith."* [4]

God's Wrath on Unrighteousness

18 For the wrath of God is revealed from heaven against all ungodliness and unrighteousness of men, who suppress the truth in unrighteousness,

19 because what may be known of God is manifest in them, for God has shown it to them.

20 For since the creation of the world His invisible attributes are clearly seen, being understood by the things that are made, even His eternal power and Godhead, so that they are without excuse,

21 because, although they knew God, they did not glorify Him as God, nor were thankful, but became futile in their thoughts, and their foolish hearts were darkened.

22 Professing to be wise, they became fools,

23 and changed the glory of the incorruptible God into an image made like corruptible man, birds, four-footed beasts, and creeping things.

24 Therefore God also gave them up to uncleanness, in the lusts of their hearts, to dishonor their bodies among themselves,

25 who exchanged the truth of God for the lie, and worshiped and served the creature rather than the Creator, who is blessed forever. Amen.

26 For this reason God gave

them up to vile passions. For even their women exchanged the natural use for what is against nature.

27 And likewise also the men, leaving the natural use of the woman, burned in their lust toward one another, men with men committing what is shameful, and receiving in themselves the penalty of their error which was due.

28 And even as they did not like to retain God in their knowledge, God gave them over to a debased mind, to do those things which are not fitting,

29 being filled with all unrighteousness, sexual immorality, wickedness, covetousness, maliciousness; full of envy, murder, strife, deceit, evil-mindedness; they are whisperers,

30 backbiters, haters of God, violent, proud, boasters, inventors of evil things, disobedient to parents,

31 undiscerning, untrustworthy, unloving, unforgiving, unmerciful;

32 who, knowing the righteous judgment of God, that those who practice such things are worthy of death, not only do the same but also approve of those who practice them.

God's Righteous Judgment

2 Therefore you are inexcusable, O man, whoever you are who judge, for in whatever you judge another you condemn yourself; for you who judge do the same things.

2 But we know that the judgment of God is according to truth against those who practice such things.

3 And do you think this, O

4 Habakkuk 2:4

man, you who judge those who do such things, and do the same, that you will escape the judgment of God?

4 Or do you despise the riches of His goodness, forbearance, and longsuffering, not knowing that the goodness of God leads you to repentance?

5 But in accordance with your hardness and your impenitent heart you are treasuring up for yourself wrath in the day of wrath and revelation of the righteous judgment of God,

6 who *"will render to each one according to his deeds"*: [5]

7 to those who by patient continuance in doing good seek for glory, honor, and immortality—eternal life;

8 but to those who are self-seeking and do not obey the truth, but obey unrighteousness—indignation and wrath,

9 tribulation and anguish, on every soul of man who does evil, of the Jew first and also of the Greek;

10 but glory, honor, and peace to everyone who works what is good, to the Jew first and also to the Greek.

11 For there is no partiality with God.[6]

12 For as many as have sinned without Torah will also perish without Torah, and as many as have sinned in the Torah will be judged by the Torah

13 (for not the hearers of the Torah are just in the sight of God, but the doers of the Torah will be justified;

14 for when Gentiles, who do not have the Torah, by nature do the things contained in the Torah, these, although not having the Torah, are a law to themselves,

15 who show the work of the Torah written in their hearts, their conscience also bearing witness, and between themselves their thoughts accusing or else excusing them)

16 in the day when God will judge the secrets of men by Yeshua ha Mashiach, according to my good news.

We Are All Guilty

17 Indeed, you are called a Jew, and rest on the Torah, and make your boast in God,

18 and know His will, and approve the things that are excellent, being instructed out of the Torah,

19 and are confident that you yourself are a guide to the blind, a light to those who are in darkness,

20 an instructor of the foolish, a teacher of babes, having the form of knowledge and truth in the Torah.

21 You, therefore, who teach another, do you not teach yourself? You who preach that a man should not steal, do you steal?

22 You who say a man should not commit adultery, do you commit adultery? You who abhor idols, do you rob temples?

23 You who make your boast in the Torah, do you dishonor God through breaking the Torah?

24 For *"The name of God is blasphemed among the Gentiles because of you,"* [7] as it is written.

5 Psalm 62:12 (62:13 in some versions); Proverbs 24:12 6 Deuteronomy 10:17

7 Isaiah 52:5; Ezekiel 36:22

Circumcision of No Avail
To Those Who Violate Torah

25 For circumcision is indeed profitable if you keep the Torah; but if you are a breaker of the Torah, your circumcision has become uncircumcision.

26 Therefore, if an uncircumcised man keeps the righteous requirements of the Torah, will not his uncircumcision be counted as circumcision?

27 And will not the physically uncircumcised, if he fulfills the Torah, judge you who, even with your written code and circumcision, are a transgressor of the Torah?

28 For he is not a Jew who is one outwardly, nor is that circumcision which is outward in the flesh;

29 but he is a Jew who is one inwardly, and circumcision is that of the heart,[8] in the Spirit, and not in the letter; whose praise is not from men but from God.

God's Judgment Defended

3 What advantage then has the Jew, or what is the profit of circumcision?

2 Much in every way! Chiefly because to them were committed the oracles of God.

3 For what if some did not believe? Will their unbelief make the faithfulness of God without effect?

4 Certainly not! Indeed, let God be true but every man a liar. As it is written:

"That You may be justified in
Your words,

And may overcome when
You are judged." [9]

5 But if our unrighteousness demonstrates the righteousness of God, what shall we say? Is God unjust who inflicts wrath? (I speak as a man.)

6 Certainly not! For then how will God judge the world?

7 For if the truth of God has increased through my lie to His glory, why am I also still judged as a sinner?

8 And why not say, "Let us do evil that good may come"? —as we are slanderously reported and as some affirm that we say. Their condemnation is just.

All Have Sinned

9 What then? Are we better than they? Not at all. For we have previously charged both Jews and Greeks that they are all under sin.

10 As it is written:

"There is none righteous, no,
   not one;

11 There is none who understands;
   There is none who seeks after God.

12 They have all gone out of
   the way;
   They have together become
   unprofitable;
   There is none who does
   good, no, not one." [10]

13 "Their throat is an open
   tomb;
   With their tongues they have
   practiced deceit"; [11]

8 Deuteronomy 30:6

9 Psalm 51:4 (51:6 in some versions)

10 Psalm 14:1–3; 53:1–3; Eccl. 7:20

11 Psalm 5:9 (5:10 in some versions)

*"The poison of asps is under
their lips";*[12]

14 *"Whose mouth is full of cursing and bitterness."* [13]

15 *"Their feet are swift to shed
blood;*

16 *Destruction and misery are
in their ways;*

17 *And the way of peace they
have not known."* [14]

18 *"There is no fear of God before their eyes."* [15]

19 Now we know that whatever
the Torah says, it says to those
who are under the Torah, that every mouth may be stopped, and
all the world may become guilty
before God.

20 Therefore by the deeds of the
Torah no flesh will be justified in
His sight, for by the Torah is the
knowledge of sin.

God's Righteousness Through Faith

21 But now the righteousness of
God apart from the Torah is revealed, being witnessed by the Torah and the Prophets,

22 even the righteousness of God
which is by faith in Yeshua
ha Mashiach to all and on all who
believe. For there is no difference;

23 for all have sinned and fall
short of the glory of God,

24 being justified freely by His
grace through the redemption that
is in Messiah Yeshua,

25 whom God has set forth to be
a propitiation, through faith, in
His blood, to demonstrate His
righteousness, because of the passing over of the sins that were previously committed, through the
forbearance of God;

26 to demonstrate at the present
time His righteousness, that He
might be just and the justifier of
the one who has faith in Yeshua.

Boasting Excluded

27 Where is boasting then? It is
excluded. By what law? Of
works? No, but by the law of
faith.

28 Therefore we conclude that a
man is justified by faith apart
from the deeds of the Torah.

29 Or is He the God of the Jews
only? Is He not also the God of
the Gentiles? Yes, of the Gentiles
also,

30 seeing there is one God who
will justify the circumcised by
faith and the uncircumcised
through faith.

31 Do we then make void the
Torah through faith? Certainly
not! On the contrary, we establish the Torah.

Abraham Justified by Faith

4 What then shall we say that
Abraham our father has
found according to the flesh?

2 For if Abraham was justified
by works, he has something of
which to boast, but not before
God.

3 For what does the Scripture
say? *"Abraham believed God,
and it was counted to him for
righteousness."* [16]

4 Now to him who works, the
wages are not counted as grace but
as debt.

---

12 Psalm 140:3 (140:4 in some versions)

13 Psalm 10:7   14 Isaiah 59:7, 8

15 Psalm 36:1 (36:2 in some versions)

16 Genesis 15:6

David Celebrates the Same Truth

5 But to him who does not work but believes on Him who justifies the ungodly, his faith is counted for righteousness,

6 just as David also describes the blessedness of the man to whom God imputes righteousness apart from works:

7 *"Blessed are those whose lawless deeds are forgiven,*
And whose sins are covered;

8 *Blessed is the man to whom the* LORD *shall not impute sin."* [17]

Abraham Justified Before Circumcision

9 Does this blessedness then come on the circumcised only, or on the uncircumcised also? For we say that faith was reckoned to Abraham for righteousness.

10 How then was it reckoned? While he was circumcised, or uncircumcised? Not while circumcised, but while uncircumcised.

11 And he received the sign of circumcision, a seal of the righteousness of the faith which he had while still uncircumcised, that he might be the father of all those who believe, though they are uncircumcised, that righteousness might be imputed to them also,

12 and the father of circumcision to those who not only are of the circumcision, but who also walk in the steps of the faith which our father Abraham had while still uncircumcised. [18]

The Promise Granted Through Faith

13 For the promise that he would be the heir of the world was not to Abraham or to his seed through the Torah, but through the righteousness of faith.

14 For if those who are of the Torah are heirs, faith is made void and the promise made of no effect,

15 because the Torah brings about wrath; for where there is no law there is no transgression.

16 Therefore it is of faith that it might be according to grace, so that the promise might be sure to all the seed, not only to those who are of the Torah, but also to those who are of the faith of Abraham, who is the father of us all

17 (as it is written, *"I have made you a father of many nations"* [19]) in the presence of Him whom he believed, even God, who gives life to the dead and calls those things which do not exist as though they did;

18 who, contrary to hope, in hope believed, so that he became the father of many nations, according to what was spoken, *"So shall your seed be."* [20]

19 And not being weak in faith, he did not consider his own body, already dead (since he was about a hundred years old), and the deadness of Sarah's womb.

20 He did not waver at the promise of God through unbelief, but was strengthened in faith, giving glory to God,

21 and being fully convinced that what He had promised He was also able to perform.

---

17 Psalm 32:1, 2

18 God counted Abraham's faith for righteousness in Genesis 15; He commanded Abraham to be circumcised *later*, in Genesis 17:11.

19 Genesis 17:4, 5   20 Genesis 15:5

22 And therefore *"it was imputed to him for righteousness."* [21]

23 Now it was not written for his sake alone that it was imputed to him,

24 but also for us, to whom it shall be imputed if we believe in Him who raised up Yeshua our Lord from the dead,

25 who was delivered up because of our offenses, and was raised because of our justification.

Faith Triumphs in Trouble

5 Therefore, having been justified by faith, we have peace with God through our Lord Yeshua ha Mashiach,

2 through whom also we have access by faith into this grace in which we stand, and rejoice in hope of the glory of God.

3 And not only that, but we also glory in tribulations, knowing that tribulation produces perseverance;

4 and perseverance, character; and character, hope.

5 And hope does not disappoint, because the love of God has been poured out in our hearts by the Holy Spirit who was given to us. [22]

The Messiah in Our Place

6 For when we were still without strength, in due time the Messiah died for the ungodly.

7 For scarcely for a righteous man will one die; yet perhaps for a good man someone would even dare to die.

8 But God demonstrates His own love toward us, in that while we were still sinners, the Messiah died for us.

9 Much more then, having now been justified by His blood, we shall be saved from wrath through Him.

10 For if when we were enemies we were reconciled to God by the death of His Son, much more, having been reconciled, we shall be saved by His life.

11 And not only that, but we also rejoice in God through our Lord Yeshua ha Mashiach, by whom we have now received the reconciliation. [23]

Death in Adam, Life in the Messiah

12 Therefore as by one man sin entered into the world, and death by sin, and thus death spread to all men, [24] because all sinned— [25]

13 (For until the Torah sin was in the world, but sin is not imputed when there is no Torah.

14 Nevertheless death reigned from Adam to Moses, even over those who had not sinned according to the likeness of the transgression of Adam, who is a type of Him who was to come.

15 But the free gift is not like the offense. For if by the one man's offense many died, much more the grace of God and the gift by the grace of the one Man, Yeshua ha Mashiach, have abounded to many.

16 And the gift is not like that which came through the one who sinned. For the judgment which

21 Genesis 15:6
22 Ezekiel 36:25–27; Isaiah 44:3; Joel
2:28 (3:1 in some versions)

23 See Isaiah 52:13—53:12
24 Genesis 2:16, 17; 3:1–24
25 Psalm 14:1–3; Ecclesiastes 7:20

came from one offense resulted in condemnation, but the free gift which came from many offenses resulted in justification.

17 For if by the one man's offense death reigned by the one, much more those who receive abundance of grace and of the gift of righteousness will reign in life through the One, Yeshua ha Mashiach.)

18 Therefore as by one man's offense judgment came to all men, resulting in condemnation, even so by one Man's righteous act the free gift came to all men, resulting in justification of life.

19 For as by one man's disobedience many were made sinners, so also by one Man's obedience many will be made righteous.

20 Moreover the Torah entered that the offense might abound. But where sin abounded, grace abounded much more,

21 so that as sin has reigned in death, even so grace might reign through righteousness to eternal life by Yeshua ha Mashiach our Lord.

Dead to Sin, Alive to God

6 What shall we say then? Shall we continue in sin that grace may abound?

2 Certainly not! How shall we who died to sin live any longer in it?

3 Or do you not know that as many of us as were immersed into Messiah Yeshua were immersed into His death?

4 Therefore we were buried with Him by immersion into death, that just as the Messiah was raised from the dead by the glory of the Father, even so we also should walk in newness of life.

5 For if we have been united together in the likeness of His death, certainly we also shall be in the likeness of His resurrection,

6 knowing this, that our old man was crucified with Him, that the body of sin might be done away with, that we should no longer serve sin.

7 For he who has died has been freed from sin.

8 Now if we died with the Messiah, we believe that we shall also live with Him,

9 knowing that the Messiah, having been raised from the dead, dies no more. Death no longer has dominion over Him.

10 For the death that He died, He died to sin once for all; but the life that He lives, He lives to God.

11 Likewise you also, reckon yourselves to be dead indeed to sin, but alive to God in Messiah Yeshua our Lord.

12 Therefore do not let sin reign in your mortal body, that you should obey it in its lusts.

13 And do not present your members as instruments of unrighteousness to sin, but present yourselves to God as being alive from the dead, and your members as instruments of righteousness to God.

14 For sin shall not have dominion over you, for you are not under law but under grace.

From Slaves of Sin to Servants of God

15 What then? Shall we sin because we are not under law but under grace? Certainly not!

16 Do you not know that to

whom you present yourselves servants to obey, you are that one's servants whom you obey, whether of sin to death, or of obedience to righteousness?

17 But God be thanked that though you were servants of sin, yet you have obeyed from the heart that form of doctrine to which you were delivered.

18 And having been set free from sin, you became servants of righteousness.

19 I speak in human terms because of the weakness of your flesh. For just as you have presented your members as servants to uncleanness, and to lawlessness leading to more lawlessness, even so now present your members as servants to righteousness for holiness.

20 For when you were servants of sin, you were free in regard to righteousness.

21 What fruit did you have then in the things of which you are now ashamed? For the result of those things is death.

22 But now having been set free from sin, and having become servants to God, you have your fruit to holiness, and the result, everlasting life.

23 For the wages of sin is death, but the gift of God is eternal life in Messiah Yeshua our Lord.

Freedom in the Messiah

7 Or do you not know, brethren (for I speak to those who know the Torah), that the Torah has dominion over a man as long as he lives?

2 For the woman who has a husband is bound by the Torah to her husband as long as he lives. But if the husband dies, she is released from the law of her husband.

3 So then if, while her husband lives, she marries another man, she will be called an adulteress; but if her husband dies, she is free from that law, so that she is no adulteress, though she has married another man.

4 Therefore, my brethren, you also have become dead to the law by the body of the Messiah, that you may be married to another, even to Him who has been raised from the dead, that we should bear fruit to God.

5 For when we were in the flesh, the passions of sins which were aroused by the Torah were at work in our members to bear fruit to death.

6 But now we have been delivered from the law, having died to what we were held by, so that we should serve in the newness of the Spirit and not in the oldness of the letter.

The Torah Is Holy

7 What shall we say then? Is the Torah sin? Certainly not! On the contrary, I would not have known sin except by the Torah. For I would not have known covetousness unless the Torah had said, *"You shall not covet."* [26]

8 But sin, taking opportunity by the commandment, produced in me all manner of evil desire. For apart from the Torah sin was dead.

9 For I was alive without the

---

26 Exodus 20:17; Deuteronomy 5:21
(5:18 in some versions)

Torah once, but when the commandment came, sin revived and I died.

10 And the commandment, which was to bring life, I found to bring death.

11 For sin, taking occasion by the commandment, deceived me, and by it killed me.

12 Therefore the Torah is holy, and the commandment holy and just and good.

The Torah Is Spiritual—We Are Carnal

13 Has then what is good become death to me? Certainly not! But sin, that it might appear sin, was producing death in me by what is good, so that sin by the commandment might become exceedingly sinful.

14 For we know that the Torah is spiritual, but I am carnal, sold under sin.

15 For what I am doing, I do not understand. For what I will to do, that I do not practice; but what I hate, that I do.

16 If, then, I do what I will not to do, I agree with the Torah that it is good.

17 Now then, it is no longer I who do it, but sin that dwells in me.

18 For I know that in me (that is, in my flesh) nothing good dwells; for to will is present with me, but how to perform what is good I do not find.

19 For the good that I will to do, I do not do; but the evil I will not to do, that I practice.

20 Now if I do what I will not to do, it is no longer I who do it, but sin that dwells in me.

21 I find then a law, that evil is present with me, the one who wills to do good.

22 For I delight in the Torah of God according to the inward man.

23 But I see another law in my members, warring against the law of my mind, and bringing me into captivity to the law of sin which is in my members.

24 O wretched man that I am! Who will deliver me from this body of death?

25 I thank God—through Yeshua ha Mashiach our Lord! So then, with the mind I myself serve the Torah of God, but with the flesh the law of sin.

Free from Indwelling Sin

8 There is therefore now no condemnation to those who are in Messiah Yeshua, who do not walk according to the flesh, but according to the Spirit.

2 For the law of the Spirit of life in Messiah Yeshua has made me free from the law of sin and death.

3 For what the Torah could not do in that it was weak through the flesh, God did by sending His own Son in the likeness of sinful flesh, and for sin, condemned sin in the flesh,

4 that the righteous requirement of the Torah might be fulfilled in us who do not walk according to the flesh but according to the Spirit.

5 For those who live according to the flesh set their minds on the things of the flesh, but those who live according to the Spirit, the things of the Spirit.

6 For to be carnally minded is death, but to be spiritually minded is life and peace.

7 Because the carnal mind is enmity against God; for it is not subject to the Torah of God, nor indeed can it be.

8 So then, those who are in the flesh cannot please God.

9 But you are not in the flesh but in the Spirit, if indeed the Spirit of God dwells in you. Now if anyone does not have the Spirit of the Messiah, he is not His.

10 And if the Messiah is in you, the body is dead because of sin, but the Spirit is life because of righteousness.

11 But if the Spirit of Him who raised Yeshua from the dead dwells in you, He who raised the Messiah from the dead will also give life to your mortal bodies by His Spirit who dwells in you.

Sonship Through the Spirit

12 Therefore, brethren, we are debtors not to the flesh, to live according to the flesh.

13 For if you live according to the flesh you will die; but if you through the Spirit put to death the deeds of the body, you will live.

14 For as many as are led by the Spirit of God, these are sons of God.

15 For you have not received the spirit of bondage again to fear, but you have received the Spirit of adoption by whom we cry out, "*Abba,* Father."

16 The Spirit Himself bears witness with our spirit that we are children of God,

17 and if children, then heirs—heirs of God and joint heirs with the Messiah, if indeed we suffer with Him, that we may also be glorified together.

From Suffering to Glory

18 For I consider that the sufferings of this present time are not worthy to be compared with the glory which shall be revealed in us.

19 For the earnest expectation of the creation eagerly waits for the revealing of the sons of God.

20 For the creation was subjected to futility, not willingly, but because of Him who has subjected it in hope;

21 because the creation itself also will be delivered from the bondage of corruption into the glorious liberty of the children of God.

22 For we know that the whole creation groans and labors with birth pangs together until now.

23 And not only they, but ourselves also who have the firstfruits of the Spirit, even we ourselves groan within ourselves, eagerly waiting for the adoption, the redemption of our body.

24 For we were saved in this hope, but hope that is seen is not hope; for why does one still hope for what he sees?

25 But if we hope for what we do not see, then we eagerly wait for it with perseverance.

26 Likewise the Spirit also helps in our weaknesses. For we do not know what we should pray for as we ought, but the Spirit Himself makes intercession for us with groanings which cannot be uttered.

27 And He who searches the hearts knows what the mind of the

Spirit is, because He makes intercession for the believers according to the will of God.

28 And we know that all things work together for good to those who love God, to those who are the called according to His purpose.

29 For whom He foreknew, He also predestined to be conformed to the image of His Son, that He might be the firstborn among many brethren.

30 Moreover whom He predestined, these He also called; whom He called, these He also justified; and whom He justified, these He also glorified.

God's Everlasting Love

31 What then shall we say to these things? If God is for us, who can be against us?

32 He who did not spare His own Son, but delivered Him up for us all, how shall He not with Him also freely give us all things?

33 Who shall bring a charge against God's elect? It is God who justifies.

34 Who is he who condemns? It is the Messiah who died, and furthermore is also risen, who is even at the right hand of God, who also makes intercession for us.

35 Who shall separate us from the love of the Messiah? Shall tribulation, or distress, or persecution, or famine, or nakedness, or peril, or sword?

36 As it is written:

"For Your sake we are killed all day long;
We are accounted as sheep for the slaughter." [27]

37 Yet in all these things we are more than conquerors through Him who loved us.

38 For I am persuaded that neither death nor life, nor angels nor principalities nor powers, nor things present nor things to come,

39 nor height nor depth, nor any other created thing, shall be able to separate us from the love of God which is in Messiah Yeshua our Lord.

God's Love for Israel

9 I tell the truth in the Messiah, I am not lying, my conscience also bearing me witness in the Holy Spirit,

2 that I have great heaviness and continual sorrow in my heart.

3 For I could wish that I myself were accursed from the Messiah for my brethren, my kinsmen according to the flesh,

4 who are Israelites, to whom pertain the adoption, the glory, the covenants, the giving of the Torah, the service of God, and the promises;

5 of whom are the fathers and from whom, according to the flesh, the Messiah came, who is over all, God blessed forever. Amen.

God's Purpose for Israel

6 It is not that the word of God has taken no effect. For they are not all Israel who are of Israel,

7 nor are they all children because they are the seed of Abraham; but, "In Isaac your seed will be called." [28]

8 That is, those who are the children of the flesh, these are not

---

27 Psalm 44:22 (44:23 in some versions)

28 Genesis 21:12

the children of God; but the children of the promise are counted as the seed.

9 For this is the word of promise, *"At this time I will come and Sarah shall have a son."* [29]

10 And not only this, but when Rebecca also had conceived by one man, even by our father Isaac

11 (for the children not yet being born, nor having done any good or evil, that the purpose of God according to election might stand, not of works but of Him who calls),

12 it was said to her, *"The older will serve the younger."* [30]

13 As it is written, *"Jacob I have loved, but Esau I have hated."* [31]

God's Mercy for Israel

14 What shall we say then? Is there unrighteousness with God? Certainly not!

15 For He says to Moses, *"I will have mercy on whomever I will have mercy, and I will have compassion on whomever I will have compassion."* [32]

16 So then it is not of him who wills, nor of him who runs, but of God who shows mercy.

17 For the Scripture says to Pharaoh, *"Even for this same purpose I have raised you up, that I might show My power in you, and that My name might be declared throughout all the earth."* [33]

18 Therefore He has mercy on whom He wills, and whom He wills He hardens.

19 You will say to me then,

"Why does He still find fault? For who has resisted His will?"

20 But indeed, O man, who are you to reply against God? Will the thing formed say to him who formed it, "Why have you made me like this?" [34]

21 Does not the potter have power over the clay, from the same lump to make one vessel for honor and another for dishonor?

22 What if God, wanting to show His wrath and to make His power known, endured with much longsuffering the vessels of wrath prepared for destruction,

23 and that He might make known the riches of His glory on the vessels of mercy, which He had prepared beforehand for glory,

24 even us whom He has called, not of the Jews only, but also of the Gentiles?

25 As He says also in Hosea:

"I will call them My people,
*   who were not My people,*
And her beloved, who was
*   not beloved."* [35]

26 *"And it shall come to pass in*
*   the place where it was said*
*   to them,*
*   'You are not My people,'*
There they will be called
*   sons of the living God."* [36]

27 Isaiah also cries out concerning Israel:

"Though the number of the
*   children of Israel be as the*
*   sand of the sea,*
The remnant will be saved.

28 *For He will finish the work*
*   and cut it short in righteousness,*

---

29 Genesis 18:10, 14
30 Genesis 25:23   31 Malachi 1:2, 3
32 Exodus 33:19   33 Exodus 9:16

34 Isaiah 45:9
35 Hosea 2:23 (2:25 in some versions)
36 Hosea 1:10 (2:1 in some versions)

Because the LORD will make
a short work upon the
earth." [37]

29 And as Isaiah said before:
"Unless the LORD of Sabaoth
had left us a seed,
We would have become like
Sodom,
And we would have been
made like Gomorrah." [38]

Present Condition of Israel

30 What shall we say then?
That the Gentiles, who did not follow after righteousness, have attained to righteousness, even the
righteousness of faith;

31 but Israel, following after the
Torah of righteousness, has not attained to the Torah of righteousness.

32 Why? Because they did not
seek it by faith, but as it were, by
the works of the Torah. For they
stumbled at that stumbling stone.

33 As it is written:
"Behold, I lay in Zion a
stumbling stone and rock of
offense,
And whoever believes on
Him will not be put to
shame." [39]

God's Gift to Israel

10 Brethren, my heart's desire
and prayer to God for Is-
rael is that they may be saved.

2 For I bear them witness that
they have a zeal for God, but not
according to knowledge.

3 For they being ignorant of
God's righteousness, and seeking

to establish their own righteousness, have not submitted to the
righteousness of God.

4 For the Messiah is the goal of
the Torah for righteousness to
everyone who believes.

5 For Moses writes about the
righteousness which is of the Torah, "The man who does those
things shall live by them." [40]

6 But the righteousness of faith
speaks in this way, "Do not say in
your heart, 'Who will ascend into
heaven?'" [41] (that is, to bring the
Messiah down from above)

7 or, "'Who will descend into
the abyss?'" [42] (that is, to bring
the Messiah up from the dead).

8 But what does it say? "The
word is near you, even in your
mouth and in your heart" [43] (that
is, the word of faith which we
preach):

9 that if you confess with your
mouth the Lord Yeshua and believe in your heart that God has
raised Him from the dead, you
will be saved.

10 For with the heart one believes to righteousness, and with
the mouth confession is made to
salvation.

11 For the Scripture says, "Whoever believes on Him will not be
put to shame." [44]

12 For there is no distinction between Jew and Greek, for the
same Lord over all is rich to all
who call upon Him.

13 For "whoever calls upon the
name of the LORD will be
saved." [45]

---

37 Isaiah 10:22, 23   38 Isaiah 1:9
39 Isaiah 8:14; 28:16

40 Leviticus 18:5   41 Deuteronomy 30:12
42 Deuteronomy 30:13
43 Deuteronomy 30:14   44 Isaiah 28:16
45 Joel 2:32 (3:5 in some versions)

14 How then shall they call on Him in whom they have not believed? And how shall they believe in Him of whom they have not heard? And how shall they hear without a preacher?

15 And how shall they preach unless they are sent? As it is written:

> "How beautiful are the feet of
> those who preach the good
> news of peace,
> And bring glad tidings of
> good things!" 46

16 But they have not all obeyed the good news. For Isaiah says, "Lord, who has believed our report?" 47

17 So then faith comes by hearing, and hearing by the word of God.

18 But I say, have they not heard? Yes indeed:

> "Their sound has gone out to
> all the earth,
> And their words to the ends
> of the world." 48

19 But I say, did Israel not know? First Moses says:

> "I will provoke you to jeal-
> ousy by those who are not
> a nation,
> And by a foolish nation I
> will anger you." 49

20 But Isaiah is very bold and says:

> "I was found by those who
> did not seek Me;
> I was made manifest to those
> who did not ask for Me." 50

21 But to Israel he says:

> "All day long I have stretched
> out My hands

> To a disobedient and con-
> trary people." 51

God's Faithfulness to Israel

11 I say then, has God cast away His people? Certainly not! For I also am an Israelite, of the seed of Abraham, of the tribe of Benjamin.

2 God has not cast away His people whom He foreknew. Or do you not know what the Scripture says of Elijah, how he pleads with God against Israel, saying,

3 "LORD, they have killed Your prophets and torn down Your altars, and I alone am left, and they seek my life"? 52

4 But what does the answer of God say to him? "I have reserved for Myself seven thousand men who have not bowed the knee to Baal." 53

5 Even so then, at this present time there is a remnant according to the election of grace.

6 And if by grace, then it is no longer of works; otherwise grace is no longer grace. But if it is of works, then it is no longer grace; otherwise work is no longer work.

7 What then? Israel has not obtained what it seeks; but the elect have obtained it, and the rest were hardened.

8 Just as it is written:

> "God has given them a spirit
> of stupor,
> Eyes that they should not see
> And ears that they should
> not hear,
> To this very day." 54

---

46 Isaiah 52:7; Nahum 1:15

47 Isaiah 53:1

48 Psalm 19:4 (19:5 in some versions)

49 Deuteronomy 32:21   50 Isaiah 65:1

51 Isaiah 65:2   52 1 Kings 19:10, 14

53 1 Kings 19:18

54 Deuteronomy 29:4 (29:3 in some versions); Isaiah 29:10

9 And David says:
"*Let their table become a
snare and a trap,
A stumbling block and a rec-
ompense to them;*
10 *Let their eyes be darkened,
that they may not see,
And bow down their back
always.*" [55]

Believers Grafted into Israel

11 I say then, have they stumbled that they should fall? Certainly not! But through their fall,
to provoke them to jealousy, salvation has come to the Gentiles.

12 Now if their fall is riches for
the world, and their failure riches
for the Gentiles, how much more
their fullness!

13 For I speak to you Gentiles;
inasmuch as I am an apostle [56] to
the Gentiles, I magnify my ministry,

14 if by any means I may provoke to jealousy those who are my
flesh and save some of them.

15 For if the casting away of
them is the reconciling of the
world, what will the receiving of
them be but life from the dead?

16 For if the firstfruit is holy, the
batch is also holy; and if the root is
holy, so are the branches.

17 And if some of the branches
were broken off, and you, being a
wild olive tree, were grafted in
among them, and with them became a partaker of the root and
fatness of the olive tree,

18 do not boast against the
branches. But if you boast, remember that you do not support
the root, but the root supports you.

19 You will say then, "Branches
were broken off that I might be
grafted in."

20 Well said. Because of unbelief they were broken off, and you
stand by faith. Do not be
haughty, but fear.

21 For if God did not spare the
natural branches, take heed lest
He also not spare you.

22 Therefore consider the goodness and severity of God: on those
who fell, severity; but toward you,
goodness, if you continue in His
goodness. Otherwise you also will
be cut off.

23 And they also, if they do not
continue in unbelief, will be
grafted in, for God is able to graft
them in again.

24 For if you were cut out of the
olive tree which is wild by nature,
and were grafted contrary to nature into a good olive tree, how
much more will these, who are the
natural branches, be grafted into
their own olive tree?

All Israel Will Be Saved

25 For I do not desire, brethren,
that you should be ignorant of this
mystery, lest you should be wise in
your own opinion, that hardening
in part has happened to Israel until the fullness of the Gentiles has
come in.

26 And so all Israel will be
saved, as it is written:
"*The Deliverer will come out
of Zion,
And He will turn away un-
godliness from Jacob.*
27 *For this is My covenant with
them,*

---

55 Psalm 69:22, 23 (69:23, 24 in some
versions)   56 See note 1, p. 246.

*When I shall take away
   their sins."* [57]

28 Concerning the good news
they are enemies for your sake,
but concerning the election they
are beloved for the sake of the fathers.

29 For the gifts and the calling of
God are irrevocable.

30 For as you in times past were
disobedient to God, yet have now
obtained mercy through their disobedience,

31 even so these also have now
been disobedient, that through the
mercy shown you they also may
obtain mercy.

32 For God has confined them
all in disobedience, that He might
have mercy on all.

33 O the depth of the riches
both of the wisdom and knowledge
of God! How unsearchable are
His judgments and His ways past
finding out!

34*"For who has known the
   mind of the LORD?
   Or who has become His
   counselor?"* [58]

35*"Or who has first given to
   Him
   And it shall be repaid to
   him?"* [59]

36 For of Him and through Him
and to Him are all things, to
whom be glory forever. Amen.

Living Sacrifices to God

12 I beseech you therefore,
brethren, by the mercies of
God, that you present your bodies
a living sacrifice, holy, acceptable

to God, which is your reasonable
service.

2 And do not be conformed to
this world, but be transformed by
the renewing of your mind, that
you may prove what is that good
and acceptable and perfect will of
God.

Serve God with Spiritual Gifts

3 For I say, through the grace
given to me, to everyone who is
among you, not to think of himself
more highly than he ought to
think, but to think soberly, as God
has dealt to each one a measure of
faith.

4 For as we have many members in one body, and all the
members do not have the same
function,

5 so we, being many, are one
body in the Messiah, and every
one members of one another.

6 Having then gifts differing according to the grace that is given
to us, let us use them: if prophecy,
let us prophesy in proportion to
our faith;

7 or service, let us use it in our
serving; or he who teaches, in
teaching;

8 or he who exhorts, in exhortation; he who gives, with liberality;
he who leads, with diligence; he
who shows mercy, with cheerful-
ness.

Behave Like a Believer

9 Let love be without hypocrisy. Abhor what is evil. Cling to
what is good.

10 Be kindly affectionate to one
another with brotherly love, in
honor giving preference to one another;

11 not lagging in diligence, fervent in spirit, serving the Lord;

57 Isaiah 59:20, 21
58 Isaiah 40:13; Jeremiah 23:18
59 Job 41:11

12 rejoicing in hope, patient in tribulation, continuing steadfastly in prayer;

13 distributing to the needs of the believers, given to hospitality.

14 Bless those who persecute you; bless and do not curse.

15 Rejoice with those who rejoice, and weep with those who weep.

16 Be of the same mind toward one another. Do not set your mind on high things, but associate with the humble. Do not be wise in your own opinion.

17 Repay no one evil for evil. Have regard for good things in the sight of all men.

18 If it is possible, as much as depends on you, live peaceably with all men.

19 Beloved, do not avenge yourselves, but rather give place to wrath; for it is written, *"Vengeance is Mine, I will repay,"* [60] says the Lord.

20 *"Therefore if your enemy hungers, feed him;*
If he thirsts, give him a drink;
For in so doing you will heap coals of fire on his head." [61]

21 Do not be overcome by evil, but overcome evil with good.

Submit to Government

13 Let every soul be subject to the governing authorities. For there is no authority except from God, and the authorities that exist are appointed by God.

2 Therefore whoever resists the authority resists the ordinance of God, and those who resist will bring judgment on themselves.

3 For rulers are not a terror to good works, but to evil. Do you then want to be unafraid of the authority? Do what is good, and you will have praise from the same.

4 For he is God's minister to you for good. But if you do what is evil, be afraid; for he does not bear the sword in vain; for he is God's minister, an avenger to execute wrath on him who does evil.

5 Therefore you must be subject, not only because of wrath but also for conscience' sake.

6 For because of this you also pay taxes, for they are God's ministers attending continually to this very thing.

7 Render therefore to all their due: taxes to whom taxes are due, customs to whom customs, fear to whom fear, honor to whom honor.

Love Your Neighbor

8 Owe no one anything but to love one another, for he who loves another has fulfilled the Torah;

9 and for this, *"You shall not commit adultery," "You shall not murder," "You shall not steal," "You shall not bear false witness," "You shall not covet";* [62] and if there is any other commandment, it is summed up in this saying, namely, *"You shall love your neighbor as yourself."* [63]

10 Love does no harm to a neighbor; therefore love is the fulfillment of the Torah.

---

60 Deuteronomy 32:35
61 Proverbs 25:21, 22
62 Exodus 20:13-15, 17; Deuteronomy 5:17-19, 21 (5:17, 18 in some versions)
63 Leviticus 19:18

Put on the Messiah

11 And do this, knowing the time, that now it is high time to awake out of sleep; for now our salvation is nearer than when we first believed.

12 The night is far spent, the day is at hand. Therefore let us cast off the works of darkness, and let us put on the armor of light.

13 Let us walk properly, as in the day, not in revelry and drunkenness, not in licentiousness and wantonness, not in strife and envy.

14 But put on the Lord Yeshua ha Mashiach, and make no provision for the flesh, to fulfill its lusts.

The Law of Liberty

14 Receive the one who is weak in the faith, but not to disputes over doubtful things.

2 For one believes he may eat all things, but he who is weak eats only vegetables.

3 Let not him who eats despise him who does not eat, and let not him who does not eat judge him who eats; for God has received him.

4 Who are you to judge another's servant? To his own master he stands or falls. Indeed, he will be made to stand, for God is able to make him stand.

5 One person esteems one day above another; another esteems every day alike. Let each be fully convinced in his own mind.

6 He who observes the day, observes it to the Lord; and he who does not observe the day, to the Lord he does not observe it. He who eats, eats to the Lord, for he gives God thanks; and he who does not eat, to the Lord he does not eat, and gives God thanks.

7 For none of us lives to himself, and no one dies to himself.

8 For if we live, we live to the Lord; and if we die, we die to the Lord. Therefore, whether we live or die, we are the Lord's.

9 For to this end the Messiah died and rose and lived again, that He might be Lord of both the dead and the living.

10 But why do you judge your brother? Or why do you show contempt for your brother? For we shall all stand before the judgment seat of the Messiah.

11 For it is written:

"As I live, says the LORD,
Every knee shall bow to Me,
And every tongue shall confess to God." [64]

12 So then each of us shall give account of himself to God.

13 Therefore let us not judge one another anymore, but rather resolve this, that no one put a stumbling block or a cause to fall in his brother's way.

The Law of Love

14 I know and am convinced by the Lord Yeshua that there is nothing unclean of itself; but to him who considers anything to be unclean, to him it is unclean.

15 But if your brother is offended because of your food, you are no longer walking in love. Do not destroy with your food the one for whom the Messiah died.

16 Therefore do not let your good be spoken of as evil;

17 for the kingdom of God is not food and drink, but righteousness

64 Isaiah 45:23

and peace and joy in the Holy Spirit.

18 For he who serves the Messiah in these things is acceptable to God and approved by men.

19 Therefore let us pursue the things which make for peace and the things by which one may edify another.

20 Do not destroy the work of God for the sake of food. All things indeed are pure, but it is evil for the man who eats with offense.

21 It is good neither to eat meat, nor drink wine, nor anything by which your brother stumbles, or is offended, or is made weak.

22 Do you have faith? Have it to yourself before God. Happy is he who does not condemn himself in what he approves.

23 But he who doubts is condemned if he eats, because he does not eat from faith; for whatever is not from faith is sin.

Bearing Others' Burdens

15 We then who are strong ought to bear the weaknesses of the weak, and not to please ourselves.

2 Let each of us please his neighbor for his good to edification.

3 For even the Messiah did not please Himself; but as it is written, *"The reproaches of those who reproached You fell on Me." 65*

4 For whatever things were written before were written for our learning, that we through patience and comfort of the Scriptures might have hope.

5 Now may the God of patience and consolation grant you to be like-minded toward one another, according to Messiah Yeshua,

6 that you may with one mind and one mouth glorify the God and Father of our Lord Yeshua ha Mashiach.

Glorify God Together

7 Therefore receive one another, just as the Messiah also received us, to the glory of God.

8 Now I say that Yeshua ha Mashiach became a servant to the circumcision for the truth of God, to confirm the promises made to the fathers,

9 and that the Gentiles might glorify God for His mercy, as it is written:

*"For this reason I will confess
to You among the Gentiles,
And sing to Your name." 66*

10 And again he says:

*"Rejoice, O Gentiles, with His
people!" 67*

11 And again:

*"Praise the LORD, all you
Gentiles!
Laud Him, all you peoples!" 68*

12 And again, Isaiah says:

*"There will be a root of Jesse;
And He who will rise to
reign over the Gentiles,
In Him the Gentiles will
hope." 69*

13 Now may the God of hope fill you with all joy and peace in believing, that you may abound in

---

65 Psalm 69:9 (69:10 in some versions)

66 2 Samuel 22:50; Psalm 18:49 (18:50 in some versions) 67 Deuteronomy 32:43
68 Psalm 117:1   69 Isaiah 11:10

hope through the power of the Holy Spirit.

From Jerusalem to Illyricum

14 And I myself also am confident concerning you, my brethren, that you also are full of goodness, filled with all knowledge, able also to admonish one another.

15 Nevertheless, brethren, I have written more boldly to you on some points, as reminding you, because of the grace given to me by God,

16 that I might be a minister of Yeshua ha Mashiach to the Gentiles, ministering the good news of God, that the offering of the Gentiles might be acceptable, sanctified by the Holy Spirit.

17 Therefore I have reason to glory in Messiah Yeshua in the things which pertain to God.

18 For I will not dare to speak of any of those things which the Messiah has not accomplished by me, through word and deed, to make the Gentiles obedient—

19 through mighty signs and wonders, by the power of the Spirit of God, so that from Jerusalem and round about to Illyricum I have fully preached the good news of the Messiah.

20 And so I have made it my aim to preach the good news, not where the Messiah was named, lest I should build on another man's foundation,

21 but as it is written:

"To whom He was not announced, they will see;
And those who have not heard will understand." [70]

Plan to Visit Rome

22 For this reason I also have been much hindered from coming to you.

23 But now no longer having a place in these parts, and having a great desire these many years to come to you,

24 whenever I take my journey to Spain, I shall come to you. For I hope to see you on my journey, and to be helped on my way there by you, if first I may enjoy your company for a while.

25 But now I am going to Jerusalem to minister to the believers.

26 For it has pleased those from Macedonia and Achaia to make a certain contribution for the poor believers who are in Jerusalem.

27 It has pleased them indeed, and they are their debtors. For if the Gentiles have been partakers of their spiritual things, their duty is also to minister to them in material things.

28 Therefore, when I have performed this and have sealed to them this fruit, I shall go by way of you to Spain.

29 And I am sure that when I come to you, I shall come in the fullness of the blessing of the good news of the Messiah.

30 Now I beg you, brethren, through the Lord Yeshua ha Mashiach, and through the love of the Spirit, that you strive together with me in your prayers to God for me,

31 that I may be delivered from those in Judea who do not believe, and that my service for Jerusalem may be acceptable to the believers,

32 that I may come to you with

70 Isaiah 52:15

joy by the will of God, and may be refreshed together with you.

33 Now the God of peace be with you all. Amen.

Sister Phoebe Commended

16 I commend to you Phoebe our sister, who is a servant of the congregation in Cenchrea,

2 that you receive her in the Lord in a manner worthy of the believers, and that you assist her in whatever business she has need of you; for indeed she has been a helper of many and of myself also.

Greeting Roman Believers

3 Greet Priscilla and Aquila, my fellow workers in Messiah Yeshua,

4 who have risked their own necks for my life, to whom not only I give thanks, but also all the congregations of the Gentiles.

5 Likewise greet the congregation that is in their house. Greet my beloved Epaenetus, who is the firstfruits of Achaia to the Messiah.

6 Greet Miriam, who labored much for us.

7 Greet Andronicus and Junia, my kinsmen and my fellow prisoners, who are of note among the apostles, who also were in the Messiah before me.

8 Greet Amplias, my beloved in the Lord.

9 Greet Urbanus, our fellow worker in the Messiah, and Stachys, my beloved.

10 Greet Apelles, approved in the Messiah. Greet those who are of the household of Aristobulus.

11 Greet Herodion, my kinsman. Greet those who are of the household of Narcissus who are in the Lord.

12 Greet Tryphena and Tryphosa, who labor in the Lord. Greet the beloved Persis, who labored much in the Lord.

13 Greet Rufus, chosen in the Lord, and his mother and mine.

14 Greet Asyncritus, Phlegon, Hermas, Patrobas, Hermes, and the brethren who are with them.

15 Greet Philologus and Julia, Nereus and his sister, and Olympas, and all the holy ones who are with them.

16 Greet one another with a holy kiss. The congregations of the Messiah greet you.

Avoid Divisive Persons

17 Now I urge you, brethren, note those who cause divisions and offenses, contrary to the doctrine which you have learned, and avoid them.

18 For those who are such do not serve our Lord Yeshua ha Mashiach, but their own belly, and by smooth words and flattering speech deceive the hearts of the simple.

19 For your obedience has become known to all. Therefore I am glad on your behalf, but yet I want you to be wise as to what is good, and simple concerning evil.

20 And the God of peace will crush Satan under your feet shortly. The grace of our Lord Yeshua ha Mashiach be with you. Amen.

Greetings from Paul's Friends

21 Timothy, my fellow worker, and Lucius, Jason, and Sosipater, my kinsmen, greet you.

22 I, Tertius, who wrote this letter, greet you in the Lord.

23 Gaius, my host and the host of the whole congregation, greets you. Erastus, the treasurer of the city, greets you, and Quartus, a brother.

24 The grace of our Lord Yeshua ha Mashiach be with you all. Amen.

Blessing

25 Now to Him who is able to establish you according to my good news and the preaching of Yeshua ha Mashiach, according to the revelation of the mystery which was kept secret since the world began

26 but now has been made manifest, and by the Scriptures of the prophets has been made known to all nations, according to the commandment of the everlasting God, for obedience to the faith—

27 to God, alone wise, be glory through Yeshua ha Mashiach forever. Amen.

The First Letter Of Paul To The
CORINTHIANS

Greeting

PAUL, called to be an apostle [1] of Yeshua ha Mashiach through the will of God, and Sosthenes our brother,

2 To the congregation of God which is at Corinth, to those who are sanctified in Messiah Yeshua, called to be believers, with all who in every place call on the name of Yeshua ha Mashiach our Lord, both theirs and ours:

3 Grace to you and peace from God our Father and the Lord Yeshua ha Mashiach.

Spiritual Gifts at Corinth

4 I thank my God always concerning you for the grace of God which was given to you by Messiah Yeshua,

5 that you were enriched in everything by Him in all utterance and all knowledge,

6 even as the testimony of the Messiah was confirmed in you,

7 so that you come short in no gift, eagerly waiting for the revelation of our Lord Yeshua ha Mashiach,

8 who will also confirm you to the end, that you may be blameless in the day of our Lord Yeshua ha Mashiach.

1 See note 1, p. 246.

9 God is faithful, by whom you were called into the fellowship of His Son, Yeshua ha Mashiach our Lord.

Do Not Be Divided

10 Now I plead with you, brethren, by the name of our Lord Yeshua ha Mashiach, that you all speak the same thing, and that there be no divisions among you, but that you be perfectly joined together in the same mind and in the same judgment.

11 For it has been declared to me concerning you, my brethren, by those who are of the household of Chloe, that there are contentions among you.

12 Now I say this, that each of you says, "I am of Paul," or "I am of Apollos," or "I am of Cephas," or "I am of the Messiah."

13 Is the Messiah divided? Was Paul crucified for you? Or were you immersed in the name of Paul?

14 I thank God that I immersed none of you except Crispus and Gaius,

15 lest anyone say that I had immersed in my own name.

16 And I also immersed the household of Stephanas. Besides, I do not know whether I immersed any other.

17 For the Messiah did not send

me to immerse, but to preach the gospel, not with wisdom of words, lest the cross of the Messiah be made of no effect.

The Messiah the Power and Wisdom of God

18 For the message of the cross is foolishness to those who are perishing, but to us who are being saved it is the power of God.

19 For it is written:

"I will destroy the wisdom of the wise,
And bring to nothing the understanding of the prudent." [2]

20 Where is the wise? Where is the scribe? Where is the disputer of this age? Has not God made foolish the wisdom of this world?

21 For since, in the wisdom of God, the world by wisdom did not know God, it pleased God by the foolishness of the message preached to save those who believe.

22 For the Jews request a sign, and the Greeks seek after wisdom;

23 but we preach the Messiah crucified, to the Jews a stumbling block and to the Greeks foolishness,

24 but to those who are called, both Jews and Greeks, the Messiah the power of God and the wisdom of God.

25 Because the foolishness of God is wiser than men, and the weakness of God is stronger than men.

Glory Only in the Lord

26 For you see your calling, brethren, that not many wise according to the flesh, not many mighty, not many noble, are called.

27 But God has chosen the foolish things of the world to put to shame the wise, and God has chosen the weak things of the world to put to shame the things which are mighty;

28 and the base things of the world and the things which are despised God has chosen, and the things which are not, to bring to nothing the things that are,

29 that no flesh should glory in His presence.

30 But of Him you are in Messiah Yeshua, who was made to us wisdom from God—and righteousness and sanctification and redemption—

31 that, as it is written, *"He who glories, let him glory in the* LORD." [3]

Know the Messiah

2 And I, brethren, when I came to you, did not come with excellence of speech or of wisdom declaring to you the testimony of God.

2 For I determined not to know anything among you except Yeshua ha Mashiach and Him crucified.

3 And I was with you in weakness, in fear, and in much trembling.

4 And my speech and my preaching were not with persuasive words of human wisdom, but in demonstration of the Spirit and of power,

5 that your faith should not be in the wisdom of men but in the power of God.

2 Isaiah 29:14

3 Jeremiah 9:24 (9:23 in some versions)

Spiritual Wisdom

6 However, we speak wisdom among those who are mature, yet not the wisdom of this age, nor of the rulers of this age, who are coming to nothing.

7 But we speak the wisdom of God in a mystery, even the hidden wisdom which God ordained before the ages for our glory,

8 which none of the rulers of this age knew; for had they known, they would not have crucified the Lord of glory.

9 But as it is written:

"Eye has not seen, nor ear heard,
Nor have entered into the heart of man
The things which God has prepared for those who love Him." [4]

10 But God has revealed them to us by His Spirit. For the Spirit searches all things, yes, the deep things of God.

11 For what man knows the things of a man except the spirit of the man which is in him? Even so no one knows the things of God except the Spirit of God.

12 Now we have received, not the spirit of the world, but the Spirit who is from God, that we might know the things that have been freely given to us by God.

13 These things we also speak, not in words which man's wisdom teaches but which the Holy Spirit teaches, comparing spiritual things with spiritual.

14 But the natural man does not receive the things of the Spirit of God, for they are foolishness to him; nor can he know them, because they are spiritually discerned.

15 But he who is spiritual judges all things, yet he himself is rightly judged by no one.

16 For "Who has known the mind of the LORD that he may instruct Him?" [5] But we have the mind of the Messiah.

Do Not Be Carnal

3 And I, brethren, could not speak to you as to spiritual people but as to carnal, as to babes in the Messiah.

2 I have fed you with milk and not with solid food; for until now you were not able to receive it, and even now you are still not able;

3 for you are still carnal. For where there are envy, strife, and divisions among you, are you not carnal and behaving like mere men?

4 For when one says, "I am of Paul," and another, "I am of Apollos," are you not carnal?

Watering, Working, Warning

5 Who then is Paul, and who is Apollos, but ministers by whom you believed, as the Lord gave to each one?

6 I have planted, Apollos watered, but God gave the increase.

7 So then neither he who plants is anything, nor he who waters, but God who gives the increase.

8 Now he who plants and he who waters are one, and each one will receive his own reward according to his own labor.

---

4 Isaiah 64:4 (64:3 in some versions)

5 Isaiah 40:13

9 For we are God's fellow workers; you are God's field, you are God's building.

10 According to the grace of God which was given to me, as a wise master builder I have laid the foundation, and another builds on it. But let each one take heed how he builds on it.

11 For no other foundation can anyone lay than that which is laid, which is Yeshua ha Mashiach.

12 Now if anyone builds on this foundation with gold, silver, precious stones, wood, hay, straw,

13 each one's work will become manifest; for the Day [6] will declare it, because it will be revealed by fire; and the fire will test each one's work, of what sort it is.

14 If anyone's work which he has built on it endures, he will receive a reward.

15 If anyone's work is burned, he will suffer loss; but he himself will be saved, yet so as through fire.

16 Do you not know that you are the temple of God and that the Spirit of God dwells in you?

17 If anyone defiles the temple of God, God will destroy him. For the temple of God is holy, which temple you are.

Avoid Worldly Wisdom

18 Let no one deceive himself. If anyone among you seems to be wise in this age, let him become a fool that he may become wise.

19 For the wisdom of this world is foolishness with God. For it is

written, *"He catches the wise in their own craftiness"*;[7]

20 and again, *"The LORD knows the thoughts of the wise, that they are futile."* [8]

21 Therefore let no one glory in men. For all things are yours:

22 whether Paul or Apollos or Cephas, or the world or life or death, or things present or things to come—all are yours.

23 And you are the Messiah's, and the Messiah is God's.

Stewards of the Mysteries

4 Let a man so consider us, as servants of the Messiah and stewards of the mysteries of God.

2 Moreover it is required in stewards that one be found faithful.

3 But with me it is a very small thing that I should be judged by you or by a court of man. In fact, I do not even judge myself.

4 For I know nothing against myself, yet I am not justified by this; but He who judges me is the Lord.

5 Therefore judge nothing before the time, until the Lord comes, who will both bring to light the hidden things of darkness and reveal the counsels of the hearts; and then each one's praise will come from God.

Fools for the Messiah's Sake

6 And these things, brethren, I have figuratively transferred to myself and Apollos for your sakes, that you may learn in us not to think beyond what is written, that none of you may be puffed up on behalf of one against the other.

6 Cf. Malachi 4:5, 6 (3:23, 24 in some versions)

7 Job 5:13   8 Psalm 94:11

7 For who makes you differ from another? And what do you have that you did not receive? Now if you did indeed receive it, why do you glory as if you had not received it?

8 You are already full! You are already rich! You have reigned as kings without us—and indeed I wish you did reign, that we also might reign with you!

9 For I think that God has displayed us, the apostles, last, as men condemned to death; for we have been made a spectacle to the world, both to angels and to men.

10 We are fools for the Messiah's sake, but you are wise in the Messiah! We are weak, but you are strong! You are distinguished, but we are dishonored!

11 Even to the present hour we both hunger and thirst, and we are poorly clothed, beaten, and homeless.

12 And we labor, working with our own hands. Being reviled, we bless; being persecuted, we endure it;

13 being defamed, we entreat. We have been made as the filth of the world, the offscouring of all things until this day.

Paul's Paternal Care

14 I do not write these things to shame you, but as my beloved children I warn you.

15 For though you might have ten thousand instructors in the Messiah, yet you do not have many fathers; for in Messiah Yeshua I have begotten you through the good news.

16 Therefore I urge you, be followers of me.

17 For this reason I have sent Timothy to you, who is my beloved and faithful son in the Lord, who will remind you of my ways in the Messiah, as I teach everywhere in every congregation.

18 Now some are puffed up, as though I were not coming to you.

19 But I will come to you shortly, if the Lord wills, and I will know, not the word of those who are puffed up, but the power.

20 For the kingdom of God is not in word but in power.

21 What do you want? Shall I come to you with a rod, or in love and a spirit of gentleness?

Immorality Defiles the Body of Believers

5 It is actually reported that there is sexual immorality among you, and such sexual immorality as is not even named among the Gentiles—that a man has his father's wife!

2 And you are puffed up, and have not rather mourned, that he who has done this deed might be taken away from among you.

3 For I indeed, as absent in body but present in spirit, have already judged, as though I were present, concerning him who has so done this deed.

4 In the name of our Lord Yeshua ha Mashiach, when you are gathered together, along with my spirit, with the power of our Lord Yeshua ha Mashiach,

5 deliver such a one to Satan for the destruction of the flesh, that his spirit may be saved in the day of the Lord Yeshua.

6 Your glorying is not good. Do you not know that a little leaven leavens the whole batch?

7 Therefore purge out the old leaven, that you may be a new batch, since you are unleavened. For indeed the Messiah, our Passover, was sacrificed for us.

8 Therefore let us keep the feast, not with old leaven, nor with the leaven of malice and wickedness, but with the unleavened bread of sincerity and truth.

Immorality Must Be Judged

9 I wrote to you in my letter not to keep company with sexually immoral people.

10 Yet I certainly did not mean with the sexually immoral people of this world, or with the covetous, or extortioners, or idolaters, since then you would need to go out of the world.

11 But now I have written to you not to keep company with anyone who is called a brother and is a fornicator, or covetous, or an idolater, or a reviler, or a drunkard, or an extortioner—not even to eat with such a person.

12 For what have I to do with judging those also who are outside? Do you not judge those who are inside?

13 But those who are outside God judges. Therefore *"put away from yourselves that wicked person."* [9]

Do Not Sue the Brethren

6 Dare any of you, having a matter against another, go to law before the unrighteous, and not before the believers?

2 Do you not know that the believers will judge the world? And if the world will be judged by you, are you unworthy to judge the smallest matters?

3 Do you not know that we shall judge angels? How much more, things that pertain to this life?

4 If then you have judgments of things pertaining to this life, do you appoint those who are least esteemed by the body of believers to judge?

5 I say this to your shame. Is it so, that there is not a wise man among you, not even one, who will be able to judge between his brethren?

6 But brother goes to law against brother, and that before unbelievers!

7 Now therefore it is already an utter failure for you that you go to law with one another. Why do you not rather accept wrong? Why do you not rather let yourselves be defrauded?

8 No, you yourselves do wrong and defraud, and you do these things to your brethren!

9 Do you not know that the unrighteous will not inherit the kingdom of God? Do not be deceived. Neither fornicators, nor idolaters, nor adulterers, nor effeminate homosexuals, nor sodomites,

10 nor thieves, nor covetous, nor drunkards, nor revilers, nor extortioners will inherit the kingdom of God.

11 And such were some of you. But you were washed, but you were sanctified, but you were justified in the name of the Lord Yeshua and by the Spirit of our God.

Glorify God in Body and Spirit

12 All things are lawful for me, but all things are not helpful. All

9 Deuteronomy 17:7; 19:19; 22:21, 24; 24:7

things are lawful for me, but I will not be brought under the power of any.

13 Foods for the stomach and the stomach for foods, but God will destroy both it and them. Now the body is not for sexual immorality but for the Lord, and the Lord for the body.

14 And God has both raised up the Lord and will also raise us up by His power.

15 Do you not know that your bodies are members of the Messiah? Shall I then take the members of the Messiah and make them members of a harlot? Certainly not!

16 Or do you not know that he who is joined to a harlot is one body with her? For *"The two,"* He says, *"will become one flesh."* [10]

17 But he who is joined to the Lord is one spirit with Him.

18 Flee sexual immorality. Every sin that a man does is outside the body, but he who commits sexual immorality sins against his own body.

19 Or do you not know that your body is the temple of the Holy Spirit who is in you, whom you have from God, and you are not your own?

20 For you were bought at a price; therefore glorify God in your body and in your spirit, which are God's.

Principles of Marriage

7 Now concerning the things of which you wrote to me: It is good for a man not to touch a woman.

2 Nevertheless, because of sexual immorality, let each man have his own wife, and let each woman have her own husband.

3 Let the husband render to his wife the affection due her, and likewise also the wife to her husband.

4 The wife does not have authority over her own body, but the husband does. And likewise also the husband does not have authority over his own body, but the wife does.

5 Do not deprive one another, except with consent for a time that you may give yourselves to fasting and to prayer; and come together again so that Satan does not tempt you because of your lack of self-control.

6 But I say this as a concession, not as a commandment.

7 For I wish that all men were even as I myself. But each one has his own gift from God, one in this manner and another in that.

8 But I say to the unmarried and to the widows: It is good for them if they remain even as I am;

9 but if they cannot exercise self-control, let them marry. For it is better to marry than to burn with passion.

To the Married

10 And to the married I command, yet not I but the Lord: A wife is not to depart from her husband.

11 But even if she does depart, let her remain unmarried or be reconciled to her husband. And a husband is not to divorce his wife.

12 But to the rest I, not the Lord, say: If any brother has a wife who does not believe, and she is willing to dwell with him, let him not divorce her.

10 Genesis 2:24

13 And the woman who has a husband who does not believe, if he is willing to dwell with her, let her not divorce him.

14 For the unbelieving husband is sanctified by the wife, and the unbelieving wife is sanctified by the husband; otherwise your children would be unclean, but now they are holy.

15 But if the unbeliever departs, let him depart; a brother or a sister is not under bondage in such cases. But God has called us to peace.

16 For how do you know, O wife, whether you will save your husband? Or how do you know, O man, whether you will save your wife?

Live as You Are Called

17 But as God has distributed to each one, as the Lord has called each one, so let him walk. And so I ordain in all the congregations.

18 Was anyone called while circumcised? Let him not become uncircumcised. Was anyone called while uncircumcised? Let him not be circumcised.

19 Circumcision is nothing and uncircumcision is nothing, but keeping the commandments of God is what counts.

20 Let each one remain in the same calling in which he was called.

21 Were you called while a servant? Do not be concerned about it; but if you can be made free, rather use it.

22 For he who is called in the Lord while a servant is the Lord's freedman. Likewise also he who is called while free is the Messiah's servant.

23 You were bought at a price; do not become servants of men.

24 Brethren, let each one remain with God in that calling in which he was called.

To the Unmarried and Widows

25 Now concerning virgins: I have no commandment from the Lord; yet I give judgment as one who has obtained mercy of the Lord to be trustworthy.

26 I suppose therefore that this is good because of the present distress—that it is good for a man to remain as he is:

27 Are you bound to a wife? Do not seek to be loosed. Are you loosed from a wife? Do not seek a wife.

28 But even if you do marry, you have not sinned; and if a virgin marries, she has not sinned. Nevertheless such will have trouble in the flesh, but I would spare you.

29 But this I say, brethren, the time is short; so that from now on, those also who have wives should be as though they had none,

30 those who weep as though they did not weep, those who rejoice as though they did not rejoice, those who buy as though they did not possess,

31 and those who use this world as not abusing it. For the form of this world is passing away.

32 But I want you to be without care. He who is unmarried cares for the things that belong to the Lord—how he may please the Lord.

33 But he who is married cares about the things of the world—how he may please his wife.

34 There is a difference between a wife and a virgin. The unmar-

ried woman cares about the things of the Lord, that she may be holy both in body and in spirit. But she who is married cares about the things of the world—how she may please her husband.

35 And this I say for your own profit, not that I may put a snare on you, but for what is proper, and that you may serve the Lord without distraction.

36 But if any man thinks he is behaving improperly toward his virgin, if she is past the flower of her youth, and thus it must be, let him do what he wishes; he does not sin; let them marry.

37 Nevertheless he who stands steadfast in his heart, having no necessity, but has power over his own will, and has so determined in his heart that he will keep his virgin, does well.

38 So then he who gives her in marriage does well, but he who does not give her in marriage does better.

39 A wife is bound by law as long as her husband lives; but if her husband dies, she is at liberty to be married to whom she wishes, only in the Lord.

40 But she is happier if she remains as she is, according to my judgment; and I think I also have the Spirit of God.

Be Sensitive to Conscience

8 Now concerning things offered to idols: We know that we all have knowledge. Knowledge puffs up, but love edifies.

2 And if anyone thinks that he knows anything, he knows nothing yet as he ought to know.

3 But if anyone loves God, this one is known by Him.

4 Therefore concerning the eating of things offered to idols, we know that an idol is nothing in the world,[11] and that there is no other God but one.

5 For even if there are so-called gods, whether in heaven or on earth—as there are many gods and many lords—

6 yet for us there is only one God, the Father, of whom are all things, and we for Him; and one Lord Yeshua ha Mashiach, by whom are all things, and we by Him.

7 However, there is not in everyone that knowledge; for some, with consciousness of the idol, to this hour eat it as a thing offered to an idol; and their conscience, being weak, is defiled.

8 But food does not commend us to God; for neither if we eat are we the better, nor if we do not eat are we the worse.

9 But take heed lest somehow this liberty of yours become a stumbling block to those who are weak.

10 For if anyone sees you who have knowledge eating in an idol's temple, will not the conscience of him who is weak be emboldened to eat those things offered to idols?

11 And because of your knowledge the weak brother, for whom the Messiah died, will perish.

12 But when you thus sin against the brethren, and wound their weak conscience, you sin against the Messiah.

13 Therefore, if food makes my brother stumble, I will eat no meat while the world stands, lest I make my brother stumble.

11 That is, has no real existence.

A Pattern of Self-Denial

9 Am I not an apostle? Am I not free? Have I not seen Yeshua ha Mashiach our Lord? Are you not my work in the Lord?

2 If I am not an apostle to others, yet doubtless I am to you. For you are the seal of my apostleship in the Lord.

3 My defense to those who examine me is this:

4 Do we have no right to eat and drink?

5 Do we have no right to take along a believing wife, as do also the other apostles, as the brothers of the Lord, and Cephas?

6 Or is it only Barnabas and I who have no right to refrain from working?

7 Who goes to war anytime at his own expense? Who plants a vineyard and does not eat of its fruit? Or who tends a flock and does not drink of the milk of the flock?

8 Do I say these things as a mere man? Or does not the Torah say the same also?

9 For it is written in the Torah of Moses, *"You shall not muzzle an ox while it treads out the grain."* [12] Is it oxen God is concerned about?

10 Or does He say it altogether for our sakes? For our sakes, no doubt, this is written, that he who plows should plow in hope, and he who threshes in hope should be partaker of his hope.

11 If we have sown spiritual things for you, is it a great thing if we shall reap your material things?

12 If others are partakers of this right over you, are we not even more? Nevertheless we have not used this right, but endure all things lest we hinder the good news of the Messiah.

13 Do you not know that those who minister the holy things eat of the things of the temple, and those who serve at the altar partake of the offerings of the altar?

14 Even so the Lord has commanded that those who preach the good news should live from the good news.

15 But I have used none of these things, nor have I written these things that it should be done so to me; for it would be better for me to die than that anyone should make my boasting void.

16 For though I preach the good news, I have nothing to boast of, for necessity is laid upon me; yes, woe is me if I do not preach the good news!

17 For if I do this willingly, I have a reward; but if against my will, I have been entrusted with a stewardship.

18 What is my reward then? That when I preach the good news, I may present the good news of the Messiah without charge, that I may not abuse my authority in the good news.

Serving All Men

19 For though I am free from all men, I have made myself a servant to all, that I might win the more;

20 and to the Jews I became as a Jew, that I might win Jews; to those who are under the Torah, as under the Torah, that I might win those who are under the Torah;

12 Deuteronomy 25:4

21 to those who are without Torah, as without Torah (not being without Torah to God, but under Torah to Messiah), that I might win those who are without Torah;

22 to the weak I became as weak, that I might win the weak. I have become all things to all men, that I might by all means save some.

23 And this I do for the good news' sake, that I may be partaker of it with you.

Striving for a Crown

24 Do you not know that those who run in a race all run, but one receives the prize? Run in such a way that you may obtain it.

25 And everyone who competes for the prize is temperate in all things. Now they do it to obtain a perishable crown, but we an imperishable.

26 Therefore I run thus: not with uncertainty. Thus I fight: not as one who beats the air.

27 But I discipline my body and bring it into subjection, lest, when I have preached to others, I myself should become disqualified.

Old Covenant Examples

10 Moreover, brethren, I do not want you to be ignorant that all our fathers were under the cloud, all passed through the sea,

2 all were baptized into Moses in the cloud and in the sea,

3 all ate the same spiritual food,

4 and all drank the same spiritual drink. For they drank of that spiritual Rock that followed them, and that Rock was the Messiah.

5 But with most of them God was not well pleased, for their bodies were scattered in the wilderness.

6 Now these things became our examples, to the intent that we should not lust after evil things as they also lusted,

7 and not become idolaters as were some of them; as it is written, *"The people sat down to eat and drink, and rose up to play."* [13]

8 Nor let us commit sexual immorality as some of them did, and in one day twenty-three thousand fell;

9 nor let us tempt the Messiah as some of them also tempted, and were destroyed by serpents;

10 nor murmur as some of them also murmured, and were destroyed by the destroyer.

11 Now all these things happened to them as examples, and they were written for our admonition, on whom the ends of the ages have come.

12 Therefore let him who thinks he stands take heed lest he fall.

13 No temptation has overtaken you except such as is common to man; but God is faithful, who will not allow you to be tempted beyond what you are able, but with the temptation will also make the way of escape, that you may be able to bear it.

Flee Idolatry

14 Therefore, my beloved, flee from idolatry.

15 I speak as to wise men; judge for yourselves what I say.

16 The cup of blessing which we bless, is it not the communion of

13 Exodus 32:6

the blood of the Messiah? The bread which we break, is it not the communion of the body of the Messiah?

17 For we, being many, are one bread and one body; for we are all partakers of that one bread.

18 Observe Israel after the flesh: Are not those who eat of the sacrifices partakers of the altar?

19 What am I saying then? That an idol is anything, or what is offered to idols is anything?

20 But I say that the things which the Gentiles sacrifice they sacrifice to demons and not to God, and I do not want you to have fellowship with demons.

21 You cannot drink the cup of the Lord and the cup of demons; you cannot be partakers of the Lord's table and of the table of demons.

22 Or do we provoke the Lord to jealousy? Are we stronger than He?

All to the Glory of God

23 All things are lawful for me, but all things are not helpful; all things are lawful for me, but all things do not edify.

24 Let no one seek his own, but each one the other's well-being.

25 Eat whatever is sold in the meat market, asking no questions for conscience' sake;

26 for "The earth is the LORD's, and everything in it." [14]

27 If any of those who do not believe invites you to dinner, and you desire to go, eat whatever is set before you, asking no question for conscience' sake.

28 But if anyone says to you,

"This was offered to idols," do not eat it for the sake of the one who told you, and for conscience' sake; for "The earth is the LORD's, and everything in it." [14]

29 Conscience, I say, not your own, but that of the other. For why is my liberty judged by another man's conscience?

30 But if by grace I am a partaker, why am I evil spoken of for that over which I give thanks?

31 Therefore, whether you eat or drink, or whatever you do, do all to the glory of God.

32 Give no offense, either to the Jews or to the Greeks or to the called-out ones of God,

33 just as I also please all men in all things, not seeking my own profit, but the profit of many, that they may be saved.

11 Be followers of me, just as I also am of the Messiah.

Head Coverings

2 Now I praise you, brethren, that you remember me in all things and keep the traditions as I delivered them to you.

3 But I want you to know that the head of every man is the Messiah, the head of woman is man, and the head of the Messiah is God.

4 Every man praying or prophesying, having his head covered, dishonors his head. [15]

5 But every woman who prays or prophesies with her head uncovered dishonors her head, for that is one and the same as if her head were shaved.

---

14 Psalm 24:1

14 Psalm 24:1
15 This may refer to a veil or other female headcovering.

6 For if a woman is not covered, let her also be shorn. But if it is shameful for a woman to be shorn or shaved, let her be covered.

7 For a man indeed ought not to cover his head, inasmuch as he is the image and glory of God; but woman is the glory of man.

8 For man is not from woman, but woman from man.

9 Nor was man created for the woman, but woman for the man.

10 For this reason the woman ought to have a symbol of authority on her head, because of the angels.

11 Nevertheless, neither is man independent of woman, nor woman independent of man, in the Lord.

12 For as the woman was from the man, even so the man also is through the woman; but all things are from God.

13 Judge among yourselves. Is it proper for a woman to pray to God with her head uncovered?

14 Does not even nature [16] itself teach you that if a man has long hair, it is a dishonor to him?

15 But if a woman has long hair, it is a glory to her; for her hair is given to her for a covering.

16 But if anyone seems to be contentious, we have no such custom, nor do the congregations of God.

Conduct in Worship

17 Now in giving these instructions I do not praise you, because you come together not for the better but for the worse.

18 For first of all, when you come together in congregation, I hear that there are divisions among you, and in part I believe it.

19 For there must also be heresies among you, that those who are approved may be recognized among you.

20 Therefore when you come together in one place, it is not to eat the Lord's Supper.

21 For in eating, each one takes his own supper ahead of others; and one is hungry and another is drunk.

22 What! Do you not have houses to eat and drink in? Or do you despise the congregation of God and shame those who have nothing? What shall I say to you? Shall I praise you in this? I do not praise you.

Meaning of Passover

23 For I have received from the Lord that which I also delivered to you: that the Lord Yeshua the same night [17] in which He was betrayed took matzah;

24 and when He had given thanks, He broke it and said, "Take, eat; this is My body which is broken for you; do this in remembrance of Me."

25 In the same manner He also took the cup [18] after supper, saying, "This cup is the new covenant in My blood. This do, as often as you drink it, in remembrance of Me."

26 For as often as you eat this matzah and drink this cup, you

---

16 The word used in the original language here often means "custom."

17 This was on Passover.

18 The third cup, the Cup of Redemption.

proclaim the Lord's death till He comes.

Examine Yourself

27 Therefore whoever eats this matzah and drinks this cup of the Lord in an unworthy manner will be guilty of the body and blood of the Lord.

28 But let a man examine himself, and so let him eat of that matzah and drink of that cup.

29 For he who eats and drinks in an unworthy manner eats and drinks judgment to himself, not discerning the Lord's body.

30 For this reason many are weak and sick among you, and many sleep.

31 For if we would judge ourselves, we would not be judged.

32 But when we are judged, we are chastened by the Lord, that we may not be condemned with the world.

33 Therefore, my brethren, when you come together to eat, wait for one another.

34 And if anyone is hungry, let him eat at home, that you not come together for judgment. And the rest I will set in order when I come.

Spiritual Gifts: Unity in Diversity

12 Now concerning spiritual gifts, brethren, I do not want you to be ignorant:

2 You know that you were Gentiles, carried away to these dumb idols, however you were led.

3 Therefore I make known to you that no one speaking by the Spirit of God calls Yeshua accursed, and no one can say that Yeshua is Lord except by the Holy Spirit.

4 Now there are diversities of gifts, but the same Spirit.

5 And there are differences of ministries, but the same Lord.

6 And there are diversities of activities, but it is the same God who works all in all.

7 But the manifestation of the Spirit is given to each one for mutual profit:

8 for to one is given the word of wisdom by the Spirit, to another the word of knowledge by the same Spirit,

9 to another faith by the same Spirit, to another gifts of healings by the same Spirit,

10 to another the working of miracles, to another prophecy, to another discerning of spirits, to another different kinds of tongues, to another the interpretation of tongues.

11 But one and the same Spirit works all these things, dividing to each one individually as He wills.

Unity and Diversity in One Body

12 For as the body is one and has many members, and all the members of that one body, being many, are one body, so also is the Messiah.

13 For by one Spirit we were all baptized into one body—whether Jews or Greeks, whether slaves or free—and have all been made to drink into one Spirit.

14 For in fact the body is not one member but many.

15 If the foot should say, "Because I am not a hand, I am not of the body," is it therefore not of the body?

16 And if the ear should say, "Because I am not an eye, I am

not of the body," is it therefore not of the body?

17 If the whole body were an eye, where would be the hearing? If the whole were hearing, where would be the smelling?

18 But now God has set the members, each one of them, in the body as it has pleased Him.

19 And if they were all one member, where would the body be?

20 But now they are many members, yet one body.

21 And the eye cannot say to the hand, "I have no need of you"; nor again the head to the feet, "I have no need of you."

22 No, much rather, those members of the body which seem to be weaker are necessary.

23 And those members of the body which we think to be less honorable, on these we bestow greater honor; and our unpresentable parts have greater modesty,

24 since our presentable parts have no need. But God has tempered the body together, having given greater honor to that part which lacks it,

25 that there should be no schism in the body, but that the members should have the same care for one another.

26 And if one member suffers, all the members suffer with it; or if one member is honored, all the members rejoice with it.

27 Now you are the body of the Messiah, and members individually.

28 And God has appointed these in the body of believers: first apostles, second prophets, third teachers, after that miracles, then gifts of healings, helps, administrations, different kinds of tongues.

29 Are all apostles? Are all prophets? Are all teachers? Are all workers of miracles?

30 Do all have gifts of healings? Do all speak with tongues? Do all interpret?

31 But earnestly desire the best gifts. And yet I show you a more excellent way.

The Greatest Gift

13 Though I speak with the tongues of men and of angels, but have not love, I have become as sounding brass or a clanging cymbal.

2 And though I have the gift of prophecy, and understand all mysteries and all knowledge, and though I have all faith, so that I could remove mountains, but have not love, I am nothing.

3 And though I bestow all my goods to feed the poor, and though I give my body to be burned, but have not love, it profits me nothing.

4 Love suffers long and is kind; love does not envy; love does not parade itself, is not puffed up;

5 does not behave rudely, does not seek its own, is not provoked, thinks no evil;

6 does not rejoice in iniquity, but rejoices in the truth;

7 bears all things, believes all things, hopes all things, endures all things.

8 Love never fails. But whether there are prophecies, they will fail; whether there are tongues, they will cease; whether there is knowledge, it will vanish away.

9 For we know in part and we prophesy in part.

10 But when that which is perfect has come, then that which is in part will be done away.

11 When I was a child, I spoke as a child, I understood as a child, I thought as a child; but when I became a man, I put away childish things.

12 For now we see in a mirror, dimly, but then face to face. Now I know in part, but then I shall know just as I also am known.

13 And now abide faith, hope, love, these three; but the greatest of these is love.

Prophecy and Tongues

14 Pursue love, and desire spiritual gifts, but especially that you may prophesy.

2 For he who speaks in a tongue does not speak to men but to God, for no one understands him; however, in the spirit he speaks mysteries.

3 But he who prophesies speaks to men for edification, exhortation, and comfort.

4 He who speaks in a tongue edifies himself, but he who prophesies edifies the congregation.

5 I wish you all spoke with tongues, but even more that you prophesied; for he who prophesies is greater than he who speaks with tongues, unless he interprets, that the congregation may receive edification.

Pray for Interpretation

6 But now, brethren, if I come to you speaking with tongues, what shall I profit you unless I speak to you either by revelation, by knowledge, by prophesying, or by teaching?

7 And even things without life, whether flute or harp, when they make a sound, unless they make a distinction in the sounds, how will it be known what is piped or played?

8 For if the trumpet makes an uncertain sound, who will prepare himself for battle?

9 So likewise you, unless you utter by the tongue words easy to understand, how will it be known what is spoken? For you will be speaking into the air.

10 There are, it may be, so many kinds of languages in the world, and none of them is without significance.

11 Therefore, if I do not know the meaning of the language, I shall be a foreigner to him who speaks, and he who speaks will be a foreigner to me.

12 Even so you, since you are zealous for spiritual gifts, seek that you may excel for the edifying of the congregation.

13 Therefore let him who speaks in a tongue pray that he may interpret.

14 For if I pray in a tongue, my spirit prays, but my understanding is unfruitful.

15 What is the result then? I will pray with the spirit, and I will also pray with the understanding. I will sing with the spirit, and I will also sing with the understanding.

16 Otherwise, if you bless with the spirit, how will he who occupies the place of the uninformed say "Amen" at your giving of thanks, since he does not understand what you say?

17 For you indeed give thanks well, but the other is not edified.

18 I thank my God I speak with tongues more than you all;

19 yet in the congregation I would rather speak five words with my understanding, that I may teach others also, than ten thousand words in a tongue.

Tongues a Sign to Unbelievers

20 Brethren, do not be children in understanding; however, in malice be babes, but in understanding be mature.

21 In the law it is written:

"With men of other tongues
and other lips
I will speak to this people;
And yet, for all that, they
will not hear Me," [19]

says the Lord.

22 Therefore tongues are for a sign, not to those who believe but to those who do not believe; but prophesying does not serve those who do not believe but those who believe.

23 Therefore if the whole congregation comes together in one place, and all speak with tongues, and there come in those who are uninformed or unbelievers, will they not say that you are mad?

24 But if all prophesy, and there comes in one who does not believe, or one uninformed, he is convinced by all, he is judged by all.

25 And thus the secrets of his heart are revealed; and so, falling down on his face, he will worship God and report that God is truly among you.

19 Isaiah 28:11, 12

Order in Congregational Meetings

26 How is it then, brethren? When you come together, each one of you has a psalm, has a teaching, has a tongue, has a revelation, has an interpretation. Let all things be done for edification.

27 If anyone speaks in a tongue, let there be two or at the most three, each in turn, and let one interpret.

28 But if there is no interpreter, let him keep silent in the congregation, and let him speak to himself and to God.

29 Let two or three prophets speak, and let the others judge.

30 If anything is revealed to another who sits by, let the first keep silent.

31 For you can all prophesy one by one, that all may learn and all may be encouraged.

32 And the spirits of the prophets are subject to the prophets.

33 For God is not the author of confusion but of peace, as in all the congregations of the believers.

34 Let your women keep silent in the congregations, for they are not permitted to speak; but they are to be submissive, as the Torah also says.

35 And if they want to learn something, let them ask their own husbands at home; for it is shameful for women to speak in the congregation.

36 Or did the word of God come from you? Or did it only come to you?

37 If anyone thinks himself to be a prophet or spiritual, let him acknowledge that the things which I write to you are the commandments of the Lord.

38 But if anyone is ignorant, let him be ignorant.

39 Therefore, brethren, earnestly desire to prophesy, and do not forbid to speak with tongues.

40 Let all things be done decently and in order.

The Risen Messiah, Faith's Reality

15 Moreover, brethren, I declare to you the good news which I preached to you, which also you have received and in which you stand,

2 by which also you are saved, if you hold fast that word which I preached to you—unless you have believed in vain.

3 For I delivered to you first of all that which I also received: that the Messiah died for our sins according to the Scriptures,[20]

4 and that He was buried, and that He rose again the third day according to the Scriptures,[21]

5 and that He was seen by Cephas, then by the twelve.

6 After that He was seen by over five hundred brethren at once, of whom the greater part remain to the present, but some have fallen asleep.

7 After that He was seen by James, then by all the apostles.

8 And last of all He was seen by me also, as by one born out of due time.

9 For I am the least of the apostles, who am not worthy to be called an apostle, because I persecuted the called-out ones of God.

10 But by the grace of God I am what I am, and His grace toward me was not in vain; but I labored more abundantly than they all, yet not I, but the grace of God which was with me.

11 Therefore, whether it was I or they, so we preach and so you believed.

The Risen Messiah, Our Hope

12 Now if the Messiah is preached that He has been raised from the dead, how do some among you say that there is no resurrection of the dead?

13 But if there is no resurrection of the dead, then the Messiah is not risen.

14 And if the Messiah is not risen, then our preaching is vain and your faith is also vain.

15 Yes, and we are found false witnesses of God, because we have testified of God that He raised up the Messiah, whom He did not raise up—if in fact the dead do not rise.

16 For if the dead do not rise, then the Messiah is not risen.

17 And if the Messiah is not risen, your faith is futile; you are still in your sins!

18 Then also those who have fallen asleep in the Messiah have perished.

19 If in this life only we have hope in the Messiah, we are of all men the most pitiable.

The Last Enemy Destroyed

20 But now the Messiah is risen from the dead, and has become the firstfruits[22] of those who have fallen asleep.

20 Isaiah 53:5-12
21 Psalm 16:10 (cf. Isaiah 53:10)
22 A reference to the ceremony of First Fruits (Leviticus 23:9-11), which was associated with Passover week.

21 For since by man came death, by Man also came the resurrection of the dead.

22 For as in Adam all die, even so in the Messiah all will be made alive.

23 But each one in his own order: the Messiah the firstfruits, afterward those who are of the Messiah at His coming.

24 Then comes the end, when He delivers the kingdom to God, even the Father, when He puts down all rule and all authority and power.

25 For He must reign till He has put all enemies under His feet.

26 The last enemy that will be destroyed is death.

27 For *"He has put all things under His feet." 23* But when He says "all things are put under Him," it is evident that He is excepted who put all things under Him.

28 And when all things are made subject to Him, then the Son Himself will also be subject to Him who put all things under Him, that God may be all in all.

Effects of Denying the Resurrection

29 Otherwise, what will they do who are immersed for the dead, if the dead do not rise at all? Why then are they immersed for the dead?

30 And why do we stand in jeopardy every hour?

31 I affirm, by the glorying in you which I have in Messiah Yeshua our Lord, I die daily.

32 If, to speak in the manner of men, I have fought with beasts at Ephesus, what advantage is it to me? If the dead do not rise, *"Let us eat and drink, for tomorrow we die." 24*

33 Do not be deceived: "Evil company corrupts good habits."

34 Awake to righteousness, and do not sin; for some do not have the knowledge of God. I speak this to your shame.

A Glorious Body

35 But someone will say, "How are the dead raised up? And with what body do they come?"

36 Foolish one, what you sow is not made alive unless it dies.

37 And what you sow, you do not sow that body that shall be, but mere grain—perhaps wheat or some other grain.

38 But God gives it a body as it has pleased Him, and to each seed its own body.

39 All flesh is not the same flesh, but there is one kind of flesh of men, another flesh of beasts, another of fish, and another of birds.

40 There are also celestial bodies and terrestrial bodies; but the glory of the celestial is one, and the glory of the terrestrial is another.

41 There is one glory of the sun, another glory of the moon, and another glory of the stars; for one star differs from another star in glory.

42 So also is the resurrection of the dead. The body is sown in corruption, it is raised in incorruption.

43 It is sown in dishonor, it is raised in glory. It is sown in weakness, it is raised in power.

---

23 Psalm 8:6 (8:7 in some versions)   *24* Isaiah 22:13

44 It is sown a natural body, it is raised a spiritual body. There is a natural body, and there is a spiritual body.

45 And so it is written, *"The first man Adam became a living soul."* [25] The last Adam became a life-giving spirit.

46 However, the spiritual is not first, but the natural, and afterward the spiritual.

47 The first man was of the earth, made of dust; the second Man is the Lord from heaven.[26]

48 As was the man of dust, so also are those who are made of dust; and as is the heavenly Man, so also are those who are heavenly.

49 And as we have borne the image of the man of dust, we shall also bear the image of the heavenly Man.

Our Final Victory

50 Now this I say, brethren, that flesh and blood cannot inherit the kingdom of God; nor does corruption inherit incorruption.

51 Behold, I tell you a mystery: We shall not all sleep, but we shall all be changed—

52 in a moment, in the twinkling of an eye, at the last shofar. For the shofar will sound, and the dead will be raised incorruptible, and we shall be changed.

53 For this corruptible must put on incorruption, and this mortal must put on immortality.

54 So when this corruptible has put on incorruption, and this mortal has put on immortality, then shall be brought to pass the saying that is written: *"Death is swallowed up in victory."* [27]

55 *"O death, where is your sting?*
O Hades, where is your victory?" [28]

56 The sting of death is sin, and the strength of sin is the Torah.

57 But thanks be to God, who gives us the victory through our Lord Yeshua ha Mashiach.

58 Therefore, my beloved brethren, be steadfast, immovable, always abounding in the work of the Lord, inasmuch as you know that your labor is not in vain in the Lord.

Collection for the Believers

16 Now concerning the collection for the believers, as I have given orders to the congregations of Galatia, so you do also:

2 On the first day of the week let each one of you lay something aside, storing up as he may prosper, that there be no collections when I come.

3 And when I come, whomever you approve by your letters, I will send to take your gift to Jerusalem.

4 And if it is fitting that I go also, they will go with me.

Personal Plans

5 Now I will come to you when I pass through Macedonia, for I am passing through Macedonia.

6 And it may be that I will remain, or even spend the winter with you, that you may send me on my journey wherever I go.

---

25 Genesis 2:7   *26* Cf. Daniel 7:13, 14   *27* Isaiah 25:8   *28* Hosea 13:14

7 For I do not wish to see you now on the way; but I hope to stay a while with you, if the Lord permits.

8 But I will tarry in Ephesus until Shavuot.

9 For a great and effective door has opened to me, and there are many adversaries.

10 Now if Timothy comes, see that he may be with you without fear; for he does the work of the Lord, as I also do.

11 Therefore let no one despise him. But send him on his journey in peace, that he may come to me; for I am waiting for him with the brethren.

12 Now concerning our brother Apollos, I strongly urged him to come to you with the brethren, but he was quite unwilling to come at this time; however, he will come when he has a convenient time.

Final Exhortations

13 Watch, stand fast in the faith, be brave, be strong.

14 Let all that you do be done with love.

15 I urge you, brethren—you know the household of Stephanas, that it is the firstfruits of Achaia, and that they have devoted themselves to the ministry of the believers—

16 that you also submit to such, and to everyone who works with us and labors.

17 I am glad about the coming of Stephanas, Fortunatus, and Achaicus, for what was lacking on your part they have supplied.

18 For they have refreshed my spirit and yours; therefore acknowledge those who are such.

Greetings and a Solemn Farewell

19 The congregations of Asia greet you. Aquila and Priscilla greet you heartily in the Lord, with the congregation that is in their house.

20 All the brethren greet you. Greet one another with a holy kiss.

21 The salutation with my own hand—Paul.

22 If anyone does not love the Lord Yeshua ha Mashiach, let him be accursed. O Lord, come!

23 The grace of our Lord Yeshua ha Mashiach be with you.

24 My love be with you all in Messiah Yeshua. Amen.

The Second Letter Of Paul To The
CORINTHIANS

Greeting

PAUL, an apostle [1] of Yeshua ha Mashiach by the will of God, and Timothy our brother,

To the congregation of God which is at Corinth, with all the believers who are in all Achaia:

2 Grace to you and peace from God our Father and the Lord Yeshua ha Mashiach.

Comfort in Suffering

3 Blessed be the God and Father of our Lord Yeshua ha Mashiach, the Father of mercies and God of all comfort,

4 who comforts us in all our tribulation, that we may be able to comfort those who are in any trouble, by the comfort with which we ourselves are comforted by God.

5 For as the sufferings of the Messiah abound in us, so our consolation also abounds by the Messiah.

6 And if we are afflicted, it is for your consolation and salvation, which is effective for enduring the same sufferings which we also suffer. Or if we are comforted, it is for your consolation and salvation.

7 And our hope for you is steadfast, knowing that as you are partakers of the sufferings, so you also will be of the consolation.

Delivered from Suffering

8 For we do not want you to be ignorant, brethren, of our trouble which came to us in Asia: that we were burdened beyond measure, above strength, so that we despaired even of life.

9 But we had the sentence of death in ourselves, that we should not trust in ourselves but in God who raises the dead,

10 who delivered us from so great a death, and does deliver us; in whom we trust that He will still deliver us,

11 you also helping together by prayer for us, that thanks may be given by many persons on our behalf for the gift granted to us through many.

Paul's Sincerity

12 For our boasting is this: the testimony of our conscience that we conducted ourselves in the world in simplicity and godly sincerity, not with fleshly wisdom but by the grace of God, and more abundantly toward you.

13 For we are not writing any other things to you than what you read or understand; and I trust you will understand, even to the end

14 (as also you have understood us in part), that we are your boast

as you also are ours, in the day of the Lord Yeshua.

Sparing the Congregation

15 And in this confidence I intended to come to you before, that you might have a second benefit—

16 to pass by way of you to Macedonia, to come again from Macedonia to you, and be helped by you on my way to Judea.

17 Therefore, when I was planning this, did I do it lightly? Or the things I plan, do I plan according to the flesh, that with me there should be Yes, Yes and No, No?

18 But as God is faithful, our word to you was not Yes and No.

19 For the Son of God, Yeshua ha Mashiach, who was preached among you by us—by me, Silvanus, and Timothy—was not Yes and No, but in Him was Yes.

20 For all the promises of God in Him are Yes, and in Him Amen, to the glory of God by us.

21 Now He who establishes us with you in the Messiah and has anointed us is God,

22 who also has sealed us and given us the Spirit in our hearts as a deposit.

23 Moreover I call God as witness against my soul, that to spare you I came no more to Corinth.

24 Not that we have dominion over your faith, but are fellow workers for your joy; for by faith you stand.

2 But I determined this within myself, that I would not come again to you in sorrow.

2 For if I make you sorrowful, then who is he who makes me glad but the one who is made sorrowful by me?

Forgive the Offender

3 And I wrote this very thing to you, lest, when I came, I should have sorrow over those from whom I ought to have joy, having confidence in you all that my joy is the joy of you all.

4 For out of much affliction and anguish of heart I wrote to you, with many tears, not that you should be grieved, but that you might know the love which I have so abundantly for you.

5 But if anyone has caused grief, he has not grieved me, but to some extent—not to be too severe—all of you.

6 This punishment which was inflicted by the majority is sufficient for such a man,

7 so that, on the contrary, you ought rather to forgive and comfort him, lest perhaps such a one be swallowed up with too much sorrow.

8 Therefore I urge you to confirm your love to him.

9 For to this end I also wrote, that I might put you to the test, whether you are obedient in all things.

10 Now whom you forgive anything, I also forgive. For if indeed I have forgiven anything, whom I have forgiven I have forgiven it for your sakes in the presence of the Messiah,

11 lest Satan should take advantage of us; for we are not ignorant of his devices.

Triumph in the Messiah

12 Furthermore, when I came to Troas to preach the Messiah's

good news, and a door was opened to me by the Lord,

13 I had no rest in my spirit, because I did not find Titus my brother; but taking my leave of them, I went from there to Macedonia.

14 Now thanks be to God who always leads us in triumph in the Messiah, and makes manifest the aroma of His knowledge by us in every place.

15 For we are to God the fragrance of the Messiah among those who are being saved and among those who are perishing.

16 To the one we are the aroma of death to death, and to the other the aroma of life to life. And who is sufficient for these things?

17 For we are not, as so many, peddling the word of God; but as of sincerity, but as from God, we speak in the sight of God in the Messiah.

A Letter of the Messiah

3 Do we begin again to commend ourselves? Or do we need, as some others, letters of commendation to you or commendations from you?

2 You are our letter written in our hearts, known and read by all men,

3 inasmuch as you are manifestly declared to be a letter of the Messiah, ministered by us, written not with ink but by the Spirit of the living God, not on tablets of stone but on tablets of flesh, that is, of the heart.

The Spirit, Not the Letter

4 And we have such trust through the Messiah toward God.

5 Not that we are sufficient of ourselves to think of anything as being from ourselves, but our sufficiency is from God,

6 who also has made us sufficient as ministers of the new covenant, not of the letter but of the Spirit; for the letter kills, but the Spirit gives life.

Glory of the New Covenant

7 But if the ministry of death, written and engraved on stones, was glorious, so that the children of Israel could not look steadily at the face of Moses because of the glory of his countenance, which glory was passing away,[2]

8 how will the ministry of the Spirit not be more glorious?

9 For if the ministry of condemnation had glory, the ministry of righteousness exceeds much more in glory.

10 For even what was made glorious had no glory in this respect, because of the glory that excels.

11 For if what is passing away was glorious, what remains is much more glorious.

12 Seeing then that we have such hope, we use great boldness of speech—

13 unlike Moses, who put a veil over his face so that the children of Israel could not look steadily at the end of what was passing away.

14 But their minds were hardened. For until this day the same veil remains unlifted in the reading of the Old Covenant, because the veil is taken away in the Messiah.

15 But even to this day, when

2 Exodus 34:29-35

Moses is read, a veil lies on their heart.

16 Nevertheless when one turns to the Lord, the veil is taken away.

17 Now the Lord is the Spirit; and where the Spirit of the Lord is, there is liberty.

18 But we all, with unveiled face, beholding as in a mirror the glory of the Lord, are being transformed into the same image from glory to glory, just as by the Spirit of the Lord.

The Light of the Messiah's Good News

4 Therefore, seeing we have this service, as we have received mercy, we do not lose heart.

2 But we have renounced the hidden things of shame, not walking in craftiness nor handling the word of God deceitfully, but by manifestation of the truth commending ourselves to every man's conscience in the sight of God.

3 But even if our good news is veiled, it is veiled to those who are perishing,

4 in whom the god of this age has blinded the minds of those who do not believe, lest the light of the good news of the glory of the Messiah, who is the image of God, should shine on them.

5 For we do not preach ourselves, but Messiah Yeshua the Lord, and ourselves your servants for Yeshua's sake.

6 For it is the God who commanded light to shine out of darkness who has shone in our hearts to give the light of the knowledge of the glory of God in the face of Yeshua ha Mashiach.

Cast Down but Unconquered

7 But we have this treasure in earthen vessels, that the excellence of the power may be of God and not of us.

8 We are hard pressed on every side, yet not crushed; we are perplexed, but not in despair;

9 persecuted, but not forsaken; struck down, but not destroyed—

10 always carrying about in the body the dying of the Lord Yeshua, that the life of Yeshua may also be manifested in our body.

11 For we who live are always delivered to death for Yeshua's sake, that the life of Yeshua may also be manifested in our mortal flesh.

12 So then death is working in us, but life in you.

13 But since we have the same spirit of faith, according to what is written, *"I believed and therefore I spoke,"* [3] we also believe and therefore speak,

14 knowing that He who raised up the Lord Yeshua will also raise us up by Yeshua, and will present us with you.

15 For all things are for your sakes, that grace, having spread through the many, may cause thanksgiving to abound to the glory of God.

Seeing the Invisible

16 Therefore we do not lose heart. But though our outward man is perishing, yet the inward man is being renewed day by day.

17 For our light affliction, which is but for a moment, is working for us a far more exceeding and eternal weight of glory,

3 Psalm 116:10

18 while we do not look at the things which are seen, but at the things which are not seen. For the things which are seen are temporary, but the things which are not seen are eternal.

Assurance of the Resurrection

5 For we know that if our earthly house, this tent, is destroyed, we have a building from God, a house not made with hands, eternal in the heavens.

2 For in this we groan, earnestly desiring to be clothed with our habitation which is from heaven,

3 if indeed, having been clothed, we shall not be found naked.

4 For we who are in this tent groan, being burdened, not because we want to be unclothed, but further clothed, that mortality may be swallowed up by life.

5 Now He who has prepared us for this very thing is God, who also has given us the Spirit as a deposit.

6 Therefore we are always confident, knowing that while we are at home in the body we are absent from the Lord.

7 For we walk by faith, not by sight.

8 We are confident, I say, and well pleased rather to be absent from the body and to be present with the Lord.

The Judgment Seat of the Messiah

9 Therefore we make it our aim, whether present or absent, to be well pleasing to Him.

10 For we must all appear before the judgment seat of the Messiah, that each one may receive the things done in his body, according to what he has done, whether it is good or bad.

11 Knowing, therefore, the terror of the Lord, we persuade men; but we are well-known to God, and I also trust are well-known in your consciences.

Be Reconciled to God

12 For we do not commend ourselves again to you, but give you opportunity to glory on our behalf, that you may have something to answer those who glory in appearance and not in heart.

13 For if we are beside ourselves, it is for God; or if we are of sound mind, it is for you.

14 For the love of the Messiah constrains us, because we judge thus: that if One died for all, then all died;

15 and He died for all, that those who live should no longer live for themselves, but for Him who died for them and rose again.

16 Therefore, from now on, we know no one according to the flesh. Even though we have known the Messiah according to the flesh, yet now we know Him thus no longer.

17 Therefore, if anyone is in the Messiah, he is a new creation; old things have passed away; behold, all things have become new.

18 And all things are of God, who has reconciled us to Himself through Yeshua ha Mashiach, and has given us the ministry of reconciliation,

19 that is, that God was in the Messiah reconciling the world to Himself, not imputing their trespasses to them, and has committed to us the word of reconciliation.

20 Therefore we are ambassadors for the Messiah, as though God were pleading by us: we implore you in the Messiah's behalf, be reconciled to God.

21 For He has made Him who knew no sin to be sin for us, that we might become the righteousness of God in Him.

Marks of the Service

6 We then, as workers together with Him, plead with you also that you not receive the grace of God in vain.

2 For He says:

"*I have heard you in an accepted time,*
And in the day of salvation I have helped you."[4]

Behold, now is the accepted time; behold, now is the day of salvation.

3 We give no offense in anything, that our service not be blamed.

4 But in all things we commend ourselves as servants of God: in much patience, in tribulations, in needs, in distresses,

5 in stripes, in imprisonments, in tumults, in labors, in sleeplessness, in fastings;

6 by purity, by knowledge, by longsuffering, by kindness, by the Holy Spirit, by unfeigned love,

7 by the word of truth, by the power of God, by the armor of righteousness on the right hand and on the left,

8 by honor and dishonor, by evil report and good report; as deceivers, and yet true;

9 as unknown, and yet well-known; as dying, and behold we live; as chastened, and yet not killed;

10 as sorrowful, yet always rejoicing; as poor, yet making many rich; as having nothing, and yet possessing all things.

The Unequal Yoke: Be Holy

11 O Corinthians! We have spoken openly to you, our heart is wide open.

12 You are not restricted by us, but you are restricted by your own affections.

13 Now in return for the same (I speak as to children), you also be open.

14 Do not be unequally yoked together with unbelievers. For what fellowship has righteousness with lawlessness? And what communion has light with darkness?

15 And what accord has the Messiah with Belial?[5] Or what part has he who believes with an unbeliever?

16 And what agreement has the temple of God with idols? For you are the temple of the living God. As God has said:

"*I will dwell in them*
And walk among them.
I will be their God,
And they shall be My people."[6]

17"*Therefore come out from among them*
And be separate, says the Lord.
Do not touch what is unclean,
And I will receive you."[7]

---

5 Hebrew: "worthlessness, wickedness," a name of Satan (cf. Deuteronomy 13:13).
6 Leviticus 26:12; Jeremiah 32:38; Ezekiel 37:27
7 Isaiah 52:11; Ezekiel 20:34, 41

4 Isaiah 49:8

18"*I will be a Father to you,
And you shall be My sons
and daughters,
Says the* L*ORD* *Almighty."* [8]

7

Therefore, having these promises, beloved, let us cleanse ourselves from all filthiness of the flesh and spirit, perfecting holiness in the fear of God.

The Corinthians' Repentance

2 Open your hearts to us. We have wronged no one, we have corrupted no one, we have defrauded no one.

3 I do not say this to condemn you; for I have said before that you are in our hearts, to die together and to live together.

4 Great is my boldness of speech toward you, great is my boasting on your behalf. I am filled with comfort. I am exceedingly joyful in all our tribulation.

5 For indeed, when we came to Macedonia, our flesh had no rest, but we were troubled on every side. Outside were conflicts, inside were fears.

6 Nevertheless God, who comforts the downcast, comforted us by the coming of Titus,

7 and not only by his coming, but also by the consolation with which he was comforted in you, when he told us your earnest desire, your mourning, your zeal for me, so that I rejoiced even more.

8 For though I made you sorry with my letter, I do not regret it; though I did regret it. For I perceive that the same letter has made you sorry, though only for a while.

9 Now I rejoice, not that you were made sorry, but that your sorrow led to repentance. For you were made sorry in a godly manner, that you might suffer loss from us in nothing.

10 For godly sorrow produces repentance to salvation, not to be regretted; but the sorrow of the world produces death.

11 For observe this very thing, that you sorrowed in a godly manner: What diligence it produced in you, what clearing of yourselves, what indignation, what fear, what vehement desire, what zeal, what vindication! In all things you have proved yourselves to be clear in this matter.

12 Therefore, although I wrote to you, I did not do it for the sake of him who had done the wrong, nor for the sake of him who suffered wrong, but that our care for you in the sight of God might appear to you.

The Joy of Titus

13 Therefore we have been comforted in your comfort. And we rejoiced exceedingly more for the joy of Titus, because his spirit has been refreshed by you all.

14 For if in anything I have boasted to him about you, I am not ashamed. But as we spoke all things to you in truth, even so our boasting to Titus was found true.

15 And his affections are greater for you as he remembers the obedience of you all, how with fear and trembling you received him.

16 Therefore I rejoice that I have confidence in you in everything.

8 2 Samuel 7:14

Excel in Giving

8 Moreover, brethren, we make known to you the grace of God bestowed on the congregations of Macedonia:

2 that in a great trial of affliction the abundance of their joy and their deep poverty abounded to the riches of their liberality.

3 For I bear witness that according to their ability, yes, and beyond their ability, they were freely willing,

4 imploring us with much urgency that we would receive the gift and the fellowship of the service to the believers.

5 And this they did, not as we had hoped, but first gave themselves to the Lord, and then to us by the will of God.

6 So we urged Titus, that as he had begun, so he would also complete this grace in you as well.

7 But as you abound in everything—in faith, in speech, in knowledge, in all diligence, and in your love for us—see that you abound in this grace also.

The Messiah Our Pattern

8 I speak not by commandment, but by occasion of the diligence of others and to prove the sincerity of your love.

9 For you know the grace of our Lord Yeshua ha Mashiach, that though He was rich, yet for your sakes He became poor, that you through His poverty might become rich.

10 And in this I give my advice: It is to your advantage not only to be doing what you began and were desiring to do a year ago,

11 but now also complete the doing of it; that as there was a readiness to desire it, so there also may be a completion out of what you have.

12 For if there is first a willing mind, it is accepted according to what one has, and not according to what he does not have.

13 For I do not mean that others should be eased and you burdened,

14 but by an equality, that now at this time your abundance may supply their lack, that their abundance also may supply your lack—that there may be equality.

15 As it is written, *"He who gathered much had nothing left over, and he who gathered little had no lack."* [9]

Collection for the Judean Believers

16 But thanks be to God who put the same earnest care into the heart of Titus for you.

17 For he not only accepted the exhortation, but being more diligent, he has gone to you of his own accord.

18 And we have sent with him the brother whose praise is in the good news throughout all the congregations,

19 and not only that, but who was also chosen by the congregations to travel with us with this gift, which is administered by us to the glory of the same Lord and declaration of your ready mind,

20 avoiding this: that anyone should blame us in this lavish gift which is administered by us—

21 providing for honorable

9 Exodus 16:18

things, not only in the sight of the Lord, but also in the sight of men.

22 And we have sent with them our brother whom we have often proved diligent in many things, but now much more diligent, because of the great confidence which we have in you.

23 If anyone inquires about Titus, he is my partner and fellow worker concerning you. Or if our brethren are inquired about, they are messengers of the congregations, the glory of the Messiah.

24 Therefore show to them, and before the congregations, the proof of your love and of our boasting on your behalf.

Administering the Gift

9 Now concerning the service to the believers, it is superfluous for me to write to you;

2 for I know your willingness, about which I boast of you to the Macedonians, that Achaia was ready a year ago; and your zeal has stirred up the majority.

3 Yet I have sent the brethren, lest our boasting of you should be in vain in this respect, that, as I said, you may be ready;

4 lest perhaps if some Macedonians come with me and find you unprepared, we (not to mention you!) should be ashamed in this same confident boasting.

5 Therefore I thought it necessary to exhort the brethren to go to you ahead of time, and prepare your bountiful gift beforehand, which you had previously pledged, that it may be ready as a matter of bounty and not as covetousness.

The Cheerful Giver

6 But this I say: He who sows sparingly will also reap sparingly, and he who sows bountifully will also reap bountifully.

7 So let each one give as he purposes in his heart, not grudgingly or of necessity; for God loves a cheerful giver.

8 And God is able to make all grace abound toward you, that you, always having all sufficiency in all things, may abound to every good work.

9 As it is written:
*"He has dispersed abroad,
He has given to the poor;
His righteousness remains
forever."* [10]

10 Now may He who supplies seed to the sower, and bread for food, supply and multiply the seed you have sown and increase the fruits of your righteousness,

11 being enriched in everything for all liberality, which causes thanksgiving through us to God.

12 For the administration of this service not only supplies the needs of the believers, but is also abounding by many thanksgivings to God,

13 while, through the proof of this ministry, they glorify God for the obedience of your confession to the good news of the Messiah, and for your liberal sharing with them and all men,

14 and by their prayer for you, who long for you because of the exceeding grace of God in you.

15 Thanks be to God for His unspeakable gift!

10 Psalm 112:9

The Spiritual War

10 Now I, Paul, myself am pleading with you by the meekness and gentleness of Messiah—who in presence am lowly among you, but being absent am bold toward you.

2 But I beg you that when I am present I may not be bold with that confidence by which I intend to be bold against some, who think of us as if we walked according to the flesh.

3 For though we walk in the flesh, we do not war according to the flesh.

4 For the weapons of our warfare are not carnal but mighty through God for pulling down strongholds,

5 casting down arguments and every high thing that exalts itself against the knowledge of God, bringing every thought into captivity to the obedience of the Messiah,

6 and being ready to punish all disobedience when your obedience is fulfilled.

Reality of Paul's Authority

7 Do you look at things according to the outward appearance? If anyone is convinced in himself that he is the Messiah's, let him consider this again in himself, that just as he is the Messiah's, even so we are the Messiah's.

8 For even if I should boast somewhat more about our authority, which the Lord has given us for edification and not for your destruction, I shall not be ashamed—

9 lest I seem to terrify you by letters.

10 "For his letters," they say, "are weighty and powerful, but his bodily presence is weak, and his speech contemptible."

11 Let such a person consider this, that what we are in word by letters when we are absent, such we will also be in deed when we are present.

Limits of Paul's Authority

12 For we dare not make ourselves of the number, or compare ourselves with some, who commend themselves. But they, measuring themselves by themselves, and comparing themselves among themselves, are not wise.

13 But we will not boast beyond measure, but within the limits of the sphere which God appointed us—a sphere reaching even to you.

14 For we are not extending ourselves beyond our sphere, as though not reaching you, for we came even to you with the good news of the Messiah;

15 not boasting of things beyond measure, that is, in other men's labors, but having hope, that as your faith is increased, we shall be greatly enlarged by you in our sphere,

16 to preach the good news in the regions beyond you, and not to boast in another man's sphere of accomplishment.

17 But *"He who glories, let him glory in the LORD."* [11]

18 For not he who commends himself is approved, but whom the Lord commends.

---

11 Jeremiah 9:23, 24 (9:22, 23 in some versions)

Concern for Their Faithfulness

11 Oh, that you would bear with me in a little folly—and indeed you do bear with me.

2 For I am jealous for you with godly jealousy. For I have betrothed you to one husband, that I may present you as a chaste virgin to the Messiah.

3 But I fear, lest somehow, as the serpent deceived Eve by his craftiness, so your minds may be corrupted from the simplicity that is in the Messiah.[12]

4 For if he who comes preaches another Yeshua whom we have not preached, or if you receive a different spirit which you have not received, or a different good news which you have not accepted, you may well put up with it.

Paul and False Apostles

5 For I consider that I am not a bit behind the most eminent apostles.

6 And though I am untrained in speech, yet I am not in knowledge. But we have been thoroughly made manifest among you in all things.

7 Have I committed sin in abasing myself that you might be exalted, because I have preached the good news of God to you free of charge?

8 I robbed other congregations, taking wages from them to minister to you.

9 And when I was present with you, and in need, I was a burden to no one, for what was lacking to me the brethren who came from Macedonia supplied. And in all things I have kept myself from being burdensome to you, and so I will keep myself.

10 As the truth of the Messiah is in me, no one shall stop me from this boasting in the regions of Achaia.

11 Why? Because I do not love you? God knows!

12 But what I do, I also will continue to do, that I may cut off the opportunity from those who desire an opportunity that in what they boast they also may be regarded just as we are.

13 For such are false apostles, deceitful workers, transforming themselves into apostles of the Messiah.

14 And no wonder! For Satan himself transforms himself into an angel of light.

15 Therefore it is no great thing if his servants also transform themselves into servants of righteousness, whose end will be according to their works.

Reluctant Boasting

16 I say again, let no one think me a fool. If otherwise, at least receive me as a fool, that I also may boast a little.

17 What I speak, I speak not according to the Lord, but as it were, foolishly, in this confidence of boasting.

18 Seeing that many boast according to the flesh, I also will boast.

19 For you put up with fools gladly, seeing you yourselves are wise!

20 For you put up with it if one brings you into bondage, if one devours you, if one takes from you, if

---

12 Genesis 3:1-13

one exalts himself, if one strikes you on the face.

21 To our shame, I say that we were too weak for that! But in whatever anyone is bold—I speak foolishly—I am bold also.

Suffering for the Messiah

22 Are they Hebrews? So am I. Are they Israelites? So am I. Are they the seed of Abraham? So am I.

23 Are they servants of the Messiah?—I speak as a fool—I am more: in labors more abundant, in stripes above measure, in prisons more frequently, in deaths often.

24 From the Jews five times I received forty stripes minus one.

25 Three times I was beaten with rods, once I was stoned, three times I was shipwrecked, a night and a day I have been in the deep;

26 in journeys often, in perils of waters, in perils of robbers, in perils by my own countrymen, in perils by the Gentiles, in perils in the city, in perils in the wilderness, in perils in the sea, in perils among false brethren;

27 in weariness and toil, in sleeplessness often, in hunger and thirst, in fastings often, in cold and nakedness—

28 besides the other things, what comes upon me daily: my anxiety for all the congregations.

29 Who is weak, and I am not weak? Who is made to stumble, and I do not burn with indignation?

30 If I must boast, I will boast in the things which concern my infirmity.

31 The God and Father of our Lord Yeshua ha Mashiach, who is

blessed forever, knows that I am not lying.

32 In Damascus the governor, under Aretas the king, was guarding the city of the Damascenes with a garrison, desiring to apprehend me;

33 and I was let down in a basket through a window in the wall, and escaped his hands.

The Vision of Paradise

12 It is doubtless not profitable for me to boast. I will come to visions and revelations of the Lord:

2 I know a man in the Messiah who fourteen years ago—whether in the body I do not know, or whether out of the body I do not know, God knows—such a one was caught up to the third heaven.

3 And I know such a man—whether in the body or out of the body I do not know, God knows—

4 how he was caught up into Paradise and heard inexpressible words, which it is not lawful for a man to utter.

5 Of such a one I will boast; yet of myself I will not boast, except in my infirmities.

6 For though I might desire to boast, I will not be a fool; for I will speak the truth. But now I forbear, lest anyone should think of me above what he sees me to be or what he hears from me.

The Thorn in the Flesh

7 And lest I be exalted above measure by the abundance of the revelations, a thorn in the flesh was given to me, a messenger of Satan to buffet me, lest I be exalted above measure.

8 For this thing I pleaded with the Lord three times that it might depart from me.

9 And He said to me, "My grace is sufficient for you, for My strength is made perfect in weakness." Therefore most gladly I will rather boast in my infirmities, that the power of the Messiah may rest upon me.

10 Therefore I take pleasure in infirmities, in reproaches, in needs, in persecutions, in distresses, for the Messiah's sake. For when I am weak, then I am strong.

The Signs

11 I have become a fool in boasting; you have compelled me. For I ought to have been commended by you, for in nothing was I behind the most eminent apostles, though I am nothing.

12 Truly the signs of an apostle were accomplished among you with all perseverance, in signs and wonders and mighty deeds.

13 For what is it in which you were inferior to other congregations, except that I myself was not burdensome to you? Forgive me this wrong!

Love for the Body of Believers

14 Now the third time I am ready to come to you. And I will not be burdensome to you; for I do not seek yours, but you. For the children ought not to lay up for the parents, but the parents for the children.

15 And I will very gladly spend and be spent for you; though the more abundantly I love you, the less I am loved.

16 But be that as it may, I did not burden you. Nevertheless, being crafty, I caught you with guile!

17 Did I take advantage of you by any of those whom I sent to you?

18 I urged Titus, and sent our brother with him. Did Titus take advantage of you? Did we not walk in the same spirit? Did we not walk in the same steps?

19 Again, do you think that we excuse ourselves to you? We speak before God in the Messiah. But we do all things, beloved, for your edification.

20 For I fear lest, when I come, I shall not find you such as I wish, and that I shall be found by you such as you do not wish; lest there be contentions, jealousies, outbursts of wrath, selfish ambitions, backbitings, whisperings, conceits, tumults;

21 and lest, when I come again, my God will humble me among you, and I shall mourn for many who have sinned before and have not repented of the uncleanness, fornication, and licentiousness which they have committed.

Coming with Authority

13 This will be the third time I am coming to you. "*In the mouth of two or three witnesses every word shall be established.*" [13]

2 I have told you before, and foretell as if I were present the second time, and now being absent I write to those who have sinned before, and to all the rest, that if I come again I will not spare,

13 Deuteronomy 19:15

3 since you seek a proof of the Messiah speaking in me, who is not weak toward you, but mighty in you.

4 For though He was crucified in weakness, yet He lives by the power of God. For we also are weak in Him, but we shall live with Him by the power of God toward you.

5 Examine yourselves, whether you are in the faith. Prove yourselves. Do you not know yourselves that Yeshua ha Mashiach is in you, unless you are disqualified?

6 But I trust that you will know that we are not disqualified.

Paul Prefers Gentleness

7 Now I pray to God that you do no evil, not that we should appear approved, but that you should do what is honorable, though we may seem disqualified.

8 For we can do nothing against the truth, but for the truth.

9 For we are glad when we are weak and you are strong. And this also we pray, that you may be made complete.

10 Therefore I write these things being absent, lest being present I should use sharpness, according to the authority which the Lord has given me for edification and not for destruction.

Greetings and Blessings

11 Finally, brethren, farewell. Become complete. Be of good comfort, be of one mind, live in peace; and the God of love and peace will be with you.

12 Greet one another with a holy kiss.

13 All the believers greet you.

14 The grace of the Lord Yeshua ha Mashiach, and the love of God, and the fellowship of the Holy Spirit be with you all. Amen.

The Letter Of Paul To The
GALATIANS

Greeting

PAUL, an apostle[1] (not from men nor by man, but by Yeshua ha Mashiach and God the Father who raised Him from the dead),

2 and all the brethren who are with me,

To the congregations of Galatia:

3 Grace to you and peace from God the Father and our Lord Yeshua ha Mashiach,

4 who gave Himself for our sins, that He might deliver us from this present evil age, according to the will of our God and Father,

5 to whom be glory forever and ever. Amen.

Only One good news

6 I marvel that you are turning away so soon from Him who called you in the grace of the Messiah, to a different good news,

7 which is not another; but there are some who trouble you and want to pervert the good news of the Messiah.

8 But even if we, or an angel from heaven, preach any other good news to you than what we have preached to you, let him be accursed.

1 See note 1, p. 246.

9 As we said before, so now I say again, if anyone preaches any other good news to you than what you have received, let him be accursed.

10 For do I now persuade men, or God? Or do I seek to please men? For if I still pleased men, I would not be a servant of the Messiah.

The Call

11 But I make known to you, brethren, that the good news which was preached by me is not according to man.

12 For I neither received it from man, nor was I taught it, but it came by the revelation of Yeshua ha Mashiach.

13 For you have heard of my former conduct in Judaism, how I persecuted the called-out ones of God beyond measure and tried to destroy them.

14 And I advanced in Judaism beyond many of my contemporaries in my own nation, being more exceedingly zealous for the traditions of my fathers.

15 But when it pleased God, who separated me from my mother's womb and called me by His grace,

16 to reveal His Son in me that I might preach Him among the Gentiles, I did not immediately confer with flesh and blood,

17 nor did I go up to Jerusalem to those who were apostles before me; but I went to Arabia, and returned again to Damascus.

Contacts at Jerusalem

18 Then after three years I went up to Jerusalem to see Peter, and remained with him fifteen days.

19 But no other of the apostles did I see except James, the Lord's brother.

20 (Now concerning the things which I write to you, indeed, before God, I do not lie.)

21 Afterward I came into the regions of Syria and Cilicia;

22 and I was unknown by face to the congregations of Judea which were in the Messiah.

23 But they were hearing only, "He who formerly persecuted us now preaches the faith which he once tried to destroy."

24 And they glorified God in me.

Defending the Good News

2 Then after fourteen years I went up again to Jerusalem with Barnabas, and also took Titus with me.

2 And I went up by revelation, and communicated to them that good news which I preach among the Gentiles, but privately to those who were of reputation, lest by any means I might run, or had run, in vain.

3 Yet not even Titus who was with me, being a Greek, was compelled to be circumcised.

4 But this occurred because of false brethren secretly brought in (who came in by stealth to spy out our liberty which we have in Messiah Yeshua, that they might bring us into bondage),

5 to whom we did not yield submission even for an hour, that the truth of the good news might continue with you.

6 But of those who seemed to be something—whatever they were, it makes no difference to me; God shows personal favoritism to no man—for those who seemed to be something added nothing to me.

7 But on the contrary, when they saw that the good news for the uncircumcised had been committed to me, as the good news for the circumcised was to Peter

8 (for He who worked effectively in Peter for the apostleship to the circumcised also worked effectively in me toward the Gentiles),

9 and when James, Cephas, and John, who seemed to be pillars, perceived the grace that had been given to me, they gave me and Barnabas the right hand of fellowship, that we should go to the Gentiles and they to the circumcised.

10 They only desired that we remember the poor, the very thing which I also was eager to do.

The Torah of Faith

11 But when Peter had come to Antioch, I withstood him to his face, because he was to be blamed;

12 for before certain men came from James, he would eat with the Gentiles; but when they came, he withdrew and separated himself, fearing those who were of the circumcision.

13 And the rest of the Jews also played the hypocrite with him, so that even Barnabas was carried away with their hypocrisy.

14 But when I saw that they were not straightforward about the truth of the good news, I said to Peter before them all, "If you, being a Jew, live in the manner of Gentiles and not as the Jews, why do you compel Gentiles to live as Jews?

15 "We who are Jews by nature, and not sinners of the Gentiles,

16 "knowing that a man is not justified by the works of the Torah but by faith in Yeshua ha Mashiach, even we have believed in Messiah Yeshua, that we might be justified by faith in the Messiah and not by the works of the Torah; for by the works of the Torah no flesh will be justified.

17 "But if, while we seek to be justified by the Messiah, we ourselves also are found sinners, is the Messiah therefore a minister of sin? Certainly not!

18 "For if I build again those things which I destroyed, I make myself a transgressor.

19 "For I through the Torah died to the Torah that I might live to God.

20 "I have been crucified with the Messiah; it is no longer I who live, but the Messiah lives in me; and the life which I now live in the flesh I live by faith in the Son of God, who loved me and gave Himself for me.

21 "I do not set aside the grace of God; for if righteousness comes by the Torah, then the Messiah died in vain."

Justification by Faith

3 O foolish Galatians! Who has bewitched you that you should not obey the truth, before whose eyes Yeshua ha Mashiach has been clearly portrayed among you as crucified?

2 This only I want to learn from you: Did you receive the Spirit by the works of the Torah, or by hearing with faith?

3 Are you so foolish? Having begun in the Spirit, are you now being made perfect by the flesh?

4 Have you suffered so many things in vain—if indeed it was in vain?

5 Therefore He who supplies the Spirit to you and works miracles among you—does He do it by the works of the Torah, or by hearing with faith?

6 Just as Abraham *"believed God, and it was accounted to him for righteousness."* [2]

7 Therefore know that only those who are of faith are sons of Abraham.

8 And the Scripture, foreseeing that God would justify the nations by faith, preached the good news to Abraham beforehand, saying, *"In you all the nations will be blessed."* [3]

9 So then those who are of faith are blessed with believing Abraham.

The Blessing and the Promise

10 For as many as are of the works of the Torah are under the curse; for it is written, *"Cursed is everyone who does not continue in*

2 Genesis 15:6
3 Genesis 12:3; 18:18; 22:18; 26:4; 28:14

all things which are written in the book of the Torah, to do them." [4]

11 But that no one is justified by the Torah in the sight of God is evident, for *"The just shall live by faith."* [5]

12 And the Torah is not of faith, but *"The man who does them shall live by them."* [6]

13 The Messiah has redeemed us from the curse of the Torah, having become a curse for us; for it is written, *"Cursed is everyone who hangs on a tree"* [7] —

14 that the blessing of Abraham might come upon the Gentiles in Messiah Yeshua, that we might receive the promise of the Spirit through faith. [8]

The Changeless Promise

15 Brethren, I speak in the manner of men: Though it is only a man's covenant, yet if it is confirmed, no one annuls or adds to it.

16 Now to Abraham and his Seed were the promises made. He does not say, "And to seeds," as of many, but as of one, *"And to your Seed,"* [9] who is the Messiah.

17 And this I say, that the Torah, which was four hundred and thirty years later, cannot annul the covenant that was confirmed before by God in the Messiah, that it should make the promise of no effect.

18 For if the inheritance is of the Torah, it is no longer of promise; but God gave it to Abraham by promise.

Purpose of the Torah

19 What purpose then does the Torah serve? It was added because of transgressions, till the Seed should come to whom the promise was made; and it was appointed through angels by the hand of a mediator.

20 Now a mediator does not mediate for one only, but God is one.

21 Is the Torah then against the promises of God? Certainly not! For if there had been a Torah given which could have given life, truly righteousness would have been by the Torah.

22 But the Scripture has confined all under sin, [10] that the promise by faith in Yeshua ha Mashiach might be given to those who believe.

23 But before faith came, we were kept under guard by the Torah, kept for the faith which would afterward be revealed.

24 Therefore the Torah was our schoolmaster to bring us to the Messiah, that we might be justified by faith.

25 But after faith has come, we are no longer under a schoolmaster.

Sons and Heirs

26 For you are all sons of God by faith in Messiah Yeshua.

27 For as many of you as have been immersed into Messiah have put on Messiah.

28 There is neither Jew nor

4 Deuteronomy 27:26   5 Habakkuk 2:4
6 Leviticus 18:5   7 Deuteronomy 21:23
8 Ezekiel 36:25–27
9 Genesis 13:15; 22:18; 24:7

10 Psalm 14:1–3

Greek,[11] there is neither slave nor free, there is neither male nor female; for you are all one in Messiah Yeshua.

29 And if you are Messiah's, then you are Abraham's seed, and heirs according to the promise.

4 Now I say that the heir, as long as he is a child, does not differ at all from a servant, though he is master of all,

2 but is under guardians and stewards until the time appointed by the father.

3 Even so we, when we were children, were in bondage under the elements of the world.

4 But when the fullness of the time had come, God sent forth His Son, born of a woman, born under the Torah,

5 to redeem those who were under the Torah, that we might receive the adoption as sons.

6 And because you are sons, God has sent forth the Spirit of His Son into your hearts, crying out, "*Abba*, Father!"

7 Therefore you are no longer a servant but a son, and if a son, then an heir of God through the Messiah.

True Freedom

8 But then, indeed, when you did not know God, you served those who by nature are not gods.

9 But now after you have known God, or rather are known by God, how is it you turn again to the weak and beggarly elemental

spirits;[12] to which you desire again to be in bondage?

10 You observe days and months and seasons and years.

11 I am afraid for you, lest I have labored for you in vain.

12 Brethren, I urge you to become as I am, for I am as you are. You have not injured me at all.

13 You know that because of physical infirmity I preached the good news to you at the first.

14 And my trial which was in my flesh you did not despise or reject, but you received me as an angel of God, even as Messiah Yeshua.

15 What then was the blessedness you spoke of? For I bear you witness that, if it had been possible, you would have plucked out your own eyes and given them to me.

16 Have I therefore become your enemy because I tell you the truth?

17 They zealously court you, but for no good; yes, they want to exclude you, that you may be zealous for them.

18 But it is good to be zealous in a good thing always, and not only when I am present with you.

19 My little children, for whom

---

11 Spiritually we are all one, but physically God has a plan for Jew and Gentile, male and female.

12 Modern biblical scholarship indicates that the heresy spoken of in Galatians 4:9, 10 may well have been some form of astrological or other pagan superstition conjoined with a superstitious appropriation of Jewish days into this pagan viewpoint. This is evidenced by the danger that they would fall into demonic bondage through this superstition. This does not seem to forbid proper respect for Jewish heritage on the part of Jews. (See Colossians 2:16.)

I labor in birth again until the Messiah is formed in you,

20 I desire to be present with you now and to change my tone; for I have doubts about you.

Two Covenants

21 Tell me, you who desire to be under the Torah, do you not hear the Torah?

22 For it is written that Abraham had two sons: the one by a bondwoman, the other by a freewoman.

23 But he who was of the bondwoman was born according to the flesh, and he of the freewoman was by promise,

24 which things are an allegory. For these are the two covenants: the one from Mount Sinai which engenders bondage, which is Hagar—

25 for this Hagar is Mount Sinai in Arabia, and corresponds to Jerusalem which now is, and is in bondage with her children;

26 but the Jerusalem above is free, which is the mother of us all.

27 For it is written:

"Rejoice, O barren,
You who do not bear!
Break forth and shout,
You who do not travail!
For the desolate has many
   more children
Than she who has a husband." [13]

28 Now we, brethren, as Isaac was, are children of promise.

29 But, as he who was born according to the flesh then persecuted him who was born according to the Spirit, even so it is now.

30 Nevertheless what does the Scripture say? "Cast out the bondwoman and her son, for the son of the bondwoman shall not be heir with the son of the freewoman." [14]

31 So then, brethren, we are not children of the bondwoman but of the free.

The Torah of Liberty

5 Stand fast therefore in the liberty with which the Messiah has made us free, and do not be entangled again with a yoke of bondage.

2 Indeed I, Paul, say to you that if you become circumcised, the Messiah will profit you nothing. [15]

3 For I testify again to every man who becomes circumcised that he is a debtor to keep the whole Torah.

4 You have become estranged from the Messiah, whoever of you would be justified by Torah; you have fallen from grace.

5 For we through the Spirit eagerly wait for the hope of righteousness by faith.

6 For in Messiah Yeshua neither circumcision nor uncircumcision avails anything, but faith working by love.

The Torah of Love

7 You ran well. Who hindered you from obeying the truth?

8 This persuasion does not come from Him who calls you.

9 A little leaven leavens the whole batch.

---

13 Isaiah 54:1

14 Genesis 21:10

15 Remember that Paul is here speaking to non-Jewish believers in the Messiah—see Acts 15.

10 I have confidence in you, in the Lord, that you will have no other mind; but he who troubles you will bear his judgment, whoever he is.

11 And I, brethren, if I still preach circumcision, why do I still suffer persecution? Then the offense of the cross has ceased.

12 I wish those who trouble you were also cut off!

13 For you, brethren, have been called to liberty; only do not use liberty as an opportunity for the flesh, but by love serve one another.

14 For all the Torah is fulfilled in one word, even in this: *"You shall love your neighbor as yourself."* [16]

15 But if you bite and devour one another, take heed that you are not consumed by one another.

Walking in the Spirit

16 This I say then: Walk in the Spirit, and you shall not fulfill the lust of the flesh.

17 For the flesh lusts against the Spirit, and the Spirit against the flesh; and these are contrary to one another, so that you do not do the things you want.

18 But if you are led by the Spirit, you are not under the law.

19 Now the works of the flesh are evident, which are these: adultery, fornication, uncleanness, licentiousness,

20 idolatry, sorcery, hatred, contention, jealousy, outbursts of wrath, selfish ambition, dissensions, heresies,

21 envy, murders, drunkenness, revelry, and the like; of which I

[16] Leviticus 19:18

tell you beforehand, just as I have also told you in time past, that those who practice such things will not inherit the kingdom of God.

22 But the fruit of the Spirit is love, joy, peace, longsuffering, kindness, goodness, faithfulness,

23 gentleness, self-control. Against such there is no law.

24 And those who are of the Messiah have crucified the flesh with its passions and desires.

25 If we live in the Spirit, let us also walk in the Spirit.

26 Let us not become conceited, provoking one another, envying one another.

Bear and Share the Burdens

6 Brethren, if a man is overtaken in any trespass, you who are spiritual restore such a one in the spirit of gentleness, considering yourself lest you also be tempted.

2 Bear one another's burdens, and so fulfill the law of the Messiah.

3 For if anyone thinks himself to be something, when he is nothing, he deceives himself.

4 But let each one examine his own work, and then he will have rejoicing in himself alone, and not in another.

5 For each one shall bear his own load.

Be Generous and Do Good

6 Let him who is taught the word share in all good things with him who teaches.

7 Do not be deceived, God is not mocked; for whatever a man sows, that he will also reap.

8 For he who sows to his flesh will of the flesh reap corruption, but he who sows to the Spirit will

of the Spirit reap everlasting life.

9 And let us not grow weary while doing good, for in due season we shall reap if we do not lose heart.

10 Therefore, as we have opportunity, let us do good to all, especially to those who are of the household of faith.

Glory Only in Messiah

11 See with what large letters I have written to you with my own hand!

12 As many as desire to make a good showing in the flesh, these try to compel you to be circumcised, only lest they suffer persecution for the cross of the Messiah.

13 For not even those who are circumcised keep the Torah, but they desire to have you circumcised that they may glory in your flesh.

14 But God forbid that I should glory except in the cross of our Lord Yeshua ha Mashiach, by whom the world has been crucified to me, and I to the world.

15 For in Messiah Yeshua neither circumcision nor uncircumcision avails anything, but a new creation.

Blessing and a Plea

16 And as many as walk according to this rule, peace and mercy be upon them, and upon the Israel of God.

17 From now on let no one trouble me, for I bear in my body the marks of the Lord Yeshua.

18 Brethren, the grace of our Lord Yeshua ha Mashiach be with your spirit. Amen.

The Letter Of Paul To The
EPHESIANS

Greeting

PAUL, an apostle [1] of Yeshua ha Mashiach by the will of God,

To the holy ones who are in Ephesus, and faithful in Messiah Yeshua:

2 Grace to you and peace from God our Father and the Lord Yeshua ha Mashiach.

Redemption in the Messiah

3 Blessed be the God and Father of our Lord Yeshua ha Mashiach, who has blessed us with every spiritual blessing in the heavenly places in the Messiah,

4 just as He has chosen us in Him before the foundation of the world, that we should be holy and without blame before Him in love,

5 having predestined us to adoption as sons by Yeshua ha Mashiach to Himself, according to the good pleasure of His will,

6 to the praise of the glory of His grace, by which He has made us accepted in the Beloved.

7 In Him we have redemption through His blood, the forgiveness of sins, according to the riches of His grace

8 which He has made to abound toward us in all wisdom and prudence,

9 having made known to us the mystery of His will, according to His good pleasure which He purposed in Himself,

10 that in the dispensation of the fullness of the times He might gather together in one all things in the Messiah, both which are in heaven and which are on earth—in Him,

11 in whom also we have obtained an inheritance, being predestined according to the purpose of Him who works all things according to the counsel of His will,

12 that we who first trusted in the Messiah should be to the praise of His glory.

13 In Him you also trusted, after you heard the word of truth, the good news of your salvation; in whom also, having believed, you were sealed with the Holy Spirit of promise,

14 who is the guarantee of our inheritance until the redemption of the purchased possession, to the praise of His glory.

Prayer for Spiritual Wisdom

15 Therefore I also, after I heard of your faith in the Lord Yeshua and your love for all the believers,

16 do not cease to give thanks for

---

1 See note 1, page 246.

you, making mention of you in my prayers:

17 that the God of our Lord Yeshua ha Mashiach, the Father of glory, may give to you the spirit of wisdom and revelation in the knowledge of Him,

18 the eyes of your understanding being enlightened; that you may know what is the hope of His calling, what are the riches of the glory of His inheritance in the believers,

19 and what is the exceeding greatness of His power toward us who believe, according to the working of His mighty power

20 which He worked in the Messiah when He raised Him from the dead and set Him at His right hand in the heavenly places,

21 far above all principality and power and might and dominion, and every name that is named, not only in this age but also in that which is to come.

22 And He has put all things under His feet, and gave Him to be head over all things to the body of believers,

23 which is His body, the fullness of Him who fills all in all.

By Grace Through Faith

2 And you He has made alive, who were dead in trespasses and sins,

2 in which you once walked according to the course of this world, according to the prince of the power of the air, the spirit who now works in the sons of disobedience,

3 among whom also we all once conducted ourselves in the lusts of our flesh, fulfilling the desires of the flesh and of the mind, and were by nature children of wrath, just as the others.

4 But God, who is rich in mercy, because of His great love with which He loved us,

5 even when we were dead in trespasses, has made us alive together with the Messiah (by grace you have been saved),

6 and has raised us up together, and made us sit together in the heavenly places in Messiah Yeshua,

7 that in the ages to come He might show the exceeding riches of His grace in His kindness toward us through Messiah Yeshua.

8 For by grace you have been saved through faith, and that not of yourselves; it is the gift of God,

9 not of works, lest anyone should boast.

10 For we are His workmanship, created in Messiah Yeshua for good works, which God has prepared beforehand that we should walk in them.

Brought Near by His Blood

11 Therefore remember that you, once Gentiles in the flesh— who are called Uncircumcision by what is called the Circumcision made in the flesh by hands—

12 that at that time you were without the Messiah, being aliens from the commonwealth of Israel and strangers from the covenants of promise, having no hope and without God in the world.

13 But now in Messiah Yeshua you who once were far off have been made near by the blood of the Messiah.

Messiah Our Peace

14 For He Himself is our peace, who has made both one, and has broken down the middle wall of division between us,

15 having abolished in His flesh the enmity, that is, the law of commandments contained in ordinances, so as to create in Himself one new man from the two, thus making peace,

16 and that He might reconcile them both to God in one body by the cross, by it having put to death the enmity.

17 And He came and preached peace to you who were afar off and to those who were near.

18 For through Him we both have access by one Spirit to the Father.

The Messiah Our Cornerstone

19 Now, therefore, you are no longer strangers and foreigners, but fellow citizens with the believers and of the household of God,

20 and have been built on the foundation of the apostles and prophets, Yeshua ha Mashiach Himself being the chief cornerstone,

21 in whom the whole building, being joined together, grows into a holy temple in the Lord,

22 in whom you also are being built together for a habitation of God in the Spirit.

The Mystery Revealed

3 For this reason I, Paul, the prisoner of Yeshua ha Mashiach for you Gentiles—

2 if indeed you have heard of the dispensation of the grace of God which was given to me for you,

3 how that by revelation He made known to me the mystery (as I wrote before in a few words,

4 by which, when you read, you may understand my knowledge in the mystery of the Messiah),

5 which in other ages was not made known to the sons of men, as it has now been revealed by the Spirit to His holy apostles and prophets,

6 that the Gentiles should be fellow heirs, of the same body, and partakers of His promise in the Messiah by the good news,

7 of which I became a servant according to the gift of the grace of God given to me by the effective working of His power.

Purpose of the Mystery

8 To me, who am less than the least of all the believers, this grace was given, that I should preach among the Gentiles the unsearchable riches of the Messiah,

9 and to make all people see what is the fellowship of the mystery, which from the beginning of the ages has been hidden in God who created all things by Yeshua ha Mashiach;

10 to the intent that now the manifold wisdom of God might be made known by the body of believers to the principalities and powers in the heavenly places,

11 according to the eternal purpose which He purposed in Messiah Yeshua our Lord,

12 in whom we have boldness and access with confidence by faith in Him.

13 Therefore I ask that you do

not lose heart at my tribulations for you, which is your glory.

Appreciation of the Mystery

14 For this reason I bow my knees to the Father of our Lord Yeshua ha Mashiach,

15 from whom the whole family in heaven and earth is named,

16 that He would grant you, according to the riches of His glory, to be strengthened with might by His Spirit in the inner man,

17 that the Messiah may dwell in your hearts by faith; that you, being rooted and grounded in love,

18 may be able to comprehend with all the believers what is the breadth and length and depth and height—

19 to know the love of the Messiah which passes knowledge; that you may be filled with all the fullness of God.

20 Now to Him who is able to do exceedingly abundantly above all that we ask or think, according to the power that works in us,

21 to Him be glory in the body of believers by Messiah Yeshua throughout all ages, world without end. Amen.

Walk in Unity

4 I, therefore, the prisoner of the Lord, beseech you to walk worthy of the calling with which you were called,

2 with all lowliness and gentleness, with longsuffering, bearing with one another in love,

3 endeavoring to keep the unity of the Spirit in the bond of peace.

4 There is one body and one Spirit, just as you were called in one hope of your calling;

5 one Lord, one faith, one immersion;

6 one God and Father of all, who is above all, and through all, and in you all.

Spiritual Gifts

7 But to each one of us grace was given according to the measure of the Messiah's gift.

8 Therefore He says:

"When He ascended on high,
He led captivity captive,
And gave gifts to men." [2]

9 (Now this, *"He ascended"*—what does it mean but that He also first descended into the lower parts of the earth?

10 He who descended is also the One who ascended far above all the heavens, that He might fill all things.)

11 And He Himself gave some to be apostles, some prophets, some evangelists, and some pastors and teachers,

12 for the perfecting of the believers for the work of service, for the edifying of the body of the Messiah,

13 till we all come to the unity of the faith and the knowledge of the Son of God, to a perfect man, to the measure of the stature of the fullness of the Messiah;

14 that we should no longer be children, tossed to and fro and carried about with every wind of doctrine, by the trickery of men, in the cunning craftiness by which they lie in wait to deceive,

15 but, speaking the truth in love, may grow up in all things into Him who is the head—the Messiah—

---

2 Psalm 68:18 (68:19 in some versions)

16 from whom the whole body, joined and knit together by what every joint supplies, according to the effective working by which every part does its share, causes growth of the body for the edifying of itself in love.

The New Man

17 This I say, therefore, and testify in the Lord, that you should no longer walk as the rest of the Gentiles walk, in the futility of their mind,

18 having their understanding darkened, being alienated from the life of God, because of the ignorance that is in them, because of the hardening of their heart;

19 who, being past feeling, have given themselves over to licentiousness, to work all uncleanness with greediness.

20 But you have not so learned the Messiah,

21 if indeed you have heard Him and have been taught by Him, as the truth is in Yeshua:

22 that you put off, concerning your former conduct, the old man which is corrupt according to the deceitful lusts,

23 and be renewed in the spirit of your mind,

24 and that you put on the new man which was created according to God, in righteousness and true holiness.

Do Not Grieve the Spirit

25 Therefore, putting away lying, each one speak truth with his neighbor, for we are members of one another.

26 *"Be angry and do not sin"*:[3]

3 Psalm 4:4 (4:5 in some versions)

do not let the sun go down on your wrath,

27 nor give place to the devil.

28 Let him who stole steal no longer, but rather let him labor, working with his hands what is good, that he may have something to give him who has need.

29 Let no corrupt communication proceed out of your mouth, but what is good for necessary edification, that it may impart grace to the hearers.

30 And do not grieve the Holy Spirit of God, by whom you were sealed for the day of redemption.

31 Let all bitterness, wrath, anger, clamor, and evil speaking be put away from you, with all malice.

32 And be kind to one another, tenderhearted, forgiving one another, just as God in the Messiah also has forgiven you.

Walk in Love

5 Therefore be followers of God as dear children.

2 And walk in love, as the Messiah also has loved us and given Himself for us, an offering and a sacrifice to God for a sweet-smelling aroma.

3 But fornication and all uncleanness or covetousness, let it not even be named among you, as is fitting for believers;

4 neither filthiness, nor foolish talking, nor coarse jesting, which are not fitting, but rather giving of thanks.

5 For this you know, that no fornicator, unclean person, nor covetous man, who is an idolater, has any inheritance in the kingdom of the Messiah and God.

6 Let no one deceive you with empty words, for because of these things the wrath of God comes on the sons of disobedience.

7 Therefore do not be partakers with them.

Walk in Light

8 For you were once darkness, but now you are light in the Lord. Walk as children of light

9 (for the fruit of the Spirit is in all goodness, righteousness, and truth),

10 proving what is acceptable to the Lord.

11 And have no fellowship with the unfruitful works of darkness, but rather expose them.

12 For it is shameful even to speak of those things which are done by them in secret.

13 But all things that are exposed are made manifest by the light, for whatever makes manifest is light.

14 Therefore He says:

"Awake, you who sleep;
Arise from the dead,
And the Messiah will give
    you light." [4]

Walk in Wisdom

15 See then that you walk circumspectly, not as fools but as wise,

16 redeeming the time, because the days are evil.

17 Therefore do not be unwise, but understanding what the will of the Lord is.

18 And do not be drunk with wine, in which is dissipation; but be filled with the Spirit,

19 speaking to one another in psalms, hymns, and spiritual songs, singing and making melody in your heart to the Lord,

20 giving thanks always for all things to God the Father in the name of our Lord Yeshua ha Mashiach,

21 submitting to one another in the fear of God.

Marriage—Messiah and the Congregation

22 Wives, submit yourselves to your own husbands, as to the Lord.

23 For the husband is head of the wife, as also the Messiah is head of the congregation; and He is the Savior of the body.

24 Therefore, just as the congregation is subject to the Messiah, so let the wives be to their own husbands in everything.

25 Husbands, love your wives, just as the Messiah also loved the congregation and gave Himself for it,

26 that He might sanctify and cleanse it with the washing of water by the word,

27 that He might present it to Himself a glorious congregation, not having spot or wrinkle or any such thing, but that it should be holy and without blemish.

28 So men ought to love their own wives as their own bodies; he who loves his wife loves himself.

29 For no one ever hated his own flesh, but nourishes and cherishes it, just as the Lord does the congregation.

30 For we are members of His body, of His flesh and of His bones.

4 Isaiah 60:1, 2

31 *"For this reason a man shall leave his father and mother, and be joined to his wife; and the two shall become one flesh."* 5

32 This is a great mystery, but I speak concerning the Messiah and the congregation.

33 Nevertheless let each one of you in particular so love his own wife as himself, and let the wife see that she respects her husband.

Children and Parents

6 Children, obey your parents in the Lord, for this is right.

2 *"Honor your father and mother,"* 6 which is the first commandment with promise:

3 *"that it may be well with you and you may live long on the earth."* 6 7

4 And you fathers, do not provoke your children to wrath, but bring them up in the training and admonition of the Lord.

Servants and Masters

5 Servants, be obedient to those who are your masters according to the flesh, with fear and trembling, in sincerity of your heart, as to the Messiah;

6 not with eyeservice, as menpleasers, but as servants of the Messiah, doing the will of God from the heart,

7 with good will doing service, as to the Lord, and not to men,

8 knowing that whatever good anyone does, he will receive the same from the Lord, whether he is a slave or free.

9 And you, masters, do the same things to them, giving up threatening, knowing that your own Master also is in heaven, and there is no partiality with Him.

The Whole Armor of God

10 Finally, my brethren, be strong in the Lord and in the power of His might.

11 Put on the whole armor of God, that you may be able to stand against the wiles of the devil.

12 For we do not wrestle against flesh and blood, but against principalities, against powers, against the rulers of the darkness of this age, against spiritual wickedness in the heavenly places.

13 Therefore take up the whole armor of God, that you may be able to withstand in the evil day, and having done all, to stand.

14 Stand therefore, having girded your waist with truth, having put on the breastplate of righteousness,

15 and having shod your feet with the preparation of the good news of peace;

16 above all, taking the shield of faith with which you will be able to quench all the fiery darts of the wicked one.

17 And take the helmet of salvation, and the sword of the Spirit, which is the word of God;

18 praying always with all prayer and supplication in the Spirit, being watchful to this end with all perseverance and supplication for all the believers—

19 and for me, that utterance may be given to me, that I may

5 Genesis 2:24   6 Deuteronomy 5:16
7 Exodus 20:12

open my mouth boldly to make known the mystery of the good news,

20 for which I am an ambassador in chains; that in it I may speak boldly, as I ought to speak.

A Gracious Greeting

21 But that you also may know my affairs and how I am doing, Tychicus, a beloved brother and faithful servant in the Lord, will make all things known to you;

22 whom I have sent to you for this very purpose, that you may know our affairs, and that he may comfort your hearts.

23 Peace to the brethren, and love with faith, from God the Father and the Lord Yeshua ha Mashiach.

24 Grace be with all those who love our Lord Yeshua ha Mashiach in sincerity. Amen.

The Letter Of Paul To The

PHILIPPIANS

Greeting

PAUL and Timothy, servants of Yeshua ha Mashiach,

To all the believers in Messiah Yeshua who are in Philippi, with the overseers and deacons:

2 Grace to you and peace from God our Father and the Lord Yeshua ha Mashiach.

Thankfulness and Prayer

3 I thank my God upon every remembrance of you,

4 always in every prayer of mine making request for you all with joy,

5 for your fellowship in the good news from the first day until now,

6 being confident of this very thing, that He who has begun a good work in you will complete it until the day of Yeshua ha Mashiach;

7 just as it is right for me to think this of you all, because I have you in my heart, inasmuch as both in my chains and in the defense and confirmation of the good news, you all are partakers with me of grace.

8 For God is my witness, how greatly I long for you all with the affection of Yeshua ha Mashiach.

9 And this I pray, that your love may abound still more and more in knowledge and in all discernment,

10 that you may approve the things that are excellent, that you may be sincere and without offense till the day of the Messiah,

11 being filled with the fruits of righteousness which are by Yeshua ha Mashiach, to the glory and praise of God.

The Messiah Is Proclaimed

12 But I want you to know, brethren, that the things which happened to me have actually turned out for the furtherance of the good news,

13 so that it has become evident to the whole palace guard, and to all the rest, that my chains are in the Messiah;

14 and most of the brethren in the Lord, having become confident by my chains, are much more bold to speak the word without fear.

15 Some indeed preach the Messiah even from envy and strife, and some also from good will:

16 The former preach the Messiah from selfish ambition, not sincerely, supposing to add affliction to my chains;

17 but the latter out of love, knowing that I am appointed for the defense of the good news.

18 What then? Only that in every way, whether in pretense or in truth, the Messiah is preached; and in this I rejoice, yes, and will rejoice.

To Live Is the Messiah

19 For I know that this will turn out for my salvation through your prayer and the supply of the Spirit of Yeshua ha Mashiach,

20 according to my earnest expectation and hope that in nothing I shall be ashamed, but that with all boldness, as always, so now also the Messiah will be magnified in my body, whether by life or by death.

21 For to me, to live is the Messiah, and to die is gain.

22 But if I live on in the flesh, this will mean fruit from my labor; yet what I shall choose I cannot tell.

23 For I am hard pressed between the two, having a desire to depart and be with the Messiah, which is far better.

24 Nevertheless to remain in the flesh is more needful for you.

25 And being confident of this, I know that I shall remain and continue with you all for your progress and joy of faith,

26 that your rejoicing for me may be more abundant in Yeshua ha Mashiach by my coming to you again.

Striving and Suffering for the Messiah

27 Only let your conduct be worthy of the good news of the Messiah, so that whether I come and see you or am absent, I may hear of your affairs, that you stand fast in one spirit, with one mind striving together for the faith of the good news,

28 and not in any way terrified by your adversaries, which is to them a proof of perdition, but to you of salvation, and that from God.

29 For to you it has been granted on behalf of the Messiah, not only to believe in Him, but also to suffer for His sake,

30 having the same conflict which you saw in me and now hear is in me.

Unity Through Humility

2 Therefore if there is any consolation in the Messiah, if any comfort of love, if any fellowship of the Spirit, if any affection and mercy,

2 fulfill my joy by being likeminded, having the same love, being of one accord, of one mind.

3 Let nothing be done through selfish ambition or conceit, but in lowliness of mind let each esteem another better than himself.

4 Let each of you look out not only for his own interests, but also for the interests of others.

The Humbled and Exalted Messiah

5 Let this mind be in you which was also in Messiah Yeshua,

6 who, being in the form of God, did not consider equality with God something to be grasped,

7 but emptied Himself by taking the form of a servant, and coming in the likeness of men.[1]

8 And being found in appearance as a man, He humbled Him-

---

1 That is, He laid aside His privileges.

self and became obedient to the point of death, even the death of the cross.

9 Therefore God also has highly exalted Him and given Him the name which is above every name,

10 that at the name of Yeshua every knee should bow,[2] of those in heaven, and of those on earth, and of those under the earth,

11 and that every tongue should confess that Yeshua ha Mashiach is Lord, to the glory of God the Father.

Light Bearers

12 Therefore, my beloved, as you have always obeyed, not as in my presence only, but now much more in my absence, work out your own salvation with fear and trembling;

13 for it is God who works in you both to will and to do for His good pleasure.

14 Do all things without murmuring and disputing,

15 that you may become blameless and harmless, children of God without fault in the midst of a crooked and perverse generation, among whom you shine as lights in the world,

16 holding fast the word of life, so that I may rejoice in the day of the Messiah that I have not run in vain or labored in vain.

17 Yes, and if I am being poured out as a drink offering on the sacrifice and service of your faith, I am glad and rejoice with you all.

18 For the same reason you also be glad and rejoice with me.

2 Isaiah 45:23

Timothy Commended

19 But I trust in the Lord Yeshua to send Timothy to you shortly, that I also may be encouraged when I know your state.

20 For I have no one likeminded, who will sincerely care for your state.

21 For all seek their own, not the things which are of Messiah Yeshua.

22 But you know his proven character, that as a son with his father he has served with me in the good news.

23 Therefore I hope to send him at once, as soon as I see how it goes with me.

24 But I trust in the Lord that I myself shall also come shortly.

Epaphroditus Praised

25 Yet I considered it necessary to send to you Epaphroditus, my brother, fellow worker, and fellow soldier, but your messenger and the one who ministered to my need;

26 since he was longing for you all, and was distressed because you had heard that he was sick.

27 For indeed he was sick almost to death; but God had mercy on him, and not only on him but on me also, lest I should have sorrow upon sorrow.

28 Therefore I sent him the more eagerly, that when you see him again you may rejoice, and I may be less sorrowful.

29 Receive him therefore in the Lord with all gladness, and hold such men in esteem;

30 because for the work of the Messiah he came close to death,

not regarding his life, to supply what was lacking in your service toward me.

All for the Messiah

3 Finally, my brethren, rejoice in the Lord. For me to write the same things to you is not tedious, but for you it is safe.

2 Beware of dogs, beware of evil workers, beware of the mutilation!

3 For we are the circumcision, who worship God in the Spirit, rejoice in Messiah Yeshua, and have no confidence in the flesh,

4 though I might also have confidence in the flesh. If anyone else thinks he may have confidence in the flesh, I more so:

5 circumcised the eighth day, of the stock of Israel, of the tribe of Benjamin, a Hebrew of the Hebrews; concerning the Torah, a Pharisee;

6 concerning zeal, persecuting the body of believers; concerning the righteousness which is in the Torah, blameless.

7 But what things were gain to me, these I have counted loss for the Messiah.

8 But indeed I also count all things loss for the excellence of the knowledge of Messiah Yeshua my Lord, for whom I have suffered the loss of all things, and count them as rubbish, that I may gain the Messiah

9 and be found in Him, not having my own righteousness, which is from the Torah, but that which is through faith in the Messiah, the righteousness which is from God by faith;

10 that I may know Him and the power of His resurrection, and the fellowship of His sufferings, being conformed to His death,

11 if, by any means, I may attain to the resurrection from the dead.

Pressing Toward the Goal

12 Not that I have already attained, or am already perfected; but I press on, that I may lay hold of that for which I also was laid hold of by Messiah Yeshua.

13 Brethren, I do not count myself to have apprehended; but one thing I do, forgetting those things which are behind and reaching forward to those things which are ahead,

14 I press toward the goal for the prize of the upward call of God in Messiah Yeshua.

15 Therefore let us, as many as are mature, have this mind; and if in anything you think otherwise, God will reveal even this to you.

16 Nevertheless, to the degree we have already attained, let us walk by the same rule, let us be of the same mind.

Our Citizenship in Heaven

17 Brethren, join in following my example, and note those who so walk, as you have us for a pattern.

18 For many walk, of whom I have told you often, and now tell you even weeping, that they are the enemies of the cross of the Messiah:

19 whose end is destruction, whose god is their belly, and

whose glory is in their shame—who set their mind on earthly things.

20 For our citizenship is in heaven, from which we also eagerly wait for the Savior, the Lord Yeshua ha Mashiach,

21 who will transform our lowly body that it may be conformed to His glorious body, according to the working by which He is able even to subdue all things to Himself.

4 Therefore, my beloved and longed for brethren, my joy and crown, so stand fast in the Lord, beloved.

Be United, Joyful, and in Prayer

2 I beg Euodia and I beg Syntyche to be of the same mind in the Lord.

3 And I urge you also, true companion, help these women who labored with me in the good news, with Clement also, and the rest of my fellow workers, whose names are in the Book of Life.

4 Rejoice in the Lord always. Again I will say, rejoice!

5 Let your gentleness be known to all men. The Lord is at hand.

6 Be anxious for nothing, but in everything by prayer and supplication, with thanksgiving, let your requests be made known to God;

7 and the peace of God, which surpasses all understanding, will guard your hearts and minds through Messiah Yeshua.

Meditate on These Things

8 Finally, brethren, whatever things are true, whatever things are noble, whatever things are just, whatever things are pure, whatever things are lovely, whatever things are of good report, if there is any virtue and if there is anything praiseworthy—meditate on these things.

9 The things which you have learned and received and heard and seen in me—these do, and the God of peace will be with you.

Philippian Generosity

10 But I rejoiced in the Lord greatly that now at last your care for me has flourished again; though surely you also did care, but you lacked opportunity.

11 Not that I speak in regard to need, for I have learned in whatever state I am, to be content:

12 I know how to be abased, and I know how to abound. Everywhere and in all things I have learned both to be full and to be hungry, both to abound and to suffer need.

13 I can do all things through the Messiah who strengthens me.

14 Nevertheless you have done well that you shared in my distress.

15 Now you Philippians know also that in the beginning of the good news, when I departed from Macedonia, no congregation shared with me concerning giving and receiving but you only.

16 For even in Thessalonica you sent aid once and again for my necessities.

17 Not that I seek the gift, but I seek the fruit that abounds to your account.

18 Indeed I have all and abound. I am full, having re-

ceived from Epaphroditus the things which were sent from you, a sweet-smelling aroma, an acceptable sacrifice, well pleasing to God.

19 And my God shall supply all your need according to His riches in glory by Messiah Yeshua.

20 Now to our God and Father be glory forever and ever. Amen.

Greeting and Blessing

21 Greet every believer in Messiah Yeshua. The brethren who are with me greet you.

22 All the believers greet you, but especially those who are of Caesar's household.

23 The grace of our Lord Yeshua ha Mashiach be with you all. Amen.

The Letter Of Paul To The
COLOSSIANS

Greeting

PAUL, an apostle[1] of Yeshua ha Mashiach by the will of God, and Timothy our brother,

2 To the believers and faithful brethren in the Messiah who are in Colosse:

Grace to you and peace from God our Father and the Lord Yeshua ha Mashiach.

Their Faith in the Messiah

3 We give thanks to the God and Father of our Lord Yeshua ha Mashiach, praying always for you,

4 since we heard of your faith in Messiah Yeshua and of your love for all the believers;

5 because of the hope which is laid up for you in heaven, of which you heard before in the word of the truth of the good news,

6 which has come to you, as it has also in all the world, and is bringing forth fruit, as also among you since the day you heard and knew the grace of God in truth;

7 as you also learned from Epaphras, our dear fellow servant, who is a faithful minister of the Messiah on your behalf,

8 who also declared to us your love in the Spirit.

Preeminence of the Messiah

9 For this reason we also, since the day we heard it, do not cease to pray for you, and to ask that you may be filled with the knowledge of His will in all wisdom and spiritual understanding;

10 that you may walk worthy of the Lord, fully pleasing Him, being fruitful in every good work and increasing in the knowledge of God;

11 strengthened with all might, according to His glorious power, for all patience and longsuffering with joy;

12 giving thanks to the Father who has qualified us to be partakers of the inheritance of the believers in the light.

13 He has delivered us from the power of darkness and translated us into the kingdom of the Son of His love,

14 in whom we have redemption through His blood, the forgiveness of sins.[2]

15 He is the image of the invisible God, the firstborn over all creation.

16 For by Him all things were created that are in heaven and that are on earth, visible and invisible, whether thrones or dominions or principalities or powers.

1 See note 1, p. 246.

2 Cf. Leviticus 17:11

All things were created by Him and for Him.

17 And He is before all things, and in Him all things hold together.

18 And He is the head of the body, the body of believers, who is the beginning, the firstborn from the dead, that in all things He may have the preeminence.

Reconciled in the Messiah

19 For it pleased the Father that in Him all fullness should dwell,

20 and by Him to reconcile all things to Himself, by Him, whether things on earth or things in heaven, having made peace through the blood of His cross.

21 And you, who once were alienated and enemies in your mind by wicked works, yet now He has reconciled

22 in the body of His flesh through death, to present you holy, and blameless, and irreproachable in His sight—

23 if indeed you continue grounded and steadfast in the faith, and are not moved away from the hope of the good news which you have heard, which was preached to every creature under heaven, of which I, Paul, became a servant.

Sacrificial Service for the Messiah

24 I now rejoice in my sufferings for you, and fill up in my flesh what is lacking in the afflictions of the Messiah, for the sake of His body, which is the body of believers,

25 of which I became a servant according to the stewardship from God which was given to me for you, to fulfill the word of God,

26 the mystery which has been hidden from ages and from generations, but now has been revealed to His believers.

27 To them God willed to make known what are the riches of the glory of this mystery among the Gentiles: which is the Messiah in you, the hope of glory.

28 Him we preach, warning every man and teaching every man in all wisdom, that we may present every man perfect in Messiah Yeshua.

29 To this end I also labor, striving according to His working which works in me mightily.

Not Philosophy but Messiah

2 For I want you to know what a great conflict I have for you and those in Laodicea, and for as many as have not seen my face in the flesh,

2 that their hearts may be encouraged, being knit together in love, and attaining to all riches of the full assurance of understanding, to the knowledge of the mystery of God, both of the Father and of the Messiah,

3 in whom are hidden all the treasures of wisdom and knowledge.

4 And this I say lest anyone deceive you with persuasive words.

5 For though I am absent in the flesh, yet I am with you in spirit, rejoicing to see your good order and the steadfastness of your faith in the Messiah.

6 As you have therefore received Messiah Yeshua the Lord, so walk in Him,

7 rooted and built up in Him and established in the faith, as you

have been taught, abounding in it
with thanksgiving.

8 Beware lest anyone take you
captive through philosophy and
empty deceit, according to the tradition of men, according to the ba-
sic principles of the world, and not
according to the Messiah.

9 For in Him dwells all the fullness of the Godhead bodily;

10 and you are complete in
Him, who is the head of all principality and power.

Not Legalism but the Messiah

11 In Him you were also circumcised with the circumcision made
without hands, by putting off the
body of the sins of the flesh, by the
circumcision of the Messiah,

12 buried with Him in immersion, in which you also were raised
with Him through faith in the
working of God, who has raised
Him from the dead.

13 And you, being dead in your
sins and the uncircumcision of
your flesh, He has made alive together with Him, having forgiven
you all trespasses,

14 having wiped out the hand-
writing of requirements that was
against us, which was contrary to
us. And He has taken it out of
the way, having nailed it to His
cross.

15 Having disarmed principalities and powers, He made a public spectacle of them, triumphing
over them in it.

16 Therefore let no one judge
you in food or in drink, or regarding a festival or a new moon or
sabbaths,[3]

17 which are a shadow of things
to come, but the substance is of the
Messiah.

18 Let no one defraud you of
your reward, taking delight in
false humility and worship of angels, intruding into those things
which he has not seen, vainly
puffed up by his fleshly mind,

19 and not holding fast to the
Head, from whom all the body,
nourished and knit together by
joints and ligaments, increases
with the increase which is from
God.

20 Therefore, if you died with
the Messiah from the elemental
spirits[4] of the world, why, as
though living in the world, do you
subject yourselves to regulations—

21 "Do not touch, do not taste,
do not handle,"

22 which all concern things
which perish with the using—according to the commandments
and doctrines of men?[4]

23 These things indeed have an
appearance of wisdom in self-im-
posed religion, false humility, and
neglect of the body—not of any
value against the indulgence of the
flesh.

Not Carnality but the Messiah

3 If then you were raised with
the Messiah, seek those things
which are above, where the Messiah is, sitting at the right hand of
God.

2 Set your mind on things
above, not on things on the earth.

---

3 Paul is speaking to a Gentile
congregation. See Acts 15:28, 29.

4 See footnote to Galatians 4:9, 10.
Modern scholarship tends toward the
view that the heresy here includes ascetic
rules not a part of the Torah but of pagan
superstition. They are thus called
commands of men.

3 For you died, and your life is hidden with the Messiah in God.

4 When the Messiah who is our life appears, then you also will appear with Him in glory.

5 Therefore put to death your members which are on the earth: fornication, uncleanness, passion, evil desire, and covetousness, which is idolatry.

6 Because of these things the wrath of God is coming on the sons of disobedience,

7 in which you also once walked when you lived in them.

8 But now you also put off all these: anger, wrath, malice, blasphemy, filthy language out of your mouth.

9 Do not lie to one another, seeing that you have put off the old man with his deeds,

10 and have put on the new man who is renewed in knowledge according to the image of Him who created him,

11 where there is neither Greek nor Jew, circumcised nor uncircumcised, barbarian, Scythian, slave nor free, but the Messiah is all and in all.

Character of the New Man

12 Therefore, as the elect of God, holy and beloved, put on tender mercies, kindness, humbleness of mind, meekness, longsuffering;

13 bearing with one another, and forgiving one another, if anyone has a complaint against another; even as the Messiah forgave you, so you do also.

14 And above all these things put on love, which is the bond of perfection.

15 And let the peace of God rule in your hearts, to which also you were called in one body; and be thankful.

16 Let the word of the Messiah dwell in you richly in all wisdom, teaching and admonishing one another in psalms, hymns, and spiritual songs, singing with grace in your hearts to the Lord.

17 And whatever you do in word or deed, do all in the name of the Lord Yeshua, giving thanks to God the Father through Him.

The Believer's Home

18 Wives, submit yourselves to your own husbands, as is fitting in the Lord.

19 Husbands, love your wives and do not be bitter toward them.

20 Children, obey your parents in all things, for this is well pleasing to the Lord.

21 Fathers, do not provoke your children, lest they become discouraged.

22 Servants, obey in all things your masters according to the flesh, not with eyeservice, as menpleasers, but in sincerity of heart, fearing God.

23 And whatever you do, do it heartily, as to the Lord and not to men,

24 knowing that from the Lord you will receive the reward of the inheritance; for you serve the Lord Messiah.

25 But he who does wrong will be repaid for the wrong which he has done, and there is no partiality.

4 Masters, give your servants what is just and fair, knowing that you also have a Master in heaven.

Speak the Mystery

2 Continue in prayer, being vigilant in it with thanksgiving;

3 meanwhile praying also for us, that God would open to us a door for the word, to speak the mystery of the Messiah, for which I am also in chains,

4 that I may make it manifest, as I ought to speak.

5 Walk in wisdom toward those who are outsiders, redeeming the time.

6 Let your speech always be with grace, seasoned with salt, that you may know how you ought to answer each one.

Final Greetings

7 Tychicus, who is a beloved brother, a faithful minister, and a fellow servant in the Lord, will tell you all the news about me.

8 I am sending him to you for this very purpose, that he may know your circumstances and comfort your hearts,

9 with Onesimus, a faithful and beloved brother, who is one of you. They will make known to you all things which are happening here.

10 Aristarchus my fellow prisoner greets you, with Mark the cousin of Barnabas (about whom you received instructions: if he comes to you, welcome him),

11 and Yeshua who is called Justus. These are my only fellow workers for the kingdom of God who are of the circumcision; they have proved to be a comfort to me.

12 Epaphras, who is one of you, a servant of the Messiah, greets you, always laboring fervently for you in prayers, that you may stand perfect and complete in all the will of God.

13 For I bear him witness that he has a great zeal for you, those who are in Laodicea, and those in Hierapolis.

14 Luke the beloved physician and Demas greet you.

15 Greet the brethren who are in Laodicea, and Nymphas and the congregation that is in his house.

Closing Exhortations and Blessing

16 And when this letter is read among you, see that it is read also in the congregation of the Laodiceans, and that you likewise read the letter from Laodicea.

17 And say to Archippus, "Take heed to the ministry which you have received in the Lord, that you fulfill it."

18 This salutation by my own hand—Paul. Remember my chains. Grace be with you. Amen.

The First Letter Of Paul To The
THESSALONIANS

PAUL, Silvanus, and Timothy,

To the congregation of the Thessalonians in God the Father and the Lord Yeshua ha Mashiach:

Grace to you and peace from God our Father and the Lord Yeshua ha Mashiach.

Their Good Example

2 We give thanks to God always for you all, making mention of you in our prayers,

3 remembering without ceasing your work of faith, labor of love, and patience of hope in our Lord Yeshua ha Mashiach in the sight of our God and Father,

4 knowing, beloved brethren, your election by God.

5 For our good news did not come to you in word only, but also in power, in the Holy Spirit, and in much assurance, as you know what kind of men we were among you for your sake.

6 And you became followers of us and of the Lord, having received the word in much affliction, with joy of the Holy Spirit,

7 so that you became examples to all in Macedonia and Achaia who believe.

8 For from you the word of the Lord has sounded forth, not only in Macedonia and Achaia, but also in every place your faith toward God has gone out, so that we do not need to say anything.

9 For they themselves declare concerning us what manner of entry we had to you, and how you turned to God from idols to serve the living and true God,

10 and to wait for His Son from heaven, whom He raised from the dead, even Yeshua who delivers us from the wrath to come.

Paul's Conduct

2 For you yourselves know, brethren, that our coming to you was not in vain.

2 But even after we had suffered before and were spitefully treated at Philippi, as you know, we were bold in our God to speak to you the good news of God in much conflict.

3 For our exhortation did not come from deceit or uncleanness, nor was it in guile.

4 But as we have been approved by God to be entrusted with the good news, even so we speak, not as pleasing men, but God who tests our hearts.

5 For neither at any time did we use flattering words, as you know, nor a cloak for covetousness—God is witness.

6 Nor did we seek glory from

men, neither from you nor from others, when we might have made demands as apostles[1] of the Messiah.

7 But we were gentle among you, just as a nursing mother cherishes her own children.

8 So, affectionately longing for you, we were well pleased to impart to you not only the good news of God, but also our own lives, because you have become dear to us.

9 For you remember, brethren, our labor and toil; for laboring night and day so as not to be a burden to any of you, we preached to you the good news of God.

10 You are witnesses, and God also, how devoutly, justly, and blamelessly we behaved ourselves among you who believe;

11 as you know how we exhorted, comforted, and charged every one of you, as a father does his own children,

12 that you would walk worthy of God who calls you into His own kingdom and glory.

Receiving the Word of God

13 For this reason we also thank God without ceasing, because when you received the word of God which you heard from us, you welcomed it not as the word of men, but as it is in truth, the word of God, which also effectively works in you who believe.

14 For you, brethren, became imitators of the congregations of God which are in Judea in Messiah Yeshua. For you also have suffered the same things from your own countrymen, just as they did from the Judeans,

15 who killed both the Lord Yeshua and their own prophets, and have persecuted us; and they do not please God and are contrary to all men,

16 forbidding us to speak to the Gentiles that they may be saved, so as always to fill up the measure of their sins; but wrath has come on them to the uttermost.

Longing to See Them

17 But we, brethren, having been taken away from you for a short time in presence, not in heart, endeavored more eagerly to see your face with great desire.

18 Therefore we wanted to come to you—even I, Paul, time and again—but Satan hindered us.

19 For what is our hope, or joy, or crown of rejoicing? Is it not even you in the presence of our Lord Yeshua ha Mashiach at His coming?

20 For you are our glory and joy.

Anxiety in Athens

3 Therefore, when we could no longer endure it, we thought it good to be left in Athens alone,

2 and sent Timothy, our brother and minister of God, and our fellow laborer in the good news of the Messiah, to establish you and encourage you concerning your faith,

3 that no one should be shaken by these afflictions; for you yourselves know that we are appointed to this.

4 For, in fact, we told you before when we were with you that

1 See note 1, p. 246.

we would suffer tribulation, just as it happened, and you know.

5 For this reason, when I could no longer endure it, I sent to know your faith, lest by some means the tempter had tempted you, and our labor might be in vain.

Encouraged by Timothy

6 But now that Timothy has come to us from you, and brought us good news of your faith and love, and that you always have good remembrance of us, greatly desiring to see us, as we also to see you—

7 therefore, brethren, we were comforted concerning you in all our affliction and distress by your faith.

8 For now we live, if you stand fast in the Lord.

9 For what thanks can we render to God for you, for all the joy with which we rejoice for your sake before our God,

10 night and day praying exceedingly that we may see your face and perfect what is lacking in your faith?

Prayer for the Congregation

11 Now may our God and Father Himself, and our Lord Yeshua ha Mashiach, direct our way to you.

12 And may the Lord make you increase and abound in love to one another and to all, just as we do to you,

13 so that He may establish your hearts blameless in holiness before our God and Father at the coming of our Lord Yeshua ha Mashiach with all His believers.

Plea for Purity

4 Finally then, brethren, we urge and exhort you by the Lord Yeshua, that as you have received from us how you ought to walk and to please God, you would abound more and more;

2 for you know what commandments we gave you through the Lord Yeshua.

3 For this is the will of God, your sanctification: that you should abstain from sexual immorality;

4 that each of you should know how to possess his own vessel in sanctification and honor,

5 not in passion of lust, like the Gentiles who do not know God;

6 that no one take advantage of and defraud his brother in this matter, because the Lord is the avenger of all such, as we also have forewarned you and testified.

7 For God has not called us to uncleanness, but in holiness.

8 Therefore he who rejects this does not reject man, but God, who has also given us His Holy Spirit.

A Brotherly and Orderly Life

9 But concerning brotherly love you do not need that I write to you, for you yourselves are taught by God to love one another;

10 and indeed you do this to all the brethren who are in all Macedonia. But we urge you, brethren, that you increase more and more;

11 that you also aspire to lead a quiet life, to mind your own business, and to work with your own hands, as we commanded you,

12 that you may walk properly

toward those who are outsiders, and that you may lack nothing.

The Comfort of the Messiah's Coming

13 But I do not want you to be ignorant, brethren, concerning those who have fallen asleep, lest you sorrow as others who have no hope.

14 For if we believe that Yeshua died and rose again, so also God will bring with Him those who sleep in Yeshua.

15 For this we say to you by the word of the Lord, that we who are alive and remain until the coming of the Lord will by no means precede those who are asleep.

16 For the Lord Himself will descend from heaven with a shout, with the voice of an archangel, and with the shofar of God. And the dead in the Messiah will rise first.

17 Then we who are alive and remain shall be caught up together with them in the clouds to meet the Lord in the air. And thus we shall always be with the Lord.

18 Therefore comfort one another with these words.

The Day of the Lord

5 But concerning the times and the seasons, brethren, you have no need that I write to you.

2 For you yourselves know perfectly that the day of the Lord [2] so comes as a thief in the night.

3 For when they say, "Peace and safety!" then sudden destruction comes on them, as labor pains on a pregnant woman. And they shall not escape.

4 But you, brethren, are not in darkness, that this Day should overtake you as a thief.

5 You are all sons of light and sons of the day. We are not of the night nor of darkness.

6 Therefore let us not sleep, as others do, but let us watch and be sober.

7 For those who sleep, sleep at night, and those who get drunk are drunk at night.

8 But let us who are of the day be sober, putting on the breastplate of faith and love, and as a helmet the hope of salvation.

9 For God has not appointed us to wrath, but to obtain salvation by our Lord Yeshua ha Mashiach,

10 who died for us, that whether we wake or sleep, we should live together with Him.

11 Therefore comfort each other and edify one another, just as you also are doing.

Various Exhortations

12 And we urge you, brethren, to recognize those who labor among you, and are over you in the Lord and admonish you,

13 and to esteem them very highly in love for their work's sake. Be at peace among yourselves.

14 Now we exhort you, brethren, warn those who are unruly, comfort the fainthearted, uphold the weak, be patient with all.

15 See that no one renders evil for evil to anyone, but always pursue what is good both for yourselves and for all.

16 Rejoice always;

17 pray without ceasing;

2 Cf. Malachi 4:5, 6 (3:23, 24 in some versions)

18 in everything give thanks; for this is the will of God in Messiah Yeshua for you.

19 Do not quench the Spirit.

20 Do not despise prophecies.

21 Test all things; hold fast what is good.

22 Abstain from every form of evil.

Blessing and Admonition

23 Now may the God of peace Himself sanctify you completely; and may your whole spirit, soul, and body be preserved blameless at the coming of our Lord Yeshua ha Mashiach.

24 He who calls you is faithful, who also will do it.

25 Brethren, pray for us.

26 Greet all the brethren with a holy kiss.

27 I charge you by the Lord that this letter be read to all the holy brethren.

28 The grace of our Lord Yeshua ha Mashiach be with you. Amen.

The Second Letter Of Paul To The
THESSALONIANS

Greeting

PAUL, Silvanus, and Timothy,

To the congregation of the Thessalonians in God our Father and the Lord Yeshua ha Mashiach:

2 Grace to you and peace from God our Father and the Lord Yeshua ha Mashiach.

God's Final Judgment and Glory

3 We are bound to thank God always for you, brethren, as it is fitting, because your faith grows exceedingly, and the love of every one of you all abounds toward each other,

4 so that we ourselves boast of you among the congregations of God for your patience and faith in all your persecutions and tribulations that you endure,

5 which is manifest evidence of the righteous judgment of God, that you may be counted worthy of the kingdom of God, for which you also suffer;

6 seeing it is a righteous thing with God to repay with tribulation those who trouble you,

7 and to give you who are troubled rest with us when the Lord Yeshua is revealed from heaven with His mighty angels,

8 in flaming fire taking vengeance on those who do not know God, and on those who do not obey the good news of our Lord Yeshua ha Mashiach.

9 These will be punished with everlasting destruction from the presence of the Lord and from the glory of His power,

10 when He comes, in that Day, to be glorified in His believers and to be admired among all those who believe,[1] because our testimony among you was believed.

11 Therefore we also pray always for you that our God would count you worthy of this calling, and fulfill all the good pleasure of His goodness and the work of faith with power,

12 that the name of our Lord Yeshua ha Mashiach may be glorified in you, and you in Him, according to the grace of our God and the Lord Yeshua ha Mashiach.

The Falling Away

2 Now we ask you, brethren, by the coming of our Lord Yeshua ha Mashiach and our gathering together to Him,

2 not to be soon shaken in mind or be troubled, neither by spirit, nor by word, nor by letter, as if from us, as though the day of the Messiah had come.

1 Cf. Daniel 7:13, 14

3 Let no one deceive you by any means; for that Day will not come unless the falling away comes first, and the man of sin is revealed, the son of perdition,

4 who opposes and exalts himself above all that is called God or that is worshiped, so that he sits as God in the temple of God, showing himself that he is God.

5 Do you not remember that when I was still with you I told you these things?

6 And now you know what is restraining, that he may be revealed in his own time.

7 For the mystery of lawlessness is already at work; only he who now restrains will do so until he is taken out of the way.

8 And then the lawless one will be revealed, whom the Lord will consume with the breath of His mouth and destroy with the brightness of His coming.

9 The coming of the lawless one is according to the working of Satan with all power, signs, and lying wonders,

10 and with all deception of unrighteousness in those who perish, because they did not receive the love of the truth, that they might be saved.

11 And for this reason God will send them strong delusion, that they should believe the lie,

12 that they all might be condemned who did not believe the truth but had pleasure in unrighteousness.

Stand Fast

13 But we are bound to give thanks to God always for you, brethren beloved by the Lord, because God has from the beginning

chosen you for salvation through sanctification by the Spirit and belief in the truth,

14 to which He called you by our good news, for the obtaining of the glory of our Lord Yeshua ha Mashiach.

15 Therefore, brethren, stand fast and hold the traditions which you have been taught, whether by word or our letter.

16 Now may our Lord Yeshua ha Mashiach Himself, and our God and Father, who has loved us and given us everlasting consolation and good hope by grace,

17 comfort your hearts and establish you in every good word and work.

Pray for Us

3 Finally, brethren, pray for us, that the word of the Lord may have free course and be glorified, just as with you,

2 and that we may be delivered from unreasonable and wicked men; for not all have faith.

3 But the Lord is faithful, who will establish you and guard you from the evil one.

4 And we have confidence in the Lord concerning you, both that you do and will do the things we command you.

5 And may the Lord direct your hearts into the love of God and into the patience of the Messiah.

Warning Against Idleness

6 Now we command you, brethren, in the name of our Lord Yeshua ha Mashiach, that you withdraw from every brother who walks disorderly and not accord-

ing to the tradition which he received from us.

7 For you yourselves know how you ought to follow us, for we were not disorderly among you;

8 nor did we eat anyone's bread free of charge, but worked with labor and toil night and day, that we might not be a burden to any of you,

9 not because we do not have authority, but to make ourselves an example of how you should follow us.

10 For even when we were with you, we commanded you this: If anyone will not work, neither shall he eat.

11 For we hear that there are some who walk among you in a disorderly manner, not working at all, but are busybodies.

12 Now those who are such we command and exhort by our Lord Yeshua ha Mashiach that with quietness they work and eat their own bread.

13 But you, brethren, do not grow weary in doing good.

14 And if anyone does not obey our word in this letter, note that person and do not keep company with him, that he may be ashamed.

15 Yet do not count him as an enemy, but admonish him as a brother.

Blessing

16 Now may the Lord of peace Himself give you peace always in every way. The Lord be with you all.

17 The salutation of Paul with my own hand, which is a sign in every letter; so I write.

18 The grace of our Lord Yeshua ha Mashiach be with you all. Amen.

The First Letter Of Paul To

TIMOTHY

Greeting

PAUL, an apostle [1] of Yeshua ha Mashiach, by the commandment of God our Savior and the Lord Yeshua ha Mashiach, our hope,

2 To Timothy, my true son in the faith:

Grace, mercy, and peace from God our Father and Yeshua ha Mashiach our Lord.

No Other Doctrine

3 As I urged you when I went into Macedonia—remain in Ephesus that you may charge some that they teach no other doctrine,

4 nor give heed to fables and endless genealogies, which cause disputes rather than godly edification which is in faith.

5 Now the purpose of the commandment is love from a pure heart, from a good conscience, and from unfeigned faith.

6 from which some, having strayed, have turned aside to idle talk,

7 desiring to be teachers of the Torah, understanding neither what they say nor the things which they affirm.

8 But we know that the Torah is good if one uses it lawfully,

1 See note 1, p. 246.

9 knowing this: that the law is not made for a righteous person, but for the lawless and insubordinate, for the ungodly and for sinners, for the unholy and profane, for murderers of fathers and murderers of mothers, for manslayers,

10 for fornicators, for sodomites, for kidnappers, for liars, for perjurers, and if there is any other thing that is contrary to sound doctrine,

11 according to the glorious good news of the blessed God which was committed to my trust.

A Faithful Saying

12 And I thank Messiah Yeshua our Lord who has enabled me, because He counted me faithful, putting me into service,

13 although I was formerly a blasphemer, a persecutor, and an insolent man; but I obtained mercy because I did it ignorantly in unbelief.

14 And the grace of our Lord was exceedingly abundant, with faith and love which are in Messiah Yeshua.

15 This is a faithful saying and worthy of all acceptance, that Messiah Yeshua came into the world to save sinners, of whom I am chief.

16 However, for this reason I obtained mercy, that in me first Yeshua ha Mashiach might show

all longsuffering, as a pattern to those who are going to believe on Him for everlasting life.

17 Now to the King eternal, immortal, invisible, to God who alone is wise, be honor and glory forever and ever. Amen.

Fight the Good Fight

18 This charge I commit to you, son Timothy, according to the prophecies previously made concerning you, that by them you may wage the good warfare,

19 holding faith and a good conscience, which some having rejected, concerning the faith have suffered shipwreck,

20 of whom are Hymenaeus and Alexander, whom I have delivered to Satan that they may learn not to blaspheme.

Pray for All Men

2 Therefore I exhort first of all that supplications, prayers, intercessions, and giving of thanks be made for all men,

2 for kings and all who are in authority, that we may lead a quiet and peaceable life in all godliness and reverence.

3 For this is good and acceptable in the sight of God our Savior,

4 who desires all men to be saved and to come to the knowledge of the truth.

5 For there is one God and one Mediator between God and men, the Man Messiah Yeshua,

6 who gave Himself a ransom for all, to be testified in due time,

7 for which I was appointed a preacher and an apostle—I am speaking the truth in the Messiah

and not lying—a teacher of the Gentiles in faith and truth.

Men and Women in the Congregation

8 Therefore I desire that the men pray everywhere, lifting up holy hands, without wrath and doubting;

9 in like manner also, that the women adorn themselves in modest apparel, with propriety and moderation, not with braided hair or gold or pearls or costly clothing,

10 but, which is proper for women professing godliness, with good works.

11 Let a woman learn in silence with all submission.

12 And I do not permit a woman to teach or to have authority over a man, but to be in silence.

13 For Adam was formed first, then Eve.

14 And Adam was not deceived, but the woman being deceived, fell into transgression.

15 Nevertheless she will be saved in childbearing if they continue in faith, love, and holiness, with self-control.

Qualifications of Overseers

3 This is a true saying: If a man desires the position of an overseer, he desires a good work.

2 An overseer then must be blameless, the husband of one wife, temperate, sober-minded, of good behavior, hospitable, able to teach;

3 not given to wine, not violent, not greedy for money, but gentle, not quarrelsome, not covetous;

4 one who rules his own house well, having his children in submission with all reverence

5 (for if a man does not know how to rule his own house, how will he take care of the congregation of God?);

6 not a novice, lest being puffed up with pride he fall into the same condemnation as the devil.

7 Moreover he must have a good testimony among those who are outsiders, lest he fall into reproach and the snare of the devil.

Qualifications of Deacons

8 Likewise the deacons must be reverent, not double-tongued, not given to much wine, not greedy for money,

9 holding the mystery of the faith with a pure conscience.

10 And let these also first be proved; then let them serve as deacons, being found blameless.

11 Likewise their wives must be reverent, not slanderers, temperate, faithful in all things.

12 Let deacons be the husbands of one wife, ruling their children and their own houses well.

13 For those who have served well as deacons obtain for themselves a good standing and great boldness in the faith which is in Messiah Yeshua.

The Great Mystery

14 These things I write to you, hoping to come to you shortly,

15 but if I am delayed, that you may know how you ought to conduct yourself in the house of God, which is the congregation of the living God, the pillar and ground of the truth.

16 And without controversy great is the mystery of godliness:

God was manifested in the flesh,
Justified in the Spirit,
Seen by angels,
Preached among the Gentiles,
Believed on in the world,
Received up in glory.

The Falling Away

4 Now the Spirit expressly says that in latter times some will depart from the faith, giving heed to deceiving spirits and doctrines of demons,

2 speaking lies in hypocrisy, having their own conscience seared with a hot iron,

3 forbidding to marry, and commanding to abstain from foods which God has created to be received with thanksgiving by those who believe and know the truth.

4 For every creature of God is good, and nothing is to be refused if it is received with thanksgiving;

5 for it is sanctified by the word of God and prayer.

A Good Servant of Yeshua ha Mashiach

6 If you instruct the brethren in these things, you will be a good servant of Yeshua ha Mashiach, nourished in the words of faith and of the good doctrine which you have carefully followed.

7 But reject profane and old wives' fables, and exercise yourself rather to godliness.

8 For bodily exercise profits a little, but godliness is profitable for all things, having promise of the life that now is and of that which is to come.

9 This is a faithful saying and worthy of all acceptance.

10 For to this end we both labor and suffer reproach, because we trust in the living God, who is the Savior of all men, especially of those who believe.

Take Heed to Your Service

11 These things command and teach.

12 Let no one despise your youth, but be an example to the believers in word, in conduct, in love, in spirit, in faith, in purity.

13 Till I come, give attention to reading, to exhortation, to doctrine.

14 Do not neglect the gift that is in you, which was given to you by prophecy with the laying on of the hands of the presbytery.

15 Meditate on these things; give yourself entirely to them, that your progress may be evident to all.

16 Take heed to yourself and to the doctrine. Continue in them, for in doing this you will save both yourself and those who hear you.

Treatment of Congregation Members

5 Do not rebuke an older man, but exhort him as a father, the younger men as brothers,

2 the older women as mothers, the younger as sisters, with all purity.

Honor True Widows

3 Honor widows who are really widows.

4 But if any widow has children or grandchildren, let them first learn to show piety at home and to repay their parents; for this is good and acceptable before God.

5 Now she who is really a widow, and left alone, trusts in God and continues in supplications and prayers night and day.

6 But she who lives in pleasure is dead while she lives.

7 And these things command, that they may be blameless.

8 But if anyone does not provide for his own, and especially for those of his household, he has denied the faith and is worse than an unbeliever.

9 Do not let a widow under sixty years old be taken into the number, and not unless she has been the wife of one man,

10 well reported for good works: if she has brought up children, if she has lodged strangers, if she has washed the believers' feet, if she has relieved the afflicted, if she has diligently followed every good work.

11 But refuse the younger widows; for when they have begun to grow wanton against the Messiah, they desire to marry,

12 having condemnation because they have cast off their first faith.

13 And besides they learn to be idle, wandering about from house to house, and not only idle but also gossips and busybodies, saying things which they ought not.

14 Therefore I desire that the younger widows marry, bear children, manage the house, give no opportunity to the adversary to speak reproachfully.

15 For some have already turned aside after Satan.

16 If any believing man or woman has widows, let them re-

lieve them, and do not let the congregation be burdened, that it may relieve those who are really widows.

Honor the Elders

17 Let the elders who rule well be counted worthy of double honor, especially those who labor in the word and doctrine.

18 For the Scripture says, *"You shall not muzzle an ox while it treads out the grain,"* [2] and, "The laborer is worthy of his wages." [3]

19 Do not receive an accusation against an elder except from two or three witnesses.

20 Those who are sinning rebuke in the presence of all, that the rest also may fear.

21 I charge you before God and the Lord Yeshua ha Mashiach and the elect angels that you observe these things without prejudice, doing nothing with partiality.

22 Do not lay hands on anyone hastily, nor share in other people's sins; keep yourself pure.

23 No longer drink only water, but use a little wine for your stomach's sake and your frequent infirmities.

24 Some men's sins are clearly evident, preceding them to judgment, but those of some men follow later.

25 Likewise, also, the good works of some are clearly evident, and those that are otherwise cannot be hidden.

Honor Masters

6 Let as many servants as are under the yoke count their own masters worthy of all honor, that the name of God and His doctrine not be blasphemed.

2 And those who have believing masters, let them not despise them because they are brethren, but rather serve them because those who are benefited are believers and beloved. Teach and exhort these things.

Error and Greed

3 If anyone teaches otherwise and does not consent to wholesome words, even the words of our Lord Yeshua ha Mashiach, and to the doctrine which is according to godliness,

4 he is proud, knowing nothing, but obsessed with disputes and arguments over words, from which come envy, strife, reviling, evil suspicions,

5 useless wranglings of men of corrupt minds and destitute of the truth, who suppose that godliness is a means of gain. From such withdraw yourself.

6 But godliness with contentment is great gain.

7 For we brought nothing into this world, and it is certain we can carry nothing out.

8 And having food and clothing, with these we shall be content.

9 But those who desire to be rich fall into temptation and a snare, and into many foolish and harmful lusts which drown men in destruction and perdition.

10 For the love of money is a root of all kinds of evil, for which some have strayed from the faith in their greediness, and pierced themselves through with many sorrows.

2 Deuteronomy 25:4   *3* Leviticus 19:13

The Good Confession

11 But you, O man of God, flee these things and pursue righteousness, godliness, faith, love, patience, gentleness.

12 Fight the good fight of faith, lay hold on eternal life, to which you were also called and have confessed the good confession in the presence of many witnesses.

13 I urge you in the sight of God who gives life to all things, and before Messiah Yeshua who witnessed the good confession before Pontius Pilate,

14 that you keep this commandment without spot, blameless until our Lord Yeshua ha Mashiach's appearing,

15 which He will show in His own time, He who is the blessed and only Potentate, the King of kings and Lord of lords,

16 who only has immortality, dwelling in unapproachable light, whom no man has seen or can see, to whom be honor and everlasting power. Amen.

Instructions to the Rich

17 Command those who are rich in this present age that they not be haughty, nor trust in uncertain riches but in the living God, who gives us richly all things to enjoy;

18 that they do good, that they be rich in good works, ready to give, willing to share,

19 storing up for themselves a good foundation for the time to come, that they may lay hold on eternal life.

Guard the Faith

20 O Timothy, guard what was committed to your trust, avoiding the profane and vain babblings and contradictions of what is falsely called knowledge—

21 by professing it, some have strayed concerning the faith. Grace be with you. Amen.

The Second Letter Of Paul To
TIMOTHY

Greeting

PAUL, an apostle[1] of Yeshua ha Mashiach by the will of God, according to the promise of life which is in Messiah Yeshua,

2 To Timothy, my beloved son:

Grace, mercy, and peace from God the Father and Messiah Yeshua our Lord.

Timothy's Faith and Heritage

3 I thank God, whom I serve with a pure conscience, as my forefathers did, as without ceasing I remember you in my prayers night and day,

4 greatly desiring to see you, being mindful of your tears, that I may be filled with joy,

5 when I call to remembrance the unfeigned faith that is in you, which dwelt first in your grandmother Lois and your mother Eunice, and I am persuaded is in you also.

6 Therefore I remind you to stir up the gift of God which is in you through the laying on of my hands.

7 For God has not given us a spirit of fear, but of power and of love and of a sound mind.

1 See note 1, p. 246.

Not Ashamed of the Good News

8 Therefore do not be ashamed of the testimony of our Lord, nor of me His prisoner, but share with me in the sufferings for the good news according to the power of God,

9 who has saved us and called us with a holy calling, not according to our works, but according to His own purpose and grace which was given to us in Messiah Yeshua before time began,

10 but has now been revealed by the appearing of our Savior Yeshua ha Mashiach, who has abolished death and brought life and immortality to light through the good news,

11 to which I was appointed a preacher, an apostle, and a teacher of the Gentiles.

12 For this reason I also suffer these things; nevertheless I am not ashamed, for I know whom I have believed and am persuaded that He is able to keep what I have committed to Him until that Day.

Be Loyal to the Faith

13 Hold fast the pattern of sound words which you have heard from me, in faith and love which are in Messiah Yeshua.

14 That good thing which was

committed to you, keep by the Holy Spirit who dwells in us.

15 This you know, that all those in Asia have turned away from me, among whom are Phygellus and Hermogenes.

16 The Lord give mercy to the household of Onesiphorus, for he often refreshed me, and was not ashamed of my chain.

17 But when he arrived in Rome, he sought me out very diligently and found me.

18 The Lord grant to him that he may find mercy from the Lord in that Day—and you know very well how many ways he ministered to me at Ephesus.

Be Strong

2 You therefore, my son, be strong in the grace that is in Messiah Yeshua.

2 And the things that you have heard from me among many witnesses, commit these to faithful men who will be able to teach others also.

3 You therefore endure hardship as a good soldier of Yeshua ha Mashiach.

4 No one engaged in warfare entangles himself with the affairs of this life, that he may please him who enlisted him as a soldier.

5 And if anyone also competes in athletics, he is not crowned unless he competes according to the rules.

6 The hard-working farmer must be first to partake of the crops.

7 Consider what I say, and may the Lord give you understanding in all things.

8 Remember that Yeshua ha Mashiach of the seed of David [2] was raised from the dead according to my good news, [3]

9 for which I suffer trouble as an evildoer, even to the point of chains; but the word of God is not chained.

10 Therefore I endure all things for the sake of the elect, that they also may obtain the salvation which is in Messiah Yeshua with eternal glory.

11 This is a faithful saying:
For if we died with Him,
  We shall also live with
    Him.
12 If we endure,
  We shall also reign with
    Him.
If we deny Him,
  He also will deny us.
13 If we are faithless,
  He remains faithful;
  He cannot deny Himself.

Approved and Disapproved Workers

14 Remind them of these things, charging them before the Lord that they not strive about words to no profit, to the ruin of the hearers.

15 Be diligent to present yourself approved to God, a worker who does not need to be ashamed, rightly dividing the word of truth.

16 But shun profane and vain babblings, for they will increase to more ungodliness.

17 And their message will spread like cancer. Hymenaeus and Philetus are of this sort,

18 who have strayed concerning

2 Matthew 1:1; cf. Jeremiah 23:5, 6
3 Psalm 16:10

the truth, saying that the resurrection is already past, and they overthrow the faith of some.

19 Nevertheless the solid foundation of God stands, having this seal: "The Lord knows those who are His," and, "Let everyone who names the name of the Messiah depart from iniquity."

20 But in a great house there are not only vessels of gold and silver, but also of wood and clay, some for honor and some for dishonor.

21 Therefore if anyone cleanses himself from these, he will be a vessel for honor, sanctified and useful for the Master, prepared for every good work.

22 Flee also youthful lusts; but pursue righteousness, faith, love, peace with those who call on the Lord out of a pure heart.

23 But avoid foolish and ignorant disputes, knowing that they generate strife.

24 And a servant of the Lord must not quarrel but be gentle to all, able to teach, patient,

25 in humility correcting those who are in opposition, if God perhaps will give them repentance to the acknowledgment of the truth,

26 and they may come to their senses and escape the snare of the devil, having been taken captive by him to do his will.

Perilous Times and Perilous Men

3 But know this, that in the last days perilous times will come:

2 For men will be lovers of themselves, lovers of money, boasters, proud, blasphemers, disobedient to parents, unthankful, unholy,

3 unloving, unforgiving, slanderers, without self-control, brutal, despisers of good,

4 traitors, headstrong, haughty, lovers of pleasure rather than lovers of God,

5 having a form of godliness but denying its power. And from such people turn away!

6 For of this sort are those who creep into households and make captives of gullible women loaded down with sins, led away by various lusts,

7 always learning and never able to come to the knowledge of the truth.

8 Now as Jannes and Jambres resisted Moses, so do these also resist the truth: men of corrupt minds, disapproved concerning the faith;

9 but they will progress no further, for their folly will be manifest to all, as theirs also was.

The Man of God and the Word of God

10 But you have carefully followed my doctrine, manner of life, purpose, faith, longsuffering, love, perseverance,

11 persecutions, afflictions, which happened to me in Antioch, in Iconium, in Lystra—what persecutions I endured. And out of them all the Lord delivered me.

12 Yes, and all who desire to live godly in Messiah Yeshua will suffer persecution.

13 But evil men and impostors will grow worse and worse, deceiving and being deceived.

14 But you continue in the things which you have learned and been assured of, knowing from whom you have learned them,

15 and that from childhood you have known the Holy Scriptures, which are able to make you wise for salvation through faith which is in Messiah Yeshua.

16 All Scripture is given by inspiration of God, and is profitable for doctrine, for reproof, for correction, for instruction in righteousness,

17 that the man of God may be complete, thoroughly equipped for every good work.

Proclaim the Word

4 I charge you therefore before God and the Lord Yeshua ha Mashiach, who will judge the living and the dead at His appearing and His kingdom:

2 Preach the word! Be ready in season, out of season. Convince, rebuke, exhort with all longsuffering and teaching.

3 For the time will come when they will not endure sound doctrine, but according to their own desires, because they have itching ears, they will heap up for themselves teachers;

4 and they will turn their ears away from the truth, and be turned aside to fables.

5 But you be watchful in all things, endure afflictions, do the work of an evangelist, fulfill your service.

Paul's Valedictory

6 For I am already being poured out as a drink offering, and the time of my departure is at hand.

7 I have fought the good fight, I have finished the race, I have kept the faith.

8 Finally, there is laid up for me the crown of righteousness, which the Lord, the righteous Judge, will give me on that Day; and not to me only, but also to all who have loved His appearing.

Abandoned

9 Be diligent to come to me quickly;

10 for Demas has forsaken me, having loved this present world, and has departed for Thessalonica—Crescens for Galatia, Titus for Dalmatia.

11 Only Luke is with me. Get Mark and bring him with you, for he is useful to me for service.

12 And Tychicus I have sent to Ephesus.

13 Bring the cloak that I left with Carpus at Troas when you come—and the books, especially the parchments.

14 Alexander the coppersmith did me much harm. May the Lord repay him according to his works—

15 of whom you also beware, for he has greatly resisted our words.

16 At my first defense no one stood with me, but all forsook me. May it not be charged against them.

The Lord Is Faithful

17 But the Lord stood with me and strengthened me, so that the message might be preached fully through me, and that all the Gentiles might hear. And I was delivered out of the mouth of the lion.

18 And the Lord will deliver me from every evil work and preserve me for His heavenly kingdom.

To Him be glory forever and ever. Amen!

Come Before Winter

19 Greet Prisca and Aquila, and the household of Onesiphorus.

20 Erastus stayed in Corinth, but Trophimus I have left in Miletus sick.

21 Do your utmost to come before winter. Eubulus greets you, as well as Pudens, Linus, Claudia, and all the brethren.

Farewell

22 The Lord Yeshua ha Mashiach be with your spirit. Grace be with you. Amen.

The Letter Of Paul To
TITUS

Greeting

PAUL, a servant of God and an apostle [1] of Yeshua ha Mashiach, according to the faith of God's elect and the acknowledgment of the truth which is according to godliness,

2 in hope of eternal life which God, who cannot lie, promised before time began,

3 but has in due time manifested His word through preaching, which was committed to me according to the commandment of God our Savior;

4 To Titus, my true son in our common faith:

Grace, mercy, and peace from God the Father and the Lord Yeshua ha Mashiach our Savior.

Qualified Elders

5 For this reason I left you in Crete, that you should set in order the things that are lacking, and appoint elders in every city as I commanded you—

6 if a man is blameless, the husband of one wife, having faithful children not accused of dissipation or insubordination.

7 For an overseer must be blameless, as a steward of God, not

self-willed, not quick-tempered, not given to wine, not violent, not greedy for money,

8 but hospitable, a lover of what is good, sober-minded, just, holy, self-controlled,

9 holding fast the faithful word as he has been taught, that he may be able, by sound doctrine, both to exhort and to convict those who contradict.

The Elders' Task

10 For there are many insubordinate, both idle talkers and deceivers, especially those of the circumcision,

11 whose mouths must be stopped, who subvert whole households, teaching things which they ought not, for the sake of dishonest gain.

12 One of them, a prophet of their own, said, "Cretans are always liars, evil beasts, lazy gluttons."

13 This testimony is true. Therefore rebuke them sharply, that they may be sound in the faith,

14 not giving heed to Jewish fables and commandments of men who turn from the truth.

15 To the pure all things are pure, but to those who are defiled and unbelieving nothing is pure;

1 See note 1, p. 246.

but even their mind and conscience are defiled.

16 They profess that they know God, but in works they deny Him, being abominable, disobedient, and disqualified for every good work.

Qualities of a Sound Congregation

2 But as for you, speak the things which are proper for sound doctrine:

2 that the older men be sober, reverent, temperate, sound in faith, in love, in patience;

3 the older women likewise, that they be reverent in behavior, not slanderers, not given to much wine, teachers of good things—

4 that they admonish the young women to love their husbands, to love their children,

5 to be discreet, chaste, homemakers, good, obedient to their own husbands, that the word of God may not be blasphemed.

6 Likewise exhort the young men to be sober-minded,

7 in all things showing yourself to be a pattern of good works; in doctrine showing integrity, reverence, incorruptibility,

8 sound speech that cannot be condemned, that he who is of the opposition may be ashamed, having nothing evil to say of you.

9 Exhort servants to be obedient to their own masters, to be well pleasing in all things, not answering back,

10 not pilfering, but showing all good fidelity, that they may adorn the doctrine of God our Savior in all things.

11 For the grace of God that brings salvation has appeared to all men,

12 teaching us that, denying ungodliness and worldly lusts, we should live soberly, righteously, and godly in the present age,

13 looking for the blessed hope and glorious appearing of our great God and Savior Yeshua ha Mashiach,

14 who gave Himself for us, that He might redeem us from every lawless deed and purify for Himself His own special people, zealous for good works.

15 Speak these things, exhort, and rebuke with all authority. Let no one despise you.

3 Remind them to be subject to rulers and authorities, to obey, to be ready for every good work,

2 to speak evil of no one, to be peaceable, gentle, showing all humility to all men.

3 For we ourselves were also once foolish, disobedient, deceived, serving various lusts and pleasures, living in malice and envy, hateful and hating one another.

4 But when the kindness and the love of God our Savior toward man appeared,

5 not by works of righteousness which we have done, but according to His mercy He saved us, by the washing of regeneration and renewing of the Holy Spirit,

6 whom He poured out on us abundantly through Yeshua ha Mashiach our Savior,

7 that having been justified by His grace we should become heirs according to the hope of eternal life.

8 This is a faithful saying, and these things I want you to affirm constantly, that those who have believed in God should be careful to maintain good works. These things are good and profitable to men.

Avoid Dissension

9 But avoid foolish disputes, genealogies, contentions, and strivings about the Torah; for they are unprofitable and useless.

10 Reject a divisive man after the first and second admonition,

11 knowing that such a person is warped and sinning, being self-condemned.

Final Messages

12 When I send Artemas to you, or Tychicus, be diligent to come to me to Nicopolis, for I have decided to spend the winter there.

13 Send Zenas the lawyer and Apollos on their journey with diligence, that they may lack nothing.

14 And let our people also learn to maintain good works, to meet urgent needs, that they may not be unfruitful.

Farewell

15 All who are with me greet you. Greet those who love us in the faith. Grace be with you all. Amen.

The Letter Of Paul To
PHILEMON

Greeting

PAUL, a prisoner of Messiah Yeshua, and Timothy our brother,

To Philemon our dearly beloved, and fellow laborer,

2 to the beloved Apphia, Archippus our fellow soldier, and to the congregation in your house:

3 Grace to you and peace from God our Father and the Lord Yeshua ha Mashiach.

Philemon's Love and Faith

4 I thank my God, making mention of you always in my prayers,

5 hearing of your love and faith which you have toward the Lord Yeshua and toward all the believers,

6 that the sharing of your faith may become effective by the acknowledgment of every good thing which is in you in Messiah Yeshua.

7 For we have great joy and consolation in your love, because the hearts of the believers have been refreshed by you, brother.

The Plea for Onesimus

8 Therefore, though I might be very bold in the Messiah to command you what is fitting,

9 yet for love's sake I rather appeal to you—being such a one as Paul, the aged, and now also a prisoner of Yeshua ha Mashiach—

10 I appeal to you for my son Onesimus, whom I have begotten while in my chains,

11 who once was unprofitable to you, but now is profitable to you and to me.[1]

12 I am sending him back. You therefore receive him, that is, my own heart,

13 whom I wished to keep with me, that in your behalf he might serve me in my chains for the good news.

14 But without your consent I wanted to do nothing, that your good deed might not be by compulsion, as it were, but voluntary.

15 For perhaps he departed for a while for this purpose, that you might receive him forever,

16 no longer as a slave but more than a slave, as a beloved brother, especially to me but how much more to you, both in the flesh and in the Lord.

Philemon's Obedience Encouraged

17 If then you count me as a partner, receive him as you would me.

1 The name "Onesimus" means "Useful" or "Profitable."

18 If he has wronged you or owes you anything, put that on my account.

19 I, Paul, am writing with my own hand. I will repay—not to mention to you that you owe me even your own self besides.

20 Yes, brother, let me have joy from you in the Lord; refresh my heart in the Lord.

21 Having confidence in your obedience, I write to you, knowing that you will do even more than I say.

22 But, meanwhile, also prepare a guest room for me, for I trust that through your prayers I shall be granted to you.

Farewell

23 Epaphras, my fellow prisoner in Messiah Yeshua, greets you,

24 as do Mark, Aristarchus, Demas, Luke, my fellow laborers.

25 The grace of our Lord Yeshua ha Mashiach be with your spirit. Amen.

The Letter To The
HEBREWS

God's Supreme Revelation

GOD, who at various times and in different ways spoke in time past to the fathers by the prophets,

2 has in these last days spoken to us by His Son, whom He has appointed heir of all things, by whom also He made the worlds;

3 who being the brightness of His glory and the express image of His person, and upholding all things by the word of His power, when He had by Himself purged our sins, sat down at the right hand of the Majesty on high,

4 having become so much better than the angels, as He has by inheritance obtained a more excellent name than they.

The Son Exalted Above Angels

5 For to which of the angels did He ever say:

"You are My Son,
Today I have begotten
You"? [1]

And again:

"I will be to Him a Father,
And He shall be to Me a
Son"? [2]

6 And when He again brings the firstborn into the world, He says:

"And let all the angels of God
worship Him." [3]

7 And of the angels He says:

"Who makes His angels spirits
And His ministers a flame of
fire." [4]

8 But to the Son He says:

"Your throne, O God, is forever and ever;
A scepter of righteousness is
the scepter of Your Kingdom.

9 You have loved righteousness
and hated lawlessness;
Therefore God, even Your
God, has anointed You
With the oil of gladness
more than Your companions." [5]

10 And:

"You, LORD, in the beginning
laid the foundation of the
earth,
And the heavens are the
work of Your hands;

11 They will perish, but You
remain;
And they will all grow old
like a garment,

12 And like a cloak You will
fold them up,
And they will be changed.
But You are the same,

---

1 Psalm 2:7   2 2 Samuel 7:14

3 Psalm 97:7   4 Psalm 104:4

5 Psalm 45:6, 7 (45:7, 8 in some versions)

*And Your years will not
   fail."*[6]

13 But to which of the angels has
He ever said:

*"Sit at My right hand,
   Till I make Your enemies
   Your footstool"*?[7]

14 Are they not all ministering
spirits sent forth to minister for
those who will inherit salvation?

Do Not Neglect Salvation

2 Therefore we must give the
more earnest heed to the
things we have heard, lest we let
them slip.

2 For if the word spoken
through angels proved steadfast,
and every transgression and disobedience received a just reward,

3 how shall we escape if we neglect so great a salvation, which at
the first began to be spoken by the
Lord, and was confirmed to us by
those who heard Him,

4 God also bearing witness with
both signs and wonders, with various miracles, and gifts of the Holy
Spirit, according to His own will?

The Son Made Lower than Angels

5 For He has not put the world
to come, of which we speak, in
subjection to angels.

6 But one testified in a certain
place, saying:

*"What is man that You are
   mindful of him,
   Or the son of man that You
   take care of him?*

7 *You made him a little lower
   than the angels;
   You crowned him with glory
   and honor,*

*And set him over the works
   of Your hands.*

8 *You have put all things in
   subjection under his feet."*[8]

For in that He put all in subjection under him, He left nothing
that is not put under him. But
now we do not yet see all things
put under him.

9 But we see Yeshua, who was
made a little lower than the angels
for the suffering of death, crowned
with glory and honor, that He, by
the grace of God, might taste
death for everyone.

Bringing Many Sons to Glory

10 For it was fitting for Him, for
whom are all things and by whom
are all things, in bringing many
sons to glory, to make the author
of their salvation perfect through
sufferings.

11 For both He who sanctifies
and those who are being sanctified
are all of one, for which reason He
is not ashamed to call them brethren,

12 saying:

*"I will declare Your name to
   My brethren;
   In the midst of the congrega-
   tion I will sing praise to
   You."*[9]

13 And again:

*"I will put My trust in
   Him."*[10]

And again:

*"Here am I and the children
   whom God has given
   Me."*[11]

---

6 Psalm 102:25–27 (102:26–28 in some
versions)   7 Psalm 110:1

8 Psalm 8:4–6 (8:5–7 in some versions)
9 Psalm 22:22 (22:23 in some versions)
10 2 Samuel 22:3; Isaiah 8:17
11 Isaiah 8:17, 18

14 Inasmuch then as the children have partaken of flesh and blood, He also Himself likewise shared in the same, that through death He might destroy him who had the power of death, that is, the devil,

15 and deliver those who through fear of death were all their lifetime subject to bondage.

16 For indeed He does not give help to angels, but He does give help to the seed of Abraham.

17 Therefore, in all things He was obligated to be made like His brethren, that He might be a merciful and faithful High Priest in things pertaining to God, to make propitiation for the sins of the people.

18 For in that He Himself has suffered, being tempted, He is able to aid those who are tempted.

The Son Was Faithful

3 Therefore, holy brethren, partakers of the heavenly calling, consider the Apostle[12] and High Priest of our confession, Messiah Yeshua,

2 who was faithful to Him who appointed Him, as also Moses was faithful in all His house.

3 For this One has been counted worthy of more glory than Moses, inasmuch as He who has built the house has more honor than the house.

4 For every house is built by someone, but He who built all things is God.

5 And Moses indeed was faithful in all His house as a servant, for a testimony of those things which were to be spoken afterward,

6 but the Messiah as a Son over His own house, whose house we are if we hold fast the confidence and the rejoicing of the hope firm to the end.

Be Faithful

7 Therefore, as the Holy Spirit says:

"Today, if you will hear His
    voice,
8 Do not harden your hearts
    as in the rebellion,
In the day of trial in the wilderness,
9 Where your fathers tested
    Me, proved Me,
And saw My works forty
    years.
10 Therefore I was angry with
    that generation,
And said, 'They always go
    astray in their heart,
And they have not known
    My ways.'
11 So I swore in My wrath,
They shall not enter My
    rest."[13]

12 Take heed, brethren, lest there be in any of you an evil heart of unbelief in departing from the living God;

13 but exhort one another daily, while it is called "Today," lest any of you be hardened through the deceitfulness of sin.

14 For we have become partakers of the Messiah if we hold the beginning of our confidence steadfast to the end,

15 while it is said:

"Today, if you will hear His
    voice,

---

12 See note 1, p. 246.

13 Psalm 95:7–11

*Do not harden your hearts
as in the rebellion."* [14]

Failure of the Wilderness Wanderers

16 For who, having heard, rebelled? Indeed, was it not all who came out of Egypt, led by Moses?

17 And with whom was He angry forty years? Was it not with those who had sinned, whose corpses fell in the wilderness?

18 And to whom did He swear that they would not enter His rest, but to those who did not obey?

19 So we see that they could not enter in because of unbelief.

The Promise of Rest

4 Therefore, since a promise remains of entering His rest, let us fear lest any of you seem to come short of it.

2 For indeed the good news was preached to us as well as to them; but the word which they heard did not profit them, not being mixed with faith in those who heard it.

3 For we who have believed do enter that rest, as He has said:

*"As I have sworn in My
  wrath,
They shall not enter My
  rest,"* [15]

although the works were finished from the foundation of the world.

4 For He spoke in a certain place of the seventh day in this way: *"And God rested the seventh day from all His works"*;[16]

5 and again in this place: *"They shall not enter My rest."* [17]

6 Since therefore it remains that some must enter it, and those to whom it was first preached did not enter because of disobedience,

7 again He designates a certain day, saying in David, *"Today,"* after such a long time, as it has been said:

*"Today, if you will hear His
  voice,
Do not harden your
  hearts."* [18]

8 For if Joshua had given them rest, then He would not afterward have spoken of another day.

9 There remains therefore a rest for the people of God.

10 For he who has entered His rest has himself also ceased from his works as God did from His.

The Word Discovers Our Condition

11 Let us therefore be diligent to enter that rest, lest anyone fall after the same example of disobedience.

12 For the word of God is living and powerful, and sharper than any two-edged sword, piercing even to the division of soul and spirit, and of joints and marrow, and is a discerner of the thoughts and intents of the heart.

13 And there is no creature hidden from His sight, but all things are naked and open to the eyes of Him to whom we must give account.

Our Compassionate High Priest

14 Seeing then that we have a great High Priest who has passed through the heavens, Yeshua the Son of God, let us hold fast our confession.

---

14 Psalm 95:7, 8   *15* Psalm 95:11
16 Genesis 2:2   *17* Psalm 95:11

18 Psalm 95:7, 8

15 For we do not have a High Priest who cannot sympathize with our weaknesses, but was in all points tempted as we are, yet without sin.

16 Let us therefore come boldly to the throne of grace, that we may obtain mercy and find grace to help in time of need.

Qualifications for High Priesthood

5 For every priest taken from among men is appointed for men in things pertaining to God, that he may offer both gifts and sacrifices for sins.

2 He can have compassion on those who are ignorant and going astray, since he himself is also beset by weakness.

3 And because of this he is obligated as for the people, so also for himself, to offer for sins.[19]

4 And no man takes this honor to himself, but he who is called by God, just as Aaron was.[20]

A Priest Forever

5 So also the Messiah did not glorify Himself to become High Priest, but it was He who said to Him:

"You are My Son,
  Today I have begotten
    You." [21]

6 As He also says in another place:

"You are a priest forever
According to the order of
  Melchizedek"; [22]

7 who, in the days of His flesh, when He had offered up prayers and supplications, with strong crying and tears, to Him who was able to save Him from death, and was heard because of His godly fear,

8 though He was a Son, yet He learned obedience by the things which He suffered.

9 And having been perfected, He became the author of eternal salvation to all who obey Him,

10 called by God as High Priest "according to the order of Melchizedek,"

11 of whom we have much to say, and hard to explain, since you have become dull of hearing.

Spiritual Immaturity

12 For though by this time you ought to be teachers, you need someone to teach you again the first principles of the oracles of God; and you have come to need milk and not solid food.

13 For everyone who partakes only of milk is unskilled in the word of righteousness, for he is a babe.

14 But solid food belongs to those who are of full age, even those who by reason of use have their senses exercised to discern both good and evil.

The Peril of Not Progressing

6 Therefore, leaving the discussion of the elementary principles of the Messiah, let us go on to perfection, not laying again the foundation of repentance from dead works and of faith toward God,

2 of the doctrine of immersions, of laying on of hands, of resurrec-

19 Leviticus 4:3, 13, 14
20 Exodus 28:1   21 Psalm 2:7
22 Psalm 110:4

tion of the dead, and of eternal judgment.

3 And this we will do if God permits.

4 For it is impossible for those who were once enlightened, and have tasted the heavenly gift, and have become partakers of the Holy Spirit,

5 and have tasted the good word of God and the powers of the age to come,

6 if they fall away, to renew them again to repentance, seeing they crucify again for themselves the Son of God, and put Him to an open shame.

7 For the earth which drinks in the rain that often comes upon it, and bears herbs useful for those by whom it is cultivated, receives blessing from God;

8 but if it bears thorns and briars, it is rejected and near to being cursed, whose end is to be burned.

A Better Estimate

9 But, beloved, we are confident of better things concerning you, the things that accompany salvation, though we speak in this manner.

10 For God is not unjust to forget your work and labor of love which you have shown toward His name, in that you have served the believers and do serve.

11 And we desire that each one of you show the same diligence to the full assurance of hope until the end,

12 that you do not become sluggish, but followers of those who through faith and patience inherit the promises.

God's Infallible Purpose in the Messiah

13 For when God made a promise to Abraham, because He could swear by no one greater, He swore by Himself,

14 saying, *"Surely blessing I will bless you, and multiplying I will multiply you."* [23]

15 And so, after he had patiently endured, he obtained the promise.

16 For men indeed swear by the greater, and an oath for confirmation is for them an end of all strife.

17 Therefore God, determining to show more abundantly to the heirs of promise the immutability of His counsel, confirmed it by an oath,

18 that by two immutable things, in which it was impossible for God to lie, we might have strong consolation, who have fled for refuge to lay hold of the hope set before us.

19 This hope we have as an anchor of the soul, both sure and steadfast, and which enters into that behind the curtain,

20 where the forerunner has entered for us, even Yeshua, having become High Priest forever according to the order of Melchizedek.[24]

The King of Righteousness

7 For this Melchizedek, king of Salem, priest of the Most High God, who met Abraham returning from the slaughter of the kings and blessed him,

23 Genesis 22:16, 17
24 One significant group of first-century Jews, the Essenes, expected a Melchizedek-type figure as part of the Messianic age.

2 to whom also Abraham gave a tenth part of all, first being translated king of righteousness, and then also king of Salem, that is, king of peace,[25]

3 without father, without mother, without genealogy, having neither beginning of days nor end of life, but made like the Son of God, remains a priest continually.

4 Now consider how great this man was, to whom even the patriarch Abraham gave a tenth of the spoils.

5 And indeed those who are of the sons of Levi, who receive the priesthood, have a commandment to receive tithes from the people according to the Torah, that is, from their brethren, though they have come from the body of Abraham;

6 but he whose genealogy is not derived from them received tithes from Abraham and blessed him who had the promises.

7 And, beyond all contradiction, the lesser is blessed by the better.

8 And here mortal men receive tithes, but there he receives them, of whom it is witnessed that he lives.

9 And even Levi, who receives tithes, paid tithes through Abraham, so to speak,

10 for he was still in the body of his father when Melchizedek met him.

Need for a New Priesthood

11 Therefore, if perfection were through the Levitical priesthood (for under it the people received the Torah), what further need was there that another priest should rise according to the order of Melchizedek, and not be called according to the order of Aaron?

12 For the priesthood being changed, of necessity there is also a change of the Torah.

13 For He of whom these things are spoken belongs to another tribe, from which no man has officiated at the altar.

14 For it is evident that our Lord arose out of Judah,[26] of which tribe Moses spoke nothing concerning priesthood.

15 And it is yet far more evident if, in the likeness of Melchizedek, there arises another priest

16 who has come, not according to the law of a fleshly commandment, but according to the power of an endless life.

17 For He testifies:

"You are a priest forever
According to the order of
Melchizedek." [27]

18 For on the one hand there is an annulling of the former commandment because of its weakness and unprofitableness,

19 for the Torah made nothing perfect; on the other hand, there is the bringing in of a better hope, through which we draw near to God.

Greatness of the New Priest

20 And inasmuch as He was not made priest without an oath

21 (for they have become priests without an oath, but He with an oath by Him who said to Him:

---

25 Genesis 14:18-20

26 Genesis 49:10 (cf. Matthew 1:1)

27 Psalm 110:4

"The LORD has sworn
And will not change His
    mind,
'You are a priest forever
According to the order of
    Melchizedek' "),[28]

22 by so much Yeshua has become a surety of a better covenant.

23 And there were many priests, because they were prevented by death from continuing.

24 But He, because He continues forever, has an unchangeable priesthood.

25 Therefore He is also able to save to the uttermost those who come to God by Him, seeing He ever lives to make intercession for them.

26 For such a High Priest was fitting for us, who is holy, harmless, undefiled, separate from sinners, and has become higher than the heavens;

27 who does not need daily, as those high priests, to offer up sacrifices, first for His own sins and then for the people's, for this He did once for all when He offered up Himself.

28 For the Torah appoints as high priests men who have weakness, but the word of the oath, which came after the Torah, appoints the Son who has been perfected forever.

The New Priestly Service

8 Now this is the main point of the things we are saying: We have such a High Priest, who is seated at the right hand of the throne of the Majesty in the heavens,

2 a Minister of the sanctuary and of the true tabernacle which the Lord set up, and not man.

3 For every high priest is appointed to offer both gifts and sacrifices. Therefore it is necessary that this One also have something to offer.

4 For if He were on earth, He would not be a priest, seeing that there are priests who offer the gifts according to the Torah;

5 who serve the copy and shadow of the heavenly things, as Moses was admonished by God when he was about to make the tabernacle. For He said, "See that you make all things according to the pattern shown to you on the mountain." [29]

6 But now He has obtained a more excellent ministry, inasmuch as He is also Mediator of a better covenant, which was established on better promises.

A New Covenant

7 For if that first covenant had been faultless, then no place would have been sought for a second.

8 Because finding fault with them, He says: "Behold, the days come, says the LORD, when I will make a new covenant with the house of Israel and with the house of Judah;

9 "not according to the covenant that I made with their fathers in the day when I took them by the hand to lead them out of the land of Egypt; because they did not continue in My covenant, and I disregarded them, says the LORD.

28 Psalm 110:4

29 Exodus 25:40

10 *"For this is the covenant that I will make with the house of Israel after those days, says the* Lord: *I will put My laws into their mind and write them on their hearts; I will be their God, and they shall be My people.*

11 *"None of them shall teach his neighbor, and none his brother, saying, 'Know the* Lord,*' for all shall know Me, from the least to the greatest.*

12 *"For I will be merciful to their unrighteousness, and their sins and their lawless deeds I will remember no more."* [30]

13 In that He says, *"A new covenant,"* He has made the first obsolete. Now what is obsolete and growing old is ready to vanish away.

The Earthly Sanctuary

9 Then indeed, even the first covenant had ordinances of divine service and the earthly sanctuary.

2 For a tabernacle was made: the first part, in which was the lampstand, the table, and the showbread, which is called the sanctuary; [31]

3 and behind the second curtain, the part of the tabernacle which is called the Holiest of All,

4 which had the golden altar of incense and the ark of the covenant overlaid on all sides with gold, in which were the golden pot that had the manna, Aaron's rod that budded, and the tablets of the covenant;

5 and above it were the cheru-bim of glory overshadowing the mercy seat. Of these things we cannot now speak in detail.

Limitations of the Earthly Service

6 Now when these things had been thus prepared, the priests always went into the first part of the tabernacle, performing the service of God.

7 But into the second part the high priest went alone once a year, not without blood, which he offered for himself and for the people's sins committed in ignorance; [32]

8 the Holy Spirit indicating this, that the way into the Holiest of All was not yet made manifest while the first tabernacle was still standing.

9 It was a figure for that time then present, in which both gifts and sacrifices were offered that could not make him who performed the service perfect in regard to the conscience—

10 concerned only with foods and drinks, various washings, and fleshly ordinances imposed until the time of reformation.

The Heavenly Sanctuary

11 But the Messiah having come as a High Priest of the good things to come, by the greater and more perfect tabernacle not made with hands, that is, not of this creation,

12 nor by the blood of goats and calves, but by His own blood He entered the Most Holy Place once for all, having obtained eternal redemption.

13 For if the blood of bulls and goats and the ashes of a heifer,

30 Jeremiah 31:31-34 (31:30-33 in some versions) *31* Exodus 25:8

32 Leviticus 16:14-17, 34

sprinkling the unclean, sanctifies to the purifying of the flesh,[33]

14 how much more shall the blood of the Messiah, who through the eternal Spirit offered Himself without spot to God, purge your conscience from dead works to serve the living God?

15 And for this reason He is the Mediator of the new covenant, by means of death, for the redemption of the transgressions under the first covenant, that those who are called may receive the promise of the eternal inheritance.

The Mediator's Death Necessary

16 For where there is a testament, there must also of necessity be the death of the testator.

17 For a testament is in force after men are dead, since it has no power at all while the testator lives.

18 Therefore not even the first covenant was dedicated without blood.[34]

19 For when Moses had spoken every precept to all the people according to the Torah, he took the blood of calves and goats, with water, scarlet wool, and hyssop, and sprinkled both the book itself and all the people,

20 saying, *"This is the blood of the covenant which God has commanded you."*[35]

21 And likewise he sprinkled with blood both the tabernacle and all the vessels of the service.

22 And almost all things according to the Torah are purged with blood, and without shedding of blood there is no remission.

Greatness of Messiah's Sacrifice

23 Therefore it was necessary that the copies of the things in the heavens should be purified with these, but the heavenly things themselves with better sacrifices than these.

24 For the Messiah has not entered the holy places made with hands, which are figures of the true, but into heaven itself, now to appear in the presence of God for us;

25 nor yet that He should offer Himself often, as the high priest enters into the holy place every year with blood of another,

26 for then He would have had to suffer often since the foundation of the world; but now, once at the end of the ages, He has appeared to put away sin by the sacrifice of Himself.

27 And as it is appointed for men to die once, but after this the judgment,

28 so the Messiah was offered once to bear the sins of many.[36] And to those who eagerly wait for Him He will appear a second time, apart from sin, for salvation.

Animal Sacrifices Insufficient

10 For the Torah, having a shadow of the good things to come, and not the very image of the things, can never with those sacrifices, which they offered continually year by year, make those who approach perfect.

2 For then would they not have ceased to be offered, because the

---

33 Numbers 19:1–22

34 Exodus 24:3–8   35 Exodus 24:8

36 Isaiah 53:12

worshipers, once purged, would have had no more consciousness of sins?

3 But in those sacrifices there is a remembrance of sins every year.[37]

4 For it is not possible that the blood of bulls and goats could take away sins.

Messiah's Death Fulfills God's Will

5 Therefore, when He came into the world, He said:

"Sacrifice and offering You
　　did not desire,
But a body You have pre-
　　pared for Me.

6 In burnt offerings and sacri-
　　fices for sin
You have had no pleasure.

7 Then I said, 'Behold, I have
　　come—
In the volume of the book it
　　is written of Me—
To do Your will, O
　　God.' "[38]

8 Previously saying, "Sacrifice and offering, burnt offerings, and offerings for sin You did not desire, nor had pleasure in them" (which are offered according to the Torah),

9 then He said, "Behold, I have come to do Your will, O God." He takes away the first that He may establish the second.

10 By that will we have been sanctified through the offering of the body of Yeshua ha Mashiach once for all.

Messiah's Death Perfects the Sanctified

11 And every priest stands min-istering daily and offering repeat-edly the same sacrifices, which can never take away sins.

12 But this Man, after He had offered one sacrifice for sins for-ever, sat down at the right hand of God,

13 from that time waiting till His enemies are made His foot-stool.[39]

14 For by one offering He has perfected forever those who are being sanctified.

15 And the Holy Spirit also wit-nesses to us; for after He had said before:

16 *"This is the covenant that I will make with them after those days, says the* LORD: *I will put My laws into their hearts, and in their minds I will write them,"* [40]

17 then He adds: *"And their sins and their lawless deeds I will remember no more."* [41]

18 Now where there is remission of these, there is no longer an of-fering for sin.

Hold Fast Your Confession

19 Therefore, brethren, having boldness to enter the Holiest by the blood of Yeshua,

20 by a new and living way which He has consecrated for us, through the curtain, that is, His flesh,

21 and having a High Priest over the house of God,

22 let us draw near with a true heart in full assurance of faith, having our hearts sprinkled from an evil conscience and our bodies washed with pure water.

---

37 Leviticus 16:34
38 Psalm 40:6-8 (40:7-9 in some versions)
39 Psalm 110:1
40 Jeremiah 31:33 (31:32 in some versions)
41 Jeremiah 31:34 (31:33 in some versions)

23 Let us hold fast the confession of our hope without wavering, for He who promised is faithful.

24 And let us consider one another so as to stir up love and good works,

25 not forsaking the assembling of ourselves together, as is the manner of some, but exhorting one another, and so much the more as you see the Day[42] approaching.

The Just Live by Faith

26 For if we sin willfully after we have received the knowledge of the truth, there no longer remains a sacrifice for sins,[43]

27 but a certain fearful expectation of judgment, and fiery indignation which will devour the adversaries.

28 He who despised Moses' Torah died without mercy on the testimony of two or three witnesses.[44]

29 Of how much worse punishment, do you suppose, will he be thought worthy who has trampled the Son of God underfoot, counted the blood of the covenant by which he was sanctified a common thing, and insulted the Spirit of grace?

30 For we know Him who has said, "Vengeance is Mine; I will repay,"[45] says the Lord." And again, "The LORD will judge His people."[46]

31 It is a fearful thing to fall into the hands of the living God!

32 But recall the former days in which, after you were illuminated, you endured a great struggle with sufferings:

33 partly while you were made a spectacle both by reproaches and tribulations, and partly while you became companions of those who were so treated;

34 for you had compassion on me in my chains, and joyfully accepted the plundering of your goods, knowing in yourselves that you have a better and an enduring possession in heaven.

35 Therefore do not cast away your confidence, which has great reward.

36 For you have need of endurance, so that after you have done the will of God, you may receive the promise:

37 "For yet a little while,
    And He who is coming will
        come and will not tarry.

38 Now the just shall live by
        faith;
    But if he draws back,
    My soul has no pleasure in
        him."[47]

39 But we are not of those who draw back to perdition, but of those who believe to the saving of the soul.

By Faith We Understand

11 Now faith is the substance of things hoped for, the evidence of things not seen.

2 For by it the elders obtained a good testimony.

3 By faith we understand that the worlds were framed by the word of God, so that the things

---

42 Cf. Malachi 4:4–5 (3:23, 24 in some versions)

43 Numbers 15:30

44 Deuteronomy 17:2–6

45 Deuteronomy 32:35

46 Deuteronomy 32:36

47 Habakkuk 2:3, 4

which are seen were not made of things which are visible.

Faith at the Dawn of History

4 By faith Abel offered to God a more excellent sacrifice than Cain, by which he obtained witness that he was righteous, God testifying to his gifts; and by it he, being dead, still speaks.[48]

5 By faith Enoch was translated so that he did not see death, *"and was not found because God had translated him";*[49] for before his translation he had this testimony, that he pleased God.[50]

6 But without faith it is impossible to please Him, for he who comes to God must believe that He is, and that He is a rewarder of those who diligently seek Him.

7 By faith Noah, being warned by God of things not yet seen, moved with fear, prepared an ark for the saving of his household, by which he condemned the world and became heir of the righteousness which is according to faith.[51]

Faithful Abraham

8 By faith Abraham obeyed when he was called to go out into the place which he would afterward receive as an inheritance. And he went out, not knowing where he was going.[52]

9 By faith he sojourned in the land of promise as in a foreign country, dwelling in tents with Isaac and Jacob, the heirs with him of the same promise;

10 for he waited for the city which has foundations, whose builder and maker is God.

11 By faith Sarah herself also received strength to conceive seed, and she bore a child when she was past the age, because she judged Him faithful who had promised.[53]

12 Therefore from one man, and him as good as dead, were born as many as the stars of the sky in multitude, and innumerable as the sand which is by the seashore.

The Heavenly Hope

13 These all died in faith, not having received the promises, but having seen them afar off were assured of them, embraced them, and confessed that they were strangers and pilgrims on the earth.

14 For those who say such things declare plainly that they seek a country.

15 And truly if they had called to mind that country from which they came out, they would have had opportunity to return.

16 But now they desire a better, that is, a heavenly country. Therefore God is not ashamed to be called their God, for He has prepared a city for them.

The Faith of the Patriarchs

17 By faith Abraham, when he was tested, offered up Isaac, and he who had received the promises offered up his only begotten son,[54]

48 Genesis 4:4, 5   49 Genesis 5:24
50 Genesis 5:22–24
51 Genesis 6:13; 7:1
52 Genesis 12:1–4

53 Genesis 18:10, 11; 21:1, 2
54 Genesis 22:1–18

18 of whom it was said, *"In Isaac your seed shall be called,"*[55]

19 accounting that God was able to raise him up, even from the dead, from which he also received him in a figurative sense.

20 By faith Isaac blessed Jacob and Esau concerning things to come.[56]

21 By faith Jacob, when he was dying, blessed each of the sons of Joseph, and worshiped, leaning on the top of his staff.[57]

22 By faith Joseph, when he was dying, made mention of the departure of the children of Israel, and gave instructions concerning his bones.[58]

The Faith of Moses

23 By faith Moses, when he was born, was hidden three months by his parents, because they saw he was a beautiful child; and they were not afraid of the king's command.

24 By faith Moses, when he had come of age, refused to be called the son of Pharaoh's daughter,

25 choosing rather to suffer affliction with the people of God than to enjoy the passing pleasures of sin,

26 esteeming the reproach of the Messiah greater riches than the treasures in Egypt; for he looked to the reward.

27 By faith he forsook Egypt, not fearing the wrath of the king; for he endured as seeing Him who is invisible.[59]

28 By faith he kept the Passover and the sprinkling of blood, lest he who destroyed the firstborn should touch them.[60]

29 By faith they passed through the Red Sea as by dry land, whereas the Egyptians, attempting to do so, were drowned.[61]

By Faith They Overcame

30 By faith the walls of Jericho fell down after they were encircled for seven days.[62]

31 By faith the harlot Rahab did not perish with those who did not believe, when she had received the spies with peace.[63]

32 And what more shall I say? For the time would fail me to tell of Gideon and Barak and Samson and Jephthah, also of David and Samuel and the prophets:

33 who through faith subdued kingdoms, worked righteousness, obtained promises, stopped the mouths of lions,

34 quenched the violence of fire, escaped the edge of the sword, out of weakness were made strong, became valiant in battle, turned to flight the armies of the aliens.

35 Women received their dead raised to life again. And others were tortured, not accepting deliverance, that they might obtain a better resurrection.

36 And others had trial of mockings and scourgings, yes, and of chains and imprisonment.

37 They were stoned, they were sawn in two, were tempted, were

---

55 Genesis 21:12   56 Genesis 27:26-40
57 Genesis 28:9-20
58 Genesis 50:24, 25   59 Exodus 2:2-15

60 Exodus 12:1-28   61 Exodus 14:13-31
62 Joshua 6:15-20   63 Joshua 6:25

slain with the sword. They wandered about in sheepskins and goatskins, being destitute, afflicted, tormented—

38 of whom the world was not worthy. They wandered in deserts and mountains, in dens and caves of the earth.

39 And all these, having obtained a good testimony through faith, did not receive the promise,

40 God having provided something better for us, that they should not be made perfect apart from us.

The Race of Faith

12 Therefore, seeing we also are surrounded by so great a cloud of witnesses, let us lay aside every weight, and the sin which so easily ensnares us, and let us run with endurance the race that is set before us,

2 looking to Yeshua, the author and finisher of our faith, who for the joy that was set before Him endured the cross, despising the shame, and has sat down at the right hand of the throne of God.

The Discipline of God

3 For consider Him who endured such hostility from sinners against Himself, lest you become weary and discouraged in your minds.

4 You have not yet resisted to blood, striving against sin.

5 And you have forgotten the exhortation which speaks to you as to sons:

"My son, do not despise the chastening of the LORD,
Nor be discouraged when you are rebuked by Him.

6 For whom the LORD loves He chastens,
And scourges every son whom He receives." [64]

7 If you endure chastening, God deals with you as with sons; for what son is he whom a father does not chasten?

8 But if you are without chastening, of which all are partakers, then you are illegitimate and not sons.

9 Furthermore, we have had human fathers who corrected us, and we paid them respect. Shall we not much rather be in subjection to the Father of spirits and live?

10 For they indeed for a few days chastened us as they deemed best, but He for our profit, that we may be partakers of His holiness.

11 Now no chastening seems to be joyous for the present, but grievous; nevertheless, afterward it yields the peaceable fruit of righteousness to those who have been trained by it.

Renew Your Spiritual Vitality

12 Therefore lift up the hands which hang down, and the feeble knees,[65]

13 and make straight paths for your feet, so that what is lame may not be turned from the way, but rather be healed.

14 Pursue peace with all men, and holiness, without which no one will see the Lord:

15 looking diligently lest anyone fall short of the grace of God; lest any root of bitterness springing up

64 Proverbs 3:11, 12
65 Isaiah 35:3

trouble you, and by this many be defiled;

16 lest there be any fornicator or profane person like Esau, who for one morsel of food sold his birthright.[66]

17 For you know that afterward, when he wanted to inherit the blessing, he was rejected, for he found no place for repentance, though he sought it diligently with tears.[67]

The Glorious Company

18 For you have not come to the mountain that may be touched and that burned with fire, and to blackness and darkness and tempest,

19 and the sound of a shofar and the voice of words, so that those who heard it begged that the word should not be spoken to them anymore.

20 (For they could not endure what was commanded: *"And if so much as a beast touches the mountain, it shall be stoned or thrust through with a javelin."* [68]

21 And so terrifying was the sight that Moses said, *"I am exceedingly afraid and trembling."* [69])

22 But you have come to Mount Zion and to the city of the living God, the heavenly Jerusalem, to an innumerable company of angels,

23 to the general assembly and congregation of the firstborn who are registered in heaven, to God

the Judge of all, to the spirits of just men made perfect,

24 to Yeshua the Mediator of the new covenant, and to the blood of sprinkling that speaks better things than that of Abel.

Hear the Heavenly Voice

25 See that you do not refuse Him who speaks. For if they did not escape who refused Him who spoke on earth, much more shall we not escape if we turn away from Him who speaks from heaven,

26 whose voice then shook the earth; but now He has promised, saying, *"Yet once more I shake not only the earth, but also heaven."* [70]

27 And this word, *"Yet once more,"* indicates the removal of those things that are being shaken, as of things that are made, that the things which cannot be shaken may remain.

28 Therefore, since we are receiving a kingdom which cannot be shaken, let us have grace, by which we may serve God acceptably with reverence and godly fear.

29 For our God is a consuming fire.

Concluding Moral Directions

13 Let brotherly love continue.

2 Do not forget to entertain strangers, for by this some have unwittingly entertained angels.[71]

3 Remember the prisoners as if chained with them, and those who are mistreated, since you yourselves are also in the body.

---

66 Genesis 25:29-34   *67* Genesis 27:34
68 Exodus 19:12-19; 20:18, 19
69 Deuteronomy 9:19

70 Haggai 2:6, 7
71 Genesis 18:1f.; 19:1f.

4 Marriage is honorable among all, and the bed undefiled; but fornicators and adulterers God will judge.

5 Let your conduct be without covetousness, and be content with such things as you have. For He Himself has said, *"I will never leave you nor forsake you."* [72]

6 So that we may boldly say:
"The LORD is my helper,
And I will not fear.
What shall man do to me?" [73]

Concluding Directions

7 Remember those who have the rule over you, who have spoken the word of God to you, whose faith follow, considering the outcome of their conduct.

8 Yeshua ha Mashiach is the same yesterday, today, and forever.

9 Do not be carried about with various and strange doctrines. For it is a good thing that the heart be established by grace, not with foods which have not profited those who have been occupied with them.

10 We have an altar from which those who serve the tabernacle have no right to eat.

11 For the bodies of those beasts whose blood is brought into the sanctuary by the high priest for sin are burned outside the camp. [74]

12 Therefore Yeshua also, that He might sanctify the people with His own blood, suffered outside the gate.

13 Therefore let us go forth to Him, outside the camp, [75] bearing His reproach.

14 For here we have no continuing city, but we seek the one to come.

15 Therefore by Him let us continually offer the sacrifice of praise to God, that is, the fruit of our lips giving thanks to His name.

16 But do not forget to do good and to share, for with such sacrifices God is well pleased.

17 Obey those who have the rule over you, and submit yourselves, for they watch out for your souls, as those who must give account. Let them do it with joy and not with grief, for that would be unprofitable for you.

Prayer Requested

18 Pray for us; for we are confident that we have a good conscience, in all things desiring to live honorably.

19 But I urge you much more to do this, that I may be restored to you the sooner.

Blessing, Final Exhortation, Farewell

20 Now may the God of peace, who brought up our Lord Yeshua from the dead, that great Shepherd of the sheep, [76] through the blood of the everlasting covenant,

21 make you complete in every good work to do His will, working in you that which is well pleasing in His sight, through Yeshua ha Mashiach, to whom be glory forever and ever. Amen.

---

72 Deuteronomy 31:6, 8; Joshua 1:5
73 Psalm 118:6
74 Leviticus 16:27

75 Exodus 33:7
76 Exodus 37:24–28; Isaiah 40:11; Micah 5:2–4 (5:1–3 in some versions)

22 And I appeal to you, brethren, bear with the word of exhortation, for I have written to you in few words.

23 Know that our brother Timothy has been set free, with whom I shall see you if he comes shortly.

24 Greet all those who rule over you, and all the believers. Those from Italy greet you.

25 Grace be with you all. Amen.

The Letter Of
JAMES

Greeting to the Twelve Tribes

JAMES, a servant of God and of the Lord Yeshua ha Mashiach,

To the twelve tribes which are scattered abroad:

Greetings.

Profiting from Trials

2 My brethren, count it all joy when you fall into various trials,

3 knowing that the testing of your faith produces patience.

4 But let patience have its perfect work, that you may be perfect and complete, lacking nothing.

5 If any of you lacks wisdom, let him ask of God, who gives to all liberally and without reproach, and it will be given to him.

6 But let him ask in faith, with no doubting, for he who doubts is like a wave of the sea driven and tossed by the wind.

7 For let not that man suppose that he will receive anything from the Lord;

8 he is a double-minded man, unstable in all his ways.

The Perspective of Rich and Poor

9 Let the lowly brother glory in his exaltation,

10 but the rich in his humiliation, because as a flower of the field he will pass away.

11 For no sooner has the sun risen with a burning heat than it withers the grass; its flower falls, and its beautiful appearance perishes. So the rich man will also fade away in his pursuits.

Loving God Under Trials

12 Blessed is the man who endures temptation; for when he has been proved, he will receive the crown of life which the Lord has promised to those who love Him.

13 Let no one say when he is tempted, "I am tempted by God"; for God cannot be tempted by evil, nor does He Himself tempt anyone.

14 But each one is tempted when he is drawn away by his own desires and enticed.

15 Then, when desire has conceived, it gives birth to sin; and sin, when it is full-grown, brings forth death.

16 Do not be deceived, my beloved brethren.

17 Every good gift and every perfect gift is from above, and comes down from the Father of lights, with whom there is no variation or shadow of turning.

18 Of His own will He brought us forth by the word of truth, that we might be a kind of firstfruits of His creatures.

Qualities Needed in Trials

19 Therefore, my beloved brethren, let every man be swift to hear, slow to speak, slow to wrath;

20 for the wrath of man does not produce the righteousness of God.

Doers—Not Hearers

21 Therefore lay aside all filthiness and overflow of wickedness, and receive with meekness the implanted word, which is able to save your souls.

22 But be doers of the word, and not hearers only, deceiving yourselves.

23 For if anyone is a hearer of the word and not a doer, he is like a man observing his natural face in a mirror;

24 for he observes himself, goes away, and immediately forgets what kind of man he was.

25 But he who looks into the perfect Torah of liberty and continues in it, and is not a forgetful hearer but a doer of the work, this one will be blessed in what he does.

26 If anyone among you thinks he is religious, and does not bridle his tongue but deceives his own heart, this one's religion is useless.

27 Pure and undefiled religion before God and the Father is this: to visit orphans and widows in their trouble, and to keep oneself unspotted from the world.

Beware of Personal Favoritism

2 My brethren, do not hold the faith of our Lord Yeshua ha Mashiach, the Lord of glory, with partiality.

2 For if there should come into your synagogue a man with gold rings, in fine apparel, and there should also come in a poor man in filthy clothes,

3 and you pay attention to the one wearing the fine clothes and say to him, "You sit here in a good place," and say to the poor man, "You stand there," or, "Sit here at my footstool,"

4 have you not shown partiality among yourselves, and become judges with evil thoughts?

5 Listen, my beloved brethren: Has God not chosen the poor of this world to be rich in faith and heirs of the kingdom which He has promised to those who love Him?

6 But you have dishonored the poor man. Do not the rich oppress you and drag you into the courts?

7 Do they not blaspheme that noble name by which you are called?

8 If you really fulfill the royal Torah according to the Scripture, *"You shall love your neighbor as yourself,"[1]* you do well;

9 but if you show partiality, you commit sin, and are convicted by the Torah as transgressors.

10 For whoever shall keep the whole Torah, and yet stumble in one point, he is guilty of all.

11 For He who said, *"Do not commit adultery,"[2]* also said, *"Do not murder."[3]* Now if you do not commit adultery, but you do murder, you have become a transgressor of the Torah.

12 So speak and so do as those who will be judged by the Torah of liberty.

1 Leviticus 19:18

2 Exodus 20:14; Deuteronomy 5:18 (5:17 in some versions)

3 Exodus 20:13; Deuteronomy 5:17

13 For judgment is without mercy to the one who has shown no mercy. Mercy triumphs over judgment.

Faith Without Works Is Dead

14 What does it profit, my brethren, if someone says he has faith but does not have works? That faith cannot save him, can it?

15 If a brother or sister is naked and destitute of daily food,

16 and one of you says to them, "Depart in peace, be warmed and filled," but you do not give them the things which are needed for the body, what does it profit?

17 Thus also faith by itself, if it does not have works, is dead.

18 But someone will say, "You have faith, and I have works." Show me your faith without your works, and I will show you my faith by my works.

19 You believe that there is one God. You do well. The demons also believe—and tremble!

20 But do you want to know, O foolish man, that faith without works is dead?

21 Was not Abraham our father justified by works when he offered Isaac his son on the altar?[4]

22 Do you see that faith was working together with his works, and by works faith was made perfect?

23 And the Scripture was fulfilled which says, *"Abraham believed God, and it was imputed to him for righteousness."*[5] And he was called the friend of God.[6]

24 You see then that by works a man is justified, and not by faith only.

25 Likewise, was not Rahab the harlot also justified by works when she received the messengers and sent them out another way?[7]

26 For as the body without the spirit is dead, so faith without works is dead also.

The Untamable Tongue

3 My brethren, let not many of you become teachers, knowing that we shall receive a stricter judgment.

2 For we all stumble in many things. If anyone does not stumble in word, he is a perfect man, able also to bridle the whole body.

3 Indeed, we put bits in horses' mouths that they may obey us, and we turn their whole body.

4 Look also at ships: Although they are so large and are driven by fierce winds, they are turned by a very small rudder wherever the pilot desires.

5 Even so the tongue is a little member and boasts great things. See how great a forest a little fire kindles!

6 And the tongue is a fire, a world of iniquity. The tongue is so set among our members that it defiles the whole body, and sets on fire the course of nature; and it is set on fire by hell.

7 For every kind of beast and bird, of reptile and creature of the sea, is tamed and has been tamed by mankind.

8 But no man can tame the tongue. It is an unruly evil, full of deadly poison.

4 Genesis 22:1-18   5 Genesis 15:6
6 Isaiah 41:8

7 Joshua 6:25

9 With it we bless our God and Father, and with it we curse men, who have been made in the similitude of God.

10 Out of the same mouth proceed blessing and cursing. My brethren, these things ought not to be so.

11 Does a spring send forth fresh water and bitter from the same opening?

12 Can a fig tree, my brethren, bear olives, or a grapevine bear figs? Thus no spring can yield both salt water and fresh.

Heavenly Versus Demonic Wisdom

13 Who is wise and understanding among you? Let him show by good conduct that his works are done in the meekness of wisdom.

14 But if you have bitter envy and self-seeking in your hearts, do not boast and lie against the truth.

15 This wisdom does not descend from above, but is earthly, sensual, demonic.

16 For where envy and self-seeking exist, confusion and every evil thing will be there.

17 But the wisdom that is from above is first pure, then peaceable, gentle, willing to yield, full of mercy and good fruits, without partiality, and without hypocrisy.

18 And the fruit of righteousness is sown in peace by those who make peace.

Pride Promotes Strife

4 Where do wars and fights come from among you? Do they not come from your desires for pleasure that war in your members?

2 You lust and do not have. You murder and covet and cannot obtain. You fight and war. Yet you do not have because you do not ask.

3 You ask and do not receive, because you ask amiss, that you may spend it on your pleasures.

4 Adulterers and adulteresses! Do you not know that friendship with the world is enmity with God? Whoever therefore wants to be a friend of the world makes himself an enemy of God.

5 Or do you think that the Scripture says in vain, "The Spirit who dwells in us yearns jealously"?

6 But He gives more grace. Therefore He says:

> "God resists the proud,
> But gives grace to the humble." [8]

Humility Cures Worldliness

7 Therefore submit to God. Resist the devil and he will flee from you.

8 Draw near to God and He will draw near to you. Cleanse your hands, you sinners; and purify your hearts, you double-minded.

9 Lament and mourn and weep! Let your laughter be turned to mourning and your joy to gloom.

10 Humble yourselves in the sight of the Lord, and He will lift you up.

Do Not Judge a Brother

11 Do not speak evil of one another, brethren. He who speaks evil of a brother and judges his brother, speaks evil of the Torah and judges the Torah. But if you

8 Proverbs 3:34

judge the Torah, you are not a doer of the Torah but a judge.

12 There is one Lawgiver, who is able to save and to destroy. Who are you to judge another?

Do Not Boast About Tomorrow

13 Come now, you who say, "Today or tomorrow we will go to such and such a city, spend a year there, buy and sell, and make a profit";

14 whereas you do not know what will happen tomorrow. For what is your life? It is even a vapor that appears for a little time and then vanishes away.

15 Instead you ought to say, "If the Lord wills, we shall live and do this or that."

16 But now you boast in your arrogance. All such boasting is evil.

17 Therefore, to him who knows to do good and does not do it, to him it is sin.

Rich Oppressors Will Be Judged

5 Come now, you rich, weep and howl for your miseries that are coming upon you!

2 Your riches are corrupted, and your garments are motheaten.

3 Your gold and silver are corroded, and their corrosion will be a witness against you and will eat your flesh like fire. You have heaped up treasure in the last days.

4 Indeed, the wages of the laborers who have mowed your fields, which you kept back by fraud, cry out; and the cries of the reapers have reached the ears of the Lord of Hosts.

5 You have lived on the earth in pleasure and luxury; you have fattened your hearts as in a day of slaughter.

6 You have condemned, you have murdered the just; he does not resist you.

Be Patient and Persevering

7 Therefore be patient, brethren, until the coming of the Lord. See how the farmer waits for the precious fruit of the earth, waiting patiently for it until it receives the early and latter rain.

8 You also be patient. Establish your hearts, for the coming of the Lord is at hand.

9 Do not grumble against one another, brethren, lest you be condemned. Behold, the Judge is standing at the door![9]

10 My brethren, take the prophets, who have spoken in the name of the Lord, as an example of suffering and patience.

11 Indeed, we count them blessed who endure. You have heard of the perseverance of Job and seen the purpose of the Lord, that the Lord is very compassionate and merciful.

12 But above all, my brethren, do not swear, neither by heaven nor by earth nor with any other oath. But let your "Yes" be "Yes," and your "No," "No," lest you fall into judgment.

Meeting Specific Needs

13 Is anyone among you suffering? Let him pray. Is anyone cheerful? Let him sing psalms.

14 Is anyone among you sick? Let him call for the elders of the

9 Isaiah 46:13; Jeremiah 23:5, 6; Isaiah 9:6, 7 (9:5, 6 in some versions); cf. John 5:21-23

congregation, and let them pray over him, anointing him with oil in the name of the Lord.

15 And the prayer of faith will save the sick, and the Lord will raise him up. And if he has committed sins, he will be forgiven.

16 Confess your trespasses to one another, and pray for one another, that you may be healed. The effective, fervent prayer of a righteous man avails much.

17 Elijah was a man with a nature like ours, and he prayed earnestly that it would not rain; and it did not rain on the land for three years and six months.

18 And he prayed again, and the heaven gave rain, and the earth produced its fruit.[10]

Bring Back the Erring One

19 Brethren, if anyone among you should wander from the truth, and someone turns him back,

20 let him know that he who turns a sinner from the error of his way will save a soul from death and cover a multitude of sins.

10 1 Kings 18:42-46

The First Letter Of
PETER

Greetings

PETER, an apostle [1] of Yeshua ha Mashiach,

To the pilgrims scattered throughout Pontus, Galatia, Cappadocia, Asia, and Bithynia,

2 elect according to the foreknowledge of God the Father, in sanctification of the Spirit, for obedience and sprinkling of the blood of Yeshua ha Mashiach:

Grace to you and peace be multiplied.

A Heavenly Inheritance

3 Blessed be the God and Father of our Lord Yeshua ha Mashiach, who according to His abundant mercy has begotten us again to a living hope by the resurrection of Yeshua ha Mashiach from the dead,

4 to an inheritance incorruptible and undefiled and that does not fade away, reserved in heaven for you,

5 who are kept by the power of God through faith for salvation ready to be revealed in the last time.

6 In this you greatly rejoice, though now for a little while, if need be, you have been grieved by manifold temptations,

7 that the genuineness of your faith, being much more precious than gold that perishes, though it is tested with fire, may be found to praise, honor, and glory at the revelation of Yeshua ha Mashiach,

8 whom having not seen you love. Though now you do not see Him, yet believing, you rejoice with joy unspeakable and full of glory,

9 receiving the end of your faith—the salvation of your souls.

10 Of this salvation the prophets have inquired and searched diligently, who prophesied of the grace that would come to you,

11 searching what, or what manner of time, the Spirit of the Messiah who was in them was indicating when He testified beforehand the sufferings of the Messiah and the glories that would follow. [2]

12 To them it was revealed that not to themselves, but to us, they were ministering the things which now have been reported to you through those who have preached the good news to you by the Holy Spirit sent down from heaven—things which angels desire to look into.

---

1 See note 1, p. 246.

2 Cf. Isaiah 52:13—53:12

Living Before God Our Father

13 Therefore gird up the loins of your mind, be sober, and hope to the end for the grace that is to be brought to you at the revelation of Yeshua ha Mashiach;

14 as obedient children, not conforming yourselves to the former lusts, as in your ignorance;

15 but as He who has called you is holy, you also be holy in all your conduct,

16 because it is written, *"Be holy, for I am holy."* [3]

17 And if you call on the Father, who without partiality judges according to each one's work, conduct yourselves throughout the time of your sojourning here in fear;

18 inasmuch as you know that you were not redeemed with corruptible things, like silver or gold, from your futile conduct received by tradition from your fathers,

19 but with the precious blood of the Messiah, [4] as of a lamb without blemish and without spot. [5]

20 He indeed was foreordained before the foundation of the world, but was manifest in these last times for you

21 who through Him believe in God, who raised Him from the dead and gave Him glory, so that your faith and hope are in God.

The Enduring Word

22 Seeing you have purified your souls in obeying the truth through the Spirit in unfeigned love of the brethren, love one another fervently with a pure heart,

23 having been born again, not of corruptible seed but incorruptible, through the word of God which lives and abides forever,

24 because

"All flesh is as grass,
    And all the glory of man as
        the flower of the grass.
    The grass withers,
    And its flower falls away,
25 But the word of the LORD
    endures forever." [6]

And this is the word which by the good news was preached to you.

2 Therefore, laying aside all malice, all guile, hypocrisy, envy, and all evil speaking,

2 as newborn babes, desire the pure milk of the word, that you may grow thereby,

3 if indeed you have tasted that the Lord is gracious.

The Chosen Stone and His Chosen People

4 Coming to Him as to a living stone, rejected indeed by men, but chosen by God and precious,

5 you also, as living stones, are being built up a spiritual house, a holy priesthood, to offer up spiritual sacrifices acceptable to God through Yeshua ha Mashiach.

6 Therefore it is also contained in the Scripture,

"Behold, I lay in Zion
    A chief cornerstone, elect,
        precious,
    And he who believes on Him
        will by no means be put to
        shame." [7]

7 Therefore, to you who believe, He is precious; but to those who are disobedient,

---

3 Leviticus 11:44, 45; 19:2; 20:7

4 Cf. Isaiah 52:13—53:12

5 Exodus 12:5-7, 13

6 Isaiah 40:6-8   7 Isaiah 28:16

*"The stone which the builders
    rejected
Has become the chief corner-
    stone,"* [8]

8 and

*"A stone of stumbling
And a rock of offense."* [9]

They stumble, being disobedient
to the word, to which they also
were appointed.

9 But you are a chosen generation, a royal priesthood, a holy nation, His own special people, that
you may proclaim the praises of
Him who has called you out of
darkness into His marvelous
light;[10]

10 who once were not a people
but are now the people of God,
who had not obtained mercy but
now have obtained mercy.[11]

Living Before the World

11 Beloved, I beg you as sojourn-
ers and pilgrims, abstain from
fleshly lusts which war against the
soul,

12 having your conduct honorable among the Gentiles, that
when they speak against you as
evildoers, they may, by your good
works which they observe, glorify
God in the day of visitation.

Submission to Government

13 Therefore submit yourselves
to every ordinance of man for the
Lord's sake, whether to the king as
supreme,

14 or to governors, as to those
who are sent by him for the pun-

ishment of evildoers and for the
praise of those who do good.

15 For so is the will of God that
by doing good you may put to silence the ignorance of foolish
men—

16 as free, yet not using your liberty as a cloak for vice, but as servants of God.

17 Honor all people.   Love the
brotherhood. Fear God. Honor
the king.

Submission to Masters

18 Servants, be submissive to
your masters with all fear, not
only to the good and gentle, but
also to the harsh.

19 For this is commendable, if
because of conscience toward God
one endures grief, suffering wrong-
fully.

20 For what credit is it if, when
you are beaten for your faults, you
take it patiently?   But when you
do good and suffer for it, if you
take it patiently, this is commendable before God.

21 For to this you were called,
because the Messiah also suffered
for us, leaving us an example, that
you should follow His steps:

22*"Who committed no sin,
    Nor was guile found in His
        mouth"*;[12]

23 who, when He was reviled,
did not revile in return; when He
suffered, He did not threaten, but
committed Himself to Him who
judges righteously;[13]

24 who Himself bore our sins in
His own body on the tree, that we,
having died to sins, might live for

---

8 Psalm 118:22   9 Isaiah 8:14

10 Exodus 19:5, 6

11 Hosea 1:10; 2:23 (2:1; 2:25 in some
versions)

12 Isaiah 53:9

13 Isaiah 53:7

righteousness—by whose stripes you were healed.[14]

25 For you were like sheep going astray, but have now returned to the Shepherd and Overseer of your souls.[15]

Submission to Husbands

3 Likewise you wives, be submissive to your own husbands, that even if some do not obey the word, they, without a word, may be won by the conduct of their wives,

2 when they observe your chaste conduct accompanied by fear.

3 Do not let your beauty be that outward adorning of arranging the hair, of wearing gold, or of putting on fine apparel;

4 but let it be the hidden person of the heart, with the incorruptible ornament of a gentle and quiet spirit, which is very precious in the sight of God.

5 For in this manner, in former times, the holy women who trusted in God also adorned themselves, being submissive to their own husbands,

6 as Sarah obeyed Abraham, calling him lord, whose daughters you are as long as you do good and are not afraid with any terror.

A Word to Husbands

7 Likewise you husbands, dwell with them with understanding, giving honor to the wife, as to the weaker vessel, and as being heirs together of the grace of life, that your prayers not be hindered.

Called to Blessing

8 Finally, all of you be of one mind, having compassion for one another; love as brothers, be tenderhearted, be courteous;

9 not rendering evil for evil or reviling for reviling, but on the contrary bless, knowing that you were called to this, that you may inherit a blessing.

10 For

*"He who would love life
And see good days,
Let him refrain his tongue
from evil,
And his lips that they speak
no guile;*

11 *Let him turn away from evil
and do good;
Let him seek peace and pursue it.*

12 *For the eyes of the LORD are
on the righteous,
And his ears are open to
their prayers;
But the face of the LORD is
against those who do
evil."* [16]

Suffering for Right and Wrong

13 And who is he who will harm you if you become followers of what is good?

14 But even if you should suffer for righteousness' sake, you are blessed. *"And do not be afraid of their threats, nor be troubled."* [17]

15 But sanctify the Lord God in your hearts, and always be ready to give a defense to everyone who asks you a reason for the hope that is in you, with meekness and fear;

16 having a good conscience, that when they speak evil of you

---

14 Isaiah 53:5
15 Isaiah 53:6

16 Psalm 34:12-16 (34:13-17 in some versions)   *17* Isaiah 8:12

as evildoers, those who revile your good conduct in the Messiah may be ashamed.

17 For it is better, if it is the will of God, that you suffer for doing good than for doing evil.

Of Messiah's Suffering and Ours

18 For the Messiah also has suffered once for sins, the just for the unjust, that He might bring us to God, being put to death in the flesh but made alive by the Spirit,

19 by whom also He went and preached to the spirits in prison,

20 who formerly were disobedient, when once the longsuffering of God waited in the days of Noah, while the ark was being prepared, in which a few, that is, eight souls, were saved through water.

21 There is also an antitype which now saves us, namely immersion (not the removal of the filth of the flesh, but the answer of a good conscience toward God), through the resurrection of Yeshua ha Mashiach,

22 who has gone into heaven and is at the right hand of God, angels and authorities and powers having been made subject to Him.[18]

4 Therefore, since the Messiah has suffered for us in the flesh, arm yourselves likewise with the same mind, for he who has suffered in the flesh has ceased from sin,

2 that he no longer should live the rest of his time in the flesh for the lusts of men, but for the will of God.

3 For it should be sufficient that we did the will of the Gentiles in the former time of our lives—when we walked in licentiousness, lusts, drunkenness, revelry, drinking parties, and abominable idolatries,

4 in which they think it strange that you do not run with them in the same flood of dissipation, speaking evil of you.

5 They will give an account to Him who is ready to judge the living and the dead.

6 For this reason the good news was preached also to those who are dead, that they might be judged according to men in the flesh, but live according to God in the spirit.

Serving for God's Glory

7 But the end of all things is at hand; therefore be serious and watchful in your prayers.

8 And above all things have fervent love among yourselves, for *"love will cover a multitude of sins."* [19]

9 Be hospitable to one another without grumbling.

10 As each one has received a gift, minister it to one another, as good stewards of the manifold grace of God.

11 If anyone speaks, let him speak as the oracles of God. If anyone serves, let him do it as with the ability which God supplies, that in all things God may be glorified through Yeshua ha Mashiach, to whom is the praise and the dominion forever and ever. Amen.

18 Psalm 110:1

19 Proverbs 10:12

Suffering for God's Glory

12 Beloved, do not think it strange concerning the fiery trial which is to try you, as though some strange thing happened to you;

13 but rejoice, insofar as you are partakers of the Messiah's sufferings, that when His glory is revealed, you may also be glad with exceeding joy.

14 If you are reproached for the name of the Messiah, blessed are you, for the Spirit of glory and of God rests on you. On their part He is blasphemed, but on your part He is glorified.

15 But let none of you suffer as a murderer, a thief, an evildoer, or as a busybody in other people's matters.

16 Yet if anyone suffers as a follower of the Messiah, let him not be ashamed, but let him glorify God in this matter.

17 For the time has come for judgment to begin at the house of God. And if it begins with us first, what will be the end of those who do not obey the good news of God?

18 And

*"If the righteous one is
  scarcely saved,
  Where will the ungodly and
  the sinner appear?"* [20]

19 Therefore let those who suffer according to the will of God commit their souls to Him in doing good, as to a faithful Creator.

Shepherd the Flock

5 The elders who are among you I exhort, I who am a fellow elder and a witness of the suf-

ferings of the Messiah, and also a partaker of the glory that will be revealed:

2 Shepherd the flock of God which is among you, serving as overseers, not by constraint but willingly, not for monetary gain but eagerly;

3 nor as being lords over those entrusted to you, but being examples to the flock;

4 and when the Chief Shepherd[21] appears, you will receive the crown of glory that does not fade away.

Submit to God, Resist the Devil

5 Likewise you younger people, submit yourselves to your elders. Yes, all of you be submissive to one another, and be clothed with humility, for

*"God resists the proud,
  But gives grace to the humble."* [22]

6 Therefore humble yourselves under the mighty hand of God, that He may exalt you in due time,

7 casting all your care upon Him, for He cares for you.

8 Be sober, be vigilant; because your adversary the devil walks about like a roaring lion, seeking whom he may devour.

9 Resist him, steadfast in the faith, knowing that the same sufferings are experienced by your brotherhood in the world.

10 But may the God of all grace, who has called us to His eternal glory by Messiah Yeshua, after

20 Proverbs 11:31

21 Ezekiel 37:24–28; Isaiah 40:11; Micah 5:2–4 (5:1–3 in some versions)

22 Proverbs 3:34

you have suffered a while, perfect,
establish, strengthen, and settle
you.

11 To Him be the glory and the
dominion forever and ever.
Amen.

Farewell and Peace

12 By Silvanus, our faithful
brother as I consider him, I have
written to you briefly, exhorting
and testifying that this is the true
grace of God in which you stand.

13 She who is in Babylon, elect
together with you, greets you; and
so does Mark my son.

14 Greet one another with a kiss
of love. Peace be with you all
who are in Messiah Yeshua.
Amen.

The Second Letter Of
PETER

Greeting the Faithful

SIMON PETER, a servant and an apostle[1] of Yeshua ha Mashiach,

To those who have obtained like precious faith with us by the righteousness of our God and Savior Yeshua ha Mashiach:

2 Grace and peace be multiplied to you in the knowledge of God and of Yeshua our Lord,

3 as His divine power has given to us all things that pertain to life and godliness, through the knowledge of Him who has called us by glory and virtue,

4 by which have been given to us exceedingly great and precious promises, that by these you may be partakers of the divine nature, having escaped the corruption that is in the world through lust.

Fruitful Growth in the Faith

5 But also for this very reason, giving all diligence, add to your faith virtue, to virtue knowledge,

6 to knowledge self-control, to self-control perseverance, to perseverance godliness,

7 to godliness brotherly kindness, and to brotherly kindness love.

1 See note 1, p. 246.

8 For if these things are yours and abound, they keep you from being either barren or unfruitful in the knowledge of our Lord Yeshua ha Mashiach.

9 For he who lacks these things is blind, cannot see afar off, and has forgotten that he was purged from his old sins.

10 Therefore, brethren, be even more diligent to make your calling and election sure, for if you do these things you will never stumble;

11 for so an entrance will be supplied to you abundantly into the everlasting kingdom of our Lord and Savior Yeshua ha Mashiach.

Peter's Approaching Death

12 Therefore I will not be negligent to remind you always of these things, though you know them, and are established in the present truth.

13 Yes, I think it is right, as long as I am in this tent, to stir you up by reminding you,

14 knowing that shortly I must put off my tent, just as our Lord Yeshua ha Mashiach has shown me.

15 Moreover I will endeavor that you always may be able to have a reminder of these things after my decease.

The Trustworthy Prophetic Word

16 For we have not followed cunningly devised fables when we made known to you the power and coming of our Lord Yeshua ha Mashiach, but were eyewitnesses of His majesty.

17 For He received from God the Father honor and glory when such a voice came to Him from the Excellent Glory: "This is My beloved Son, in whom I am well pleased."

18 And we heard this voice which came from heaven when we were with Him on the holy mountain.

19 We also have the prophetic word made more sure, which you do well to heed as a light that shines in a dark place, until the day dawns and the morning star rises in your hearts;

20 knowing this first, that no prophecy of Scripture is of any private interpretation;

21 for prophecy never came by the will of man, but holy men of God spoke as they were moved by the Holy Spirit.[2]

Destructive Doctrines

2 But there were also false prophets among the people, even as there will be false teachers among you, who will secretly bring in destructive heresies, even denying the Lord who bought them, and bring on themselves swift destruction.

2 And many will follow their destructive ways, because of whom the way of truth will be blasphemed.

3 And by covetousness they will exploit you with deceptive words, whose judgment for a long time has not been idle, and their destruction does not slumber.

Doom of False Teachers

4 For if God did not spare the angels who sinned, but cast them down to hell and delivered them into chains of darkness, to be reserved for judgment;

5 and did not spare the ancient world, but saved Noah, one of eight people, a preacher of righteousness, bringing in the flood on the world of the ungodly;[3]

6 and turning the cities of Sodom and Gomorrah into ashes, condemned them to destruction, making them an example to those who afterward would live ungodly;

7 and delivered righteous Lot, who was oppressed with the filthy conduct of the wicked[4]

8 (for that righteous man, dwelling among them, tormented his righteous soul from day to day by seeing and hearing their unlawful deeds),

9 the Lord knows how to deliver the godly out of temptations and to reserve the unjust under punishment for the day of judgment,

10 and especially those who walk according to the flesh in the lust of uncleanness and despise authority. They are presumptuous, self-willed; they are not afraid to speak evil of dignitaries,

11 whereas angels, who are greater in power and might, do

2 2 Samuel 23:2

3 Genesis 6:5; 7:21-24
4 Genesis 19:1-26

not bring a reviling accusation against them before the Lord.

Depravity of False Teachers

12 But these, like natural brute beasts made to be caught and destroyed, speak evil of the things that they do not understand, and will utterly perish in their own corruption,

13 and will receive the wages of unrighteousness, as those who count it pleasure to carouse in the daytime. They are spots and blemishes, carousing in their own deceptions while they feast with you,

14 having eyes full of adultery and that cannot cease from sin, beguiling unstable souls. They have a heart trained in covetous practices, and are accursed children.

15 They have forsaken the right way and gone astray, following the way of Balaam the son of Beor, who loved the wages of unrighteousness;

16 but he was rebuked for his iniquity: a dumb donkey speaking with a man's voice restrained the madness of the prophet.[5]

17 These are wells without water, clouds carried by a tempest, to whom the gloom of darkness is reserved forever.

Deceptions of False Teachers

18 For when they speak great swelling words of emptiness, they allure through the lusts of the flesh, through licentiousness, those who have actually escaped from those who live in error.

19 While they promise them liberty, they themselves are slaves of corruption; for by whom a person is overcome, by him also he is brought into bondage.

20 For if, after they have escaped the pollutions of the world through the knowledge of the Lord and Savior Yeshua ha Mashiach, they are again entangled in them and overcome, the latter end is worse for them than the beginning.

21 For it would have been better for them not to have known the way of righteousness, than after they have known it, to turn from the holy commandment delivered to them.

22 But it has happened to them according to the true proverb: *"The dog returns to his own vomit,"* [6] and, "the sow that had washed, to her wallowing in the mire."

God's Promise Is Not Slack

3 Beloved, I now write to you this second letter (in both of which I stir up your pure minds by way of reminder),

2 that you may be mindful of the words which were spoken before by the holy prophets, and of the commandment of us the apostles of the Lord and Savior,

3 knowing this first: that scoffers will come in the last days, walking according to their own lusts,

4 and saying, "Where is the promise of His coming? For since the fathers fell asleep, all things continue as they were from the beginning of creation."

---

5 Numbers 22:5-33   6 Proverbs 26:11

5 For this they willfully forget: that by the word of God the heavens were of old, and the earth standing out of water and in the water,

6 by which the world that then was, being flooded with water, perished.

7 But the heavens and the earth which now exist are kept in store by the same word, reserved for fire until the day of judgment and perdition of ungodly men.[7]

8 But, beloved, do not forget this one thing, that one day is with the Lord as a thousand years, and a thousand years as one day.

9 The Lord is not slack concerning His promise, as some count slackness, but is longsuffering toward us, not desiring that any should perish but that all should come to repentance.

The Day of the Lord

10 But the day of the Lord will come as a thief in the night, in which the heavens will pass away with a great noise, and the elements will melt with fervent heat; both the earth and the works that are in it will be burned up.[8]

11 Seeing then that all these things will be dissolved, what manner of persons ought you to be in holy conduct and godliness,

12 looking for and hastening the coming of the day of God, because of which the heavens, being on fire, will be dissolved, and the elements will melt with fervent heat?

13 Nevertheless we, according to His promise, look for new heavens and a new earth in which righteousness dwells.[9]

Be Steadfast

14 Therefore, beloved, seeing that you look for such things, be diligent that you may be found by Him in peace, without spot, and blameless;

15 and account that the longsuffering of our Lord is salvation—as also our beloved brother Paul, according to the wisdom given to him, has written to you,

16 as also in all his letters, speaking in them of these things, in which are some things hard to understand, which those who are untaught and unstable twist to their own destruction, as they do also the rest of the Scriptures.

17 You therefore, beloved, seeing you know these things beforehand, beware lest you also, being led away with the error of the wicked, fall from your own steadfastness;

18 but grow in the grace and knowledge of our Lord and Savior Yeshua ha Mashiach. To Him be the glory both now and forever. Amen.

7 Isaiah 66:15, 16
8 Isaiah 34:4; Micah 1:4

9 Isaiah 65:17-25

The First Letter Of
JOHN

What Was Heard, Seen, and Touched

THAT which was from the beginning, which we have heard, which we have seen with our eyes, which we have looked upon, and our hands have handled, concerning the Word of life—

2 for the life was manifested, and we have seen, and bear witness, and declare to you that eternal life which was with the Father and was manifested to us—

3 that which we have seen and heard we declare to you, that you also may have fellowship with us; and truly our fellowship is with the Father and with His Son Yeshua ha Mashiach.

4 And these things we write to you that your joy may be full.

The Basis of Fellowship with Him

5 And this is the message which we have heard from Him and declare to you, that God is light and in Him is no darkness at all.

6 If we say that we have fellowship with Him, and walk in darkness, we lie and do not practice the truth.

7 But if we walk in the light as He is in the light, we have fellowship with one another, and the blood of Yeshua ha Mashiach His Son cleanses us from all sin.

8 If we say that we have no sin, we deceive ourselves, and the truth is not in us.

9 If we confess our sins, He is faithful and just to forgive us our sins and to cleanse us from all unrighteousness.[1]

10 If we say that we have not sinned, we make Him a liar, and His word is not in us.

2 My little children, these things I write to you so that you may not sin. And if anyone sins, we have an Advocate with the Father, Yeshua ha Mashiach the righteous.

2 And He Himself is the propitiation for our sins, and not for ours only but also for the whole world.

The Test of Knowing Him

3 And by this we know that we know Him, if we keep His commandments.

4 He who says, "I know Him," and does not keep His commandments, is a liar, and the truth is not in him.

5 But whoever keeps His word, truly the love of God is perfected in him. By this we know that we are in Him.

6 He who says he abides in

1 Proverbs 28:13

Him ought himself also to walk just as He walked.

7 Brethren, I write no new commandment to you, but an old commandment which you have had from the beginning. The old commandment is the word which you heard from the beginning.

8 Again, a new commandment I write to you, which thing is true in Him and in you, because the darkness is passing away, and the true light is already shining.

9 He who says he is in the light, and hates his brother, is in darkness until now.

10 He who loves his brother abides in the light, and there is no cause for stumbling in him.

11 But he who hates his brother is in darkness and walks in darkness, and does not know where he is going, because the darkness has blinded his eyes.

Their Spiritual State

12 I write to you, little children,
    Because your sins are for-
        given you for His name's
        sake.
13 I write to you, fathers,
    Because you have known
        Him who is from the be-
        ginning.
    I write to you, young men,
    Because you have overcome
        the wicked one.
    I write to you, little children,
    Because you have known
        the Father.
14 I have written to you, fa-
        thers,
    Because you have known
        Him who is from the be-
        ginning.

I have written to you, young
        men,
    Because you are strong,
        and the word of God
        abides in you,
    And you have overcome
        the wicked one.

Do Not Love the World

15 Do not love the world or the things in the world. If anyone loves the world, the love of the Father is not in him.

16 For all that is in the world—the lust of the flesh, the lust of the eyes, and the pride of life—is not of the Father but is of the world.

17 And the world is passing away, and the lust of it; but he who does the will of God abides forever.

Deceptions of the Last Hour

18 Little children, it is the last hour; and as you have heard that the Antichrist is coming, even now many antichrists have come, by which we know that it is the last hour.

19 They went out from us, but they were not of us; for if they had been of us, they would have continued with us; but they went out that they might be made manifest, that none of them were of us.

20 But you have an anointing from the Holy One, and you know all things.

21 I have not written to you because you do not know the truth, but because you know it, and that no lie is of the truth.

22 Who is a liar but he who denies that Yeshua is the Messiah? He is antichrist who denies the Father and the Son.

23 Whoever denies the Son does not have the Father either; he who acknowledges the Son also has the Father.

Let Truth Abide in You

24 Therefore let that abide in you which you have heard from the beginning. If what you have heard from the beginning abides in you, you also will abide in the Son and in the Father.

25 And this is the promise that He has promised us—eternal life.

26 These things I have written to you concerning those who try to deceive you.

27 But the anointing which you have received from Him abides in you, and you do not need that anyone teach you; but as the same anointing teaches you concerning all things, and is true, and is not a lie, and just as it has taught you, you will abide in Him.

The Children of God

28 And now, little children, abide in Him, that when He appears, we may have confidence and not be ashamed before Him at His coming.

29 If you know that He is righteous, you know that everyone who practices righteousness is born of Him.

3 Behold what manner of love the Father has bestowed on us, that we should be called children of God! Therefore the world does not know us, because it did not know Him.

2 Beloved, now we are children of God; and it has not yet been revealed what we shall be, but we know that when He is revealed, we shall be like Him, for we shall see Him as He is.

3 And everyone who has this hope in Him purifies himself, just as He is pure.

Sin and the Child of God

4 Whoever commits sin also commits lawlessness, and sin is lawlessness.

5 And you know that He was manifested to take away our sins, and in Him there is no sin.

6 Whoever abides in Him does not sin. Whoever sins has neither seen Him nor known Him.

7 Little children, let no one deceive you. He who practices righteousness is righteous, just as He is righteous.

8 He who practices sin is of the devil, for the devil has sinned from the beginning. For this purpose the Son of God was manifested, that He might destroy the works of the devil.

9 Whoever has been born of God does not practice sin, for His seed remains in him; and he cannot sin, because he has been born of God.

The Imperative of Love

10 In this the children of God and the children of the devil are manifest: Whoever does not practice righteousness is not of God, nor is he who does not love his brother.

11 For this is the message that you heard from the beginning, that we should love one another,

12 not as Cain who was of the wicked one and murdered his brother. And why did he murder

him? Because his works were evil and his brother's righteous.[2]

13 Do not marvel, my brethren, if the world hates you.

14 We know that we have passed from death to life, because we love the brethren. He who does not love his brother abides in death.

15 Whoever hates his brother is a murderer, and you know that no murderer has eternal life abiding in him.

The Outworking of Love

16 By this we know love, because He laid down His life for us. And we ought to lay down our lives for the brethren.

17 But whoever has this world's goods, and sees his brother in need, and shuts up his heart from him, how does the love of God dwell in him?

18 My little children, let us not love in word or in tongue, but in deed and in truth.

19 And by this we know that we are of the truth, and shall assure our hearts before Him.

20 For if our heart condemns us, God is greater than our heart, and knows all things.

21 Beloved, if our heart does not condemn us, we have confidence toward God.

22 And whatever we ask we receive from Him, because we keep His commandments and do those things that are pleasing in His sight.

23 And this is His commandment: that we should believe on the name of His Son Yeshua ha Mashiach and love one another, as He gave us commandment.

The Spirit of Truth and the Spirit of Error

24 And he who keeps His commandments dwells in Him, and He in him. And by this we know that He abides in us, by the Spirit whom He has given us.[3]

4 Beloved, do not believe every spirit, but test the spirits, whether they are of God; because many false prophets have gone out into the world.

2 By this you know the Spirit of God: Every spirit that confesses that Yeshua ha Mashiach has come in the flesh is of God,

3 and every spirit that does not confess that Yeshua ha Mashiach has come in the flesh is not of God. And this is the spirit of the Antichrist, which you have heard was coming, and even now it is already in the world.

4 You are of God, little children, and have overcome them, because He who is in you is greater than he who is in the world.

5 They are of the world. Therefore they speak as of the world, and the world hears them.

6 We are of God. He who knows God hears us; he who is not of God does not hear us. By this we know the spirit of truth and the spirit of error.

Knowing God Through Love

7 Beloved, let us love one another, for love is of God; and

---

2 Genesis 4:4–8

3 Ezekiel 36:25–27; Isaiah 44:3; Joel 2:28 (3:1 in some versions)

everyone who loves is born of God and knows God.

8 He who does not love does not know God, for God is love.

9 In this the love of God was manifested toward us, that God has sent His only begotten Son into the world, that we might live through Him.

10 In this is love, not that we loved God, but that He loved us and sent His Son to be the propitiation for our sins.

11 Beloved, if God so loved us, we also ought to love one another.

Seeing God Through Love

12 No one has seen God at any time. If we love one another, God dwells in us, and His love has been perfected in us.

13 By this we know that we dwell in Him, and He in us, because He has given us of His Spirit.

14 And we have seen and testify that the Father has sent the Son as Savior of the world.

15 Whoever confesses that Yeshua is the Son of God, God dwells in him, and he in God.

16 And we have known and believed the love that God has for us. God is love, and he who dwells in love dwells in God, and God in him.

The Consummation of Love

17 In this our love has been made perfect, that we may have boldness in the day of judgment; because as He is, so are we in this world.

18 There is no fear in love; but perfect love casts out fear, because fear involves torment. But he who fears has not been made perfect in love.

19 We love Him because He first loved us.

Obedience by Faith

20 If someone says, "I love God," and hates his brother, he is a liar; for he who does not love his brother whom he has seen, how can he love God whom he has not seen?

21 And this commandment we have from Him: that he who loves God love his brother also.

5 Whoever believes that Yeshua is the Messiah is born of God, and everyone who loves Him who begot also loves him who is begotten of Him.

2 By this we know that we love the children of God, when we love God and keep His commandments.

3 For this is the love of God, that we keep His commandments. And His commandments are not burdensome.

4 For whatever is born of God overcomes the world. And this is the victory that has overcome the world—our faith.

5 Who is he who overcomes the world, but he who believes that Yeshua is the Son of God?

The Certainty of God's Witness

6 This is He who came by water and blood—Yeshua ha Mashiach; not only by water, but by water and blood. And it is the Spirit who bears witness, because the Spirit is truth.

7 For there are three who bear witness in heaven: the Father, the

Word, and the Holy Spirit; and these three are one.

8 And there are three that bear witness on earth: the Spirit, the water, and the blood; and these three agree as one.

9 If we receive the witness of men, the witness of God is greater; for this is the witness of God which He has testified of His Son.

10 He who believes in the Son of God has the witness in himself; he who does not believe God has made Him a liar, because he has not believed the testimony that God has given of His Son.

11 And this is the testimony: that God has given us eternal life, and this life is in His Son.

12 He who has the Son has life; he who does not have the Son of God does not have life.

13 These things I have written to you who believe in the name of the Son of God, that you may know that you have eternal life, and that you may continue to believe in the name of the Son of God.

Confidence and Compassion in Prayer

14 And this is the confidence that we have in Him, that if we ask anything according to His will, He hears us.

15 And if we know that He hears us, whatever we ask, we know that we have the petitions that we have asked of Him.

16 If anyone sees his brother sinning a sin which does not lead to death, he shall ask, and He will give him life for those who commit sin not leading to death. There is sin leading to death. I do not say that he should pray about that.

17 All unrighteousness is sin, and there is sin not leading to death.

Knowing the True—Rejecting the False

18 We know that whoever is born of God does not sin; but he who has been born of God keeps himself, and the wicked one does not touch him.

19 We know that we are of God, and the whole world lies in the power of the wicked one.

20 And we know that the Son of God has come and has given us an understanding, that we may know Him who is true; and we are in Him who is true, in His Son Yeshua ha Mashiach. This is the true God and eternal life.

21 Little children, keep yourselves from idols. Amen.

The Second Letter Of
JOHN

Greetings

THE ELDER,

To the elect lady and her children, whom I love in truth, and not only I, but also all those who have known the truth,

2 because of the truth which abides in us and will be with us forever:

3 Grace, mercy, and peace will be with you from God the Father and from the Lord Yeshua ha Mashiach, the Son of the Father, in truth and love.

Walk in the Messiah's Commandments

4 I rejoiced greatly that I found some of your children walking in truth, as we have received commandment from the Father.

5 And now I plead with you, lady, not as though I wrote a new commandment to you, but that which we have had from the beginning: that we love one another.

6 And this is love, that we walk according to His commandments. This is the commandment, that as you have heard from the beginning, you should walk in it.

Beware of Deceivers

7 For many deceivers have gone out into the world who do not confess Yeshua ha Mashiach as coming in the flesh. This is a deceiver and an antichrist.

8 Look to yourselves, that we not lose those things we have worked for, but that we receive a full reward.

9 Whoever transgresses and does not abide in the doctrine of the Messiah does not have God. He who abides in the doctrine of the Messiah has both the Father and the Son.

10 If anyone comes to you and does not bring this doctrine, do not receive him into your house nor greet him;

11 for he who greets him shares in his evil deeds.

John's Farewell Greeting

12 Having many things to write to you, I did not wish to do so with paper and ink; but I hope to come to you and speak face to face, that our joy may be full.

13 The children of your elect sister greet you. Amen.

The Third Letter Of
JOHN

Greeting to Gaius

THE ELDER,

To the beloved Gaius, whom I love in truth:

2 Beloved, I pray that you may prosper in all things and be in health, just as your soul prospers.

3 For I rejoiced greatly when brethren came and testified of the truth that is in you, as you do walk in the truth.

4 I have no greater joy than to hear that my children walk in truth.

Gaius Commended for Generosity

5 Beloved, you do faithfully whatever you do for the brethren and for strangers,

6 who have borne witness of your love before the congregation. If you send them forward on their journey in a manner worthy of God, you will do well,

7 because they went forth for His name's sake, taking nothing from the Gentiles.

8 We therefore ought to receive such, that we may become fellow workers for the truth.

Diotrephes and Demetrius

9 I wrote to the congregation, but Diotrephes, who loves to have the preeminence among them, does not receive us.

10 Therefore, if I come, I will call to mind his deeds which he does, prating against us with malicious words. And not content with that, he himself does not receive the brethren, and forbids those who wish to, putting them out of the congregation.

11 Beloved, do not follow what is evil, but what is good. He who does good is of God, but he who does evil has not seen God.

12 Demetrius has a good testimony from all, and from the truth itself. And we also bear witness, and you know that our testimony is true.

Farewell Greeting

13 I had many things to write, but I do not wish to write to you with pen and ink;

14 but I hope to see you shortly, and we shall speak face to face. Peace to you. Our friends greet you. Greet the friends by name.

The Letter Of

JUDE

Greeting to the Called

JUDE, a servant of Yeshua ha Mashiach, and brother of James,

To those who are called, sanctified by God the Father, and preserved in Yeshua ha Mashiach:

2 Mercy, peace, and love be multiplied to you.

Contend for the Faith

3 Beloved, while I was very diligent to write to you concerning our common salvation, I found it necessary to write to you exhorting that you should earnestly contend for the faith which was once for all delivered to the believers.

4 For certain men have crept in unnoticed, who long ago were marked out for this condemnation, ungodly men, who turn the grace of our God into licentiousness and deny the only Lord God and our Lord Yeshua ha Mashiach.

Old and New Apostates

5 But I want to remind you, though you once knew this, that the Lord, having saved the people out of the land of Egypt, afterward destroyed those who did not believe.

6 And the angels who did not keep their proper domain, but left their own habitation, He has reserved in everlasting chains under darkness for the judgment of the great day;

7 as Sodom and Gomorrah, and the cities around them in a similar manner to these, having given themselves over to sexual immorality and gone after strange flesh, are set forth as an example, suffering the vengeance of eternal fire.

8 Likewise also these dreamers defile the flesh, reject authority, and speak evil of dignitaries.

9 Yet Michael the archangel, in contending with the devil, when he disputed about the body of Moses, dared not bring against him a reviling accusation, but said, "The Lord rebuke you!"

10 But these speak evil of whatever they do not know; and whatever they know naturally, like brute beasts, in these things they corrupt themselves.

11 Woe to them! For they have gone in the way of Cain, run greedily in the error of Balaam for profit, and perished in the rebellion of Korah.

Apostates Depraved and Doomed

12 These are spots in your love feasts, while they feast with you

without fear, tending only themselves; they are clouds without water, carried about by the winds;
late autumn trees without fruit,
twice dead, pulled up by the roots;

13 raging waves of the sea, foaming up their own shame; wandering stars for whom is reserved the
blackness of darkness forever.

14 And Enoch, the seventh from
Adam, prophesied about these
men also, saying, "Behold, the
Lord comes with ten thousands of
His holy ones,

15 "to execute judgment on all,
to convict all who are ungodly
among them of all their ungodly
deeds which they have committed
in an ungodly way, and of all the
harsh things which ungodly sinners have spoken against Him."

Apostates Predicted

16 These are murmurers, com-
plainers, walking according to
their own lusts; and their mouth
speaks great swelling words, flattering people to gain advantage.

17 But you, beloved, remember
the words which were spoken before by the apostles[1] of our Lord
Yeshua ha Mashiach:

1 See note 1, p. 246.

18 how they told you that there
would be mockers in the last time
who would walk according to their
own ungodly lusts.

19 These are the sensual ones,
who cause divisions, not having
the Spirit.

Maintain Your Life with God

20 But you, beloved, building
yourselves up on your most holy
faith, praying in the Holy Spirit,

21 keep yourselves in the love of
God, looking for the mercy of our
Lord Yeshua ha Mashiach to eter-
nal life.

22 And on some have compassion, making a distinction;

23 and save others with fear,
pulling them out of the fire, hating
even the garment defiled by the
flesh.

Glory to God

24 Now to Him who is able to
   keep you from stumbling,
   And to present you faultless
   Before the presence of His
   glory with exceeding joy,

25 To God our Savior,
   Who alone is wise,
   Be glory and majesty,
   Dominion and power,
   Both now and forever.
   Amen.

THE REVELATION
Of Yeshua Ha Mashiach

Introduction

THE Revelation of Yeshua ha Mashiach, which God gave Him to show His servants—things which must shortly take place. And He sent and signified it by His angel to His servant John,

2 who bore witness to the word of God, and to the testimony of Yeshua ha Mashiach, and to all things that he saw.

3 Blessed is he who reads, and those who hear the words of this prophecy, and keep those things which are written in it; for the time is near.

Greeting the Seven Congregations

4 John, to the seven congregations which are in Asia:

Grace to you and peace from Him who is and who was and who is to come, and from the seven Spirits who are before His throne,

5 and from Yeshua ha Mashiach who is the faithful witness, the firstborn from the dead, and the ruler over the kings of the earth. To Him who loved us and washed us from our sins in His own blood,

6 and has made us kings and priests to His God and Father, to Him be glory and dominion forever and ever. Amen.

7 Behold, He is coming with clouds,[1] and every eye will see Him, and they also who pierced Him.[2] And all the tribes of the earth will mourn because of Him. Even so, Amen.

8 "I am the Alpha and the Omega, the Beginning and the End," says the Lord, "who is and who was and who is to come, the Almighty."

Vision of the Son of Man

9 I, John, both your brother and companion in tribulation, and in the kingdom and patience of Yeshua ha Mashiach, was on the island that is called Patmos for the word of God and for the testimony of Yeshua ha Mashiach.

10 I was in the Spirit on the Lord's Day, and I heard behind me a loud voice, as of a shofar,

11 saying, "I am the Alpha and the Omega, the First and the Last," and, "What you see, write in a book and send it to the seven congregations which are in Asia: to Ephesus, to Smyrna, to Pergamos, to Thyatira, to Sardis, to Philadelphia, and to Laodicea."

12 And I turned to see the voice that spoke with me. And having

1 Daniel 7:13 2 Zechariah 12:10

turned I saw seven golden lamp-stands,[3]

13 and in the midst of the seven lampstands One like the Son of Man,[4] clothed with a garment down to the feet and girded about the chest with a golden belt.

14 His head and His hair were white like wool, as white as snow; His eyes were like a flame of fire.[5]

15 His feet were like fine brass, as if refined in a furnace, and His voice as the sound of many waters.

16 He had in His right hand seven stars, out of His mouth went a sharp two-edged sword, and His countenance was like the sun shining in its strength.

17 And when I saw Him, I fell at His feet as dead. And He laid His right hand on me, saying to me, "Do not be afraid; I am the First and the Last.[6]

18 "I am He who lives, and was dead, and behold, I am alive for-evermore. Amen. And I have the keys of Hades and of Death.

19 "Write the things which you have seen, and the things which are, and the things which will take place after this.

20 "The mystery of the seven stars which you saw in My right hand, and the seven golden lamp-stands: The seven stars are the an-gels of the seven congregations, and the seven lampstands which you saw are the seven congrega-tions.

---

3 Zechariah 4:2, 3

4 Daniel 7:13, 14; 10:5

5 Daniel 7:9

6 Isaiah 41:4; 44:6; 48:12-16

The Loveless Congregation

2 "To the angel of the congre-gation of Ephesus write,

'These things says He who holds the seven stars in His right hand, who walks in the midst of the seven golden lampstands:

2 "I know your works, your la-bor, your patience, and how you cannot bear those who are evil. And you have tested those who say they are apostles and are not, and have found them liars;

3 "and you have persevered and have patience, and have la-bored for My name's sake and have not become weary.

4 "Nevertheless I have this against you, that you have left your first love.

5 "Remember therefore from what you have fallen; repent and do the first works, or else I will come to you quickly and remove your lampstand from its place—unless you repent.

6 "But this you have, that you hate the deeds of the Nicolaitans, which I also hate.

7 "He who has an ear, let him hear what the Spirit says to the congregations. To him who over-comes I will give to eat of the tree of life, which is in the midst of the Paradise of God." '[7]

The Persecuted Congregation

8 "And to the angel of the con-gregation in Smyrna write,

'These things says the First and the Last, who was dead, and came to life:

---

7 Genesis 2:9; 3:24

9 "I know your works, tribulation, and poverty (but you are rich); and I know the blasphemy of those who say they are Jews and are not, but are a synagogue of Satan.

10 "Do not fear any of those things which you are about to suffer. Indeed, the devil is about to throw some of you into prison, that you may be tested, and you will have tribulation ten days. Be faithful until death, and I will give you the crown of life.

11 "He who has an ear, let him hear what the Spirit says to the congregations. He who overcomes shall not be hurt by the second death." '

The Compromising Congregation

12 "And to the angel of the congregation in Pergamos write,

'These things says He who has the sharp two-edged sword:

13 "I know your works, and where you dwell, where Satan's throne is. And you hold fast to My name, and have not denied My faith even in the days in which Antipas was My faithful martyr, who was killed among you, where Satan dwells.

14 "But I have a few things against you, because you have there those who hold the doctrine of Balaam, who taught Balak to put a stumbling block before the children of Israel, to eat things sacrificed to idols, and to commit sexual immorality.[8]

15 "Thus you also have those who hold the doctrine of the Nicolaitans, which thing I hate.

16 "Repent, or else I will come to you quickly and will fight against them with the sword of My mouth.

17 "He who has an ear, let him hear what the Spirit says to the congregations. To him who overcomes I will give some of the hidden manna to eat. And I will give him a white stone, and on the stone a new name written which no one knows except him who receives it." '

The Corrupt Congregation

18 "And to the angel of the congregation in Thyatira write,

'These things says the Son of God, who has eyes like a flame of fire, and His feet like fine brass:

19 "I know your works, love, service, faith, and your patience; and as to your works, the last are more than the first.

20 "Nevertheless I have a few things against you, because you allow that woman Jezebel, who calls herself a prophetess, to teach and beguile My servants to commit sexual immorality and to eat things sacrificed to idols.

21 "And I gave her time to repent of her sexual immorality, and she did not repent.

22 "Indeed, I will cast her into a sickbed, and those who commit adultery with her into great tribulation, unless they repent of their deeds.

23 "And I will kill her children with death. And all the congregations shall know that I am He who searches the minds and hearts. And I will give to each one of you according to your works.

8 Numbers 25:1ff.

24 "But to you I say, and to the rest in Thyatira, as many as do not have this doctrine, and who have not known the depths of Satan, as they call them, I will put on you no other burden.

25 "But hold fast what you have till I come.

26 "And he who overcomes, and keeps My works until the end, to him I will give power over the nations—

27 'And he shall rule them with
a rod of iron;
As the vessels of a potter
they shall be broken to
pieces'[9]—

"as I also received from My Father.

28 "And I will give him the morning star.

29 "He who has an ear, let him hear what the Spirit says to the congregations." '

The Dead Congregation

3 "And to the angel of the congregation in Sardis write,
'These things says He who has the seven Spirits of God and the seven stars: "I know your works, that you have a name that you are alive, and yet you are dead.

2 "Be watchful, and strengthen the things which remain, that are ready to die, for I have not found your works perfect before God.

3 "Remember therefore how you have received and heard; hold fast and repent. Therefore if you will not watch, I shall come upon you as a thief, and you shall not know what hour I shall come upon you.

4 "You have a few names even in Sardis who have not defiled their garments; and they shall walk with Me in white, for they are worthy.

5 "He who overcomes shall be clothed in white garments, and I will not blot out his name from the Book of Life; but I will confess his name before My Father and before His angels.

6 "He who has an ear, let him hear what the Spirit says to the congregations." '

The Faithful Congregation

7 "And to the angel of the congregation in Philadelphia write,
'These things says He who is holy, He who is true, "*He who has the key of David, He who opens and no one shuts, and shuts and no one opens*":[10]

8 "I know your works. See, I have set before you an open door, and no one can shut it; for you have a little strength, have kept My word, and have not denied My name.

9 "Indeed, I will make those of the synagogue of Satan, who say they are Jews and are not, but lie—indeed, I will make them come and worship before your feet, and to know that I have loved you.

10 "Because you have kept My command to persevere, I also will keep you from the hour of trial which shall come upon all the world, to test those who dwell on the earth.

11 "Behold, I come quickly! Hold fast what you have, that no one take your crown.

9 Psalm 2:9

10 Isaiah 22:22

12 "He who also overcomes, I will make him a pillar in the temple of My God, and he shall go out no more. And I will write on him the name of My God and the name of the city of My God, the New Jerusalem, which comes down out of heaven from My God. And I will write on him My new name.

13 "He who has an ear, let him hear what the Spirit says to the congregations." '

The Lukewarm Congregation

14 "And to the angel of the congregation of the Laodiceans write, 'These things says the Amen, the Faithful and True Witness, the Beginning[11] of the creation of God:

15 "I know your works, that you are neither cold nor hot. I wish you were cold or hot.

16 "So then, because you are lukewarm, and neither cold nor hot, I will spew you out of My mouth.

17 "Because you say, I am rich, have become wealthy, and have need of nothing—and do not know that you are wretched, miserable, poor, blind, and naked—

18 "I counsel you to buy from Me gold refined in the fire, that you may be rich; and white garments, that you may be clothed, that the shame of your nakedness not be revealed; and anoint your eyes with eye salve, that you may see.

19 "As many as I love, I rebuke and chasten. Therefore be zealous and repent.

20 "Behold, I stand at the door and knock. If anyone hears My voice and opens the door, I will come in to him and dine with him, and he with Me.

21 "To him who overcomes I will grant to sit with Me on My throne, as I also overcame and sat down with My Father on His throne.

22 "He who has an ear, let him hear what the Spirit says to the congregations." ' "

The Throne Room of Heaven

4 After these things I looked, and behold, a door standing open in heaven. And the first voice which I heard was like a shofar speaking with me, saying, "Come up here, and I will show you things which must take place after this."

2 And immediately I was in the Spirit, and behold, a throne set in heaven, and One sat on the throne.

3 And He who sat there was like a jasper and a sardius stone in appearance; and there was a rainbow around the throne, in appearance like an emerald.[12]

4 And around the throne were twenty-four thrones, and on the thrones I saw twenty-four elders sitting, clothed in white robes; and they had crowns of gold on their heads.

5 And out of the throne proceeded lightnings, thunderings, and voices. And there were seven lamps of fire burning before the throne, which are the seven Spirits of God.

6 And before the throne there

---

11 That is, the origin or source.

12 Ezekiel 1:26-28

was a sea of glass like crystal. And in the midst of the throne, and around the throne, were four living creatures full of eyes in front and in back.

7 And the first living creature was like a lion, the second living creature like a calf, the third living creature had a face like a man, and the fourth living creature was like a flying eagle.[13]

8 And the four living creatures, full of eyes around and within, each had six wings. And they do not rest day or night, saying:

"Holy, holy, holy,
Lord God Almighty,
Who was and is and is to
come!"[14]

9 And whenever the living creatures give glory and honor and thanks to Him who sits on the throne, who lives forever and ever,

10 the twenty-four elders fall down before Him who sits on the throne and worship Him who lives forever and ever, and cast their crowns before the throne, saying:

11"You are worthy, O Lord,
To receive glory and honor
and power;
For You have created all
things,
And by Your will they exist
and were created!"

The Lamb Takes the Scroll

5 And I saw in the right hand of Him who sat on the throne a scroll written inside and on the back, sealed with seven seals.

2 And I saw a strong angel proclaiming with a loud voice, "Who is worthy to open the scroll and to loose its seals?"

3 And no one in heaven or on the earth or under the earth was able to open the scroll, or to look at it.

4 And I wept greatly, because no one was found worthy to open and read the scroll, or to look at it.

5 And one of the elders said to me, "Do not weep. Behold, the Lion of the tribe of Judah,[15] the Root of David,[16] has prevailed to open the scroll and to loose its seven seals."

6 And I looked, and behold, in the midst of the throne and of the four living creatures, and in the midst of the elders, stood a Lamb as it had been slain, having seven horns and seven eyes, which are the seven Spirits of God sent out into all the earth.

7 And He came and took the scroll out of the right hand of Him who sat on the throne.

Worthy Is the Lamb

8 And when He had taken the scroll, the four living creatures and the twenty-four elders fell down before the Lamb, each having a harp, and golden bowls full of incense, which are the prayers of the believers.

9 And they sang a new song, saying:

"You are worthy to take the
scroll,
And to open its seals;
For You were slain,
And have redeemed us to
God by Your blood

---

13 Ezekiel 1:10   14 Isaiah 6:1-3

15 Genesis 49:9, 10

16 Jeremiah 23:5, 6

Out of every tribe and
tongue and people and na-
tion,

10 And have made us kings and
priests to our God;
And we shall reign on the
earth."

11 And I looked, and I heard
the voice of many angels around
the throne, the living creatures,
and the elders; and the number of
them was ten thousand times ten
thousand, and thousands of thousands,[17]

12 saying with a loud voice:
"Worthy is the Lamb who
was slain
To receive power and riches
and wisdom,
And strength and honor and
glory and blessing!"

13 And every creature which is
in heaven, on the earth, under the
earth, and such as are in the sea,
and all that are in them, I heard
saying:
"Blessing and honor and glory
and power
Be to Him who sits on the
throne,
And to the Lamb, forever
and ever. Amen!"[18]

14 And the four living creatures
said, "Amen!" And the twenty-
four elders fell down and worshiped Him who lives forever and
ever.

First Seal: The Conqueror

6 And I saw when the Lamb
opened one of the seals; and I
heard, like the noise of thunder,
one of the four living creatures
saying, "Come and see."

2 And I looked, and behold, a
white horse. And he who sat on it
had a bow; and a crown was given
to him, and he went out conquer-
ing and to conquer.

Second Seal: Conflict on Earth

3 And when He opened the
second seal, I heard the second living creature saying, "Come and
see."

4 And another horse that was
fiery red went out. And power
was given to him who sat on it to
take peace from the earth, and
that they should kill one another;
and there was given to him a great
sword.

Third Seal: Scarcity on Earth

5 And when He opened the
third seal, I heard the third living
creature say, "Come and see."
And I looked, and behold, a black
horse, and he who sat on it had a
pair of scales in his hand.

6 And I heard a voice in the
midst of the four living creatures
saying, "A measure of wheat for a
denarius,[19] and three measures of
barley for a denarius; and do not
harm the oil and the wine."

Fourth Seal: Widespread Death on Earth

7 And when He opened the
fourth seal, I heard the voice of
the fourth living creature saying,
"Come and see."

8 And I looked, and behold, a
pale horse. And the name of him
who sat on it was Death, and
Hades followed with him. And

17 Daniel 7:10　18 Daniel 7:13, 14

19 Approximately one day's wage for a
worker.

power was given to them over a fourth of the earth, to kill with sword, with hunger, with death, and by the beasts of the earth.

Fifth Seal: The Cry of the Martyrs

9 And when He opened the fifth seal, I saw under the altar the souls of those who had been slain for the word of God and for the testimony which they held.

10 And they cried with a loud voice, saying, "How long, O Lord, holy and true, until You judge and avenge our blood on those who dwell on the earth?"

11 And white robes were given to each of them; and it was said to them that they should rest a little while longer, until both the number of their fellow servants and their brethren, who would be killed as they were, was completed.

Sixth Seal: Cosmic Disturbances

12 And I looked when He opened the sixth seal, and behold, there was a great earthquake; and the sun became black as sackcloth of hair, and the moon became like blood.[20]

13 And the stars of heaven fell to the earth, as a fig tree drops its late figs when it is shaken by a mighty wind.

14 And the sky receded as a scroll when it is rolled together, and every mountain and island was moved out of its place.[21]

15 And the kings of the earth, the great men, the rich men, the commanders, the mighty men, ev-

ery slave and every free man, hid themselves in the caves and in the rocks of the mountains,

16 and said to the mountains and rocks, "Fall on us and hide us from the face of Him who sits on the throne and from the wrath of the Lamb![22]

17 "For the great day of His wrath has come, and who is able to stand?"[23]

The Sealed of Israel

7 And after these things I saw four angels standing at the four corners of the earth, holding the four winds of the earth, that the wind should not blow on the earth, on the sea, or on any tree.

2 And I saw another angel ascending from the east, having the seal of the living God. And he cried with a loud voice to the four angels to whom it was given to harm the earth and the sea,

3 saying, "Do not harm the earth, the sea, or the trees till we have sealed the servants of our God on their foreheads."

4 And I heard the number of those who were sealed. One hundred and forty-four thousand of all the tribes of the children of Israel were sealed:

5 of the tribe of Judah twelve thousand were sealed;
of the tribe of Reuben twelve thousand were sealed;
of the tribe of Gad twelve thousand were sealed;
6 of the tribe of Asher twelve thousand were sealed;

---

20 Joel 2:10, 31 (3:4 in some versions)
21 Isaiah 34:4

22 Isaiah 2:19-21   23 Malachi 3:2

of the tribe of Naphtali twelve thousand were sealed; of the tribe of Manasseh twelve thousand were sealed;

7 of the tribe of Simeon twelve thousand were sealed; of the tribe of Levi twelve thousand were sealed; of the tribe of Issachar twelve thousand were sealed;

8 of the tribe of Zebulun twelve thousand were sealed; of the tribe of Joseph twelve thousand were sealed; of the tribe of Benjamin twelve thousand were sealed.

A Multitude from the Great Tribulation

9 After these things I looked, and behold, a great multitude which no one could number, of all nations, tribes, peoples, and tongues, standing before the throne and before the Lamb, clothed with white robes, with palm branches in their hands,

10 and crying out with a loud voice, saying, "Salvation to our God who sits on the throne, and to the Lamb!"

11 And all the angels stood around the throne, and around the elders and the four living creatures, and fell on their faces before the throne and worshiped God,

12 saying:

"Amen! Blessing and glory and wisdom,

And thanksgiving and honor and power and might,
Be to our God forever and ever. Amen."

13 And one of the elders answered, saying to me, "Who are these arrayed in white robes, and where did they come from?"

14 And I said to him, "Sir, you know." And he said to me, "These are the ones who come out of the great tribulation, and have washed their robes and made them white in the blood of the Lamb.

15 "Therefore they are before the throne of God, and serve Him day and night in His temple. And He who sits on the throne will dwell among them.

16 "They will neither hunger anymore, nor thirst anymore; the sun shall not strike them, nor any heat;[24]

17 "for the Lamb who is in the midst of the throne will shepherd[25] them and lead them to living fountains of waters. And God will wipe away every tear from their eyes." [26]

Seventh Seal: Prelude to the Seven Shofars

8 And when He opened the seventh seal, there was silence in heaven for about half an hour.

2 And I saw the seven angels who stand before God, and to them were given seven shofars.

3 And another angel, having a

24 Isaiah 49:10
25 Ezekiel 37:24-28; Isaiah 40:11; Micah 5:2-4 (5:1-3 in some versions)
26 Isaiah 25:8

golden censer, came and stood at the altar. And he was given much incense, that he should offer it with the prayers of all the believers on the golden altar which was before the throne.

4 And the smoke of the incense, with the prayers of the believers, ascended before God out of the angel's hand.

5 And the angel took the censer, filled it with fire from the altar, and threw it to the earth. And there were noises, thunderings, lightnings, and an earthquake.

6 And the seven angels who had the seven shofars prepared themselves to sound.

First Shofar: Vegetation Struck

7 The first angel sounded: And hail and fire followed, mingled with blood, and they were thrown to the earth; and a third of the trees were burned up, and all green grass was burned up.

Second Shofar: The Seas Struck

8 And the second angel sounded: And something like a great mountain burning with fire was thrown into the sea, and a third of the sea became blood;

9 and a third of the living creatures in the sea died, and a third of the ships were destroyed.

Third Shofar: The Waters Struck

10 And the third angel sounded: And a great star fell from heaven, burning like a torch, and it fell on a third of the rivers and on the springs of water;

11 and the name of the star is Wormwood; and a third of the waters became wormwood; and many men died from the waters, because the waters were made bitter.

Fourth Shofar: The Heavens Struck

12 And the fourth angel sounded: And a third of the sun was struck, a third of the moon, and a third of the stars, so that a third of them were darkened; and a third of the day did not shine, and the night likewise.

13 And I looked, and I heard an angel flying through the midst of heaven, saying with a loud voice, "Woe, woe, woe to the inhabitants of the earth, because of the remaining blasts of the shofar of the three angels who are about to sound!"

Fifth Shofar: The Locusts from the Bottomless Pit

9 And the fifth angel sounded: And I saw a star fall from heaven to the earth. And to him was given the key to the bottomless pit.

2 And he opened the bottomless pit, and smoke arose out of the pit like the smoke of a great furnace. And the sun and the air were darkened because of the smoke of the pit.

3 And locusts came out of the smoke onto the earth. And to them was given power, as the scorpions of the earth have power.

4 And they were commanded that they should not harm the grass of the earth, any green thing, nor any tree, but only those men who do not have the seal of God on their foreheads.

5 And it was granted to them that they should not kill them, but that they should be tormented five months. And their torment was like the torment of a scorpion when it strikes a man.

6 And in those days men will seek death and shall not find it; they will desire to die, and death will flee from them.

7 And the shapes of the locusts were like horses prepared for battle; and on their heads, as it were, crowns like gold, and their faces were like the faces of men.

8 And they had hair like women's hair, and their teeth were like lions' teeth.

9 And they had breastplates like breastplates of iron, and the sound of their wings was like the sound of chariots with many horses running into battle.

10 And they had tails like scorpions, and there were stings in their tails. And their power was to hurt men five months.

11 And they had a king over them who is the angel of the bottomless pit, whose name in Hebrew is *Abaddon,* but in Greek he has the name *Apollyon.*

12 One woe is past. Behold, still two more woes are coming after these things.

Sixth Shofar: The Angels from the Euphrates

13 And the sixth angel sounded: And I heard a voice from the four horns of the golden altar which is before God,

14 saying to the sixth angel who had the shofar, "Release the four angels who are bound at the great river Euphrates."

15 And the four angels, who had been prepared for the hour and day and month and year, were released to kill a third of mankind.

16 And the number of the army of the horsemen was two hundred million, and I heard the number of them.

17 And thus I saw the horses in the vision: those who sat on them had breastplates of fiery red, hyacinth blue, and sulfur yellow; and the heads of the horses were like the heads of lions; and out of their mouths came fire, smoke, and brimstone.

18 By these three plagues a third of mankind was killed—by the fire, by the smoke, and by the brimstone which came out of their mouths.

19 For their power is in their mouth and in their tails; for their tails are like serpents, having heads; and with them they do harm.

20 And the rest of mankind, who were not killed by these plagues, still did not repent of the works of their hands, that they should not worship demons, and idols of gold, silver, brass, stone, and wood, which can neither see nor hear nor walk;

21 and they did not repent of their murders nor their sorceries nor their sexual immorality nor their thefts.

The Mighty Angel with the Scroll

10 And I saw another mighty angel coming down from heaven, clothed with a cloud.

And a rainbow was on his head, his face was like the sun, and his feet like pillars of fire.

2 And he had a little book open in his hand. And he set his right foot on the sea and his left foot on the land,

3 and cried with a loud voice, as when a lion roars. And when he cried out, seven thunders uttered their voices.

4 And when the seven thunders uttered their voices, I was about to write; and I heard a voice from heaven saying to me, "Seal up those things which the seven thunders uttered, and do not write them."

5 And the angel whom I saw standing on the sea and on the land lifted up his hand to heaven

6 and swore by Him who lives forever and ever, who created heaven and the things that are in it, the earth and the things that are in it, and the sea and the things that are in it, that there should be delay no longer,

7 but in the days of the sounding of the seventh angel, when he is about to sound, the mystery of God would be finished, as He has declared to His servants the prophets.[27]

John Consumes the Scroll

8 And the voice which I heard from heaven spoke to me again and said, "Go, take the little book which is open in the hand of the angel who stands on the sea and on the earth."

9 And I went to the angel and said to him, "Give me the little book." And he said to me, "Take and eat it; and it will make your stomach bitter, but it will be as sweet as honey in your mouth."[28]

10 And I took the little book out of the angel's hand and ate it, and it was as sweet as honey in my mouth. And when I had eaten it, my stomach became bitter.

11 And he said to me, "You must prophesy again about many peoples, nations, tongues, and kings."

The Two Witnesses

11 And there was given to me a reed like a measuring rod.[29] And the angel stood, saying, "Rise and measure the temple of God, the altar, and those who worship there.

2 "But leave out the court which is outside the temple, and do not measure it, for it has been given to the Gentiles. And they will tread the holy city under foot forty-two months.

3 "And I will give power to my two witnesses, and they will prophesy one thousand two hundred and sixty days, clothed in sackcloth."

4 These are the two olive trees and the two lampstands standing before the God of the earth.[30]

5 And if anyone wants to harm them, fire proceeds out of their mouth and devours their enemies. And if anyone wants to harm them, he must be killed in this manner.

27 Daniel 12:6, 7

28 Ezekiel 2:8—3:3

29 Ezekiel 40:3—42:20; Zechariah 2:1f. (2:5f. in some versions)

30 Zechariah 4:3, 11-14

6 These have power to shut heaven, so that no rain falls in the days of their prophecy; and they have power over waters to turn them to blood, and to strike the earth with all plagues, as often as they desire.

The Witnesses Killed

7 And when they finish their testimony, the beast that ascends out of the bottomless pit will make war against them, overcome them, and kill them.

8 And their dead bodies will lie in the street of the great city which spiritually is called Sodom and Egypt, where also our Lord was crucified.

9 And those from the peoples, tribes, tongues, and nations will see their dead bodies three and a half days, and not allow their dead bodies to be put into graves.

10 And those who dwell on the earth will rejoice over them, make merry, and send gifts to one another, because these two prophets tormented those who dwell on the earth.

The Witnesses Resurrected

11 And after three and a half days the breath of life from God entered them, and they stood on their feet, and great fear fell on those who saw them.

12 And they heard a loud voice from heaven saying to them, "Come up here." And they ascended to heaven in a cloud, and their enemies saw them.

13 And in the same hour there was a great earthquake, and a tenth of the city fell; and in the earthquake seven thousand men were killed. And the rest were afraid and gave glory to the God of heaven.

14 The second woe is past. Behold, the third woe is coming quickly.

Seventh Shofar: The Kingdom Proclaimed

15 And the seventh angel sounded: And there were loud voices in heaven, saying, "The kingdoms of this world have become the kingdoms of our Lord and of His Messiah, and He shall reign forever and ever!" [31]

16 And the twenty-four elders who sat before God on their thrones fell on their faces and worshiped God,

17 saying:

"We give You thanks, O Lord
   God Almighty,
The One who is and who
   was and who is to come,
Because You have taken
   Your great power and have
   reigned.
18 And the nations were angry,
   and Your wrath has come,
And the time of the dead,
   that they should be judged,
And that You should reward
   Your servants the prophets
   and the believers,
And those who fear Your
   name, small and great,
And should destroy those
   who destroy the earth."

19 And the temple of God was opened in heaven, and the ark of His covenant was seen in His temple. And there came lightnings,

31 Daniel 7:13, 14; Psalm 2:2f.

noises, thunderings, an earthquake, and great hail.

The Woman, the Child,
and the Dragon

12 And a great sign appeared
in heaven: a woman
clothed with the sun, with the
moon under her feet, and on her
head a crown of twelve stars.

2 And being with child, she
cried out in labor and in pain to
give birth.

3 And another sign appeared
in heaven: behold, a great, fiery
red dragon having seven heads
and ten horns,[32] and seven crowns
on his heads.

4 And his tail drew a third of
the stars of heaven and threw
them to the earth. And the
dragon stood before the woman
who was ready to give birth, to devour her Child as soon as it was
born.

5 And she brought forth a male
Child who was to rule all nations
with a rod of iron.[33] And her
Child was caught up to God and
to His throne.[34]

6 And the woman fled into the
wilderness where she has a place
prepared by God, that they should
feed her there one thousand two
hundred and sixty days.

Satan Thrown Out of Heaven

7 And there was war in
heaven: Michael and his angels
fought against the dragon; and the
dragon and his angels fought,

8 and they did not prevail, nor
was a place found for them in
heaven any longer.

9 And the great dragon was
cast out, that serpent of old, called
the Devil and Satan, who deceives
the whole world; he was cast to
the earth, and his angels were cast
out with him.

10 And I heard a loud voice saying in heaven, "Now salvation,
and strength, and the kingdom of
our God, and the power of His
Messiah have come, for the ac-
cuser of our brethren, who accused
them before our God day and
night, has been cast down.

11 "And they overcame him by
the blood of the Lamb and by the
word of their testimony, and they
did not love their lives to the
death.

12 "Therefore rejoice, O heavens, and you who dwell in them!
Woe to the inhabitants of the
earth and the sea! For the devil
has come down to you, having
great wrath, because he knows
that he has only a short time."

The Woman Persecuted

13 And when the dragon saw
that he had been cast to the earth,
he persecuted the woman who
gave birth to the male Child.

14 And the woman was given
two wings of a great eagle, that she
might fly into the wilderness to her
place, where she is nourished for a
time and times and half a time,
from the face of the serpent.

15 And the serpent spewed water out of his mouth like a flood
after the woman, that he might
cause her to be carried away by
the flood.

32 Cf. Daniel 7:7, 20, 24
33 Psalm 2:8, 9   34 Psalm 110:1

16 And the earth helped the woman, and the earth opened its mouth and swallowed up the flood which the dragon spewed out of his mouth.

17 And the dragon was enraged with the woman, and he went to make war with the rest of her off-spring who keep the command-ments of God and have the testi-mony of Yeshua ha Mashiach.

The Beast from the Sea

13 And I stood on the sand of the sea. And I saw a beast rising up out of the sea, having seven heads and ten horns,[35] and on his horns ten crowns, and on his heads the name of blasphemy.

2 And the beast which I saw was like a leopard, his feet were like the feet of a bear, and his mouth like the mouth of a lion.[36] And the dragon gave him his power, his throne, and great au-thority.

3 And I saw one of his heads as if it had been wounded to death, and his deadly wound was healed. And all the world marveled and followed the beast.

4 And they worshiped the dragon who gave authority to the beast; and they worshiped the beast, saying, "Who is like the beast? Who is able to make war with him?"

5 And he was given a mouth speaking great things and blasphe-mies, and authority was given to him to continue forty-two months.

6 And he opened his mouth in blasphemy against God, to blas-pheme His name, His tabernacle, and those who dwell in heaven.

7 And it was granted to him to make war with the believers and to overcome them. And authority was given him over every tribe, tongue, and nation.[37]

8 And all who dwell on the earth will worship him, whose names have not been written in the Book of Life of the Lamb who was slain from the foundation of the world.

9 If anyone has an ear, let him hear.

10 He who leads into captivity shall go into captivity; he who kills with the sword must be killed with the sword. Here is the patience and the faith of the believers.

The Beast from the Land

11 And I saw another beast com-ing up out of the earth, and he had two horns like a lamb[38] and spoke like a dragon.

12 And he exercises all the au-thority of the first beast in his pres-ence, and causes the earth and those who dwell in it to worship the first beast, whose deadly wound was healed.

13 And he performs great signs, so that he makes fire come down from heaven on the earth in the sight of men.

14 And he deceives those who dwell on the earth by those signs which he had power to do in the sight of the beast, saying to those who dwell on the earth that they should make an image to the beast who was wounded by the sword and lived.

---

35 Daniel 7:7, 20, 24   36 Daniel 7:4-6   37 Daniel 7:21, 25   38 Cf. Daniel 8:3

15 And he had power to give breath to the image of the beast, that the image of the beast should both speak and cause as many as would not worship the image of the beast to be killed.

16 And he causes all, both small and great, rich and poor, free and slave, to receive a mark on their right hand or on their foreheads,

17 and that no one may buy or sell except the one who has the mark or the name of the beast, or the number of his name.

18 Here is wisdom. Let him who has understanding calculate the number of the beast, for it is the number of man: And his number is six hundred and sixty-six.

The Lamb and the 144,000

14 And I looked, and behold, a Lamb standing on Mount Zion, and with Him one hundred and forty-four thousand, having His Father's name written on their foreheads.

2 And I heard a voice from heaven, like the voice of many waters, and like the voice of loud thunder. And I heard the sound of harpists playing their harps.

3 And they sang a new song before the throne, before the four living creatures, and the elders; and no one could learn that song except the hundred and forty-four thousand who were redeemed from the earth.

4 These are the ones who were not defiled with women, for they are virgins. These are the ones who follow the Lamb wherever He goes. These were redeemed from among men, being firstfruits to God and to the Lamb.

5 And in their mouth was found no guile, for they are without fault before the throne of God.

The Proclamations of Three Angels

6 And I saw another angel flying in the midst of heaven, having the everlasting good news to preach to those who dwell on the earth—to every nation, tribe, tongue, and people—

7 saying with a loud voice, "Fear God and give glory to Him, for the hour of His judgment has come; and worship Him who made heaven and earth, the sea and the springs of water."

8 And another angel followed, saying, "Babylon is fallen, is fallen, that great city, because she made all nations drink of the wine of the wrath of her fornication."

9 And a third angel followed them, saying with a loud voice, "If anyone worships the beast and his image, and receives his mark on his forehead or on his hand,

10 "he himself shall also drink of the wine of the wrath of God, which is poured out full strength into the cup of His indignation. And he shall be tormented with fire and brimstone in the presence of the holy angels and in the presence of the Lamb.

11 "And the smoke of their torment ascends forever and ever; and they have no rest day or night, who worship the beast and his image, and whoever receives the mark of his name."

12 Here is the patience of the holy ones; here are those who keep the commandments of God and the faith of Yeshua.

13 And I heard a voice from

heaven saying to me, "Write: 'Blessed are the dead who die in the Lord from now on.'" "Yes," says the Spirit, "that they may rest from their labors, and their works follow them."

Reaping the Earth's Harvest

14 And I looked, and behold, a white cloud, and on the cloud sat One like the Son of Man,[39] having on His head a golden crown, and in His hand a sharp sickle.

15 And another angel came out of the temple, crying with a loud voice to Him who sat on the cloud, "Thrust in Your sickle and reap, for the time has come for You to reap, for the harvest of the earth is ripe."[40]

16 And He who sat on the cloud thrust in His sickle on the earth, and the earth was reaped.

Reaping the Grapes of Wrath

17 And another angel came out of the temple which is in heaven, he also having a sharp sickle.

18 And another angel came out from the altar, who had power over fire, and he cried with a loud cry to him who had the sharp sickle, saying, "Thrust in your sharp sickle and gather the clusters of the vine of the earth, for her grapes are fully ripe."

19 And the angel thrust his sickle into the earth and gathered the vine of the earth, and threw it into the great winepress of the wrath of God.

20 And the winepress was trampled outside the city, and blood came out of the winepress, up to the horses' bridles, for one thousand six hundred furlongs.[41]

Prelude to the Bowl Judgments

15 And I saw another sign in heaven, great and marvelous: seven angels having the seven last plagues, for in them the wrath of God is complete.

2 And I saw something like a sea of glass mingled with fire, and those who have the victory over the beast, over his image, over his mark, and over the number of his name, standing on the sea of glass, having harps of God.

3 And they sing the song of Moses, the servant of God, and the song of the Lamb, saying:

"Great and marvelous are Your works,
Lord God Almighty!
Just and true are Your ways,
O King of the holy ones!
4 Who shall not fear You, O Lord, and glorify Your name?
For You alone are holy.
For all nations will come and worship before You,
For Your judgments have been manifested."

5 And after these things I looked, and behold, the temple of the tabernacle of the testimony in heaven was opened.

6 And out of the temple came the seven angels having the seven plagues, clothed in pure bright linen, and having their chests girded with golden belts.

7 And one of the four living

---

39 Daniel 7:13, 14
40 Joel 3:13 (4:13 in some versions)

41 Lit. 1,600 stadia, equal to about 200 miles.

creatures gave to the seven angels seven golden bowls full of the wrath of God who lives forever and ever.

8 And the temple was filled with smoke from the glory of God and from His power,[42] and no one was able to enter the temple till the seven plagues of the seven angels were completed.

16 And I heard a loud voice out of the temple saying to the seven angels, "Go and pour out the bowls of the wrath of God on the earth."

First Bowl: Malignant Sores

2 And the first went and poured out his bowl on the earth, and a foul and loathsome sore came on the men who had the mark of the beast and on those who worshiped his image.

Second Bowl: The Sea Turns to Blood

3 And the second angel poured out his bowl on the sea, and it became like the blood of a dead man; and every living creature in the sea died.

Third Bowl: The Waters Turn to Blood

4 And the third angel poured out his bowl on the rivers and springs of water, and they became blood.

5 And I heard the angel of the waters saying:

"You are righteous, O Lord,
The One who is and who
was and who is to come,
Because You have judged
these things.

6 For they have shed the blood
of holy ones and prophets,
And You have given them
blood to drink.
For they are worthy of it."

7 And I heard another out of the altar saying, "Even so, Lord God Almighty, true and righteous are Your judgments."

Fourth Bowl: Men Are Scorched

8 And the fourth angel poured out his bowl on the sun, and power was given to him to scorch men with fire.

9 And men were scorched with great heat, and they blasphemed the name of God who has power over these plagues; and they did not repent to give Him glory.

Fifth Bowl: Darkness and Pain

10 And the fifth angel poured out his bowl on the throne of the beast, and his kingdom became full of darkness; and they gnawed their tongues because of the pain.

11 And they blasphemed the God of heaven because of their pains and their sores, and did not repent of their deeds.

Sixth Bowl: Euphrates Dried Up

12 And the sixth angel poured out his bowl on the great river Euphrates, and its water was dried up, so that the way of the kings from the east might be prepared.

13 And I saw three unclean spirits like frogs coming out of the mouth of the dragon, out of the mouth of the beast, and out of the mouth of the false prophet.

14 For they are the spirits of demons, working signs, which go out to the kings of the earth and of the whole world, to gather them to the

42 Cf. Isaiah 6:1-5

battle of that great day of God Almighty.

15 "Behold, I am coming as a thief. Blessed is he who watches, and keeps his garments, lest he walk naked and they see his shame." [43]

16 And they gathered them together to the place called in Hebrew, *Armageddon.*

Seventh Bowl: The Earth Utterly Shaken

17 And the seventh angel poured out his bowl into the air, and a loud voice came out of the temple of heaven, from the throne, saying, "It is done!"

18 And there were noises, thunderings, and lightnings; and there was a great earthquake, so mighty and so great an earthquake, such as had not been since men were on the earth.

19 And the great city was divided into three parts, and the cities of the nations fell. And great Babylon was remembered before God, to give her the cup of the wine of the fierceness of His wrath.

20 And every island fled away, and the mountains were not found.

21 And great hail out of heaven fell on men, every stone about the weight of a talent. And men blasphemed God because of the plague of the hail, since that plague was exceedingly great.

The Scarlet Woman and the Scarlet Beast

17 And one of the seven angels who had the seven bowls came and talked with me, saying to me, "Come! I will show you the judgment of the great harlot who sits on many waters,

2 "with whom the kings of the earth committed fornication, and the inhabitants of the earth were made drunk with the wine of her fornication."

3 So he carried me away in the Spirit into the wilderness. And I saw a woman sitting on a scarlet beast, full of names of blasphemy, having seven heads and ten horns.[44]

4 And the woman was arrayed in purple and scarlet, and adorned with gold, precious stones, and pearls, having in her hand a golden cup full of abominations and the filthiness of her fornication.

5 And on her forehead a name was written:

MYSTERY,
BABYLON THE GREAT,
THE MOTHER OF
HARLOTS AND OF THE
ABOMINATIONS OF THE
EARTH.

6 And I saw the woman, drunk with the blood of the believers and with the blood of the martyrs of Yeshua. And when I saw her, I marveled with great amazement.

The Meaning of the Woman and the Beast

7 And the angel said to me, "Why did you marvel? I will tell you the mystery of the woman and of the beast that carries her, which has the seven heads and the ten horns.

---

43 Matthew 24:43f.; Luke 12:37f.

44 Daniel 7:7, 20-25

8 "The beast that you saw was, and is not, and will ascend out of the bottomless pit and go to perdition. And those who dwell on the earth will marvel, whose names are not written in the Book of Life from the foundation of the world, when they see the beast that was, and is not, and yet is.

9 "Here is the mind which has wisdom: The seven heads are seven mountains on which the woman sits.

10 "And there are seven kings. Five have fallen, one is, and the other has not yet come. And when he comes, he must continue a short time.

11 "And the beast that was, and is not, is himself also the eighth, and is of the seven, and is going to perdition.

12 "And the ten horns which you saw are ten kings who have received no kingdom as yet, but they receive authority for one hour as kings with the beast.

13 "These have one mind, and they will give their power and authority to the beast.

14 "These will make war with the Lamb, and the Lamb will overcome them, for He is Lord of lords and King of kings; and those who are with Him are called, chosen, and faithful."

15 And he said to me, "The waters which you saw, where the harlot sits, are peoples, multitudes, nations, and tongues.

16 "And the ten horns which you saw on the beast, these will hate the harlot, make her desolate and naked, eat her flesh, and burn her with fire.

17 "For God has put it into their hearts to fulfill His purpose, to have one purpose, and to give their kingdom to the beast, until the words of God are fulfilled.

18 "And the woman whom you saw is that great city which reigns over the kings of the earth."

The Fall of Babylon the Great

18 And after these things I saw another angel coming down from heaven, having great authority, and the earth was illuminated with his glory.

2 And he cried mightily with a loud voice, saying, "Babylon the great is fallen, is fallen, and has become a habitation of demons, a prison for every foul spirit, and a cage for every unclean and hated bird.

3 "For all the nations have drunk of the wine of the wrath of her fornication, the kings of the earth have committed fornication with her, and the merchants of the earth have become rich through the abundance of her luxury."

4 And I heard another voice from heaven saying, "Come out of her, my people, lest you share in her sins, and lest you receive of her plagues.

5 "For her sins have reached to heaven, and God has remembered her iniquities.

6 "Render to her just as she rendered to you, and repay her double according to her works; in the cup which she has mixed, mix for her double.

7 "As much as she has glorified herself and lived luxuriously, so much torment and sorrow give

her; for she says in her heart, 'I sit as queen, and am no widow, and will not see sorrow.'

8 "Therefore her plagues will come in one day—death, mourning, and famine. And she will be utterly burned with fire, for strong is the Lord God who judges her.

The World Mourns Babylon's Fall

9 "And the kings of the earth who have committed fornication and lived luxuriously with her will weep and lament for her, when they see the smoke of her burning,

10 "standing at a distance for fear of her torment, saying, 'Alas, alas, that great city Babylon, that mighty city! For in one hour your judgment has come.'

11 "And the merchants of the earth will weep and mourn over her, for no one buys their merchandise anymore:

12 "merchandise of gold and silver, precious stones and pearls, fine linen and purple, silk and scarlet, every kind of citron wood, every kind of object of ivory, every kind of object of most precious wood, bronze, iron, and marble;

13 "and cinnamon and incense, fragrant oil and frankincense, wine and oil, fine flour and wheat, cattle and sheep, horses and chariots, and bodies and souls of men.

14 "And the fruit that your soul longed for has gone from you, and all the things which are rich and splendid have gone from you, and you shall find them no more at all.

15 "The merchants of these things, who became rich by her, will stand at a distance for fear of her torment, weeping and wailing,

16 "and saying, 'Alas, alas, that great city that was clothed in fine linen, purple, and scarlet, and adorned with gold, precious stones, and pearls!

17 'For in one hour such great riches have come to nothing.' And every shipmaster, all who travel by ship, sailors, and as many as trade on the sea, stood at a distance

18 "and cried out when they saw the smoke of her burning, saying, 'What is like this great city!'

19 "And they threw dust on their heads and cried out, weeping and wailing, and saying, 'Alas, alas, that great city, in which all who had ships on the sea became rich by her wealth! For in one hour she is made desolate.'

20 "Rejoice over her, O heaven, and you holy apostles and prophets, for God has avenged you on her!"

Finality of Babylon's Fall

21 And a mighty angel took up a stone like a great millstone and threw it into the sea, saying, "Thus with violence the great city Babylon shall be thrown down, and shall not be found anymore.

22 "And the sound of harpists, musicians, flutists, and trumpeters shall not be heard in you anymore. And no craftsman of any craft shall be found in you anymore. And the sound of a millstone shall not be heard in you anymore.

23 "And the light of a lamp shall not shine in you anymore. And the voice of bridegroom and bride shall not be heard in you anymore. For your merchants were the great men of the earth, for by

your sorcery all the nations were deceived.

24 "And in her was found the blood of prophets and holy ones, and of all who were slain on the earth."

Heaven Exults over Babylon

19 And after these things I heard a loud voice of a great multitude in heaven, saying, "Hallelujah! Salvation and glory and honor and power to the Lord our God!

2 "For true and righteous are His judgments, because He has judged the great harlot who corrupted the earth with her fornication; and He has avenged the blood of His servants at her hand."

3 And again they said, "Hallelujah! And her smoke rises up forever and ever!"

4 And the twenty-four elders and the four living creatures fell down and worshiped God who sat on the throne, saying, "Amen! Hallelujah!"

5 And a voice came out of the throne, saying, "Praise our God, all you His servants and you who fear Him, both small and great!"

6 And I heard, as it were, the voice of a great multitude, as the sound of many waters and as the sound of mighty thunderings, saying, "Hallelujah! For the Lord God Omnipotent reigns!

7 "Let us be glad and rejoice and give Him glory, for the marriage of the Lamb has come, and His wife has made herself ready."

8 And to her was granted that she should be arrayed in fine linen, clean and bright, for the fine linen is the righteous acts of the holy ones.

9 And he said to me, "Write: 'Blessed are those who are called to the marriage supper of the Lamb!'" And he said to me, "These are the true sayings of God."

10 And I fell at his feet to worship him. And he said to me, "See that you do not do that! I am your fellow servant, and of your brethren who have the testimony of Yeshua. Worship God! For the testimony of Yeshua is the spirit of prophecy."

The Messiah on a White Horse

11 And I saw heaven opened, and behold, a white horse. And He who sat on him was called Faithful and True, and with righteousness He judges and makes war.

12 His eyes were like a flame of fire, and on His head were many crowns. And He had a name written that no one knew except Himself.

13 And He was clothed with a robe dipped in blood, and His name is called The Word of God.

14 And the armies in heaven, clothed in fine linen, white and clean, followed Him on white horses.

15 And out of His mouth goes a sharp sword, that with it He should strike the nations. And He Himself will rule them with a rod of iron. He Himself treads the winepress of the fierceness and wrath of Almighty God.[45]

45 Isaiah 11:1-5; 63:3; Psalm 2:9

16 And He has on His robe and on His thigh a name written:

KING OF KINGS
AND LORD OF LORDS.

The Beast and His Armies Defeated

17 And I saw an angel standing in the sun; and he cried with a loud voice, saying to all the birds that fly in the midst of heaven, "Come and gather together for the supper of the great God,

18 "that you may eat the flesh of kings, the flesh of captains, the flesh of mighty men, the flesh of horses and of those who sit on them, and the flesh of all people, free and slave, both small and great."

19 And I saw the beast, the kings of the earth, and their armies, gathered together to make war against Him who sat on the horse and against His army.

20 And the beast was taken, and with him the false prophet who worked signs in his presence, by which he deceived those who had received the mark of the beast and those who worshiped his image. These two were cast alive into the lake of fire burning with brimstone.

21 And the rest were killed with the sword which proceeded out of the mouth of Him who sat on the horse. And all the birds were filled with their flesh.

Satan Bound 1,000 Years

20 And I saw an angel coming down from heaven, having the key to the bottomless pit and a great chain in his hand.

2 And he laid hold of the dragon, that serpent of old, who is the Devil and Satan, and bound him for a thousand years;

3 and he cast him into the bottomless pit, and shut him up, and set a seal on him, so that he should deceive the nations no more till the thousand years were finished. And after these things he must be released for a little while.

The Believers Reign with the Messiah 1,000 Years

4 And I saw thrones, and they sat on them, and judgment was given to them. And I saw the souls of those who had been beheaded for their witness to Yeshua and for the word of God, who had not worshiped the beast or his image, and had not received his mark on their foreheads or on their hands. And they lived and reigned with the Messiah for a thousand years.

5 But the rest of the dead did not live again until the thousand years were finished. This is the first resurrection.

6 Blessed and holy is he who has part in the first resurrection.[46] Over such the second death has no power, but they will be priests of God and of the Messiah, and will reign with Him a thousand years.

Satanic Rebellion Crushed

7 And when the thousand years have expired, Satan will be released from his prison

8 and will go out to deceive the nations which are in the four corners of the earth, Gog and Magog,

46 Daniel 12:2

to gather them together to battle, whose number is as the sand of the sea.

9 And they came up on the breadth of the earth and surrounded the camp of the holy ones and the beloved city. And fire came down from God out of heaven and devoured them.[47]

10 And the devil, who deceived them, was cast into the lake of fire and brimstone where the beast and the false prophet are. And they will be tormented day and night forever and ever.

The Great White Throne Judgment

11 And I saw a great white throne and Him who sat on it, from whose face the earth and the heaven fled away. And there was found no place for them.

12 And I saw the dead, small and great, standing before God, and books were opened. And another book was opened, which is the Book of Life. And the dead were judged according to their works, by the things which were written in the books.

13 And the sea gave up the dead who were in it, and Death and Hades delivered up the dead who were in them. And they were judged, each one according to his works.

14 And Death and Hades were cast into the lake of fire. This is the second death.

15 And anyone not found written in the Book of Life was cast into the lake of fire.

[47] Ezekiel 38:2, 22

All Things Made New

21 And I saw a new heaven and a new earth, for the first heaven and the first earth had passed away. And there was no more sea.[48]

2 And I, John, saw the holy city, New Jerusalem, coming down from God out of heaven, prepared as a bride adorned for her husband.

3 And I heard a loud voice out of heaven saying, "Behold, the tabernacle of God is with men, and He shall dwell with them, and they shall be His people, and God Himself shall be with them and be their God.[49]

4 "And God shall wipe away every tear from their eyes; there shall be no more death, nor sorrow, nor crying; and there shall be no more pain, for the former things have passed away." [50]

5 And He who sat on the throne said, "Behold, I am making all things new." And He said to me, "Write, for these words are true and faithful."

6 And He said to me, "It is done! I am the Alpha and the Omega, the Beginning and the End. I will give of the fountain of the water of life freely to him who thirsts.[51]

7 "He who overcomes shall inherit all things, and I will be his God and he shall be My son.

[48] Isaiah 65:17
[49] Ezekiel 37:24-28; 36:24-29
[50] Isaiah 25:8; 35:10; 65:19
[51] Isaiah 55:1

8 "But the cowardly and unbe- lieving and abominable and mur- derers and sexually immoral and sorcerers and idolaters and all liars shall have their part in the lake which burns with fire and brim- stone, which is the second death."

The New Jerusalem

9 And one of the seven angels who had the seven bowls filled with the seven last plagues came to me and talked with me, saying, "Come! I will show you the bride, the Lamb's wife."

10 And he carried me away in the Spirit to a great and high mountain, and showed me the great city, the holy Jerusalem, de- scending out of heaven from God,

11 having the glory of God. And her light was like a most pre- cious stone, like a jasper stone, clear as crystal.

12 And she had a great and high wall, and had twelve gates, and twelve angels at the gates, and names written on them, which are the names of the twelve tribes of the children of Israel:

13 three gates on the east, three gates on the north, three gates on the south, and three gates on the west.

14 And the wall of the city had twelve foundations, and on them were the names of the twelve apos- tles of the Lamb.

15 And he who talked with me had a golden reed to measure the city, its gates, and its wall.

16 And the city is laid out as a square, and its length is as great as its breadth. And he measured the city with the reed: twelve thousand furlongs. Its length, breadth, and height are equal.

17 And he measured its wall: one hundred and forty-four cubits, according to the measure of a man, that is, of an angel.

18 And the construction of its wall was of jasper; and the city was pure gold, like clear glass.

19 And the foundations of the wall of the city were adorned with all kinds of precious stones: the first foundation was jasper, the second sapphire, the third chal- cedony, the fourth emerald,

20 the fifth sardonyx, the sixth sardius, the seventh chrysolite, the eighth beryl, the ninth topaz, the tenth chrysoprase, the eleventh ja- cinth, and the twelfth amethyst.

21 And the twelve gates were twelve pearls: each individual gate was of one pearl. And the street of the city was pure gold, like transparent glass.

The Glory of the New Jerusalem

22 And I saw no temple in it, for the Lord God Almighty and the Lamb are its temple.

23 And the city had no need of the sun or of the moon to shine in it, for the glory of God illuminated it, and the Lamb is its light.[52]

24 And the nations of those who are saved shall walk in its light, and the kings of the earth bring their glory and honor into it.

25 And its gates shall not be shut at all by day, for there shall be no night there.

26 And they shall bring the glory and the honor of the nations into it.

52 Isaiah 60:19, 20

27 And there shall by no means enter it anything that defiles, or causes an abomination or a lie, but only those who are written in the Lamb's Book of Life.

The River of Life

22 And he showed me a pure river of water of life, clear as crystal, proceeding out of the throne of God and of the Lamb.[53]

2 In the middle of its street, and on either side of the river, was the tree of life, which bore twelve fruits, yielding its fruit every month. And the leaves of the tree were for the healing of the nations.[54]

3 And there shall be no more curse, but the throne of God and of the Lamb shall be in it, and His servants shall serve Him.

4 And they shall see His face, and His name shall be on their foreheads.

5 And there shall be no night there; they need no lamp nor light of the sun, for the Lord God gives them light. And they shall reign forever and ever.[55]

The Time Is Near

6 And he said to me, "These words are faithful and true." And the Lord God of the holy prophets sent His angel to show His servants the things which must shortly take place.

7 "Behold, I am coming quickly! Blessed is he who keeps the words of the prophecy of this book."

8 And I, John, saw and heard these things. And when I had heard and seen, I fell down to worship before the feet of the angel who showed me these things.

9 Then he said to me, "See that you do not do that. For I am your fellow servant, and of your brethren the prophets, and of those who keep the words of this book. Worship God."

10 And he said to me, "Do not seal the words of the prophecy of this book, for the time is at hand.

11 "He who is unjust, let him be unjust still; he who is filthy, let him be filthy still; he who is righteous, let him be righteous still; he who is holy, let him be holy still."

Yeshua Testifies to the Congregations

12 "And behold, I am coming quickly, and My reward is with Me, to give to each one according to his work.

13 "I am the Alpha and the Omega, the Beginning and the End, the First and the Last." [56]

14 Blessed are those who do His commandments, that they may have the right to the tree of life, and may enter in through the gates into the city.

15 But outside are dogs and sorcerers and sexually immoral and murderers and idolaters, and whoever loves and practices a lie.

16 "I, Yeshua, have sent My angel to testify to you these things in the congregations. I am the Root and the Offspring of David, the Bright and Morning Star." [57]

53 Zechariah 14:8, 9
54 Cf. Ezekiel 47:12
55 Zechariah 14:6-9

56 Isaiah 44:6; 48:12-16
57 Jeremiah 23:5, 6; 33:14-16; cf. Matthew 1:1; Numbers 24:17

17 And the Spirit and the bride say, "Come!" And let him who hears say, "Come!" And let him who thirsts come. And whoever desires, let him take the water of life freely.[58]

A Warning

18 For I testify to everyone who hears the words of the prophecy of this book: if anyone adds to these things, God will add to him the

[58] Isaiah 55:1; 44:3; 12:2, 3; cf. John 7:37, 38

plagues that are written in this book.

19 And if anyone takes away from the words of the book of this prophecy, God will take away his part from the Book of Life, from the holy city, and from the things which are written in this book.

I Am Coming Quickly

20 He who testifies to these things says, "Surely I am coming quickly." Amen. Even so, come, Lord Yeshua.

21 The grace of our Lord Yeshua ha Mashiach be with you all. Amen.

Of Whom Does the Prophet Speak?

Who hath believed our report? and to whom is the arm of the Lord revealed?

For he shall grow up before him as a tender plant, and as a root out of a dry ground: he hath no form nor comeliness; and when we shall see him, *there is* no beauty that we should desire him.

He is despised and rejected of men; a man of sorrows, and acquainted with grief: and we hid as it were *our* faces from him; he was despised, and we esteemed him not.

Surely he hath borne our griefs, and carried our sorrows: yet we did esteem him stricken, smitten of God, and afflicted.

But he *was* wounded for our transgressions, *he was* bruised for our iniquities: the chastisement of our peace *was* upon him; and with his stripes we are healed.

All we like sheep have gone astray; we have turned every one to his own way; and the Lord hath laid on him the iniquity of us all.

He was oppressed, and he was afflicted, yet he opened not his mouth: he is brought as a lamb to the slaughter, and as a sheep before her shearers is dumb, so he openeth not his mouth.

He was taken from prison and from judgment: and who shall declare his generation? for he was cut off out of the land of the living: for the transgression of my people was he stricken.

And he made his grave with the wicked, and with the rich in his death; because he had done no violence, neither *was any* deceit in his mouth.

Yet it pleased the Lord to bruise him; he hath put *him* to grief: when thou shalt make his soul an offering for sin, he shall see *his* seed, he shall prolong *his* days, and the pleasure of the Lord shall prosper in his hand.

He shall see of the travail of his soul, *and* shall be satisfied: by his knowledge shall my righteous servant justify many; for he shall bear their iniquities.

Therefore will I divide him *a portion* with the great, and he shall divide the spoil with the strong; because he hath poured out his soul unto death: and he was numbered with the transgressors; and he bare the sin of many, and made intercession for the transgressors.

Isaiah 53:1-12

Dear Friend,

Because I love the Messiah, I'm extending my hand in friendship to help you answer any questions you have about Messianic Judaism, Jewish believers, or the Messiah Yeshua. So please use this card to request any more information you may want. There is no charge for any literature you receive in return. May God bless you.

— Sid Roth, founder of Messianic Vision.

☐ Please tell me more about Jewish believers.
☐ Please tell me more about Messianic Judaism.
☐ Please have someone personally contact me.
☐ Please _____
_____ .

I am ☐ Jewish ☐ Non-Jewish ☐ A Believer in Messiah

Name: _____

Address: _____

City: _____ State: _____ Zip: _____

Phone: _____

A Jewish Riddle

*Who hath ascended
up into heaven, or descended?
Who hath gathered
the wind in his fists?
Who hath established
all the ends of the earth?
What is his name,
and what is his son's name,
if thou canst tell?*

Proverbs 30:4